INDONESIA

Publisher:	Aileen Lau
Editorial Manager:	Bina Maniar
Editors:	Bina Maniar
	Emma Tan
	Aileen Lau
Design/DTP:	Sares Kanapathy
Illustrations:	Susan Harmer
Cover Artwork:	Susan Harmer
Maps:	Rebecca Fong

Published in the United States by
PRENTICE HALL GENERAL REFERENCE
15 Columbus Circle
New York, New York, 10023

PRENTICE HALL and colophon are registered trademarks
of Simon & Schuster, Inc.

ISBN 0-671-87912-X

Titles in the series:
Alaska - American Southwest - Australia - Bali - California - Canada - Caribbean - China - England - Florida - France - Germany - Greece - Hawaii - India - Indonesia - Italy - Ireland - Japan - Kenya - Malaysia - Mexico - Nepal - New England - New York - Pacific Northwest USA - Singapore - Spain - Thailand - Turkey - Vietnam

USA MAINLAND SPECIAL SALES
Bulk purchases (10+copies) of the Travel Bugs series are available at special discounts for corporate use. The publishers can produce custom publications for corporate clients to be used as premiums or for sales promotion. Copies can be produced with custom cover imprints. For more information write to Special Sales, Prentice Hall Travel, Paramount Communications Building, 15th floor, 15 Columbus Circle, New York, NY 10023.

Printed in Singapore

INDONESIA

Text by Holly Smith

With contributions by:
Emma Tan

Editors:
Bina Maniar
Emma Tan
Aileen Lau

Prentice Hall Travel

New York   London   Toronto   Sydney   Tokyo   Singapore

C O N T E N T S

C O N T E N T S

FOLLOW THAT BUG

C O N T E N T S

C O N T E N T S

Indonesia a land of

vigour and colour in its

art, variety and vitality

in its culture.

Indonesia's protected

rainforests remain

pristine habitats for an abundance of wildlife and its research.

Hundreds of islands

millions of people;

the oceans guard them and the seas provide.

island to island

Cultures may vary from

province to province, but the warm and friendly Indonesian spirit remains the same throughout.

Shelter for the body, mind and soul seen in tiered, attap

and Torajan roofing.

Introduction

I t begins with a smile, that slow, sweet Indonesian expression that welcomes you to their land. It touches your spirit for it reflects the curiosity and caring that are the country's national characteristics. Always accompanied by a hearty call of, "Hello Mister!" that smile extends an immediate cord of companionship that embraces your heart in its warmth.

But, behind the bright eyes, there is a great sense of pride in family and friendship; beyond the greeting, a genuine willingness to share the values that are an intricate part of Indonesian life. Within every face there is wisdom and kindness, each gentle curve and wrinkle revealing a culture preciously honed through tradition and time. And, contained within that smile is the very soul of the country, an archipelago of true natural beauty where visitors are always welcomed with open arms and open hearts.

Smile wide and touch the spirit of Indonesia and the warmth of its people.

1

Wecloming canoes cut the azure blue waters in Sulawesi.

An Enchanting Archipelago

There is an aura of magic about Indonesia that charms its way into the soul. Spirits are intertwined with the islands, with religion and with life. From the very first moments they encircle the senses in the pale scent of lotus perfume, in the feathered palm leaves swaying slowly at the edge of the sea and in the soft chime of bells in the *gamelan* orchestra bubbling over the evening breeze like clear water through a fresh mountain stream.

From each forest shadow, old souls watch over the world, while demons take peace in the fragrant petals scattered along gravel roads. Gods and god-

desses reflect the moods and the seasons, venting their wrath with each summer storm or bestowing joy in the perfect crimson sunset of evening. Freedom is easy to feel here, on sun-warmed skin, in wind-tossed hair, in the aroma of wistful wisps of incense that trickle up into the clear night sky. This is the essence of Indonesia, an endless, timeless beauty that stretches across the horizon in a spectacular panorama of jungle hills, misty volcanoes and the waves thundering of the surrounding seas.

Pulse of Life

However, upon your arrival, you will probably feel amazed at the sheer en-

Stand back in wonder at the centuries old majestic splendour of Borobudur.

ergy and chaos of Indonesian life. Mopeds zip down the roads between cows and crowded buses while horse-drawn carts jingle leisurely alongside. Parallel rice paddies spill over the land in pristine shades of colour, depicting scenes that could have been lifted from paintings executed several centuries before. In the cities, quickened steps click across the smooth marble floors of air-conditioned skyscrapers that stretch languorously into the clouds. Outside, the sound and scent of traffic surges through four-lane highways, urgent neon messages are splashed over buildings, while on the rough sidewalks below, a never-ending bazaar of bright shops tantalizes onlookers with inexpensive eastern bargains.

By day, culture is to be found around every corner, with museums and monuments, tombs and temples, markets and gardens tucked into the hills and alleys of each island town. After dark, the clock does not stop; the streets are lined with stands of sizzling fried rice and *satay* (charcoal grilled skewered meat), the aroma of spices filter through the dusty air while the non-stop noise of discos and after-hours bars reverberates through the night air.

Beauteous Serenity

A quiet serenity still flows throughout Java, at the temples of Prambanan and Borobudur, in Bogor's beautiful botani-

Fast Facts

Geography: With 13,667 islands, only 6,000 inhabited, Indonesia is the world's longest archipelago (15,120 kilometres). 81 percent (1.9 million square kilometres) of the country is water. In order of size, the largest main islands are Kalimantan, Sumatra, Sulawesi, Irian Jaya, Sulawesi and Java.

More than 400 volcanoes line the archipelago, about 80 of them are still active. Highest points on the islands are Irian Jaya's Mount Jaya (5,200 metres) and the Kerinci volcano (3,950 metres) in Sumatra.

Climate: Indonesia has a tropical climate with high humidity and temperature. Two equatorial monsoons travel through the islands, the dry season's "east" monsoon from May to September and the wet season's "west" monsoon from October to April. In the lowlands, the average temperature is 30°C; the mountains are several degrees cooler.

Population: 180 million, mostly living on the islands of Java, Bali and Sumatra.

Capital: Jakarta, in West Java, with a population of approximately eight million.

Government: Indonesia is a democratic state based on the 1945 Constitution and the five Pancasila Principles: belief in one God, a just and civilized humanity, the unity of Indonesia, representative government and social justice.

They represent the national outlook. The country is run by the President and the Vice-President, who are elected for five-year terms. The islands are divided into 27 regional provinces.

Coat of Arms: It is a golden bird with a shield that symbolizes the principles of the Pancasila: the centre star (Faith in God), the unbroken chain (Humanity), the buffalo head (Nationalism), the Banyan tree (Representative Government) and the sprigs of rice and cotton (Social Justice).

National Motto: *Bhinneka Tunggal Ika,* or "They are many, they are one" — usually translated to Unity in Diversity.

Religion: Indonesia is the largest Islamic nation in the world, with 87 percent professing this faith. On the island of Bali, however, Hinduism is the dominant religion, and on the island of Flores the majority of Indonesians are Catholic. Christianity has influenced areas of Irian Jaya, Kalimantan, Sulawesi and Sumatra, and there are also strong animistic beliefs intertwined within each of these religions.

People: Convenience of location and diversity of historical backgrounds has created more than 300 different ethnic groups throughout the archipelago which include: Java's Sundanese and Tenggerese, Sumatra's Acehnese, Bataks and Minangabau, as well as the Balinese, Nusa

cal gardens and in Bandung's classic "European" charm. Culture is cultivated in Yogyakarta, where graceful *gamelan* orchestras chime the liquid music of moonlight while *wayang kulit* (shadow puppets) jabber ancient Javanese tales until dawn. Inland, each footstep leads to treasures of time and ruined kingdoms stand scattered across the central plateaus. Wild coastlines and sheer, cliffside caves hide soothing cures for the spirits, while Loro Kidul, the Goddess of the Sea, rules the southern

beaches and the lush caldera of Anak Krakatau smokes silently and ominously against the distant sunset.

Better known is Bali, the island of celebration and smiles, where one is easily charmed into staying just a little bit longer. It is a place of mixed tradition and modern life, where busy shops are crammed with crafts of *batik*, silver and wood, while outside the dusty roads are littered with offerings of sweet incense and bright flower petals. Lush hillsides are stacked with thick terraces

Tenggara's Sumbanese and Timorese, Sulawesi's Toraja culture, Kalimantan's various Dayak peoples and Irian Jaya's numerous inland Dani tribes.

Economy: Major exports include: LNG, or liquified natural gas (Indonesia is the world's largest exporter), cloves, rubber, coffee, tin, timber, coal, copper and copra.

Language: The national language is Bahasa Indonesia. However, nearly 600 dialects are also spoken throughout the islands.

Flora: With more than 140 million acres of tropical jungle that covers three-fourths of the archipelago's land, Indonesia has the largest rainforest area after Brazil and Zaire. The islands also contain more than 40,000 plants, (12 percent of the estimated number of species in the world).

Fauna: Indonesia is a diverse zoological paradise, with more than 17 percent (1,500) of the world's bird species, 12 percent (about 500) of the world's mammals and 16 percent of the world's reptiles and amphibians. Endangered species include the Javan and Sumatran rhino, the Rothchild's Mynah, the orangutan, the probiscus monkey, the anoa, the babirusa and the Komodo dragon.

National Holiday: All the islands celebrate Independence Day on August 17th.

that somehow slide into the beaches of popular tourist ventures. Yet, the peaceful grace of Ubud still captures the charm of the "Emerald Island" that lingers a lifetime within each visitor's mind. Across the horizon, huge tankers chug through the Makassar Strait between the port cities along Sumatra's northern edge. Yet, encircled within the smooth, white-sand beaches of the archipelago's second-largest island, thick rainforests stretch southwards through the noble Bukit Barisan mountain range. There is

a wilder flavour to culture and life on Sumatra, felt in the serenity of Lake Toba, the merriment of Batak music, the haunting mosques of Benkulu or the Minangkabau tribal legends – an island where journeys are always accompanied by the spirit of adventure.

The islands of Nusa Tenggara lie scattered in the dry sunlight across the border of the Wallace Line to the east of Bali. More Australian than Asian in terms of its fauna, the wide channels spanning between them are connected by a chain of small ferries that link diverse cultures together in the clear blue, salty sea.

Above them, Maluku is a puzzle of nearly a thousand spice islands and bright coral reefs that for centuries have attracted traders. On the left are the central cliffside graves of Sulawesi's Torajaland and Kalimantan's river highways that snake through the thickest jungles. To the right, Irian Jaya's isolated Baliem Valley backs up against Papua New Guinea marking a slim eastern 5,200 kilometre border for the Indonesian islands.

Throughout the archipelago, more than 300 dialects are interwoven into the national Bahasa Indonesia language. Separated by only the history of kingdoms and the geography of the land, these diverse cultures exist side-by-side, sharing the islands and preserving peaceful traditions thus clearly reflecting the national motto of *Bhinneka Tunggal Ika,* or "unity in diversity" that is proudly stated in the national motto.

Bali — mountains, beaches, greenery a rest and respite for all weary souls.

Wild Indonesia

Centred within the Pacific's fiery ring of volcanoes, the Indonesian archipelago is alive with the movement of land and wildlife. Against the clear sky, more than 400 rugged peaks nudge the clouds, carrying imposing names like Leuser, Krakatau, Bromo, Agung, Rinjani and Tambora they stand in an age-old for-mation across the vista. Some have ex-ploded to life in ground-shaking erup-tions and shattering waves felt through-out the world. Close to a hundred of these volcanoes still smoke with life. And then there is "Wild Indonesia," which is situated at the very heart of Kalimantan, Sulawesi and Irian Jaya, where unknown tribes live in uninhib-ited paradise and only the rules of the jungle apply. It is a step backwards in

mystery. Protected by the deepest forests and most difficult hills, culture and custom remains unchanged as if untouched by time and the vagaries of the modern world.

A Sweet Sense of Being

And, time is gentle in Indonesia, the pulse slower, hours unhurried, each moment savoured as if a gift from the gods. Like the leisurely shuffling of sandals over dusty dirt *jalans* (roads), moves freely, unpressurized and controlled.

By day, roosters give the first bold awakening cries, rice is cooked over wood fires, children are dressed in crisp uniforms and packed off to school. Mid-morning is more like noon, where meals are consumed with mugs of hot tea, followed by a lazy retreat from the scorching sun. The splash of the *mandi* (bath) is the afternoon song, while prayers are chanted low over the sunset. And then a clear velvet sky scattered with stars appears. Beneath them, wrapped in bright *sarongs* (wrap-around skirt-like attire), families still sleep side–by–side, lulled by the soft chirping of crickets and the light breeze wafting through the palms. These are the images that will come to mind later, rich impressions that colour the mind. And the feeling that comes with it – as if the spirits themselves were encircling you in their warmth and tickling your soul with the true kindness and hope of that brilliant Indonesian smile.

time, to a land where near-extinct species still roam, where man and beast share both the paths and produce of the natural world. These are the sacred lands lined with hidden valleys and thundering rivers that twist through the world's third largest rainforest area. Here, ancient tribes linger and traditional *adat* (customs) remain, where people practice ancestor worship and animism. Modern times have not touched them; thus, little is known, for these tribes and species are still sheltered in a circle of

Along Java's lonely Solo River basin, scattered amidst layers of volcanic ash and coastal deposits, lie the ancient remains of human life fossilized by the forces of nature and time. At Trinil are the bare skulls of "Java Man", grinning mockingly at the arguments of the archaelogists over their age.

Further downriver, the younger bones of "Solo Man" lie quiet and sun-faded near Sambunmacan and Ngadong. Brought to the surface by erosion, tectonic movements and volcanic eruptions, these *homo erectus* fossils remained in place while the land around them changed. Today, they provide valuable evidence of the evolution of Indonesia's environment and human life.

Scenes from the past, a Buddhist heritage in Bali.

9

Mysteries of Early Humans

Neither Solo nor Java man were the ancestors of modern Indonesians, as both lines of human life died out for reasons still unknown to

Skeletal remnants from the past in a shelf of skulls and bones.

scientists. Nor were the fossils of *homo sapiens* that were discovered at East Java's Brantas River believed to be any relation, although their 10,000-year-old remains provided many clues about the first generations of human beings. Innovations from early eras have been found near the Solo area, many are believed to be creations of the advanced Ngandong peoples. Some of the remains found include stone tools, hand axes, bone implements and other fundamental instruments honed specifically to suit the needs of the time. Skull caps, possibly saved for drinking cups or religious and mystical rituals were also found. However, Indonesia's original ancestors are thought to have arrived from Southeast Asia before 5,000 BC.

Later, they were pushed into the remote interiors of Sumatra as others moved into the coastal lands. A secondary migration from Indochina brought with it neolithic, bronze and iron age technologies that soon spread throughout the islands. The Australoid ancestors of the Melanesians and Australian aborigines, who arrived on the islands some 30,000 years ago were also key players in Indonesia's evolutionary heritage. Settling in Java around the same time as the arrival of the Indochinese immigrants, the Austronesians enhanced the language, developed rice agriculture, propagated neolithic traditions and were also the archipelago's most revered seafarers, who had been known to sail as far as Africa, simply by using the stars!

Early Law & Government

And so, the first waves of human life on the islands developed, from small coastal groupings to inner villages and small "kingdoms", each with systems of custom and belief that had developed from the independent inheritance of tradition. Animism was the most popular religion, as the belief in spirits and ancestor worship grew stronger with unexplained occurrences in unexplored lands.

Adat (village law) evolved from these customs and beliefs, it soon became the basis for separate but very similar early government systems. In these growing villages, early "governments" arose from the organization of religious and societal systems.

However, the roles and responsibilities involved in rice farming techniques were also key factors in forming the foundations of early law and order. Most structured were Bali and Java's similar systems of *sawah* ("wet" field) cultivation, which required an intricate schedule of technique and timing to ensure continuous and abundant harvests.

The *ladang* ("dry" field) crops were not as complex. Thus, the complex organizational systems of Java and Bali allowed the islands to quickly move ahead in terms of social and agricultural development. Success in its implementation was aided by the mild climate and rich soil of the various islands,

as well as the willingness of each village to share the systems. Soon, a variety of agricultural products were being cultivated throughout the settled areas of the archipelago. What naturally followed was an interest in and the beginnings of barter.

Lure of the Islands

However, it was spices, that were best known to the traders of the east. Used as flavourings, perfumes and preservatives, they attracted merchants from all corners of the known world. Soon, the archipelago's waters were traced with billowing sails and smart schooners – but it was often a dangerous business, one in which the potential for profit and peril attracted both prospectors and pirates alike. A key area was Moluccas – made up of a chain of islands including: Ternate, Tidore, Seram and Banda – here, the attraction of nutmeg and cloves brought ships from the rest of Asia, China, India and Europe. With gold, pepper and benzoin, Sumatra joined the chain of exchange, trading her precious goods for items such as Arab aloe, sampan wood, camphor and tin.

The China trade was established in 200 BC and brought with it riches such as silk, ivory, porcelain and ebony. A little more than a century later, Indian merchants crossed the ocean to start a strong trade route that also helped to spread religion and a cultural influence which still remains in the islands today.

The massacre of Javanese royalty, the ancient prelude of years of bloodshed.

Gajah Mada: The Great Ruler of Majapahit

An anti-royalist revolt first brought this young palace guard to fame in the 1320s and displayed his natural talent for leadership. After successfully quelling the uprising, Gajah Mada's reputation for strength and intelligence eventually grew, placing him in the Majapahit seat of power. As Majapahit was the largest kingdom in Indonesian history, this made him the most influential leader to ever control the land.

The Bitter Gourd

Founded in 1294 by Prince Wijaya of the Singosari kingdom, Majapahit was the largest empire in the history of the country. Although the name "Majapahit" when translated means "bitter gourd," the kingdom was not one of tragedy as the term suggests but rather one of glory and power.

Majapahit's riches were in the rice fields, the spice trade and its unique religion – a blend of Hinduism and Buddhism (although those who practiced the new religion of Islam were also tolerated). Trowulan, the kingdom's capital whose ruins lie scattered 35 kilometres from modern Surabaya, was a centre for culture and art and was frequently compared to the cosmopolitan lifestyle of classical European cities.

Unification

However, it was the first Prime Minister, Gajah Mada, who brought the area under control during his reign from 1331 to 1364. From confusion to understanding, from chaos to peace, this charismatic leader smoothed diplomatic and cultural differences so that this small kingdom wielded both power and hope for the entire island of Java. Driven by a pledge to unite Java under the auspices of the Majapahit king-

dom, Gajah Mada increased the realm of Majapahit's power by claiming suzerainty over an area larger than modern Indonesia, within which he consolidated various smaller kingdoms and cities in the name of common rulership within the island territories.

Thus, Gajah Mada was the first ruler who introduced the idea of a united "Indonesia" with a separate "Indonesian" identity. To accomplish this, he created a new code of law throughout his land and the extensive Trowulan city area. In addition, he commissioned the writing of the epic poem *Nagarakertanagam* – now one of the major historical sources on the Singosari kingdom.

Majapahit reached its height of power under the rule of Hayam Wuruk who ruled from 1350 to 1389, although Gajah Mada remained as Prime Minister for part of this term. And, it was under Gajah Mada's influential leadership that the new kingdom encompassed an area which was larger than modern-day Indonesia, and which probably included parts of the Malay peninsula.

Probably the most revered character in Indonesian history, Gajah Mada ruled the vast Majapahit empire until his death in 1364. After which Majapahit's "Golden Age" slowly disintegrated when conflicts with disapproving Islamic states, resulted in the outbreak of civil and holy wars in the early 15th century.

Some believe it was the fall of the Islamic coastal port of Demak in 1478 that was Majapahit's crushing blow. Still, a wander through the former area of this great kingdom's ruined pools, temples and tombs inspires visions of a kingdom that stood at the centre of the country's power – and, under the guidance, of Gajah Mada was at the core of the unification of the Indonesian islands. In 1946, Yogyakarta's new **Gajah Mada University**, was named in honour of this influential historical figure.

The early kingdoms were strongly influenced by Hinduism, yet no relics remain to mark the presence of Tarumanegara, the oldest Hindu domain on the island of Java.

Surprisingly, Indonesia's first kingdom was that of the Kutai region of Kalimantan – which would later become part of East Java's powerful Majahapit empire.

A view of the volatile Ternate before erupting in 1840, Moluccas Islands.

Coastal Cities & Kingdoms

By controlling the Malaka Strait between Sumatra and the Malay peninsula during the 7th century, the Hindu-Buddhist kingdom of Srivijaya became the first Indonesian authority to wield major commercial power. Located near present-day Palembang, this coastal state shared the island of Sumatra with two other kingdoms; that of Tulang-bawang in today's Lampung area and central Jambi's kingdom of Melayu. Known for its wealth and cosmopolitan atmosphere, Srivijaya was perhaps a bit more modern than the strict agrarian empires located in the central areas. Run by the Tamils and the Chinese,

Srivijaya was not the only rich commercial state in the islands – across the Sunda Strait in central Java, historical records of China's Tang dynasty also list dealings with a powerful trading kingdom called He-ling.

With increased trading, dynasties also began to emerge in Java. The most noted being King Sanjaya's Hindu Mataram empire and the Buddhist Shaliendra, or "Kings of the Mountain" dynasty. Between the 8th and 10th centuries, both kingdoms left their marks on the central plains with two of the most magnificent temples in the country's history – Buddhist **Borobudur** and Hindu **Prambanan**. Traditional rivals, the Shaliendra controlled Mataram until C. AD 832, when an inter-kingdom mar-

BORO BOEDOR, FROM THE PASSAGRAHAN

Borobudur the magnificent temple built by the Buddhist Shaliendra dynasty c. AD 778–850.

riage restored the dominance of the Sanjaya dynasty. However, later a rebellious Shaliendra leader usurped the power of Sumatra's Srivijaya kingdom and turned it into Mataram's most powerful opponent.

Movements of Power

From the time of the first kingdoms of Sumatra and Kalimantan, Indonesia's centre of power had slowly been moving eastwards, with cultural changes being intertwined with the influence of traders and kings. Religion, too, was honing new images, with Hinduism and Buddhism cautiously melding practices and beliefs to create individual cultures with a radiance of their own.

On Java's eastern edge, the land flourished under King Sindok, a man whose legacy was so great that for generations he was claimed as an ancestor by rulers to whom he had no relation! Much of the braiding of Hinduism and Buddhism is also attributed to Sindok's great-granddaughter, who married King Vdayana of Bali several decades later, with whom she had a son named Airlangga. In the 11th century Sindok's kingdom gained the power to invade Sumatra and in 1016 the Sumatrans retaliated against the east Javan empire. Along with a band of followers, the young crown prince Airlangga fled into the mountains, where he prepared for the fight to reclaim the kingdom. Four years later, he ruled a coastal area near Surabaya, and soon afterward won the battle to reconquer the land of his ancestors. However, in 1041 he gave up the throne to become a hermit named Resi Gentayu but he is still considered to be one of the greatest kings in Balinese history. Upon Airlangga's death, Sindok's former kingdom was divided into two regions – Janggala (near Malang) and Panjalu (near Kediri).

Then, in 1222, a common labourer named Angrok assumed control over the area by overthrowing the King of Kediri and assuming the name of Rajasa. Several generations later, one of Java's most important unifications took place under Angrok's descendent Rangga Wuni, who once again reunited Airlangga's land, this time under the new name of the Kingdom of Singasari.

An incredibly violent domain, Singasari was an intimidating foe which dominated Indonesia's western islands and a bit of the Malay Peninsula as well. One of her most notorious rulers was the formidable Kertanagara, after whom Surabaya's "*Joko Dolong*" – the Fat Boy –

statue of Buddha is replicated. One of his most shocking acts was to cut off the ears of a messenger sent by China's notorious ruler Kublai Khan. When four years later, the Mongol troops finally arrived to avenge that act, they found that Kertanagara had died the previous year in a surprise attack upon the palace staged by the viceroy of Kediri. Thus, after Kertanagara's death, Kediri was once again the ruling kingdom. But, Kertanagara's son-in-law and closest heir, Prince Vijaya, cleverly escaped attack. After a few years of silence, he returned to the area west of Surabaya to build a new kingdom, and in 1293 joined forces with Kublai Khan's Mongols to destroy Kediri. Then, Prince Vijaya took the throne of his new empire that now ruled all of Java – the Majapahit kingdom or the kingdom of the "bitter gourd".

Marvels of Majapahit

Predominantly a Hindu kingdom, Majapahit was the greatest Indonesian empire of all, for it held enough power and influence to tie all of the islands together under its realm. It was hardly an empty vision, for the kingdom monopolized the trade routes between Southeast Asia and its own islands of Lombok, Moluccas, Sulawesi, Sumatra and Sumbawa. With its rich blend of art and culture, the Majapahit capital of Trowulan was comparable to European cities of the time and it was the largest commercial centre to flourish within Indonesia in pre-colonial times.

It was Gajah Mada, the premier during the reign of the Majapahit queen, whose aim it was to unite the islands of Indonesia under one rule. (see p 15). In the 30-odd years of his rule, he nearly managed to accomplish this goal, even bringing parts of Malaysia and the Philippines under Majapahit control. Majapahit was also at the centre of Indonesia's Golden Age which dawned in 1350 under the rule of Hayam Waruk. Unfortunately, this attempt at unity did not last long as the kingdom fell with the onslaught of another Kediri attack. Sea power and strategic positions were suddenly up for grabs, and after Majapahit no single power could dominate the region. The influence of Islam was slowly spreading around the island and across the trading routes. Many kingdoms reflected their attraction to the new religion by declaring themselves to be independent Muslim states. Java's *Wali Songo* (nine apostles) added to this influence by preaching Islamic doctrine throughout the island and founding the Sultanates of Banten and Cirebon. Demak's importance as a diffusion centre for "Islamization" is also well documented; the central-square mosque is Java's holiest point for Muslims, and making the trip there seven times in one's lifetime is believed to be as important as the *haj* (pilgrimage to Mecca) which should take place at least once in every Muslim's lifetime. Further inland, the kingdom of Mataram was flourishing once again, under the rule of its leader Agung, who was also responsible for introducing the Islamic calendar. Agung's domain quickly expanded as he fought battles all the way to the northeast coastline. However, what he may not have known was that ports of the other islands were being slowly taken over by a new trading player ... the fortune-hunters of distant Europe.

Dutch Dominance

The colonial struggle for eastern ports was probably started by the Portuguese who vied for control of Moluccas spice trade. Soon, they had opened new trade routes between Europe and Asia which other traders slipped through, including the English, the Spanish – and, most importantly, the Dutch, whose influence would dominate Indonesia for the following 300 years. The Dutch landed at Banten in 1596, prying open the trade route into a channel of capitalist commercial exchange. The second main port was Jakarta – or, "Jayakarta," as it

JP Coen the founder of the Dutch East India Company (VOC).

the centre for trade to secure an absolute trading monopoly over the islands. With Governor-General Marshall Daendals installed into power from 1808-1810 "Old Batavia" underwent countless changes. Daendals wanted a modern city with wide roads and stylish buildings. Thus, a new *kota* (city centre) was built in the southern area and the old harbour fortress was knocked away.

Reforms to the city continued under the British leadership of Thomas Stamford Raffles, a noted military leader and keen naturalist, who arrived in Java on a military mission. Under his guidance, Batavia was re-created as a cultural centre for art, literature and education, and the port was expanded to become Southeast Asia's largest centre

was known at the time. The major opposition to the Dutch struggle for control came from the Sultans of Mataram and Banten in Java, Sumatra's Aceh and Sulawesi's Makassar, yet the Dutch managed to maintain firm control of trade and influence the government.

To end rivalry between the traders, the Dutch East India Company (*Vereenigde Oost Indische Compagnie* or VOC) was established to give the country control over the territories between the Straits of Magellan and the Cape of Good Hope – with sovereignty rights over the "Indies". Rumours still abound about the schemes of its founder, Jan Pieterszoon Coen, who used cheap overseas labour and his newly-named capital of Batavia (formerly Jayakarta) as

The coat of arms of the Dutch VOC (Vereenigde Oost Indische Compagnie).

Ships plying the lucrative trading routes from Batavia to other parts of Indonesia and Europe.

of trade until Raffles's even greater endeavour of Singapore came to life. For the Dutch, maintaining power was of key importance to their goals of monopoly. This was easily accomplished by "dividing and conquering" the various kingdoms — including strongholds like Banten and Mataram. After the division of the land, smaller states with limited power were created, which smoothed over power struggles creating a sense of peace and unification in Java. However, in the late-1700s, the VOC fell into financial trouble which was coupled by problems of inner corruption and labour uprisings which soon took their toll on the company. Finally, the VOC handed its land over to the Netherlands and transferred its trading rights to the colonial government – in what was the largest commercial collapse of the time.

After the Napoleonic Wars, when the British occupied the Dutch East Indies post of "Jawa", but control was eventually restored to the Dutch in 1816. The 1824 treaty that followed involved the exchange of Dutch holdings in the Malay Peninsula and India for the return of Indonesian settlements by the British.

Fights to the Death

The Dutch were also at work in Bali in order to gain a foothold along the northern coast as they claimed that wrecked

Prince Diponegoro — who would
"free the people from oppression."

ships were being ransacked in Bali's northern waters. By 1906, several thousand Dutch troops occupied the northern states of Buleleng and Jembrana, with battles being fought along the beaches between Sanur and Denpasar to lay the last claim to the island.

Dutch Assaults

In September 1906, when the Dutch mounted an assault in Denpasar the three princes of Banduy knew they could not escape defeat any longer. However, rather than face their inevitable fate of surrender and exile, they chose the more honourable path of *puputan* (suicidal fight to the death). The aristocracy faced death against a background of burning temples, dressed in their best clothes with their best *krises* (daggers) in hand. A painting at one of Ubud's museums recaptures the event in intense and gruesome detail as the Balinese faced the Dutch in a fateful last stand when more than 4,000 Balinese were slaughtered after a day's fighting which once again brought the island under Dutch rule. The Sumatrans also chose to fight; in fact, "fierce Aceh" is a description directly coined from the Dutch confrontation. Some of the bloodiest battles of Indonesian history came during the civil "Padri" wars, when the Dutch sided with the traditional Muslims in 1821 and then slyly wrested control. Within a short time, they dominated the west coast of the Minangkabau districts, including Benkulu (awarded in the 1824 trade treaty with the British).

Additional areas of the large island were quickly won by battles, although the staunch Bataks resisted until the turn of the century. Even after his 1903 surrender to the Dutch, Tuanku Muhamat Dawot, the last of the Acehnese sultans, kept the fight going as it had been for the past 30 years. Guerrilla resistance lingered within the hills of the island until 1907, forcing the Dutch to keep a wary military presence for the next decade.

Diponegoro & Loro Kidul

Still, the Indonesians were far from quiet

The Dutch engaged in fierce wars on Bali.

during this time, as Sumatra's 17-year Padai War raged in 1821 and the five-year Java War was launched in 1825 by Prince Diponegoro.

Diponegoro was an intriguing character whose life seemed charmed with divine intervention – he was thought to have received a vision from Loro Kidul, the Goddess of the Seas, during a meditation before a battle. In this prophesy, Loro Kidul told Diponegoro that he was destined to restore Java to its former height of power and glory. Thus, Diponegoro was rumoured to be "the Prince who would free the people from oppression". And he did, as his rebellion against the Dutch achieved temporary success until he was finally tricked into arrest by the Dutch, who pretended to be interested in peace negotiations. Diponegoro was then exiled to Sulawesi, where he spent his last years until his death in 1855.

Located in Ujung Pandang, Diponegoro's tomb is now a national heritage site. The loyalty of him and his fellow fighters is annually commemorated on the same day as the more than 200,000 Indonesians who lost their lives to disease, famine and war are remembered on **Heroes Day** on November 10th.

Culture of Convenience

More than 90 percent of Java was now under Dutch dominion, and in 1930 the Governor General, Johannes Van den

Raden Ajeng Kartini: Catalyst of Women's Rights

Kartini and her husband
(17th December 1903).

Her face is as common as the lavender 10,000 rupiah notes, from which she nobly gazes at those who hold her. Turn the bill over and her achievements are listed: progress in education and the attainment of rights and freedom for Muslim women.

Catalyst For Independence

She is Raden Ajeng Kartini, the woman whose writings were the catalyst for the independence of Indonesian women.

Born in Mayong, East Java, in 1879, Kartini was the daughter of the Regent of the Jepara. Her privileged status granted her the freedom of a European education – nearly unheard of for girls at that time, and started her brilliant mind on a neverending journey for the continuation of learning.

However, upon puberty, she was refused permission to continue her education, as women of that era were customarily expected to learn duties of the home.

Angered over the fact that her brothers were still allowed to attend school – coupled with what she viewed as Islam's unfairness to women, she began the writings that would change the way of life of women for the next two decades.

Published in Indonesian, Dutch and English, her letters questioned Islamic customs pertaining to the rights of women, the effects of seclusion, hierarchy and polygamy inherent in the religious system and its effects on the *priyayi* (aristocratic) women of Java. Some praised her brash honesty, while others scoffed at her outspoken views against traditional Javanese etiquette and the polygamy instituted through Islamic laws.

Educate The Javanese

Her demand to "Educate the Javanese" was reminiscent of a thirst for education in her younger days and her hope for the females of future generations. Truly a trailblazer in every sense of the word she set out to not only speak her mind but followed it too. After her marriage to the Regent of Remban, a supporter of progressive social policies, they set up their own school at their home in Remang for the daughters of Regents.

Kartini's writings continued as she vocalised her "longing for freedom, independence, and to stand alone," making her one of the first and most revered Indonesian writers. *Through Darkness to Light* a collection of her letters published in Dutch in 1911, contain some of her most quoted works (the English translation is available in paperback from the Norton Publishing Company).

Her life ended suddenly after the birth of her son in 1904. Today, a commemorative tomb stands within the grounds of the old mosque close to her home of Jepara, and on each April 21 – her birthday – the Republic of Indonesia remembers her spirit by celebrating **Kartini Day**, a national holiday.

TRANSPLANTING RICE.

The backbone of the economy — paddy or rice and the principal workers — women.

Bosch introduced a new *cultuurstelsel* ("Culture System") which was aimed at "promoting peaceful interchange between the races," but was mainly introduced to prevent further outbreaks of violence by the Javanese. An exchange of customs and traditions was thus incorporated between the leaders and the common people to enhance understanding and facilitate easier relations. Knowledge of Javanese dance and customs were required learning for all Europeans, while Western education, literature and social graces were introduced to the lower classes.

The peasants learnt farming methods, deciding that allocated land would be planted with specific crops to provide the most successful — and profitable — agricultural yields for both the economic and social system.

Power & Profits

Somehow, those in power made enough profits to save the Netherlands from becoming bankrupt and boost Java to the status of economic self-sufficiency. The government and aristocracy were ecstatic over the results but managed to turn a blind eye to those most affected by the shortcomings of the system.

The most obvious one being forced labour, an inefficient agricultural plan and a miscalculation of the amount of land and people necessary, which meant that the peasants felt far different about the outcome of the Culture System; they were forced to grow government crops on huge amounts of their own land, leaving them devastated when the "cash crops" failed. Finally these peasants were forced to face the prospect of poverty and starvation.

Pride in Nationalism

However, there was a conscience, within the Dutch Parliament, who felt the strong need to improve the lives and educate the lower classes of Indonesians. And, as the need for educated workers increased the efficiency and scope of the Indonesian school system, middle and upper-class Indonesians quickly took advantage of the opportunities offered by education, soon realizing the injustices of the Dutch system — as well as the pride and power of their own culture and heritage.

Stirrings of Independence

As modern conveniences and European-influenced customs were introduced into impoverished areas of the country, the first stirrings of independence started to electrify the youth. The time was ripe for change when the Japanese invaded the islands in 1942, Dutch influence came to a downfall and the capital was renamed "Jakarta," or "City of Victory" – the first in a long line of changes towards freedom.

Early meeting of the Party Kommunist Indonesia (PKI) held in Batavia, 1925.

An early market scene in Pasar Baroe, Batavia.

View of Padang, Sumatra at the turn of the century.

Raden NaVanujara

SA Radeu the Regent of Lebak.

G o v e r n m e n t

Marching down the wide boulevards of Batavia to crisp drum beats and cries of, "Single Fatherland! Single Nation! Single Language!" hundreds of young students brashly declared their freedom in the *Sumpah Pemuda* (Oath of Youth). It was 1928, a time when many Indonesians were taking pride in their country and making statements of their belief in their heritage and self-worth. For the Dutch, who had dominated the country for nearly 300 years, it signified the beginning of the end of their power.

The Pancasila spells out the five principles adopted by the government.

Politics & Progression

As in most oppressed societies, education was the catalyst that prodded masses of Indonesians into indignant protest against the unfairness of the Dutch colonial government. And, somehow, the educated elite and the lower classes came together in preparation for the impending fight – in the form of founding the country's first government par-

The President's Palace, Jakarta on Independence Day.

ties. *Saraket Islam*, or the *Islamic Association*, was the first true mass political movement in the country. It originated in 1909 as a society set up to protect Indonesians from unscrupulous Chinese dealers. The group claimed two million members (ranging from villagers to aristocracy), many of whom strongly identified with the Islamic focus of the party. In 1914, a Marxist group known as the *Perserikatan Kommunist Indonesia (PKI)*, (Indonesian Communist Party), was born in Semarang and soon aligned itself with Sareket Islam through its shared disdainment of capitalism and support for the trade union movements. The PKI was much more aggressive, and exhibited their displeasure through the organisation of strikes and revolts in Javan and Sumatran businesses and factories. It was dissolved in the late 1920s – with nearly 20,000 arrests, detainments and deportments during the angry rebellions.

However, the organization that became the most famous, was the *Partai Nasional Indonesia (PNI)*, (Indonesian Nationalist Party). Their vision was one of an independent nation; it was amongst students belonging to this group that Indonesian "nationalism" was first defined and the *Sumpah Pemuda* (Oath of Youth) was avowed.

The PNI was a creation formed from the genius of the 1927 Bandung Study Group, and was led by a man named Sukarno – who would later rise to power as the first president of Indonesia. Two students named Hatta and Sjahrir were also instrumental in PNI dealings, but their approach to their country's freedom was very different from that of Sukarno's.

Although both of them hailed from Sumatra they were educated in the Netherlands and favoured the development of outlets such as clinics, unions and cooperatives to bring the Indonesian people together, rather than employing Sukarno's strategy of dialogue to unite Marxist and Muslims in a move towards independence.

However, it did not take the Dutch long to recognize the threat of this group's shared goals and ambitions; all three were eventually detained and imprisoned until the end of Dutch rule.

Japanese Occupation & Assistance

According to legend the prophet King Joyoboyo foretold the coming of the Japanese in a vision that the land of Indonesia would be taken over by a white buffalo with blue eyes, then a yellow chicken that would rule for a year of corn before *Ratu Adil,* (the "Just Prince") would usher in a new Golden Age. The white buffalo, they say, was the Dutch, the yellow chicken the Japanese, and the professed "year of corn," a short enough time space to provide hope for Indonesian independence. The vision was only a little off course; (four years to be exact), during which time

Political campaign fresco
of the PPP.

the nationalists – primarily Sukarno and Hatta – worked hard to free their country from the shackles of foreign domination.

To assist the Indonesian leaders in securing a stable system for independence, the Japanese sponsored mass pro-Islamic, anti-western organizations, brought Muslim factions together with the *Masyuni* group and in 1943 formed the popular *PETA,* (Volunteer Army Defenders of the Fatherland). With good timing, technology and a good communication system propaganda easily reached the people resulting in mass motivation. Sukarno soon became known throughout the nation as the country in a united stance surged towards independence. Realizing that their

Sukarno's Intriguing Legacy

He was shocking. He was sweet. He was tough and unpredictable. Yet, he was also organized, charming and strong – the right man at the right time for his country. As the leader of one of the emerging world powers, Sukarno was a formidable force whom other countries regarded with wariness, whilst his own people basked in his warmth and rejoiced in his strength which ably guided them down the new roads to independence and power.

Humble Beginnings

For the man who was to lead Indonesia through times of turmoil to independence and beyond, his early years were relatively humble. Born in the year after the turn of the 20th century, Sukarno was the son of a lower *priyayi* (established aristocratic administrative class) schoolteacher and his Balinese wife. He spent his young days involved in school studies and family responsibilities. But he always showed his leadership ambitions. In his youth, he took an active role in educational endeavours and continually pushed new ideas ahead. His mentors were often radical cultural and political figures, such as; Douwes Dekker, Tjipto Mangunjusumo and Ki Hadjan Dewantaro. As his mind slowly opened and his ambitions grew, he seemed determined to break away from the usual pattern set by the political "followers" of the time. While turning questions into answers, his visions matured into dreams of power – both for himself and for his country.

First Political Parties

Not surprisingly, Sukarno was part of the first political movement called *Sarekat Islam*, a strong Islamic party that channelled the country's young growing pains into constructive action. When barely past boyhood, Sukarno married the daughter of Tjokroaminato, one of the most influential political leaders of the time. However, after his marriage in 1922, it seemed that he quickly disentangled himself from being associated with the party. He continued his studies at the new *Bandung Engineering College*, where he created the famous Bandung Study Group that voiced the concerns of the youth of the era. A year after receiving his engineering degree in 1926, Sukarno founded the *Indonesian Nationalist Association*, from the Bandung study group, which believed that an "independent Indonesia" was the ultimate and only objective. Out of the Indonesian Nationalist Association grew Sukarno's *Indonesian Nationalist Party*, better known as the popular PNI. With programmes that stressed mass organizations, cooperation with the Dutch authorities and, of course, the eventual freedom of the country, this group soon became the strongest nationalist movement during the last days of colonial Indonesia.

The Rise to Power

During the late 1920s, Sukarno rapidly shot into the limelight of power, for his ideas and vision lit a fire beneath the young masses who were tired of living under foreign domination and were ready to create a government of their own. Rather than appealing to only the aristocracy or the educated, he tempered his views to embrace all factions of the country from rural workers to women and youth.

When – not *if* – the time came for an independent Indonesian government, Sukarno suggested that it should be based on the traditional village system which featured leadership and guidance founded on an all party discussion. This way issues were resolved whilst various factions were drawn together towards the common goal of independence for the country.

And, to Sukarno, traditional Western "majority rules" were simply the appeasement of 51 percent of the population and the oppression of the other 49 percent. Thus he wanted complete involvement from all societal factions and strata to represent all views and provide possible answers. His disdainment for the "fake" democracies of capitalist countries was reflected in his acronym language for organizations – particularly the NEFOS, which can be termed the "New Emerging Forces", and OLDEFOS, or

"Old Established Forces", which divided the world, along with the NEKOLIM, or "Neo-Colonial Imperialists" which was his special term for western powers.

Of course, the colonial Dutch rulers of the time were hardly pleased with Sukarno's outspoken statements. Recognizing a clear threat to their power in December 1929 they placed him on trial for sedition, for speaking out against the government. He was sentenced to four years in prison, but received an early release after only two years. However, in 1933, he was arrested yet again and exiled to Flores, from where he was transfered to Benkulu, Sumatra five years later.

Cult of Personality

However, Sukarno was not only admired by his own people, he was also a dashing, dangerous leader regarded with something akin to awe by top political figures abroad. His image was well toned, his own outstanding characteristics and charisma fermented by an emulation of great legendary and historical figures. During his career, Sukamo played up this role as a charismatic demagogue with his flamboyant style of rule whilst appealing to the lingering beliefs in mysticism held by his followers.

He got away with it too, for his adventuresome and determined nature gave him a strength and character few people questioned – and many admired. Despite his flippant attitude towards traditional western values such as monogamy and abstinence, he was still trusted and in fact revered – his well-known sexual exploits and unfaithfulness to his wife were all easily overlooked and forgiven. Instead, he was known as *bapak* (father), by the people; a man who could quickly assume the position of leadership without any firm goals or direction in which to move. He could look good without action, sound powerful without saying anything meaningful. He was something of a chameleon observer whose views altered to keep up with the most popular sentiments of the time. Sukarno's strategies were cool, yet crafty; he often set himself up as a mediator between two groups, with him discussions flowed freely, as if cooperation and unity were something he alone had brilliantly engineered. He wanted no enemies but to identify himself with everyone and somehow managed to simultaneously claim belief in both God and Marxism. His most emotional levers over the masses were his ideals which were intertwined with the legends of the islands – traditional stories which many Indonesians still believed. In his policies and actions, he took the role of the determined and cheerful Bina, the heroic *wayang* (puppet show) character whose friendliness and strength provided a magnetic mysticism that appealed to popular emotions and the inner beliefs of the Indonesian people.

Ego and Downfall

However, soon, intangible power was not enough for the enigmatic leader, so Sukarno began the construction of great monuments throughout the capital. There were more self-commemorations to his own status than symbols for the country and people, such as the **Merdeka** ("Freedom") **Monument** – a sparkling new sports stadium. This and other ostentatious but unnecessary works of grandeur soon formed part of the city's skyline. And, like the great energy of the leader who created them the awesome presence of these monuments could not be ignored.

Unfortunately however, by concentrating on the cultivation of his own centre of power, the inconsistencies in Sukarno's political philosophies grew at the same rate as his ego. He gave scant attention to the development of government, nor to the growth of dependable ideologies which his country could look to for guidance ... and it was during this time when he increasingly focused his energies on personal gain that Sukarno's hold on power began to slowly slip away. The Untung Coup was staged and power transfered to Suharto in 1965. No stranger to prison, Sukarno was kept under house arrest until his death in June 1970 – a humble end to one of Indonesia's most influential and charismatic leaders.

The ivory white walls and gold dome of the Presidential Palace, Bogor.

time was short, the Japanese were also preparing for eventual change, setting up "The Investigating Body for the Preparation of Indonesian Independence," to help guide the country along the path to eventual freedom.

It was at this time that Sukarno created the country's binding philosophy of the *Pancasila*, (Five Principles): Faith in One God, Humanity, Nationalism, Representative Government and Social Justice. Reflecting a unique synthesis of Islam, Marxism, democracy, bureaucracy and traditional Indonesian communications and customs, the *Pancasila* would soon provide the basis of unification for the new independent government of Indonesia.

The explosion came on August 6 1945, when Hiroshima was scattered across the seas and the Japanese emperor surrendered ten days later. It was a time of confusion for Indonesia, as the defeated Japanese still occupied the island but could not grant the Indonesian's independence whilst the Allied forces had not yet arrived.

Thus, the status of who exactly controlled the country was momentarily uncertain. Rumours still abound that there were sharp conflicts between those who wanted to wait until Indonesian independence was legally granted and those who wanted to take advantage of the state of anarchy by seizing power in the country immediately. Stories of the weeks events fly back and forth through history, but on August 16, impatient underground communist resistance

A monument to President Sukarno, Jakarta.

groups kidnapped the nationalist leaders outside Jakarta to force the proclamation of freedom for Indonesia. Some paint the picture of a reluctant Sukarno declaring independence at the gunpoint of rebel activists while others believe that it was all part of his own plan.

Nevertheless, on the 17th August, Sukarno and Hatta announced Indonesia's independence and mounted the red-and-white flag for the first time.

Final Steps Towards Freedom

If the Dutch thought they could return to their former position of colonial power, their ideas were only a hopeful dream.

Their attempts to recapture control of the country, were to no avail as the nationalists strongly held onto their fragile freedom.

In a speech made that same year Mohammed Hatta remarked, "Indonesia has achieved her own administration as a result of her own efforts ... The Dutch should not remain under the delusion that they can thwart Indonesia's desire to remain independent". And, Hatta was correct, for international pressure finally forced the Dutch out of the region in 1949, and on December 27 1949 Dutch sovereignity was conceded to create an independent Indonesian republic.

This was somewhat forced by the United States' threat to withdraw aid (through the Marshall plan) which was to help rebuild the Netherlands after WWII, if the Dutch did not agree to an Indonesian republic.

elections from 1945 to 1958. Still, under Sukarno and his often radical leadership, the country somehow managed to remain under control.

Fight for Independence

Many Indonesians died fighting for their independence, and November 10 is now known as *Heroes Day* to commemorate Indonesians who fought and continue to fight for the independence of their country.

However, there was disorder in the diversity of the new republic; a lingering history of varied customs, religions, traditions and politics now led to a confusion which was further heightened by the onslaught of economic depression. Even the strength and guidance of the *Pancasila* principles could not hold the young country together, many of the smaller islands began to fight for their own independence which resulting in guerilla warfare, falling economic productivity and increased smuggling.

During this time, the government could easily have descended into a chaotic mess, with 17 cabinets and various unorganized or frequently cancelled

Sukarno's Guiding System

Sukarno's determination, strength and implausible charm helped him to hold on to his position as president, as well as to spread his proposal for "Guided Democracy". It was a system of strength and comfort to the naive young nation, one which represented all the parties and included all social classes including youth, women and villagers.

Functional groups such as the army were also included. The strength of "Guided Democracy" was the value of having different people working together, discussing situations and creating solutions within agreed points decided upon by the leaders.

Based on the traditional village government system, Sukarno's new system of *Nas-A-Kom*; *nasionalism* (nationalism), *agaman* (religion), *kommunisme* (communism), was a welcome change from the predictable and often apathetic "puppets" created by the western parliamentary system. Still, there was cor-

Monument to commemorate Diponegoro, Jakarta.

ruption within the central government structure and rebellion seethed amongst the people.

To smooth over differences and combat outbursts, Sukarno set up a powerful system that included a president-appointed parliament of organisational representatives, a Supreme Advisory Council for policy making and a National Front that would organize demonstrations and defense.

It was a sly power move, for none of these new organizations could hold ultimate control over the President – as they were subject to his terms of agreement. However, his boldness inspired both confidence and fear, and the country was, for the time being, under Sukarno's control.

Konfrontasi

Konfrontasi is perhaps the most suitable term to describe this era of politics; which involved directly confronting every issue and every country in a series of bold nationalist movements. This included an arms agreement with the Soviet Union, pressurising the US into handing over an area of West Irian Jaya to Indonesia in 1963, as well as staging attacks upon British and American holdings within Indonesia to protest against colonial presence in the newly-formed Malaysia.

During this time, many monuments were constructed in Jakarta as testaments to Indonesias identity, such as the **Merdeka** (*Freedom*) **Monument** in the centre of Jakarta. The sense of pride was high. During this time the PKI grew to nearly three million members, with around 20 million belonging to mass affiliated organizations such as the *Central All-Indonesian Workers Organization* and the *Indonesian Peasant Front*.

The Untung Coup

But, the reforms were not moving quickly enough for some – the PKI in particular, not only wanted more control of central policy-making, but insisted that workers and peasants should also be armed for self-defense. After several months of debate, Sukarno agreed to provide the arms by forming a "fifth" branch of the

A portrait of the second and current president, Suharto.

military and arranging to purchase 100,000 rifles from China.

However, an alternative plan was soon discovered, as six top army generals who opposed the establishment of this "fifth" force were gruesomely murdered by rebel apparently with the encouragement of the PKI. Left-wing forces were also stationed in Merdeka Square and close to the Presidential palace, although there was no attempt at revolt in Jakarta or in any of the other islands. It was lucky timing and smart thinking that allowed General Suharto, leader of the army's strategic reserve division, to take command of the army and crush the attempted coup.

The coup had failed, but theories behind it still run wild; were the communists in the PKI trying to seize power from Sukarno? Was the military in cahoots from the start – or was the motive a bit deeper; was Suharto waiting to do away with his rivals in a bid for power (possibly presidential)? And then there is the question of the involvement of Sukarno, could he have staged the coup himself to show his strength to the Indonesian people?

Whatever the motive, and whoever the instigator, the effect of the outbreak was a wave of anti-communist violence that cost hundreds of thousands of PKI lives.

Anyone suspected of involvement with communist organizations or even sympathizing with the group's causes faced the threat of arrest, exile or elimination, and many innocent of the charges still died in wrongful accusations that flew through the air in this one of Indonesia's greatest purges of the time.

Suharto's Approach

After squashing down the coup and ending confrontation in Malaysia, General Suharto was waiting for just the right time to make a bid for power – and he did not have too long to wait. Appointed Commander-in-Chief of the Armed Forces in 1965 by Sukarno, he organised demonstrations to increase pressure on the President and gain the confidence of those who still controlled the unstable government system.

Bugles blow in celebration of Independence Day.

Even youngsters get into the spirit of Independence Day.

Finally, in March of 1966, he surrounded the Presidential palace and "encouraged" Sukarno to sign the 11th *March Order,* which gave Suharto the freedom to act on his own, without presidential authority. Six days later, Suharto's troops occupied communication offices, defence bases and replaced Sukarno's government offices. Still, it took almost a year – until March 27,

by the new regime. The administration shifted to Suharto's men and "democratic" elections were held with Suharto's *Golkar*, a newly-formed federation of functional groups which was mainly based on the strength of the military troops. Known as the Army party, competition to *Golkar* was either banned or disqualified. After 1971 to stand up to *Golkar's* power, the four main Muslim parties combined into the *Development Union Party (PPP)*. Sukarno's former PNI group was crushed, and the remaining satellite parties were swept under his new and long standing broad *Indonesian Democratic Party* (PDI).

Looking to the Future

Since his election, Suharto has opened Indonesia to new opportunities, by adopting modern policies which include abandoning traditional isolationism from membership in the UN.

The country is also active in the promotion of the **Association of Southeast Asian Nations (ASEAN)**, in whose campaigns and promotions Indonesia plays an integral part. Foreign investment is now being encouraged, and education and research are continued high priorities within the country. Any opposition to the system is counterbalanced by a government whose driving force is the presence and support of a military power which aims to ensure equal rights and opportunities for the citizens of the Republic of Indonesia.

1967, for Suharto to gain control of the *People's Consultative Congress* and finally be elected President. Again, the change in power brought with it political upheaval as the last communist, anti-government, pro-Sukarnoists were pursued and stamped into non-existence

Indonesia has the potential to be one of the richest countries in the world. Blessed with a rich variety of natural resources, Indonesia's economy is steadily growing stronger. In the past few years, the country has maintained an overall economic growth rate of more than 7 percent – easily surpassing the 5 percent goal outlined in Suharto's Five Year Development Plan. Within the impenetrable forests of East Kalimantan and Irian Jaya lie rich deposits of oil, minerals, gemstones and coal, all ably protected and hidden amidst massive hills. But slowly and most certainly, mining and manufacturing companies are digging closer and closer to the natural treasures of these "resource-rich" lands that have attracted the accounts of western investors.

Along with Sumatra's Aceh and Riau provinces, these areas remain virtually untapped for their coal, iron, bauxite and tin. Thus, the tribal cultures of the interior remain safe – at least for the time being.

Economy

Liquid gold – oil reserves being tapped from an offshore oil rig.

Cocoa – one of Indonesia's premier cash crops being unloaded from a cocoa bean drier.

Sparsely populated and secluded, these areas – with proper planning, excavation and recultivation – could be the islands that not only secure Indonesia's economically independent future, but also raise the standard of living for its people and become a model of a successful "eco-productive" use of the environment by humans.

Living off the Land

A neverending supply of sunshine, dependable rains and soft volcanic ash has created an excellent climate for the cultivation of cash crops in the western islands. These include; Java's tea plantations, Bali's rice fields and Sumatra's coastal rubber crops. The natural condition of the archipelago and the blessings of climate make these areas some of the most important in the nation's food production.

Unfortunately, in the eastern islands, the soil is not as fertile; dry and baked by the sunlight, it lacks the nutrients needed to cultivate crops. Farmers working the eastern islands practice "shifting" cultivation which has resulted in erosion and the destruction of the environment. To make use of the land's remaining potential, conservation and agricultural experts are now working with soil additives, experimental crops and the re-education of farming techniques used within the villages. Still, agronomy turns the economic wheels of

The verdant terraced rice fields of Bali – a green dream.

the country, as Indonesia is the top producer of cloves, second in rubber and third in coffee production in the international market place. Palm oil and spices are two other signficant industries that have supplied the country with income for centuries.

However, the most controversial land-based industry, is probably that of timber. With more than 140 million hectares of rainforest which cover nearly three-fourths of the country's land, Indonesia shelters the largest rainforest area after Brazil and Zaire – the wood that is extracted from it is a significant contribution to the country's foreign exchange earnings.

Therefore, to appease production and profit concerns while still protect-

ing the biodiversity of plants and animals within these forests, the government has set up guidelines for selective tree felling, reforestation, the development of timber estates and a ban on the export of logs.

Green Fields Forever

Indonesia's main staple is rice. Primarily a crop cultivated in Java and Bali, it has been an agricultural staple for more than 2,000 years. The perfect climate has controlled this rice tradition; the hot, wet seasons of the central islands have perfected sawah, (wet rice cultivation), in which the lush, terraced fields produce crops all year-round at two-

Coffee, one of the leading produce today, as it was in colonial times.

month intervals. *Ladang*, (shifting culti-vation), is the prefered style in the drier eastern islands, where the jungle is burned to enrich the soil by hastening both decompostion and the production of oxygen. The fields are dry and as bare as skeletons when rice cultivation be-gins, with bulls harnessed with wooden plows blundering through the rough chunks of earth. Behind them, thin

area, where rice farmers first sow a small crop which will be dug up and carefully replanted, watered and weeded until the rice reaches maturity once again. Surprisingly, irrigation has existed for thousands of years in Indonesia, an engineering technology enforced by nature because of the rugged terrain that required the construction of smooth terraces which were often built far from rivers and streams. As seen in the beautiful terraces that highlight the Balinese landscape, this intricate system of tunnels and dams brings water, the lifeblood of the rice crops to the fields.

Because of the key role played by rice in the country's economy, irrigation technology is an important government concern. Policies are being discussed to develop swamp areas whilst preserving the country's supplies of water and soil. Rehabilitation and development activities are taking place to build new irrigation networks throughout the fields, that will benefit the land and help the farmers maintain economic self-sufficiency.

Gifts of the Hills

Indonesia's rugged hills and rich earth offer unquestionable wealth to miners and investors, for the depths of bauxite, coal, copper and tin reserves are substantial. Most important is the country's supply of natural gas – the archipelago is not only the world's top liquified natural gas (LNG) producer, but it is also the largest exporter of natural gas. The main

trenches slide into the soil over old, bony stalks that were burned off after the last season's harvest. After plowing, the fields are soothingly soaked in water, then plowed over and over until the dark land is replenished and enriched. Planting begins in a small edge of the plowed

Enter the world of synthetics – metallic heavy duty machinery for processing polyester.

difference between the two is that "natural" gas is the raw form of the resource which is tapped from the ground as vapour, while "liquified natural gas" has been pressurized into liquid form to reduce its volume for shipping and transportation.

Oil is another of the area's most profitable industries, as the country is the major oil producer within Southeast Asia. On the international market, Indonesia's supplies are highly distributed, ranking sixth among OPEC nations and thirteenth in the world, with an output of more than 1.3 million barrels each day. For these resources, the government reaps a good income – around 60 percent. Furthermore 70 percent of its revenue comes from oil profits and gas earnings, respectively. Most of this oil and natural gas is mined from the remote areas of North Sumatra and East Kalimantan. Plans for research, mapping and mining the millions of unexplored hectares within these areas are being carried out under each of Suharto's successive Five Year Plans.

Jewels of the Archipelago

Two of the world's most precious islands, Sumatra and Kalimantan provide Indonesia with little-known mines of gold, silver and diamonds.

Sumatra (the archipelago's largest island) has been the prime "gold mine" since the time of explorers, who crossed

Rubber saplings being reared in a nursery before being transplanted.

the oceans in search of sparkling riches. An interesting tale from the past centres on the Dutch quest for the legendary "El Dorado" as they explored the island's western mines for gold during the 17th century. Local Minangkabau rulers protested against their efforts, warning them that it was a futile attempt to gain riches. However, the Dutch ignored them as the VOC sunk thousands of guilders into a new mine near Salinda. But, poor geological composition, the harsh tropical climate and a shortage of workers, led to the eventual collapse of this enterprise in 1732.

The main Sumatran gold mines are located in the central province of Jambi, which, until 1989, was only open to exploration by local investors. However,

now the island's potential has attracted outside markets, and to accommodate this new interest the government has issued permits allowing foreigners to explore and mine gold from Sumatra's rich reserves. Diamonds are the jewels of Kalimantan, where new deposits (expected to yield more than 250,000 carats) were recently found in the swampland surrounding Banjarmasin. Possibilities for "dry-mining" are now being explored by Indonesian, Australian and British companies to replace the current "dredging" technique.

As the largest tin producer in the world, the land is also rich in mineral content. Reserves in Irian Jaya, Kalimantan and Sulawesi provide Indonesia with the world's largest reserves of nickel-oxide. Substantial copper deposits have also been discovered in these areas as well as Sumatra and Java.

Capturing Power & Produce

A frightening sight cuts into the pleasant scenery that usually dots Java's west coastal road; a gigantic white rocket-shaped reactor surrounded by long lines of huge aeroplane turbines that loom over the palms as if threatening doomsday. This is Indonesia's new industry, the manufacturing of aeroplanes and nuclear energy – which, with the onset of technology, is becoming one of the country's most powerful investments. Inland, nature has graced the island with rushing rivers and volcanic lakes from which hydroelectric and geothermal energy are being tapped.

The surrounding lakes and seas provide for a national fishing trade that brings profits to local village markets and city superstores alike. With its vast variety of freshwater life, Indonesia's aquatic industries have always flourished. There has been substantial and continuing growth in the country's sea and inland fisheries, which has led to a near-doubling of fresh fish exports over the past decade. As world concerns concentrate on better health and nutrition, the country has also come to the market forefront with offerings such as shrimp, squid, crab, lobster and octopus, expanding the demand for the archipelago's delicious natural banquet both within its own islands and on the larger, international scale.

Economic Diversity

So far, "upward socialism, downward capitalism", has been the term coined to describe the Indonesian economic system. What this means is that the state retains control of or owns most of the natural resources such as oil and gas, as well as infrastructure such as, communication and transportation utilities. These are mostly found within the "densely populated" areas of Java, Bali and Sumatra, where the government and bureaucratic offices are located, where businesses grow, capitalist ventures are risked and tourism has the greatest economic impact. In these cities the standard of modern efficiency is part of a current debate on the merits of capitalism.

Skyscrapers soar into the clouds, money changes hands in air-conditioned banks while muzak plays and at

It is not difficult to be a rupiah millionaire.

night, neon attractions hypnotize late night shoppers into indulging in alternative pleasures. But, between the smog-filled roads and dilapidated huts standing on stilts above rubbish-filled rivers, capitalists point out that the economic payoff of commercialism is that it provides "every human with the opportunity for a better future".

In the drier, less-populated outer islands there is much that comprises the category of "barren and poor". Yet, somehow, modern conveniences have crept into the lives of the string of cities and villages stretching from Lombok to Timor; small businesses flourish, plantations manage to eke out another year's crop of tea or fruit and the coconut trucks rumble by on the hour, hawking thick, juicy shavings and sweet, watery milk along the rough roads.

Industry & Opportunity

It is small business in a small state, but one with potential – shops selling electric appliances such as refrigerators and televisions, western clothing stores and beauty parlours line the towns. Some have headed for the lights of Jakarta with promises of "better living;" others are satisfied enough to remain, living on one or two thousand rupiah a day (approximately US$1), living simply, caring for families and neighbours, meditating on the richness of life. With the help of larger state-owned and pri-

Tourism in Bali

Kuta – the beach bum's paradise on earth!

It is the clash of sizzling topless beaches and cool, quiet hills that makes Bali an ever-changing kaleidescope of solemn tradition and brash modern holiday dreams. Of the nearly three million annual visitors to Indonesia – approximately the population of Bali itself – more than half travel to this small central island.

During the school holidays' hotels are completely booked, beaches packed, western music blares from open-air pubs throughout the night, streets are clogged with tourists wobbling along on mopeds and bicycles, whilst dodging chickens and dogs in a haphazard effort to enjoy this limited experience of Indonesia available dur-

vate companies, small businesses have been able to find assistance and guidance which have helped the industry flourish as a whole. Banks have also offered a helpful hand by offering special credit policies and several industrial centres specializing in helping small organizations have also been established.

Recently recognized concepts of "independence" and "individual accomplishment" have also helped Indonesia's small-scale industries to catch on quickly within the population. Their development has added jobs and helped equalize the distribution of economic opportunities – particularly in the less wealthy, rural areas – encouraging bet-ing their vacation time.

Benefits of Tourism

Bali has come quite a long way from the "Gem of the Lesser Sunda Islands" slogan first used by the Government Tourist Bureau in the early 1900s. Three-quarters of a century later, during Suharto's first Five Year Development Plan, tourism became a national issue and the concept of *parawisata* (cultural tourism) was impressed upon Balinese minds. The idea being to bring in a steady tourist income while promoting the beauty and history of the Balinese culture. And, strangely enough, the influences of the west have created an interesting cultural exchange that has benefited both the Balinese and those who come to experience the "Emerald Island". For those born on Bali, traditions have miraculously remained staunchly unchanged, only occasionally watered down to suit the impatience of tourists. Temples are still sacred, dances revered and honed to perfection and offerings of incense and flower petals placed carefully in sight of both the spirits of evil and good. However, the greatest impact of the west is related to culture – that of Balinese art.

Naturally creative, the Balinese have traditionally practised carving, singing, dancing and drawing, weaving their talents into the hours of daily life – somewhere along the way, it was found that visitors would actually pay for their art. Suddenly, a new industry was founded for the Balinese, who could now make a lifetime career out of honing the crafts they enjoyed.

Now, *batik* clothing is the "in" style, while silver and woodcarving industries thrive. Painting is perhaps the most western-influenced art of all; which not only generates tourist revenue, but has also inspired the talents of numerous Dutch and American professionals who now reside permanently on the island.

Thus, not only has tourism resulted in the enhancement of artistry in Bali, but it has also opened the minds of Western visitors to one of the most influential cultures and oldest traditions of Indonesia.

A Bit of Every World

Perhaps what makes Bali enchanting is its ability to capture the charm of both east and west, with respect for both. In Kuta, for instance, it is rare to find a menu not filled with western food, pop and rap music fill the stores, there is the infamous "Peanut" area of Harley-Davidson, leather jacket and sequin-studded bars. Happy hours thrive in Australian-theme pubs, while guesthouses often have a distinctly French or German air.

Yet, *petit* bamboo-leaf boxes filled with spirit offerings are scattered across the ground, the scent of incense warms the evening breeze as the flash of delicate cloth moves in a lifelike way from rope lines. Lush terraced rice paddies march up the sloping hills and children crunch fried grasshopper snacks as paper kites soar through the sky.

ter production quality, more efficient sales and marketing techniques and a greater feeling of pride, individual worth and self-reliance amongst its people.

Tradeoffs of Tourism

Temples and traditions make tourism one of the country's economic strengths. In 1987, for the first time the country received more than one million visitors. Today, close to three million international tourists annually visit to experience Indonesia's exciting landscape, intriguing customs and warm-hearted people. One of the most successful promotions of Indonesia has been, "*Visit*

Oil palm being harvested on extensive estates in Sumatra, Java amd Kalimantan.

ASEAN Year", an ongoing marketing campaign that draws visitors to the Southeast Asian area. Together with Brunei, Malaysia, the Philippines, Singapore and Thailand, Indonesia has participated in international events, conferences and special travel packages that have successfully attracted many tourists to the area.

Promotion & Education

Thus, government offices, tour agencies and travel organizations are in the process of setting up local and regional promotional offices to provide printed materials, better accommodation and transportation systems for the quickly increasing number of holiday and business visitors. In addition, hundreds of English-language training and tourism schools have recently been established throughout the archipelago, not only to assist western travellers, but also to teach Indonesians how best to fulfill the growing number of job opportunities arising in the field of tourism.

One of the most convenient advantages of travelling in Indonesia is the two-month exemption that allows visitors from 38 countries to enter for 60 days visa-free. However, what is especially encouraging with the increasing number of international travellers, is the country's concern with preserving its culture and heritage while at the same time generously sharing with and educating others.

Geography & Climate

Cutting a wide, wet trench amidst the foaming blue of the sea, schooners criss-cross the six main islands of the Indonesian archipelago in search of spices, silks and gold. Faded maps of pale parchment are ink-marked with stains and dotted lines carefully retraced between the narrow straits of a half-dozen seas. On the ragged base, beneath the islands, are drawn the waves of the Indian Ocean, with the South China Sea and the Pacific Ocean surging silently above. In-between, at the tip of Sumatra, the Java Sea melts into the Flores which melts into the Banda and Arafua Seas all the way to the edge of Northern Australia ... the thin channels in between providing a path for pirate hideouts, potential raids and swiftly planned escapes. The horizontal fold of the map marks the Equator, slicing Sumatra and Kalimantan in two and looping off the arms of Sulawesi and Ternate. Waves and whirlpools are quick slashes of blue around Sumatra's rugged southern edges, the sly

Resorts and commercial development are fast evolving on Batam Island.

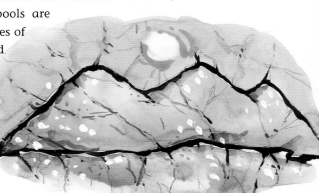

curves of Makassar are encircled by the thin Sulawesi Strait. Skulls and crossbones warn of the deep, dangerous waves between Lombok and Bali, and an imaginary boundary called the Wallace Line relinquishes Asia to the western islands and Australia to the east, thereby demarking regional divisions of flora and fauna.

A Gentle Curve of Islands

Like the curving tail of a tiger in the Java Sea, Indonesia's landscape is one of the wildest on earth. Coined by the Greeks, the name "Indonesia" stems from two words, "*indos* " – India, and "*nesi*," – islands, and of the 13,700 or so, only about 6,000 hold human life.

About 20 percent of the archipelago's territory is land, outlined by a crumpled mass of mountains that rise in sloping splendour in the midst of each of the six main islands – Kalimantan, Sumatra, Sulawesi, Java, Irian Jaya (New Guinea) and Bali.

Formed by volcanic activity, many splintered away from the main chain; some formed the Moluccas islands and Nusa Tenggara, while others were destined to face eons in desolation. With more than 30 percent of the world's active volcanoes, Indonesia is at the very core of the South Pacific's "Ring of Fire".

Standing guard all the way down the archipelago's centre, names like Sumatra's Kerinci, Java's Bromo, Semaru and Merapi, Bali's sacred Agung and Lombok's rugged Rinjani conjure memories of past shows of power and immense destruction. It is still a rare day when the breath from these heated peaks can not be seen against the blue of the sky. They remain a constant reminder of the powerful wrath contained within their sulphurous cauldrons.

The 1883 eruption of Krakatau off Java's western coast is probably the most well-known; not only were its effects seen and felt around the world, but it destroyed entire coastal villages and changed the shape of the land. On a clear night the view from the nearby Carita Beach – named *carita*, (stories), told of the explosion – glowing crimson trails of lava can sometimes still be spotted leaking out of Anak Krakatau, the smaller caldera left behind by the original explosion.

Several lakes such as the surpris-

Nipah swamps among meandering muddy rivers in Balikpapan, Borneo.

ingly azure bays of Java's Ijien crater and the ever-changing gemstones of Flores' Keli Mutu lakes now glisten red, black and green as they settle between the mountain folds.

The largest lake in Southeast Asia, Sumatra's peaceful Lake Toba separates the island of Samosir from the encircling mainland, creating a small offshore haven of Batak culture in the midst of the Bukit Barisan range.

Rivers are sometimes sources of power and fear; Sumatra's mighty Alas River that runs from north to south, offers infamous white-water rafting challenges; Java's Solo River that carried the first transport through Yogyakarta between Jakarta and Surabaya and the Mahakam River in Kalimantan, winds a river road through the jungle.

In Kalimantan, the roads are the rivers – including the Kapuas, which is more than 1,000 kilometres long! Although Java and Bali are crowded by settlements of humanity, the other islands mostly remain as jungle as they have for thousands of years. With 10 percent of the world's rainforests (only Brazil zaire have more) Indonesia's land has been targeted for some of the government's most important environmental protection programmes.

Birthmarks of Beauty

Interestingly, each area still has its own unique characteristics and landscape

The undeveloped, undiscovered in Lake Bratan, Bali.

that immediately distinguishes it from most of the other islands. Much of Java is now smoke and steel, yet its adventuresome side is well-preserved, located in lovely mountains and soft lowland plains between the solemn northern and wild southern coastlines.

Tiny Bali's northern foothills fall southwards to terraced rice fields, serrated by a central mountain chain presided over by "the Mother" Gunung Agung. Nearly three times the size of Java, Sumatra's spine is marked by more than 100 volcanoes located in the Bukit Barisan

ing into the sunrise is Nusa Tenggara, a fractured puzzle of island pieces where mountains often slide into the sea.

On the other side of the Wallace Line, the climate is dry, the land dustier, the daylight bathed in hues of beige. Resembling the Australian outback, life here is often limited to the fertile central plains. From the stunning coastal road the sight of Lombok's lush forestation around the central mountains provides a vivid glimpse of Bali's younger days.

With weathered craters and ageing volcanic escarpments that hide the lovely Dumpai plains, Sumbawa has a beauty all of its own that stretches east over Mount Tambora's two-coloured crater lake to small Sape's Islamic port. Brighter than most photographs taken of them, the islands of Komodo Rinca are woven into an embroidery of low green and gold shrubs, unpredictable hills and smooth beaches which are *de facto* far more fascinating than the hazy heat of tourist brochures usually depict.

However, the islands hold danger as well, for rough tides, waves and whirlpools guard the komodo dragons that roam within from curious ships on the outer shores. Flores means "flowers" in Portuguese and the description is accurate; the one-lane dirt roads that push up and over the roller-coaster peaks of the mountains are encircled by dry blossoms that brush over vehicles passing through the vast cliffsides and wide valleys.

At the eastern half of Flores, past the port of Ende where ships bound for

("Marching Hills") range.

On the east side is swampland; to the west, the rugged, palm-lined coast, with high, Tibet-like plateaus. In-between, a monument marking the Equator's crossing stands in the village of Bonjol, whose thick rainforest jungle sprawls out over both sides of the land. Tossed eastwards from Bali, and stretch-

Exploring Indonesia

With a bit of time and imagination, it is fairly easy to explore the varying landscapes of Indonesia's very different islands. Gravel roads and cement highways crisscross mountains and inner plateaus, while longboats silently slip down wide rivers to reach formerly unreachable areas. Tiny offshore islands make interesting jump-off spots for adventure. You can reach them by ship as many of them call in the port to drop supplies or to pick up export goods. However, throughout the most remote areas of Kalimantan, Irian Jaya, Sulawesi and Sumatra, flying is still the best way to get across the land, as well as to discover the immense expanse of its beauty. Not only does a bird's-eye view give the explorer a different look at the islands but it is still often the only available means of transport.

the Timor and Sumba Islands chug through the sea, you can see the tri-coloured lakes of Keli Mutu sparkling in the light.

Inner Timor is a mass of sweeping bare mountains and tumbled valleys, sucked dry by the sun and the winds, while the edges are ringed by the parched fields of the lower hills.

To the west, the wide grasslands of neighbouring Sumba provide sustenance for its horse-breeding tradition, although most of the population prefers the more fertile earth of its wetter western end.

Secret Inner Lands

Once known as Borneo, Kalimantan shares a common border with Malaysia's province of Sarawak and is one of the largest Indonesian islands. On a clear day the view from above shows an intricate web of surging camel-coloured rivers looping in ribbons and bows between more than 539,400 square kilometres of mountainous land.

Not surprisingly, this area wraps a tight jungle boundary around the powerful Barito River – Indonesia's largest and longest river which cuts through the midst of the southern "province of a thousand rivers". The rivers of Kalimantan provide important "roads" of travel that are the country's communication links between the busy coastal ports and the inner mountains, lakes and hot springs.

Two hundred kilometres north of Balikpapan, the eastern capital of Samarinda lies on the northern bank of the mighty Mahakam that cuts into the heart of the territory of the Dayak tribes, while at 1,143 kilometers, the western Kapuas River is one of the country's longest waterways.

The Kapuas and Landak Rivers together divide the fast-growing provincial capital of Pontianak into three separate areas. Pontianiak, just 125 kilometres from the Malaysian border lies exactly on the equator at the middle of the island's western coast and is the gateway to some of Kalimantan's most remote central areas. Because of its convenient waterways and coastal location, it has become one of the country's major harbours and trading centres.

Sulawesi's odd four-fingered peninsulas resemble whorls around the slop-

Snow in the tropics? Visit the Carstensz Range which boasts of the Merren Glacier.

ing central mountains – an area of nearly 200,000 square kilometres that is encrusted by broken coral beaches and brilliant reefs. At the tip of the island's northern edge, Manado provides some of Indonesia's most interesting offshore outcrops and reefs. Inland, stunning sheer cliffs drop upon flat, grassy fields which descend into massive folds of mountains forming a chain down to the southern capital and port of Ujung Pandang.

One of the most unusual features of this odd-shaped island are the presence of central caves in the high, grey cliffs of the central mountain areas. The largest cave in South Sulawesi is the Mampu Cave. But, by far the largest source of curiosity and a tourist attraction are the central area's eerie cliffside tombs. Here, the Toraja tribe have used the inner caves and cliff walls to carve out graves for their dead. These graves function to protect the clothing, jewels and coins that were provided for burial from thieving eyes.

Tiny Islands & Towering Mountains

Sea gardens and small islands glitter like jade across the deep blue of the Seram and Banda Seas where the 1,000 small islands of the Moluccas cluster between the coasts of Sulawesi and Irian Jaya.

Not surprisingly, close to 90 percent

Around the Fiery Circle

Smouldering calderas sitting in close proximity in Java.

Mount Tambora exhibited the ultimate power of volcanic force. Legends told that it was the sign of a marriage celebration for the child of the Sea Goddess Loro Kidul. Better-known is the smaller, but

Along the sloping grey walls of the crusty volcanic rim, the earth is like talcum powder, a fine ashen silt that settles in the pores and nostrils creating a chartreuse hue on the skin. Although chilly, the air is damp and scented with sulphur.

Above, there are nothing but misty fumes rising into the sky ... and below, only bubbling pools of crimson lava. The feeling of energy is awesome, as is the shadow of fear; one slip and life could plummet into the depths of the dreaded otherworld. Underfoot, the ground trembles with every wisp of smoke.

An Explosion of Life

Feared for centuries by the various peoples that have inhabited the islands of Indonesia, the string of more than 400 volcanoes have been a source of both legend and customs. To climb one can be a pilgrimage, to sacrifice life to one may appease the wrath of the gods that reside within. With more than 80 active volcanoes dotted throughout the islands, volcanoes have long been a part of the archipelago's history – even before there were signs of human life. Probably the largest prehistoric explosion was that of Mount Toba in Sumatra, where Southeast Asia's largest lake, Lake Toba is now settled.

In 1815, Sumbawa's enormous eruption of equally destructive Krakatau explosion some 60 odd years later. Although the power and lava was just one-tenth the strength and volume of Tambora, Krakatau changed the face of Java's western coastline; on a clear night veins of lava can still be spotted flowing from the edges of the caldera of its "child," Anak Krakatau. In 1963, the "King of Mountains," Mount Agung, erupted in Bali. The furious eruption was likened (according to legend) to the anger of the Hindu gods.

Just across the western strait, Java's Mount Bromo is home to the spirit of Joko Seger, whose unpredictable temperament that varies between benevolence and wrath prompts annual midnight offerings, at suitable times indicated by the Tenggerese calendar.

Fury Throughout Time

Throughout time there have been cycles of heat and cooling and most volcanoes seem to reserve their energy for the most feverish periods that occur just before the chill. In fact, many scientists believe that volcanoes are the key to explaining the cause of the Ice Age, as well as the distribution of land masses and species. Exploding during the most intense periods of warmth, the volcanoes destroy coastlines and create islands, while at the same time their dust and smoke hides the light of the sun. Without sunlight, the climate quickly cools and old cycles of life come to an end. Sea levels then drop as the water is frozen into glacial masses, creating land bridges over which new generations of plant, animal and human life will eventually cross.

Into the Depths

To understand the ferocious movements beneath the earth's crust, try to picture a giant kettle, filled with water covered with a tight lid and with a fire below. The water inside soon bubbles and heats to a boil – the temperature rises, steam seeps and hisses from the thin crack between the lid and kettle lip, until the contents are brought to a swift boil which will overflow down the sides of the kettle until the heat is extinguished. This is akin to the process of eruption, when the steady heating of water located at the base of the mountain leads to eruptions from the top.

Magma is contained in a spherical central chamber, and when the potential (static) energy is transformed into kinetic (dynamic) energy, a force of lava is pushed out through the upper end of the cone with an explosion. The timing of eruptions is difficult for scientists and geophysicists to predict due to differences in timing at the beginning of the heating cycle. Results also vary, depending on the length and mass of the explosion; tidal waves, the changing colour of the sky, earth trembles and a continuous thundering sound throughout the atmosphere have all been recorded throughout the world as effects of eruptions.

And Then, Life

However, after the destruction and devastation of the land, the ashen volcano slopes are soon covered with foliage once again. The lush greens of Anak Krakatau off Java's west coast stand as testimony to the life sustaining possibilities located in the fiery circle of Indonesia's islands.

of this province's area is water – the ocean here is thousands of metres deep and the Banda Sea, at 6,500 metres, is Indonesia's deepest waterway. The 10 percent of land is a myriad of airports and shipping lanes that link the small islands together in commerce and communication.

The capital of Ambon, located on the large, central island of Seram, provides a good example of the geographical location of the surrounding towns with its low hills, winding coastlines and volcanic, mountainous core. Situated in one of the world's most active and dangerous volcanic belts, many of Moluccas islands look as if they have erupted into cones straight from the depths of the sea.

Gunung Api, one of the biggest and barest islands, erupted only a few years ago, and the province has had more than 70 volcanic eruptions in the last 400 years. Cold, snow-covered mountains and sheer cliff faces suddenly jut out above the vast jungle of Irian Jaya.

Here, the highest peak in the country proudly overlooks the rest of the western islands, and at more than 5,500 metres, Gunung Jayawijaya – better-known as Mount Jaya – is overwhelming enough to cast a formidable glacial shadow that attracts climbers from all over the world. Irian Jaya was once called "West New Guinea" until Suharto's confrontation with the Dutch which resulted in Indonesia's acquistion of this territory in 1969.

Today, the former island of New

Screaming primates, thick undergrowth, leafy vines… everywhere in the tropical rainforest of Java.

Guinea has been split into two, and the nearly 422,000 square kilometres of "West Irian" shares a long border with Papua New Guinea.

You can find a hint of every kind of landscape in Irian Jaya ranging from the palm-fringed coral reefs ringing the edges to the flat central plains located close to the border of New Guinea. Offshore reefs surround the international island gateway of Biak to the north, while the peninsula that pinches the edges of the small city of Sorong is squeezed out from the island's western

edge. Swamps hem the southeastern areas, but the centre is covered with snow fields and alpine meadows which surround the solemn glacial peak of Gunung "Jaya" (5,030 metres) – Irian Jaya's main geographical attraction.

In the central plateaus, the Baliem Valley spills out between the rugged hills, its protective, jagged border sur-rounding some of the most remote areas of the archipelago.

From the central forests, humid swamps dip low to encroach the jungle surrounding the central Baliem River, which runs west from the area around Gunung Trikora about 120 kilometres through the Grand Valley to the Arafua Sea.

W hen the lone ship *Victoria* from Magellan's fleet returned to Spain from its round-the-world voyage in 1522, the delicate Moluccas bird plumes contained in the cargo's cache hold were believed to be the wings of angels. And so, it was perhaps this lust for trade with the east that first roused explorers' curiosity and acquisition instincts towards Indonesia's unique wildlife. Although already drawn by the promise of aromatics, textiles and gold, a keen interest in the archipelago's plants and animals began when stories of unusual spices and mythical unicorns circulated through European and Asian shipyards.

Bornean Gibbons swing about in Kalimantan.

73

Flora and Fauna

The Wallace Line

Of those who sailed in search of answers, it was Alfred Russell Wallace whose work was by far the most influential in the field of biology. From 1854 to 1864, Wallace explored the islands of Malaysia and clearly

A Practical Plan: Conservation in Indonesia

Free to raom the national parks.

certain species was either limited or altogether prohibited.

The first true National Park was **Ujung Kulon**, on Java's southwestern peninsula. Established by the Netherlands Indies Society for the Protection of Nature, it was declared a national reserve in 1921 and a National Park only in 1983. Today, the park is most often cited for its efforts to protect the last species of the rare Javan rhino. Along with Ujung Kulon, Komodo Island was also declared one of the country's first reserves to protect the 2000 or so lizards that roam the island. As the concern for nature grew, conservation soon became an increasing priority and other important areas, such as Sumatra's mountainous **Leuser**, Java's eastern triad of **Baluran**, **Alas Purwo** and **Mehru Betiri**, and Kalimantan's **Tanjung Pinang** were soon to follow.

Prior to 1957, the herculean task of monitoring the reserves solely rested on the small staff of the Bogor Botanic Gardens, but the Department of Forestry soon took over from duties of caring for them. In 1971, a separate directorate was established for the Department of Forestry, and in 1983 it became known as the "*Direktorat Jenderal Perlindungan Hutan dan Pelestanan Alam*" (Directorate – General of Forest Protection and Natural Conservation) – or the PHPA.

During this time, the KLH, or Ministry for the Development of the Environment, was also established by the government of Indonesia. The focus of both organizations being the protection of forests and the conservation of nature. The PHPA is responsible for the more than 100 reserves throughout the islands of the country. Wildlife organizations like the Worldwide Fund

It may come as a surprise to learn that Indonesia's first natural reserves were granted long before the 20th century. In fact, the King of Srivijaya set up the first wildlife reserve in southern Sumatra in AD 684. Since its inception, the Hindu religion and the many Hindu kingdoms have always held a deep reverence for animal life as spirits were believed to reside within. Thus, this first wildlife reserve was a symbolic gesture by the kingdom to show gratitude and respect for animal life.

What we think of as a "modern" wildlife reserve, did evolve later. Amazingly, it was the Dutch, the non-stop conquerors of Indonesian culture and kingdoms, who were the catalyst behind the new movement to set up conservation areas in West Java.

Cibodas, in West Java, was the first such "park," which was declared a reserve in 1889. However, even earlier, the **Kebon Raya Botanical Gardens** of Bogor were established under the Dutch Director CGC Rinwardt, who managed to collect and revive more than 15,000 varieties of international tropical plants within this 87-hectare area.

Before WWI, more than 100 reserves were declared throughout the archipelago to protect the vast forests and the many newly-discovered species. Many were also established as hunting preserves, where the tracking of

for Nature, the Nature Conservancy and The Asia Foundation are also involved in the various conservation projects in these areas. There are also several American, European and Southeast Asian zoos, whose research in special endangered species breeding programmes may enable the future propagation of these species.

After only a few decades as an independent republic, Indonesia is working hard to be at the forefront of conservation. The third International Parks Conference, a once in a decade event, was held in Bali in 1982, making the archipelago the largest Third World country ever to host such an event. During the conference, the government announced the creation of 10 new parks, with more being considered for the future. And, this has been only one of the many giant steps taken by the government, research firms and conservation organizations, to help preserve part of one of the largest rainforest areas in the world and the hundreds of endemic and endangered species that share their home with the tribes and cultures of the country.

However, the most important current concern is melding the concerns of the people living close to the parks with these conservation efforts. Indigenous tribes still fish and hunt – should this be legal? Others farm, and some villages are located within park boundaries. The questions are many; should the people be removed, should the park boundaries be changed, or should special laws be made for those who do not wish their home to be declared a reserve? The answers lie in compromise, and in a genuine concern for both the species and the people who reside in these areas. To fulfill the needs of both sides, local guides are being trained to take visitors through the park and local craft coop-

A new regard for wildlife and preservation.

eratives are being set up to educate people on the influences of the environment on culture. New farming techniques are being taught for better land use and poaching is greatly discouraged. Many villagers are now working as guards which helps to provide jobs and protect incomes while preserving the natural areas.

But, it is also up to the visitor to enter each park with an open mind, to view it as a special haven to learn with respect about the unique intertwining of life rather than to merely exploit it for man's own 'needs' and pleasures. Rare species often play a part in determining an area's lifestyle, creating the legends from the past and beliefs of the present and they help bridge the vast history of spiritualism inherent in Indonesia's precious cultural history.

Thus education is becoming the focus of greatest importance, both within the country and for the increasing numbers of other cultures who come to explore Indonesia's parks and reserves. Not only are the local villages learning new methods for "eco-existence," but visitors from the modern world are also learning to understand and respect the ways of life treasured there and the cultures which they encapsulate.

described the differences between plants and animals of the eastern and western regions of the Indonesian archipelago. This was the first clue to scientists that the major land masses of the world may have been broken off into separate island groups, for the species Wallace spoke of varied greatly in terms of type on either side of the Makassar and Lombok Straits.

As the silent side-partner who co-authored Darwin's **Origin of Species**, Wallace is better-known for his book **The Malay Archipelago**, (1869) which shocked the logical world. In this book, he described his travels and drew the imaginary "Wallace Line" between Sulawesi and Kalimantan to the north and Bali and Lombok to the south to mark the point at which Asian and Australian flora and fauna meet at the west and east division of the Indonesian islands.

The Wallace Line advanced theories about the depth and danger contained in the waters between these two land masses. Wallace further surmised that at one time, when the world's climate cooled and the polar ice caps froze, the sea level dropped and land bridges were formed which allowed for the transportation of seeds and animals southwards from Asia's cool mountains and northwards from Australia to Nusa Tenggara, Sulawesi, the Moluccas and Irian Jaya.

In some areas, the depth of the Lombok and Makassar Straits still can not be recorded indicating the possibility that the waves never receded which resulted in an Asian species remaining in the west Indonesian islands and an Australian species in the east. And later, when the climate warmed and ice caps melted, the sea level again rose to cover the lands bridges between the islands, leaving species from the main Asian and Australian continents to slowly evolve over centuries in a unique new world.

Today, the channels of the Wallace Line are still known for their dangers; with constant strong winds, unpredictable currents, whirlpools and choppy waves. Ferries chug slowly through the depths while smaller boats are often blown off course. But as soon as you cross the straits, the differences in plant life are obvious, reflected in the lush, wet jungle hills and mountains of the west that suddenly change to the dry, yellow grasses and fine earth of the eastern islands. Animal life between the two areas is also different; large Asian species such as the elephant, rhino, big cats and deer keep to Sumatra, Java, Bali and Kalimantan, while Nusa Tenggara, the Moluccas, Sulawesi and Irian Jaya foster Australian marsupials, large insects and many species of colourful birds – thus, this imaginary boundary is often termed the "great zoological divide."

A Diversity of Flora

From the beginning of time, Indonesia

An exotic range of plants and flowers populate Indonesia's range of landscape.

the brittle land millions of years ago. However, when "Gondwanaland" splintered and floated north to collide with Eurasia, Australian plants were added to the eastern island landscape. The distribution of these plant species depended on the vagaries of climate and landscape; namely, the altitude of the vegetation cover and the amount of rainfall distributed throughout the area. Indonesia is a mountainous archipelago and, logically, as the altitude of the landscape increases, the temperature decreases, leaving a less conducive

has always been rich in plant life. Early fossils show the islands' floral diversity, which has since multiplied into an area comprising more than 144 million hectares of tropical rainforest which occupies 10 percent of the archipelago's area. Some of these great forests are ancient – for example, scientists estimate that Kalimantan's jungle territory is at least 35 million years old. And, these sheltering rainforests preserve an incredible density and diversity of plants; more than 40,000 types of flora – nearly 15 percent of the estimated species in the world – have been recorded in the "Malaysian" area which is located from Irian Jaya westwards while many areas still remain unexplored and many species undiscovered.

The flora of Indonesia though mostly of Asian origin is similar to that of the southeast Pacific area, as many of the islands represent chips off the main continent when plate tectonics fractured

Symbolic lotuses are often found in or around temples.

Mushrooms spring in an overnight damping or monsoon weather.

support an evergreen forest. Some areas can even support a deciduous or monsoon forest if there is heavy rainfall. Rainfall comes during two "seasons" in Indonesia; the "dry" or summer monsoons from May to October and the "wet" winter winds that blow from November to April.

From May to November, Australia creates a "rainshadow" over the drier eastern islands of Nusa Tenggara, Irian Jaya, Sulawesi and East Java, leaving them full of sunlight and free from showers. However, from October to April, the brittle scrub and cactus species are cooled by heavy rains which result when the southern monsoon winds from chilly Asia, meet Australia's heated low pressure zone rising over the mountains and

climate for growth the higher one goes.

Thus, along the highest mountains of Irian Jaya, Sumatra and Java, as you ascend, several layers of vegetation can be identified: thick tropical rainforest, montane flora, moss forests below the tree line, then sub-alpine meadow, sparse alpine fields and, sometimes, bare peaks located under snowfall.

Seasons & Growth

The amount and distribution of moisture is a major contributory factor in determining the success and variety of growth. A lowland area with scarce rainfall can only support thin savannah, but, an equatorial lowland with six or more centimetres of rain each month for a year, can

Plant life takes many fascinating shapes and sizes, such as fungi and giant Rafflesias.

condensing to send wind and rainstorms that stretch from the Sunda Shelf to northern Australia.

Different types of vegetation need different amounts of rainfall; thus, different types of flora indicate the climate of an area. Kalimantan, Sumatra and Irian Jaya's thick rainforests require "everwet" moisture conditions, so their landscape is typified by plants such as the

A garden variety of the lily.

Nepenthes Pitcher Plant, "hairy" ferns and mossy forests that boast countless varieties of llianas, saprophytes and epiphytes. However, in the dry areas, the main plant species are sugar-cane and the Pychospria Eutescens ferns.

Endemic Flora

Indonesia holds a variety of unique plant species, but the best known is probably the huge, orange *Rafflesia arnoldi,* named after none other than Sir Thomas Stamford Raffles. Raffles was the Lieutenant – Governor of Java during the British occupation of Indonesia who later bought the island of Singapore from the Sultan of Johore. A keen naturalist, he led expeditions to Java and Sumatra to observe and sketch plants and wildlife, he later founded the Royal Society of London, one of the first major conservation organizations, and in 1817 ordered the establishment of the Bogor Botanical Gar-

The silent Bird of Paradise.

Treasure Trove of Medicine

Standing amidst the foliage of a rainforest is in one sense akin to visiting the local pharmacy, for each jungle is filled with thousands of curative plants that are used in everyday western medicine.

In Indonesia the hectares of wild foliage are also the archipelago's *apotik*, (apothecary) where for centuries the various island cultures have used plants to sooth away every pain from headaches to maladies of the heart.

Origins of the Cures

Probably the first guides to the medical usage of plants came from the animal world. Guided by their instincts cats chew on dog-tooth grass which acts as an emetic, while bears favour wild arum as a panacea to ease away various pains. The deer make use of the common *wartwort to* ease *parturition* and rub against the *geum* to treat certain ailments.

In Indonesia, various medicinal plants have traditionally been mixed to create cures for several different types of ailments such as minor problems like coughs, fevers and malaise. Other mixes are for treating outbreaks of the skin like mumps and measles.

Then, there is a range of herbal tonics which aid any and all sexual and reproductive situations, from male stamina to post-partum blues.

Jamu, as the Javanese versions are known, are often seen in coloured glass bottles carried in woven baskets on the backs of women. Also popular are certain powders and pills, wrapped in bright packages often accompanied by rather graphic illustrations of their powers that are a bit surprising to find in a modest Muslim country!

Some of the medicines are actually rubbed directly onto the skin, where they are absorbed by osmosis into the bloodstream. Perfumes are a good example of the speed of this method, for some can give a woman an allergic reaction in minutes. If you doubt the efficiency of "medicine through the skin," try rubbing garlic on the sole of your foot – a few minutes later it will be on your breath, where it will stay for hours.

Creating Concoctions

"Phytotherapy," or the study of modern herbalism, lists four main methods for processing medicines from plants: decoction (heating or boiling for extraction from the insides of thicker plants); maceration (pouring boiling water over the plant in a closed container and filtering); infusion (immersion in cold water) and extraction (such as with a blender). To separate the excess plant fibre from the curative juices, a process of distillation is believed to

dens in west Java.

The *Rafflesia* is only found in parts of Sumatra, where its huge, metre-wide petals make it the largest flower in the world. Its bright orange blossoms easily differentiate it from the surrounding forest areas, as does its unmistakable stench which has often been described as akin to that of rotting meat!

The clove and nutmeg trees of the Moluccas, the svelte rasamala trees of west Java and some beautiful species of

rainforest orchids including the exotic *bualangapandurata* (black orchid) found in the forests of East Kalimantan, are all unique to Indonesia. Herbal medicine is a large part of local Indonesian culture and more than 6,000 types of plants are used in traditional ceremonies, rituals and medicines.

If you are interested in exploring Indonesia's floral diversity, head for the **Botanical Gardens** in Bogor, West Java. Covering an area of 87 hectares, this

stimulate the healing properties of the organism. This, in turn, when applied to the secondary ailment (the human being), is supposed to transfer and encourage recuperation. Sweet and sour medicines produce different results. The taste is changed by the use of various flavourings such as cinnamon, mint and sugar. The heat or coldness of a medicine are also important considerations both for swallowed medicines and cures that are directly applied to the skin. Crimson betelnuts and coconut milk act to soothe, while spicy peppers and ginger stimulate action and complete the healing process.

Current Cures

Indonesia's "natural" medicine industry has expanded into more than 300 factories located all over the archipelago. For more than half a century, their popularity has expanded into a huge cult as regular use has encouraged more faith in its efficiency than foreign western cures.

Next time you are in a small *apotik* (pharmacy) – or even in one of the city supermarkets – wander over to the medicine case and have a look at all the brands.

Natural medicine gives an interesting insight into the mixture of nature and magic that permeates the islands.

lush international garden provides fertile ground for the growth of plant species from all over the world, including rare orchids, the original *"Havea Brazilliensis"* rubber tree and, of course, the unusual *Rafflesia.*

Awareness of Wildlife

Perhaps the first and most famous observations of fauna were recorded by the

Indonesia is host to a vast number of orchid species and hybrids.

explorer Marco Polo in 1292 after returning to Venice from a visit to the Mongol court of China. In his **Book of Marvels**, he tells of the strange "unicorn" sighted in the jungles of what is known as Java. This was the first documented evidence that proved the existence of the rare Javan rhino only one of the many unique and wonderful species found exclusively in the Indonesian archipelago.

Due to the shift of climate and continents, many animals crossed southwards from the Asian continent especially as sea levels lowered and temperatures cooled with the freezing of the polar ice caps. Thus, in addition to differences in plant life, the Wallace Line effectively distributed the animal world

Birding in Indonesia

The natural statistics of Indonesia are staggering: From the western tip of Sumatra to the eastern border of Irian Jaya the country stretches for 5,000 kilometres. There are altogether 17,500 islands in this widespread archipelago, almost 1,000 of which are inhabited. Indonesia spans across two different zoogeographical regions so the diversity of wildlife matches the diversity of human cultures. In fact about 250 different languages are spoken!

In terms of birdlife, 1,532 different bird species occur, 311 are restricted-range endemic species and 110 are more widely distributed Indonesian endemics. According to surveys conducted by the International Council for Bird Preservation (ICBP) 126 of these birds are regarded as threatened with extinction, Indonesia has thus more rare and endangered birds than any other nation in the world! ICBP has recently (in 1992) opened an office in Bogor, Java to work with the Indonesian authorities on protecting the many rare birds in important centres of biological diversity that are located all over the country.

Compared to many other states, Indonesia is not an easy location to go birding in. Generally, wildlife protection laws are not adequately enforced and birds near populated areas are often shy and difficult to approach. To get to the good birding spots in protected areas there are vast distances and sometimes difficult logistics to deal with, documentation on the avifauna is in many places incomplete or non-existent. But, for the keen birder who can spend the necessary time in remote places to track down these birds, the possibilities in Indonesia are unlimited.

The Sunda Subregion

Indonesia straddles two major zoological realms: the Oriental and the Australasian Regions. The western part of the archipelago belongs to the Oriental Region, namely Sumatra, Java/Bali and Borneo. This area is sometimes referred to as the Greater Sunda Islands and together with the Malay Peninsula they form the Sunda Subregion. Many of the birds found here are shared with other parts of the Oriental Region extending

Java Sparrow.

Red-throated Barbet.

east and northwards to Pakistan and South China although most of the rainforest species in the lowlands are restricted to the subregion and are labelled Sunda endemics — these are the kind of birds that visiting birders especially want to see because they can be found nowhere else in the world!

In Sumatra, the major national parks are also the most popular birding destinations. To the north of the island is the **Gunung Leuser National Park**, in central Sumatra the vast **Kerinci-Seblat National Park**, to the south the **Barisan Selatan National Park** and some smaller reserves along the coast and on offshore islands. Information on these parks is generally available from travel agents but the nature tourist who is especially interested in birds should get a copy of the British Ornithologist Union (BOU) annotated checklist No 10 on *The Birds of Sumatra*, London, 1988, it lists all the species that occur. Most are illustrated in Ben King's *A Field Guide to the Birds of Southeast Asia*", Collins, 1975. There are 600 different birds currently occuring on Sumatra and nearby islands, 12 are full endemic species and 4 more are endemic to isolated islands along the west coast. Especially typified in the Sunda Subregion are forest birds such as the families of babblers (43), bulbuls (27), flycatchers (25), sunbirds (16), woodpeckers (13) and hornbills and pittas (both 9).

In Kalimantan on the island of Borneo, the avifauna is quite similar, but there are 26 endemics mostly in the montane rainforest habitat. There are seven more island endemics in the Malaysian part of Borneo which have not yet been found in Kalimantan, large parts of which are still poorly known, especially around the interior mountains. Kalimantan is a difficult place to go birding in and unofficial rumours in the birding circles have it that the Borneo endemics are much easier to "get", (i.e. see) in Sabah and Sarawak, East Malaysia. For documentation *The Birds of Borneo* by B.E. Smythies, Malaysia, 1981, which also exists in a pocket-size edition is the book to use.

Java and Bali are easier to cover for the eco-tourist and have some good protected areas where the birdlife is still rich, especially if you go out into lowland and lower montane rainforest shortly after dawn, 7-11 a.m, this is the time when the forest birds are very active. It is a good idea to learn some of the bird calls or go with a guide who knows these calls. Cassettes with many Oriental bird calls are commercially available. Often the forest birds are difficult to see as they stay high inside the dense foliage but if you know their calls you will recognise the rare and spectacular ones that are worth going after.

Seventeen endemics are restricted to Java alone, 7 more are endemic to both Java and Bali. Bali has only one island endemic — the Bali Starling - for birding on Bali see *Trav' Bug, Bali*, Sun Tree 1992. All birds occuring in Java and Bali (488) are illustrated in the *Field Guide to the Birds of Java and Bali*, Gadjah Mada University Press 1988, which is a good example of a locally produced bird book.

The best spots for birds on Java include the **Ujong Kulon National Park** to the west where there are many lowland and coastal species, **Gede-Pangrango National Park** which holds many Javan endemics, most of which are montane and the **Baluran National Park** to the west where the climate is drier and more seasonal than in the rest of the Sunda Subregion

Sacred Kingfisher.

Chestnut-capped Laughing Thrush.

which is typically saturated with precipitation all year round and has tall, evergreen forest. As you progress eastwards a new type of more arid terrain becomes dominant with low, drought-deciduous forest and savannah type grasslands. In the Lesser Sunda Islands the birdlife is strikingly different.

Wallacea

East of Bali a deep trench in the seabed has isolated the chain of islands extending towards New Guinea, the Lesser Sunda Islands. During the Ice Age which until quite recently (15,000 years ago) caused sea-levels to drop thereby creating landbridges between the Greater Sunda Islands. Together with Sulawesi and the Moluccas to the north, the Lesser Sunda Islands constitute Wallacea which is part of the Australasian Region but with many locally endemic bird species.

The birdlife of Wallacea was studied during the last century by AR Wallace who among other things gave his name to the line seperating the two major zoogeographical regions that

...Birding in Indonesia

meet in Indonesia. Although all the birds occuring in Wallacea are known, described and named the area is still very poorly covered in popular handbooks. For instance, here is no proper identificational field guide illustrating all the species occuring, so birders have to piece information together from various sources. The new **Checklist to the Birds of Wallacea** in the BOU series (No 7), London 1986, is the best guide available for this. Another new title is ***Wallacea: A Site Guide for Birdwatchers*** by D Gibbs, 1990, which is useful for all travellers interested in the Indonesian outdoors.

The Lesser Sunda Islands has many wonderful nature locations and some travel agents arrange eco-tourism tours to offshore islands with huge seabird colonies of terns, frigatebirds and boobies. Some families and genera of birds like cockatoos, scrubfowl, cicadabirds and honey-eaters — missing in the Oriental Region — can be seen here. There are also many sometimes confusing varieties of fruit-doves, parrots, whistlers, thrushes and white-eyes in this part of Wallacea.

Probably most fascinating to birders however is the island of Sulawesi (which was called Celebes). It has no less than 72 endemic species including the enigmatic Maleo which is a chicken-like bird that incubates its large eggs in mounds of sand using solar or vulcanic heat. Many of the Sulawesi endemics can quite easily be seen in the major protected areas which include **Lore Lindu National Park** in central Sulawesi, **Morowali** to the east and **Dumoga-Bone** to the north. In the nearby Molucca Islands the largest national park is **Manusela** on

Green Imperial Pigeon.

Little Egret.

Seram Island. In the northern part of the Moluccas two endemic species of the Paradisaeidae family occur, they are birds of paradise which otherwise only occur in New Guinea.

Irian Jaya

It is not easy to spot a bird of paradise. No less than 38 different species of these colourful and active birds occur in New Guinea alone and yet you can travel for weeks on the island and not spot a single individual! You need to do your

as well. Tigers, leopards, elephants, rhino, deer, marsupials and monotremes are found in the "Greater Sunda Islands" of Sumatra, Java and Kalimantan, whereas many bird species are limited to the eastern region. Irian Jaya is an exception, for in addition to a wide variety of mammals the province is

home to an incredible diversity of bird life.

Why? Because during the Jurassic Age, when Australia became separated from Gondwanaland, pouched marsupials and egg-laying monotremes were unable to reach the island of New Guinea and what is now called Irian Jaya. How-

homework to succeed, study the literature before you go and if possible get a local guide to help you locate them.

New Guinea is a well-defined geographical entity that has been politically sliced up in an arbitrary manner making the fauna checklists per country difficult. Naturally, the birds do not recognise the new border between the Indonesian section Irian Jaya and Papua New Guinea which is now an independant nation. Altogether 725 different species occur within New Guinea and nearby islands as described in the main guide to the area — *Birds of New Guinea* by B M Beehler et al,1986. Although good documentation is available, the island still needs a lot of extensive work in order to survey the birdlife of Irian Jaya. This is a rugged and thinly populated country with remote snow-covered mountains over 5,000 metres high and huge swamps especially along the south coast where thousands of waterbirds breed or visit during the migration season. Most of its birdlife is shared with nearby Australia with which the island was linked by a landbridge until at the end of the last Ice Age. Bowerbirds, butcherbirds, logrunners and fairy-wrens are some of the bird families that are represented in only this region. The cassowaries, a small family of huge, flightless birds which live secretly inside the lowland rainforest are also found in this region.

Anybody interested in Indonesian birds would be well advised to become a member of the Oriental Bird Club based at The Lodge, Sandy, Bedfordshire SG19 2DL, UK. Amongst other things, a trip-report from Irian Jaya prepared by J Hornbuckle in 1991.

ever, hundreds of bird species were able to cross over to the area from many different islands as they did not need land bridges.

Today, Sulawesi, Nusa Tenggara and the Moluccas boast a mixture of both Asian and Australian flora and fauna. Isolated by deep ocean trenches before the Piocene Era three million years ago, these areas remained uninhabited by animal life until the action of plate tectonics shifted Sulawesi's position creating a land border between western Java and Kalimantan through to the eastern islands, allowing species from both areas to mingle.

Special Species & Reserves

Nowhere else in the world will you be able to find such a heart-warming clown as the Button-eyed Orangutan of Sumatra and Kalimantan. An honourary member of the endangered species list, they are now protected in two sites – **Bohorok Orangutan Rehabilitation Centre** in **Gunung Leuser National Park** near Medan, Sumatra and **Tanjung Puting's Camp Leakey**, near Kumai in Central Kalimantan. Here, orangutans that were formerly captive or kept as pets are taken in and cared for, before being re-released into the forest. Often wild, the orangutans will crash through the trees to join in with the early-morning and afternoon feeding programmes.

The **Kerinci-Sebelat National Park** in central Sumatra is one of Indonesia's largest and most important protected areas. Encompassing thousands of square kilometres of rainforest mountains and wistful Tibet-like plateaus, this vast area is the last home for the very rare Sumatran tiger, the small, red-haired Sumatran rhinoceros, gibbons,

Out for a dip in the sea.

leaf monkeys and the black-and-white Malaysian tapir.

One by one, the wild elephants lumber down the rough dirt road of the **Way Kambas Elephant Training Centre** in southern Sumatra. Located just a few hours north of the landing point for the ferry plying between Southern Sumatra and Java, this camp is an educational site which encourages interaction with visitors. Here, the mistreated and injured animals are rehabilitated, protected and trained to assist local farmers and workers.

Unfortunately, the click of a hidden forest camera is the only thing fast enough to catch a glimpse of the elusive Javan rhino, which is rarely seen except along the swampy riverbanks of west Java's peninsula **Ujung Kulon National Park**.

Less than 60 Javan rhinos exist, but protective park programmes are helping to increase their numbers. The Ujung Kulon Park is also abundant in other species of wildlife as well; wild *babi* (pig), *rusa* (deer) and big cats such as the swift-pawed fishing cats and the rare spotted and black leopards. Does the Javan tiger still exist? Well, the **Mehru Betiri National Park** situated at the opposite end of the island claims that about half a dozen roam its hills!

Though an endangered species, the turtles of Sukamede's beaches are more commonly sighted in the park as they slowly crawl up from the sea to lay their soft eggs in the sand. Close by, the **Alas**

More areas are designated for national parklands.

presented to zoos for educational displays and breeding pro-grammes, or re-released into the wild.

Komodo Island is a sudden step back in time to a dry, barren Jurassic world of slop-ing hills and slithering komodo dragons. With some measuring up to three or four metres long, these lizards are not as deadly as island lore would have visitors believe, but their bite can leave a nasty, festering wound. Their main prey are the wild goats, deer and pigs that roam the is-land, though legend has it that they enjoy the occasional child as well! Twice a week, a goat is slaughtered for visitors who come to "the dragons' lair." Legend also states that local villagers are de-scendents of these endangered creatures.

Purwo National Park in east Java also claims tigers and turtles as residents, even though its waves have also be-come notorious surfing territory. The **Baluran National Park** due north is a marvelous savannah home to herds of wild black and brown *banteng* (wild cat-tle) deer, and pigs. Its splendid moun-tain backdrop successfully camouflages primates, cats, birds and a variety of intriguing mountain trails.

Though Bali is no longer home to the tiger, its western **Bali Barat Na-tional Park** near Gili-manuk shelters the rare Rothchild's Mynah, also known as the "*Jalak Putih*," or the Bali Starling. Less than one hundred of these birds are left in existence, and close to a dozen are kept and cared for at a small shelter here, before being

Tropical insect life, a scientists' dream.

All puffed up with nowhere to go.

marsupials and monotremes that once crossed over from Australia. The very rare *dugong*, or *manatee*, mammal smoothly coasts through the offshore sea waters. It is easy to see why their smooth, white skin and somewhat "voluptuous" curves often caused sailors to mistake this shy mammal for a sensuous female swimmer – resulting in stories of seductive mermaids.

Shy and doe-eyed, the small Anoa Buffalo is only found in Sulawesi – as is the frightening but surprisingly gentle Babirusa pig. Both animals are extremely rare, and only found in remote parks such as the **Dua Saudara** in the northern arm of the island and the **Lore Kalamanta National Park**. The latter island is also the site for the many ancient megaliths located within the sheer mountain valleys.

On the island of New Guinea, nearly 700 species of birds can be sighted – nearly half of which are unique to Indonesia's Irian Jaya. National parks such as the **Lorentz** and **Wassur** are home to many species of apes, as well as the

Marine Marvels

With more than 13,000 islands, the marine life of Indonesia is one of the area's major attractions. The endless beauty of its beaches, bright coral gardens and variety of aquatic wildlife can be enjoyed in any part of this vast archipelago.

The sand ranges in colour from coral-white to deep black volcanic ash, the coasts from steamy mangrove swampland to open beaches leading

What's a friendly rut between friends, the common buffalo.

out to clear azure waves whose warmth make snorkeling and diving the perfect afternoon activity.

The shipwrecks located off the Riau archipelago in Sumatra and around the Moluccas, are home to hundreds of fish that drift through the currents, darting in and out of anemones, corals and sea grasses in a procession of colourful underwater sea traffic.

Popular offshore areas for underwater exploration include the **Dumoga-Bone National Park** off Manado's coast in northern Sulawesi, the reefs around the Banda and Ternate islands in the Moluccas, the **Pulau Seribu** islands just north of Jakarta in Java and the area of Nusa Tenggara somewhere between Komodo Island and Maumere, a north-

eastern port on the island of Flores.

Scenes of The Future

Indonesia's diversity of plant and animal life makes it one of the last real nature havens. And, it is one in which visitors can easily interact with nature, by simply walking through Bogor or Bandung's amazing botanical gardens or embarking on long and arduous jungle treks. Both indigenous and endangered species can easily be spotted at the *kebun binatang* (garden of animals) in Surabaya, Yogyakarta or at Jakarta's Ragunan Zoo. Or, you can go wildlife watching in the archipelago's beautiful reserves and national parks. For details

Visitors are free to visit the vast range of preservation areas.

on these areas, contact the **PHPA** (Perlindungan Hutan dan Pelestarian Alam), also known as the **Directorate General of Forest Protection and Nature Conservation** in Bogor at Jalan IR H Janda 100, Bogor; telephone (0251) 21014. Additional offices are located in Jakarta and Labuan, West Java; or, alternatively contact the organizations of; the **Worldwide Fund for Nature** (at

Jalan Pela Raya No. 3, Gandaria Utara, PO Box 7928 JKISKM, Jakarta 12079, Indonesia; telephone (21) 7203095); **The Asia Foundation** (at Jalan Darmanwangsaraya 50, Kebayoran Baril, Jakarta Selatan 12160, Indonesia). Please feel free to get in touch with these or-ganizations if you would like details on visiting Indonesia's wildlife parks and reserves. Often, special projects take place in these areas, many of which offer volunteer opportunities to help preserve and protect Indonesia's wildlife for the future.

People

Indonesia is a varied tapestry of life in which the threads of more than 300 different ethnic groups have been woven into a colourful blanket of shared culture and tradition.

The national motto of *Bhinneka Tunggal Ika,* ("They are many they are one") perfectly suits the benevolent feeling that exists among these groups who have emigrated between the islands for decades. Through sharing responsibilities, resources and friendship with one another, they have created a country where there truly is "Unity in Diversity", regardless of heritage, religion, place of birth or social strata. The binding thread is *Bahasa Indonesia,* the national language, which brings the 600 local dialects together in a vocabulary of common words and expressions. However, for many, B*ahasa Indonesia* is still very much a second language to the more familiar local dialects

Welcome to Ubud and the graceful dance of the Ramayana in mystical Bali.

93

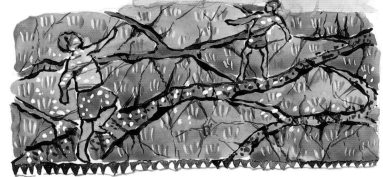

such as the Javanese, Balinese, Acehnese and Dayak languages.

First Human Life

Settled between Australia and Malaysia, Indonesia's ancestry is one of combined features and memories. The country's earliest inhabitants arrived in East Java, where the Solo River Valley has provided evidence of prehistoric life. It was here that the remains of *Pithanthropicus Erectus,* (Trinil Man), *Java Man, Solo Man* and tools of the advanced *Ngadong* culture have been unearthed. It is believed that these first humans, travelled southward to the archipelago from the area which is now called "India." Theorists suggest that the migration could have resulted because of the presence of land bridges, or with the help –and luck – of primitive vessels travelling the seas. Whatever the means, the process was slow.

But, soon the first small settlements began to thrive in east and central Java. The second wave of migration also came from the north, except this time it was China. Every wave occured over the course of several thousand years. Each cluster of arrivals from the Malay peninsula featured similar but slightly altered cultural traditions, which later developed individually within the separate islands to form local *adat* (customs and laws) that are still present and practiced in daily life. During the Neolithic era between 3,000 and 2,000

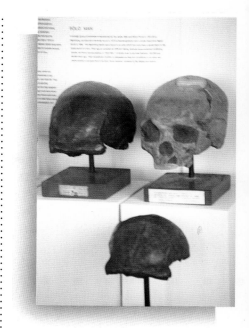

Skeletal remains of the earliest inhabitants in the National Museum.

BC the influence of the "Austronesian" seafarers from the South and from Indochina spread throughout the Indonesian archipelago. However, on arrival, they may have been surprised to find groups of "Melanesians" already settled on the land. Some, like the Dravida and Papua groups, feared the intruders and were driven away, while other tribal cultures allowed the Austronesians to meld their new traditions into their settled ways of life.

The *Dongson* people also arrived at around this time. Hailing from China and Vietnam, they brought with them the all-important technology for farming, irrigation and handicrafts. Before their arrival, Indonesian society was already skilled in metalwork, the domestication of animals and strong sea-faring traditions. Now both the settled groups and the new *Dongson* arrivals assimilated and advanced their existing cultures with the new additions.

Structure & Survival

The way of life and belief systems have remained largely unchanged over the centuries as Indonesian culture is strongly based on both religion and farming. With the arrival of Indian Hinduism and the founding of the first Hindu Kingdom in AD 78 by Aji Caka, new ideas and practices slowly filtered in and began to enrich the local developing cultures.

Many traditions of early Indonesian settlements were based on *adat* (generic local "traditions") that have been extended across all villages and islands to form a way of life based on social duty and religion. Developed out of the rigid daily organization necessary to ensure the success of farming techniques, these *adat* differ slightly from one area to the next. However, they have been instrumental in developing social structures such as; government hierarchy, fair distribution of work, equal rights and social justice – concepts that today form the basis of the "guided democracy" that rules the country.

Rice cultivation eventually helped to organize routines and form customs within these early cultures, for the planning it took to harvest a successful crop

Another weary day in Sulawesi as a lady trudges to work with heavy load.

required the persistence and cooperation of all village members. The correct timing of sowing the seeds, the design of the irrigation systems, responsibility for plowing, watering and burning of the rice fields led to a tradition of shared life that can still be seen in the rural areas.

However, on some islands, the soil was not as favourable for crop growth, so other cultures were forced into a "shifting" society that harvested an area, then burned it before moving on to the next. These societies mostly kept to the dry, eastern areas, and were less structured and stable than the shared *sawah* (wet rice cultivation cultures).

The constant migration required for the *ladang* (dry rice system) because of unpredictable soil and climate forced

itinerant tradition that did not fit into the neatly structured organization of stationary farm life.

To supplement their diet of rice, early settlers also lived off the wildlife of the land. With an abundant variety of pig, deer, birds and large game, hunting traditions were the basis for the development of innovations such as; spears, sling-shots, forest traps and blow guns. Domestic animals such as goats, sheep, chickens and cows were slowly introduced by explorers who came to the islands in search of riches and trade. The early societies also practiced "gathering" traditions as the diversity of natural fruits and vegetables provided an excellent source of added nutrition. The tropical climate nurtures bananas, pineapples, papayas, mangoes, rambutan, jackfruit and many other delicious varieties of organic foods whose trees have lined Indonesia's coastal fields and mountains for eons.

Known as strong seafarers, the early settlers had no trouble taming the surrounding waters to provide sustenance for those on the land. The nomads of the Riau archipelago, known as the *orang laut* (sea gypsies) in particular began the fishing tradition that greatly contributes to Indonesia's modern economy.

Javanese Beginnings

"Javanese" is a misleading term to describe those who live on the island of Java. In fact, there are many groups

who share the same heritage, yet whose differences are reflected through language and culture. The true Javanese, mainly live in the eastern and central regions, and account for only about 60 percent of the island's population. They are sometimes classified into two distinct groups by social status and physical features: the gentle, more refined

A charismatic speaker addressing the crowds at a rally.

culture of the educated inland *kejawen* (bourgeoisie) and the sharp-featured, hard-bodied, more aggressive *pasisir* (coastal) cultures.

The Sundanese, settled in a large area stretching from the west coast to Bandung. They make up around 20 percent of Java's population and are described as the most Islamic of the cultural groups. Known for their beauty, the western Sundanese are one of the many ethnic groups on the island. Others, such as the eastern Tenggerese, and the "brave" Madurese of Madura Island

Young schoolchildren getting ready for another day
of further education near Gianyar.

boast distinct differences in tradition.

One of the most intriguing offshoots of Sundanese culture are the *orang Kanekes* (people of Kanekes) who are better known as the Badui tribes of west Java's highlands. Claiming to be the pre-Islamic indigenous people of the area, fewer than 3,000 people are confined to 35 or so settlements just inside the central west coast. Divided into inner and outer "territories," the Badui preserve their communities by isolating them from modern society. Although members of the outer villages can receive visitors and travel to other towns, those who live within the inner village circles of the elite have successfully managed to preserve the tradition and religion of pre-Islamic times in the face of rapid modernization.

Though Hinduism has made an impact on the central and eastern cultures, it is Islam that defines practices and people of "Javan" heritage. The Badui and Tenggerese have traditionally resisted the influence of Islamic tradition, while the Madurese and Sundanese have embraced it and made various aspects of this religion the distinctive traits of their culture.

Hindu Traditions

From the road, the sight of Bali's small, modest temples and terraced hills immediately reflect the island's enchanting traditions. Warmth and creativity

A Balinese man in mid-cultural performance.

home to nearly three million people, a complex sense of family, and of privacy, that separates each household from the rest of the community by way of a surrounding wall and small, separate rooms used for different functions.

However, with a society based on the practice of rice cultivation, most of Balinese tradition is based on the community, and all responsibilities and rewards are shared between the people. A special *subak* government divides the responsibilities of running the fields, while *bajars* (organizations formed for the discussion of local community concerns and events), are also part of the village government structure.

There are celebrations for every aspect of life, from the realization of pregnancy to death rituals and beyond. Birth and funerals, puberty and menopause, marriage and ageing are events that are to be shared between the family and the village. Bali is also an animistic society, which practices the appeasement of both by offerings of scattered petals and incense on the ground.

shine through nearly every aspect of Balinese life. In the gentle smiles, it is easy to sense an appreciation of life and a deep sense of respect for spiritual tradition. Music and art are intertwined with these beliefs, as are the ceremonies that are part of daily ritual. Secluded on the smallest main island of the archipelago, the Balinese have their own way of life, with social structure and religious beliefs that reflect the deep influence of Hindu tradition. Somehow, there exists within this tiny island,

A beach hawker in Sanur displaying her wares in a most appropriate place.

Dayak Women

A natural beauty, the woman smiles gracefully, her black eyes beaming from her light, smooth skin. It is a beauty enhanced by the adornment of more than 100 gold hoops hanging from each ear — the distinctive mark of a Dayak woman.

Enhancement of Beauty

Although at first glance it looks painful, the lengthened earlobes of the women of the central Kalimantan tribes are simple lifetime configurations of the body and are comparable to the piled rings that lengthen the necks of several African groups. The hoops stretch down the lobes in a gradual progression of weight and time. The process is begun when the women are only young girls of two or three, but the age of the first piercing could vary.

After one hoop has taken well to each ear, more are added as the girls grow older. It is not uncommon for the skin of the lobes to touch the shoulders by the time these girls turn into women. The Dayak people are comprised of more than 200 tribes scattered throughout the interior of the island of Borneo – more than half of which is comprised of Kalimantan. Most of these million-plus light-skinned people share similar customs of self-enhancement including the methods in which jewellery is worn and the practice of lengthening the lobe with dozens of earrings.

Talented Metal Workers

Known for their skills in working with various metals, the Dayak people have long forged

A woman in Manado with extended earlobes to enhance their beauty.

weapons such as knives and axes from iron found in many of the hills. Brasswork is common in the southeast area, while silverwork is a specialty of the west. Both these metals are popular in the manufacture of jewellery such as leg rings, arm bands, bracelets and, of course, hoop earrings.

Questions have been raised as to whether the metal used for these rings or the number used was symbolic of stature or duty. Although rather heavy, sometimes more than ten dozen

Stories of Sumatra

Miles of rainforest, rugged mountains, whirling rivers and eons of time have separated the different ethnic groups of

Sumatra. With about 30 million people, there is, understandably, a great diversity in heritage, tradition and beliefs from one end of the long island to the other. And, it is a fascinating cultural journey north from Panjang to Banda

would jangle from each ear – which can amount to one kilogramme in weight.

Equal Rights

The reason for the stretching of the earlobes was probably to enhance beauty to attract a lover at the proper age. Men sometimes wore earrings to reflect strength and accomplishment rather than to accentuate good looks. Instead of plain hoops, males who wore earrings often chose carvings that symbolized the surrounding wildlife, or intricate designs carved from various forest materials. In addition to pierced lobes which they stretched with weights equal to those used by women, men also decorated their ears with jewellery that lined the thicker cartilage of the upper areas. As the women grew older, the lobes lengthened with the slackened elasticity of ageing skin, before sometimes actually breaking with the weight of the moving metal hoops. When this happened, a woman would usually cover the broken lobe by wrapping her head with a coloured cloth or by hiding it behind thick tresses of hair.

A Fading Practice

Today, the practice of lengthening lobes is rarely seen in the younger generation, although in interior Kalimantan many women still proudly continue this practice. However, in other areas, missionaries have encouraged the abandonment of these old traditions so fervently that some of the elder females have actually lopped off their bangled lobes to symbolize their conversion to the new faith.

Aceh for any traveller who has the time to explore the region.

Some of the most educated and independent Indonesians are part of the Minangkabau culture (including Mohommad Hatta, Sukarno's Vice-Presi-

dent). This culture is based in the area of Sumatra surrounding Padang. The Minangkabau were believed to be great traders with the Moluccas islands and probably settled in the area before the 12th century, only adopting the characteristics of modern life after the Dutch arrived some 500 years later. An unusual tale accompanies Minangkabau history as to the origin of the "buffalo head" roof on the houses; in fact, the word Minangkabau means "the buffalo wins," or "the buffalo's victory."

As the story goes, several centuries ago, the King of Java indicated that he wanted to rule Sumatra as well. Smaller and less powerful, the Sumatrans came up with an unusual plan; instead of fighting a hopeless, bloody battle, the two kingdoms decided to let a bullfight determine the outcome for rulership of the area. On the day of the contest, the Javan kingdom brought an enormous, strong bull to the field, while the Sumatrans placed only a newborn calf with sharpened sticks attached for horns into the ring.

However, while the Javan people laughed, the calf ran over to what it thought was its mother and tried to suckle the milk, piercing the huge bull with its "horns" so that the enormous animal became frightened and ran away. Thus, in thankful memory to their little hero in the cries of "Minangkabau!" and the resemblence of the tribe's headdresses and homes to buffalo horns.

Isolationism and adherence to the

Balinese cuisine and chef having a breather.

traditional *adat* (traditional customs and laws) law are the strength of the Batak tribes who inhabit the central-northern plateau near Lake Toba.

Believed to be the descendants of the hero Si Radja Batak who introduced the *adat* laws, the Bataks were fearful foes with an infamous reputation for eating the flesh of their enemies as well as that of members of their own tribe who were guilty of breaking community laws.

Siberut Island, the northernmost of the Mentawi group, is so heavily cov-

An Indonesian portrait of a mother and her adorable child.

ered with dense jungle that it has effectively isolated the Siberut culture within its midst.

Settled along the riverbanks, villages include both central *uma* (communal houses) and the *lalep* (family homes) that surround them. In the Siberut culture, the men traditionally hold most of the power, although each person takes an equal part in making decisions on important issues such as leadership and division of work. Left untouched by modern advances, the government has recently decided to resettle these tribes to make way for the needs of logging companies and tourist facilities.

"Fierce" and "staunchly Muslim" are two of the most familiar terms used to describe the Acehnese people of northern Sumatra. These characteristics were probably attributed to them when they traded with Asia, Europe and India and during the lingering guerilla hill wars that broke out during the Dutch occupation. Their light skins, smooth complexions and small frames suggest a strong Malay heritage, though many are the results of early cultural mixing with the surrounding countries.

Today, Banda Aceh's beautiful mosque is at the centre of Islamic life while a strict sense of obedience is reflected in the dappled green and yellow of hundreds of camouflage army uniforms.

However, though religion is serious and protection is top priority, do not let

A ready smile on the face of this young child from Padang.

their "ferocious" reputation fool you – the Acehnese are one of the most friendly people in the country.

Development of the Outer Islands

Religion is the defining factor for the different cultures in Nusa Tenggara; the Muslim Sasaks on Lombok, the very Islamic Sumbawanese, the Roman Catholics on Flores and Timor's incomprehensible mix of Christian and Muslim tradition.

Openness, generosity and friendliness – is an unmistakable trait of these cultures, many of whom rarely see a Westerner and are always willing to go out of their way to help others while at the same time reflecting a pride in their traditions that have been well preserved in their isolation.

Most of the people living on Lombok belong to the Sasak culture, although they think of themselves as Muslim they are better described as being followers of *wektu telu* (a religion unique to the island which encompasses a trilogy of beliefs). We*ktu telu* combines the influences of Hinduism, Islam and animism and uses the figures of Islam's Mohommad and Allah and Christianity's Adam and images of the sun, moon, stars, heaven, earth and water and other ideas to form their beliefs and concepts of local *adat* (traditional customs and laws). While the moody mosques and misty Muslim graveyards in the dry hills of Sumbawa reveal the island's Islamic beliefs, across the sea from Komodo Island to Flores the many Christian churches reflect a different culture and tradition.

Out of the one and a-half million people, more than three-fourths of the Florinese are Catholic, though they still practice strong animistic beliefs and indulge in rituals such as the sacrifical slaughtering of animals. Though the island is small, the five Manggarai, Ngada, Lio, Sikkanese and Lamaholot cultures are divided by vast mountain valleys, and by differences in physical appearance ranging from the slighter Malay to the darker Melanesian features.

Dutch influence also led to the Chris-

Away from prying eyes – Irian Jaya's children.

tianization of Ambon in the northern Moluccas. Today, crumbled churches are still found near the battle ruins of the hills, and on Sundays well-dressed worshippers head bibles in hand for Christian houses of God.

From the Depths of Time

Found in shadows of the darkest forests, the lands of the Dayak tribes are only accessible by rafting the most dangerous rivers into Kalimantan's central core. Famous for their *lamin* (longhouses) that are up to 300 metres long, there are many different ethnic "Dayak" groups; some being slash-and-burn farmers and others nomadic hunter-gatherers. Prob-

ably the descendents of ethnic groups from China and Southeast Asia, the various tribes use unusual methods of body decoration and mutilation – tattoos and long ear lobes define different aspects of their religion and life especially in the older members of the tribes.

The wood effigies of ancestors peer out from the looming cliffs of central Sulawesi. This is Torajaland, home of the huge, raised sloping-roof dwellings of the Toraja tribes, who still use hanging tree graves to mourn their dead children. They slaughter bulls, pigs and birds in traditional funeral ceremonies that take months to organize and which can last for several days.

Flying over Irian Jaya's dark, snow-covered mountains and waves of forested

Tattooing

Across his arms a line of thin dots intertwine to form an intricate pattern. Large birds fly across his light, muscled skin while his throat is marked with the rugged imprints of a forest warrior. These are the tattoos of the 200 odd Dayak tribes of Kalimantan, who for centuries have used symbols of bodily adornment to mark their social position and role. Spread across the island of Borneo, these tribes have traditionally been hunters and gatherers. Seen close up, these body markings are striking, completely spread over the skin in a seemingly painful design. Mostly, a masculine adornment the tattoos spread across the shoulders, upper arms and sometimes the upper chest and back.

Designed in bland, darkened greys and blues, these patterns range in size and form, from tiny flower petals to large and intricate mammals and birds. In several tribes, throat tattoos symbolize a successful head hunter. The thin neck skin makes the tattooing process quite painful, yet the markings seem to come to life as the man speaks and swallows. Women of different tribes were also similarly adorned, usually along their calves and forearms. Female designs were just as extensive as those of the men, usually taking the form of birds and intricate spiritual figures.

Process and Significance

In Dayak culture, these markings were often extensive and executed professionally, some designs taking more than a month before completion. A tattoo is created with the aid of several implements such as; a thin metal "needle," the sharp point of which is attached to a manoeuvrable wooden handle of wood, then carefully dipped into the "ink" for designing. The inks are created from natural materials such as soot or damar, which results in faded hues of blue, red and green as each puncture snakes over the skin in a dark, carefully tapped dot-to-dot pattern. Some Dayak tribes reserve these markings only for the aristocracy, as extensive tattoos indicate members of the upper societal levels. Other cultures allow almost anyone to wear the designs, with various motifs reflecting outstanding characteristics, such as the possession of certain tribal skills, bravery, or success in hunting and warfare. Other tattoos act as pro-

hills is the only means of reaching the cool, central Baliem Valley that is home to the various tribes of the Dani people. The men of Torajaland are usually pictured donned only in their *horim* (penis guards), the rest of their skin and hair covered in pig fat to provide warmth. The rituals practiced here such as polygamy, the bride price being paid for in terms of pigs and the men sleeping apart from the women and children are still well-preserved.

The tribal women practice several

Tattoos denote status and skill.

tective charms against sickness and disease, or as a shield against bad spirits.

The Palang

For men of the Dayak tribes, one of the most interesting and painful decorations is the *palang* ("penis pin"). Inserted through the penis glans, this form of body enhancement is considered a great symbol of prowess. Believed to be first used by the Kenyah tribe, this method is now used throughout the island of Borneo as a tool of sexual enhancement. Depending on the wealth of the wearer, the pins can be made of anything ranging from bamboo to copper, silver, bone or gold. To prevent the opening from healing over, men keep this adornment inserted at all times. Later, when with a woman, the man can then exchange the ordinary pin for the decoration to participate in greater pleasures. Items of recorded use include metal, glass shavings, pig bristles and various wires that increase the size of the member. According to men of the Dayak culture, the *palang* is an adornment demanded by women. Although dangerous and sometimes fatal this tradition is still practised by many tribes.

A man from (Toraja) Sulawesi fronting a Torajan house.

Manner & Tradition

There is a refreshing expression of honesty as well as a sparkling glint of boldness and mischief reflected in the eyes of the "Indonesian" people. This is carefully held back by a natural reserve that has been carefully cultivated over the years. This reservation is perhaps due to the islands' growing proximity to modern life. However, quiet, patient mannerisms are part of the overall traditions of Indonesia. It is a culture of kindness honed through each generation.

"Keeping face" is as important as flowing with the pace of "rubber time" – Western emotions of worry, anger and impatience are nearly non-existent as

interesting customs, such as exclusively reserving their milk for the first five years of their newborn child which also means that she cannot have intercourse during this time.

Unmarried women wear grass skirts; married women wear a skirt of seeds or fibres just below their bare breasts. Women used to amputate their finger joints to signify the death of a close relative, and often the cremation ceremony involved keeping the body as a blackened mummy for future viewing.

Children – this nation's future looks secure.

Cool waters on a hot day and sitting secure in the warmth of your mothers' arms in Samalona island.

Indonesians live by the premise that things will sort themselves out in their own unique manner.

Flexibility is their underlying attribute; if the train does not run, if the letter is not delivered, if "plans" go awry, the world does not fall apart and life can still be enjoyed.

A helpful hand, a sharing smile, a few moments in which to share tea with the neighbours or talk with a stranger on the bus are all part of the sharing and caring tradition of the Indonesian way of life.

Religion

Bare soles bent as they crouch low in prayer, rows of Muslim men in Banda Aceh chant in unison, black skullcaps perched on bowed heads, eyes downcast to the marble mosque floor. Along a gravel roadside in Bali, a young woman lights a small stick of incense on the ground, scattering petals in an offering of appeasement to the evil spirits that lurk in the nearby forest shadows.

In the jungle hills of Irian Jaya, rocks and trees are worshipped in lingering animistic beliefs. Every Sunday on the island of Flores, several thousand Catholic churchgoers stand behind stained-glass windows and sing their praises to a more familiar western God.

Shades of religion often overlap within Indonesia, for each set of beliefs plays an integral part in the intermingling of the islands' past traditions and

The Istiglal Mosque beckons in Indonesia's capital.

111

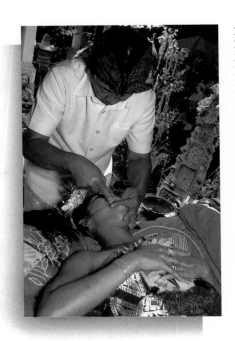

Tooth-filing ritual in Bali.

are the terms of *adat* and *animism*. Based on respect for and mystification with the surrounding world, these beliefs were probably the earliest forms of "religious" beliefs for Indonesia's ancient cultures.

The term *adat* refers to an unwritten system of laws and beliefs; a government system based on custom and respect between those in a village or culture. Originating in the hierarchies of power used to organize the early agricultural community systems, *adat* is founded on the subtle values of responsibility, humbleness, sharing and self-worth. It is a "code" borne of the earliest human settlements of the archipelago, one which flourished in similiar ways within the cultures of various islands. And somehow, these systems of leadership managed to remain throughout the centuries within each different island's villages and beliefs.

While *adat* deals with human values and earthly customs, *animism* deals instead with those of the spirits. Long practiced by tribes around the world, *animism* is the belief that there are deities living within many things, such as animals and trees of the forest.

To those of western heritage, such things may seem unusual, but for cultures such as the Dayaks of Kalimantan and the Dani of Irian Jaya, animism is a strong force within their way of life. Even in large cities such as Jakarta, Denpasar and Padang, it is not uncommon to hear tales of the benevolence and wrath of various deities.

The most modern of Indonesians

present customs. Shared gods, parallel doctrines and similarities in faith show the development of many religions, bits and pieces of beliefs exchanged with the movement and modernization of the Indonesian culture. It is first necessary to comprehend the underlying religions of the region. Like a carefully composed piece of music, notes of one set of beliefs have been intricately inlaid upon others, the melody rich and reflective, yet differing depending on the atmosphere in which it is played.

Early Adat & Animism

Two important concepts interwoven through the religions of the archipelago

still work these age-old beliefs into their way of life, knowing that it is better to pay respect to non-existent gods than incur the fury of those who might be there. Thus, offerings and prayers to spirits of the sea, mountains and nature remain alive in Indonesia today, as in many other parts of the world.

Expansion of Religion & Rumour

Throughout the islands of Indonesia, there is a certain sense of spirituality, from the intense, moody energy of Java's dark and hidden coastal caves to the simple roadside floral offerings of Bali, Sumatra's mosques, Flores' Christian crosses or the forest spirits of Irian Jaya. Though mostly Islamic, the islands have been crossed by the influence of international pirates, pilgrims and preachers, each with their own interpretations of religion – and the diversity shows within the spread of beliefs throughout the archipelago's settlement.

Hinduism & Buddhism

Besides the religions of *adat* and *animism* that naturally developed throughout the islands, the first sets of internationally accepted beliefs to reach the archipelago were Buddhism and Hinduism. The Hindu religion is one of the oldest in the world. Originating around 1,000 BC, Hinduism involves three gods

Ganesha statues confirm the Hindu influence.

- *Brahma,* the "creator", *Vishnu,* the "preserver" and *Shiva,* the "destroyer". These three gods control the balance of life. Reincarnation is inherent in the Hindu beliefs, as life is viewed as a series of repeated cycles. According to positive or negative use of one's time on earth, one is reincarnated at higher or lower levels reaching *karma,* the highest level of being. Delivered by the hands of sailors in the early 7th century, Buddhism originated in the 6th century BC when Prince Siddhartha Gautama of India became "enlightened" while sitting beneath a banyan tree. Dissatisfied with life and the weaknesses of the body despite his position of wealth, he founded an order of monks while in his early thirties and spent several decades teaching Bud-

Hindu temple architecture repeats itself in Bali, where most of the locals
practise the Balinese religion, a hybrid of Hinduism.

dhism, a religion based an eight fold path finally reaching.

The underlying guidance of Buddhism is not in a supreme god but rather in an ultimate state of being; *nirvana* (peace). One reaches *nirvana* by overcoming the constraints of "earthly de-sires," which Buddhists believe are the source of the suffering that defines all life. As shown by ancient temples and shrines throughout the island , both religions seemed to arrive on the islands in a blend of beliefs rather than two individually recognized religions. It

Stunning stupas and bidding Buddha at Borobudur.

seems that the different gods and customs were separated later as they were adopted by the area's early kingdoms.

The influence of Hinduism and Buddhism in the country is reflected in some of the greatest empires, such as Java's Hindu Majapahit and Sumatra's Buddhist Srivijaya empire that reigned within the islands in the early centuries. And, of these kingdoms, incredible edifices that still stand today were constructed to emphasize the depth of their belief – the Hindu Prambanan and Dieng Plateau temple ruins, and the awesome Buddhist building of Borobudur.

Early Hindu and Buddhist beliefs are also mirrored in epic stories that are still told today, in the forms of *wayang* (theatre) puppets and moonlight ballets. **Mahabharata**, the story of a battle in Northern India based on the epic poem the **Bhagavad Gita**, written by the great soldier Krishna, in which the duties of a warrior are explained to Prince Arjuna – a favourite of Indonesian storytelling fare. Perhaps the most well-known epic, the **Ramayana**, recounts the kidnapping of Sita, Prince Rama's wife, by the evil demon Rawana, and the prince's attempt to rescue her with the help of an army of monkeys led by Hanuman.

The Entrance of Islam

Islam entered the scene about two centuries after Buddhism and Hinduism

A rural but modern day mosque.

when the first Arabs settled the land.

Mohammed, the Arab prophet who is the founder of Islam, was the person who translated the word of God rather than a soothsayer. His message was one of peace, found in surrendering life to the one omniscient, all-powerful being.

The word "Islam" is derived from *salam,* meaning "peace," or "surrender." In fact, the name *Mohammad* is a pseudonym for the prophet, taken from an expression which means "highly praised."

Born around 570 AD, Mohammed

A medicine man outside the
Istiglal mosque.

first taught the faith of Islam in Mecca until the surrounding Arab communities forced him to flee to Medina in AD 622. Little wonder, as his beliefs of individualism, independence, monotheism and equality directly clashed with the traditional Arab polytheistic and class-structured ways of life. After leaving Mecca, Mohammad turned Medina into a political base from which he set up a powerful army. In AD 630, he marched back to Mecca and defeated the city, carrying with him victory until his death in AD 632.

In Indonesia, it was the Islamic *sufis*, or mystics who first spread the beliefs of Islam. Confronting villages already versed in Buddhist and Hindu beliefs, the *sufis* probably provided an alternative choice for those villages and kingdoms which questioned aspects of the waning early religions. It was Sumatra's province of Aceh where Islam first took hold, but seafarers were fast spreading the beliefs as they crossed over to trade with the various islands. Two centuries after Aceh's conversion, the religion took hold in the Moluccas and for the next hundred years expanded throughout Java, Sulawesi and Kalimantan.

Islam is probably most prominent in Java, due to the *Wali Songo,* or nine holy men, whom legends say wandered the island teaching others from their deep understanding of the religion. It is said they had special powers, but others argue that they were only strong rulers who used their influence to turn their kingdoms into Islamic provinces.

Ancient royal tombs on Samosir Island, Lake Toba.

The Importance Of Islam

More than 90 percent of Indonesia's population are Muslims, or followers of the Islamic beliefs, making Indonesia the largest Islamic country in the world.

Mosques are everywhere, domes shining in the late afternoon sunlight, prayers carrying down from Banda Aceh in northern Sumatra all the way across the archipelago to the mountains surrounding Jayapura, Irian Jaya. Famous places of praise are the gleaming, ostentatious mosques such as Jakarta's Izmail or the Bhaiturraman, in Banda Aceh's centre square. More commonly, however, they are small houses of worship, found in the ragged wooden floorboards of the many villages where velvet-capped men and solemn-faced women

wrapped in traditional head coverings kneel barefoot and humble to give respect and praise to Allah, their god.

Westerners often find striking parallels between Islam and Chistianity, for many of the creeds are similar and it seems as if some of the characters are known only by a different name. Islam, like Christianity, is a way of life, one in which every change in the universe is due to the will of the supreme God. Life on earth is a precursor to an eternity spent in "heaven" or "hell." The "soul" is eternal, all beings are equal and will pass before a "judgement day." There is even a holy book like the **Bible**, known as the **Koran**, the Islamic holy book of scriptures that was posthumously compiled from Mohammad's writings.

Special Islamic Rituals

In the Muslim religion, there are special

The work of Christian missionaries still continue.

rituals, such as worship five times during the day. Most important to followers is the journey back to visit Mecca — called the "Haji" for men and the "Haja" for women. During the ninth month of the Islamic calendar, the fasting period of *Ramandan*, or Bulan Puasa, is ob-

served. Followers arise before dawn and feast, then wait until after sunset to eat again. It is a time of respect and worship of ancestors and royal members who have passed away; reflected in the quiet mood of the country. At the end of the month – called *Lebaran*, or Idul Fitri – the

Borobudur Buddhist freizes, distinctly Indian in decorative flavour.

mood changes to one of forgivemess and rekindled bonds, when colourful processions, mass prayers and vast banquets are laid out to celebrate the passing of the ceremony.

Indonesian Islam

Somehow, the practices of Indonesian Islam differ slightly from those anywhere else in the world – particularly when it comes to the role of women. Here, women are given an equal role, and one of responsibility and respect; they must consent before their husbands can take second wives, they are the initiators of divorce and they, too, enjoy a good bit of freedom.

Islam has been interactive with Indonesia's government since the time of the Republic's independence. The *Sarekat Islam* was the first Islamic political party, though now all branches have been combined into the United Development Party (PPP). In west Java, the separatist movement of *Darul Islam* even tried to create a new state for believers of the religion. However, the attempt at an alternate Islamic area was foiled.

Sacred Sites of Java

In the cry of the *muezzin* that summons followers of Islam to prayer from the high, thin menara, there is a feeling of watchful spirits throughout the island of Java. Muslim beliefs have always been strong, yet an underlying animist culture still thrives in the thick forests and windy cliffs of the wildest coastlines. It may be the tingling of skin, the sensing of another presence, or simply a change in the breeze that shifts the possibilities for other worlds within the imagination. And so, although specific beliefs and spirit names may vary, even westerners will agree that there are certain places throughout the islands where strong *semengkat* (spiritual energies) can be felt.

Java is an island of wild spirits and haunted places, particularly in its temples and caves. Across the Dieng Plateau, one can almost envision past Buddhist and Hindu kingdoms, while whispers pass through the soft coastal winds. At the southern beaches around Parangkusomo, or the tips of Mount Merapi and Mount Lawu, traditional offerings are annually made by the Javanese calender. The tombs of the *wali songo* (nine original apostles) have an aura of settled grace, while the caves of southern Parangtritis and western Sanghyangsirah are havens of meditation and prayer for those who desire healing of body, heart and soul.

Sumatran Celebrations

In the towns along Sumatra's western coastline, magic is in the air on midsummer nights. A parade of huge towers and lighted floats winds its way

Making an offering at a village temple in Bali.

through the wide streets, accompanied by a haphazard marching musical orchestra and thousands of laughing, cheering followers. This is the *Tabot,* a special festival celebrated on the island's western coast, particularly in Benkulu. It is a celebration to honour Hussein, the prophet Mohammed's grandson, who was martyred in the Kerbala War while defending the Muslim religion. As with many Asian-influenced customs and celebrations in Indonesia, decorated effigies are part of this tradition. It takes days to construct these tall, tiered floats with flowers, mirrors, lights and other colourful pieces of local culture. Some floats are figures of *bouraqs* (winged horses with the faces of women who are believed to collect the souls of dead

Legend of Loro Kidul

Perhaps the most influential goddess of Java-nese culture is Loro (Ratu) Kidul, the Goddess of the Southern Seas who has been a part of spiritual belief since she guided the emergence of the Majapahit kingdom. Her strategic and amorous affair with Panembahan Senopati, founder of the second Mataram kingdom, con-ducted in her beautiful underwater palace was only the first of her continuing communications with the ruling family's descendents. Sultan Hamengkubuwono I, the founder of Yogya-karta's ruling house, actually built a stunning underwater replica of her realm.

A rush of cool wind, suddenly slowed to a caress that leaves a powerful, flowered perfume is the sign that marks her presence. She ages with the moon; young at darkness, wise at fullness, and her favourite colour is a pale yel-low-green. Swimmers near the moody beaches of Cilicap are warned of her wrath, as her servants Mbok Roro Kidul and Nyai Roro Kidul often take victims underwater to serve in her palace. It is said Loro Kidul sometimes appears as a shimmering figure during the *Bedoyo Ketawang,* the most sacred dance at the Surakarta palace. It is perhaps possible to meet her spirit at the Samudra Beach Hotel in West Java, where a room has considerately been reserved for her and an intermediary is on hand to help deliver any offerings.

heroes for heaven). The procession be-gins from the town centre and marches to the beach, where the *bouraq* towers are tossed into the sea. Followers often jump in as well to grab the remains of the floats as mementos and charms of good luck.

Bali's Special Religion

Bali is the only island in the Indonesian archipelago on which the culture is based on Hinduism. And, the Balinese have given the religion a few twists of their own – in addition to *Brahma, Vishnu* and *Shiva,* they worship many spirits and entities, along with *Sanghyang Widhi,* the supreme god of the island's unique traditions.

Like other branches of the Hindu religion, the Balinese are born into one of four *castes* in which they must remain for life. However, on Bali, the caste names differ *brahman* (priests), *satria* (soldiers and governors), *wesia* (farmers and trad-ers) or the *sudra* (menial workers).

In Bali, the images of *Garuda* (Vishnu's celestial vehicle) are common as is the *lingga* (phallic representations of Shiva that stand for the creation that arises out of destruction). In the small, road-side temples, offerings of flowers, food and incense are reminders that spiritual beings are interwoven through-out these religions.

Celebrations of Death

The funerals customs of Indonesia are a far cry from the solemn, teary eyed western affairs. Rather, they are cel-ebrations of the passing on and con-tinuation of life.

Bali's cremation ceremonies have long been a part of the island's culture, for they glorify the death of the physical and mental "bodies" in which the core of being (the soul) is kept during life. However, a proper funeral can be quite expensive, for the traditionally ostenta-

A Balinese cremation dias.

one of palm leaves and the other of sandalwood. Black is the colour of choice, seen in women's headdresses and the clothes of the relatives as they carry enormous decorated cremation towers across the rice paddies, as they dance about the twirling tower that holds the body so as to keep the soul from finding its way back to the family's home.

Later, after prayers are said, holy water is thrown about and pots are smashed at the final cremation site, a blow torch is used to set the tower on fire (as matches are considered unclean). The family watches until the pyre has turned the structure to ashes, which are later thrown into the sea.

Dying Eastern Traditions

On the remote island of Sumba in Nusa Tenggara, the culture is closely interwoven with spiritual forces.

Kateda (spirit stones), are found at the main entrances to villages to keep out bad energies that might cause misfortune to the society within. In some areas, the word *semengat* means "fighting spirit." In Sumba, it refers to the concentration of spiritual energies on specific places or things, much like the sacred pilgrim caves or forest protectors of Javanese belief. The most important concept here is *merapu*, which means all spiritual forces in Sumbanese tradition, including those of the ancestors, animist spirits and deities. The *marapu maluri* are the original spirits who have

tious ceremony includes not only the construction of ornate processional towers and sarcophagi, but food and entertainment for everyone as well. Because of the expense involved, families might keep a body for months (or years!) in a coffin, fluids drained to prevent stench and decomposition, until the money is saved. Sometimes poor families who do not have the funds to afford the luxury of a proper celebration will wait until a member of the wealthy elite dies – then the bodies will be exhumed to participate in the rich person's ceremony.

During the funeral, the corpse is placed on a tiered platform with symbols of the heart (a coconut filled with rice), the soul (a small lamp of eggshells) and two name-engraved effigies,

Rites of Passage

A bloody ritual proceeds with a 'death in the afternoon'.

in black march in circles around the squealing animal sacrifices to the incessant beat of a handmade leather drum.

Bright blood gushes from the throat of a huge bull, its black fur glistenening with foaming sweat as it stumbles to the ground, bellowing deeply in an almost mournful panic. Surrounding it are several dark boys and men who bend quickly to catch the liquid in long bamboo tubes before the animal finally dies.

Surrounding this central arena is a crowd of families, who cheer as they smoke and munch peanuts from raised bamboo ledges. In the front of the first platform is an effigy of the dead, peered at by all who enter the area. From a tree high above the scene, a priest calls out the names of relatives and their offerings for the ceremony, tossing down chunks of raw meat while below a ragged procession of men and women dressed

Ceremonial Procedures

This is a bit of the chaos at a Toraja funeral ceremony, where the rites of passage attract relatives from all parts of the archipelago. Often, it takes months to organize travel and funding for the celebration. Thus, like Bali, bodies are often drained and stored for quite awhile until the proper time for the funeral arrives.

A great funeral ceremony surrounds the coffin and the spirit of the dead.

Effigies in cliff-side graves mark the tangible point between death and belief in spirit life.

rows of bright-eyed wooden faces look out over the landscape in an eerie reminder of those who have already passed into the spirit world.

The bodies are life-sized, the clothes simple, life-like faces carved by specialists in the villages and made to closely mirror the features of the person who died. Eyes open, expressions lively, they peer out from the cliffs in rows as if standing aboard a departing ship to wave goodbye. Thin bamboo pole ladders are placed at intervals so relatives can climb up to leave offerings in the outstretched palms of the effigies.

Carved from wood, the type of tree used signifies the wealth of the family of the deceased; usually, that of the *nangka* (jackfruit) indicates the highest classes, as it is the most expensive. Rather than effigies, children who have died are instead "buried" in hanging graves within trees. In areas which have no space for carved burial caves in the rocks, bodies are instead placed in raised wooden "house" graves resembling the dwellings of the living.

Ceremonies have the overtone of animist beliefs, as well as the polytheistic customs and mythology that have been a part of Toraja tradition. Historically, the main god was known as *Puang Matua,* while deities of separate families or tribes were also observed. However, the arrival of Christian missionaries altered many of the traditional ways of worship and celebration. Now, a large portion of the Toraja culture has absorbed Christian beliefs – but without completely replacing their own. However, most of the funeral traditions are still practiced in the same manner as they were centuries ago.

Altars of area megaliths in the area are constructed from rocks brought down from the hills, while traditional dances are performed. The *Mabadong* (traditional re-enactment of the cycle of life), is the central performance to many ceremonies, as it serves to symbolize the payment of last respects and wish for good fortune in the afterlife. Sometimes the *Makatia* will also be danced as a reminder of the generosity and kindness of the one who died, while the *Maranding* war steps serve to commemorate heroic accomplishments.

The number of buffaloes and pigs sacrificed at these cememonies depends on the wealth of the deceased; usually only one for a person of common social status, while up to the hundreds for someone on the richest hierachy level. Once the relatives arrive, celebrations can last anywhere from one day to one week, with songs, dances, processions, *sisemba* (kick-fighting) and buffalo fights all being part of the proceedings.

The Tau Tau

Traditionally, people from Torajaland have carved *tau-tau,* or life-size effigies of the dead to line their sacred burial caves. To keep the various treasures buried with relatives from being ransacked by thieves, the caves were eventually moved up into the grey, cliffside hills, so now

Bersakih, the mother of all temples in Bali, receiver of endless offerings.

never "lived" human lives and who often dwell in the *semangat* sites. *Marapu mameti* are relatives who have passed into the world of the dead but can still influence the lives of their ancestors – in both helpful and harmful ways.

Upon death in Sumba, the deceased is buried with wealth and in a large stone tomb constructed through the efforts of everyone in the village. Important ancestors have their places smack in the centre of the villages. Dead enemies have traditionally earned a place in the town square as well – their severed heads strung up in the *andung* (monument, of the "skull trees") as a show of victory by the Sumbanese tribes.

Merging Beliefs & Traditions

"Belief in the one and only God," states the first principle of Indonesia's *Pancasila* state philosophy, as it is the premise that holds the country together.

In an archipelago with vastly diverse customs and often confusing mixtures of religion, this principle simply encourages belief in "one God," but also recognizes the various spiritual beings that are interwoven into Indonesia's vast background of religion and culture. And, whether Allah, Buddha, God or Mohammed is the foremost god of an island's religion, this first principle shows recognition and respect for each separate culture, binding the various faiths together within an umbrella of harmonious belief.

Life itself is a celebration in Indonesia. And, celebration is a reason for life. From the birth of a laughing Balinese baby to the last rites for a Tana Toraja *tau-tau* (funeral), Indonesia's seasons are filled with festivities. Some events, such as weddings, encompass traditional song and dance, while other rites of passage take place within the simple, quiet surroundings of village and family. But, seldom are the celebrations sombre; instead, irrespective of reason, they are frequently colourful expressions of joy and respect for human life.

A brilliant parade marks the Annual Bali Arts Festival.

Festivals

Surrounded by Celebration

When Indonesia became a Republic in 1945, to recognize the most important aspect of the country's diverse cultures certain religious and cul-

Costumed parades in Jakarta.

tural observances were declared national holidays. And so, a strange mix of titles mark the festivities for those special days that are treated with reverence throughout the archipelago.

New Year opens as showers of fireworks, sprinkle the midnight sky with glistening vibrant colours, bells and laughter emerge from carnivals and one can hear the echoing cheers and cries of revellers welcoming in the New Year. Throughout the night, the national holiday is celebrated, while in Christian Ambon and north Sulawesi, church services are held. In the large cities, special events are the central attractions; in rural areas, the celebrations are small – an exchange of goodwill and continuing friendship for the coming year. The first day in February celebrates the Prophet Mohommad's Ascension and is better-known as **Isra Mi'raj Nabi Muhammad**. Next is **Nyepi**, the Balinese Caka New Year, which is also celebrated throughout the archipelago according to its timing on the Balinese calendar.

Celebrations After Ramadan

Idul Fitri, or the end of the Muslim Ramadan fasting observation, also occurs around this time. After a month-long period of only eating after sunset and before sunrise, there is a two-day national holiday in celebration of forgiveness and friendship, with much feasting.

In Yogyakarta, the **Gerebed Syawai**

Ceremony is a special Muslim celebration in praise of God after the completion of fasting during the month of **Ramadan**. It begins with a parade of palace guards from the Sultan's palace, where they march through the city to the northern square with a procession of *gunungan* (a mound of rice decorated with vegetables, eggs and cakes) and various traditional foods. Music and chanting ward off evil spirits while the *gunungan* is being made. The food is later blessed and shared with the people.

Other areas of the archipelago also celebrate the end of Ramadan, including the Moluccas, where the festivities are called **Pukul Sapu**. The ceremonies held seven days after Idul Fitri, include contests where groups of men strike each other on their bare backs with brooms, the wounds are then "healed" with coconut oil, which is believed to possess special medicinal powers. Northern Sulawesi calls the post-Ramadan celebration **Hari Raya Ketupat** which is again, held seven days after the event. The festivities include horse and motorcycle racing.

Hari Raya Kupatan is East Java's unusual interpretation – the celebration of Idul Fitri is combined with a commemoration of the total solar eclipse in 1983 and the scientific research completed in the area.

In west Lombok, the festival is called **Lebaran Topat**, and includes the making of special *ketupat* (rice cakes) wrapped in woven coconut leaves. Fam-

Festival day at Pura Tanah Lot Bali.

Waicak Day celebrations at Borobudur to mark an anniversary to Buddha.

ily prayers are also held at many sacred graves.

Lomban, in central Java, is also a festival held a week after Idul Fitri and takes place on Kartini Beach in Jepara. This sea festival, locally known as **Bakdo Kupat**, is celebrated by village fishermen and includes boat races and contests – vessels are usually available for visitor participation as well.

Anniversaries & Independence

One of the most important public holidays is April 21 which is **Kartini Day**. It falls on the birthday of Raden Ajeng Kartini, Indonesia's pioneer of women's rights. Born in 1879, Kartini began a school in Jepara, Java, to help give the daughters of regents a better, western-style education. One of the first early nationalists, Kartini's writings provided the first stirrings of female equality in a country of restrictive social and religious traditions (see p 24).

Good Friday, which is called **Wafat Isa Al-Masih**, is a public mid-spring observance, as is **Waicak Day**, or the anniversary of the birth and death of Buddha. Many celebrations surround Waicak Day, particularly in Java. The day before, Buddhist monks travel to Mrapen in a quest for a flame from the eternal fire, which will then be burned at the Waicak ceremony the next morning. The real ceremony is then held at

Rallying to an Independence Day parade.

gelist Sunan Kalijogo, where offerings are made. The *Kyai Grubuk* and *Kutang Ontokusumo* heirlooms are cleaned and replaced, and visitors shake hands with the graveyard custodian – the belief is that by doing so, your wishes will come true.

Tahun Baru Hijriah, 1 Muharram 1413 H better known as the Muslim New Year follows soon after.

The largest celebration in the country, is **Indonesian Independence Day**, which falls on August 17 every year. Parades and festivals are held all over the nation to commemorate Sukarno's declaration of democracy and freedom for the Republic in 1945.

On this day all businesses are closed, mass speeches are made, and flags are proudly raised all over the nation. On the September 9, the anniversary of the birth of the Prophet Mohammad, known as **Malaud Nabi Mohammad** is celebrated. Also a national holiday, traditional ceremonies and festivals are held

Mendut and the Borobudur temples and draws Buddhist visitors from all over the world to participate in the mass prayers and ceremonies.

The ascension of Christ is celebrated soon afterwards and is nationally known as **Kenaikan Isa Al-Masih**. Just a few weeks later on the Islamic calendar is **Idul Adha 10 Zulhijjah 1412 H**, the Muslim day of sacrifice when goats and cattle are slaughtered and their meat given to the needy and poor. In Demak, central Java, ceremonies centre around the mosque and grave of the Muslim evan-

Presidential guests at Independence Day celebrations.

The Christians go about their celebrations in a quieter vein.

and glad tidings that precede the festivities which will usher in the New Year.

Unique Celebrations

Influenced by merging religions and cultures, the archipelago's traditions have embraced customs and beliefs which have resulted in some of the most unusual and surprising reasons for festivities and feasting.

During the Balinese year of 210 days, each temple is celebrated with at least one festival. The best time for festivities are during the full moon, in April and October when gambling, cock fights, music, dancing, flower displays and offerings of animals and colourful fruit are all part of the celebrations. Some-

to recognize the life of one of the most influential religious leaders in Indonesia. Preceding the celebrations for the Prophet Mohammed is the feast of **Sekaten**, which starts when a procession of sacred *gamelan* instruments are brought from Surakarta's Kraton palace, to the Grand Mosque. Festivities are accompanied by a fair conducted in front of the mosque, where music is played and traditional crafts are sold until the end of the week, when the instruments are again paraded back to the Kraton for the next annual celebration.

As in the west, **Christmas Day** is also celebrated as **Hari Raya Natal**. Despite differences in gods and religious traditions, the population shares the holiday with all the goodwill

Gambling, cock fights, music, dancing, offerings… all part of an Indonesian festivity.

Typical Balinese offering of fruits, sweets and flowers.

times called **Odalan**, these days of prayer and feasting are held throughout the country to celebrate the anniversaries of smaller temples in the villages, as well as the larger, well-known places of worship, such as Tanah Lot and Pura Goa Lawah.

Festivals of The Spirit

The religious ceremony of **Jalanidhipuja** is part of the Hindu tradition that focuses on spiritual and physical cleansing when offerings are thrown into the sea. A priest is also present at the festivities to bless the villages with holy water taken from a special spring called *Sumur Pitu*, which is located in the

midst of east Java's coastal forest. The event takes place three to seven days before **Nyepi** – the national celebration of the Balinese Caka New Year.

Ciwaratri, the Hindu ceremony of purification, is part of traditional practice in West Lombok and Nusa Tenggara. Held on the seventh month of the Balinese calendar when there is no moonlight in the sky, those who participate do not eat or sleep for 24 hours, which signifies the completeness of purification.

Rondang Bintang, or "full moon," is a Sumatran celebration that is held outside Medan. This festival of the Simalungun peoples includes traditional sports such as *Marja Lengkat*, *Margala* and *Marsampak Hotang*, and mainly takes place in Pematang Purba, the his-

Making homage.

Costumes are as dramatic and colourful as the rituals in Toraja land.

torical site of the former Purba kingdom of Simalungun, where many traditional tribal houses still stand.

The Roman Catholic celebration of the **Sendangsono Pilgrimage** takes place in Muntilan, central Java, during May and October. It is here that Catholi-cism first took hold on the island. Thousands of Roman Catholics travel to the holy spring of Sendangsono in the Menoreh mountains to collect some of the holy water that runs beneath the *sono* tree. The spring is dedicated to the Virgin Mary, and there is a statue of her at the edge of the Road of the Holy Cross leading to it, where followers light candles at her feet. Also celebrated in early May is Bali's **Pagerwesi Day**, when rituals and offerings are made to Sang Hyang Pramesti Guru (creator of the universe) to ward off evil spirits. Ambon's **Pattimura Day** occurs around the same time, when a flaming torch symbolizing the hero Pattimura, is carried Olympic-style by a team of relay runners through the villages to the city of Ambon, where it is kept burning until the next day.

Sulawesi Celebrations

During the dry summer season between June and September, Sulawesi is in full celebration. In Minahasa, north Sulawesi, **Hari Pengucapan Syukur** marks Thanksgiving Day.

Funeral ceremonies in Tana Toraja, are held between these months; *Rambu Tuka* is the joyful ceremony surrounding the death, while *Rambu Solo* is the lively celebration when dozens of pigs and buffalo are slaughtered in the hope that the spirit of the newly departed will be accepted by God.

At the end of June, the **Sea Festival** is held in Pelabuhan Ratu, West Java. It is celebrated by scattering flowers into the sea. A buffalo is also sacrificed, its head thrown into the waters as water sports competitions, *wayang golek* (puppet shows), *ketuk tilu* (communal dances) and *pencak silat* (martial arts) performances continue the festivities.

Javan Water Festivals

Suro Eve is the first night of the Suro month on the Javanese calendar, when all-night visits are paid to beaches and mountain peaks near Yogyakarta to give thanks for blessings and pray for physical strength and moral guidance. Also celebrated in Yogyakarta is the traditional **Filling Enceh Water Containers Ceremony** held at the start of the Suro month at the Imogiri Royal Cemetery. This ceremony consists of filling Enceh – four sacred bronze water containers, to thank God for the water of life. The Siraman Pusaka Ceremony, is a traditional cleaning of royal heirlooms kept at the palace.

Balinese Festivals

Both the Balinese and the Javanese celebrate important festive events around this time. **Galungan**, the most important Balinese holiday, celebrates the world's creation and the victory of good over evil. Later, **Kunngan Day**, the second-most important day of the Hindu Balinese year, is observed by offerings, special bathing and purification.

In Java, the **Labuhan Ceremony** near Yogyakarta marks the birth of the Sultan, and offerings at Parang Kusumo beach, Mount Merapi and Mount Lawu are made to appease Loro Kidul.

Sedekah Laut is celebrated by the fishermen of Cilacap on the southern

The cortege being prepared for cremation.

coast. It involves feasts, *tirakatan* (night wakes), and a procession of offerings which are thrown into the sea. The Permuni Cave where the Opak meets the Gajah Wong River, is where legend holds that King Senopati met Loro Kidul.

On the last Wednesday of the Sapar month of the Javanese calendar, a week-long **Water Festival** is annually held here to pray for good harvest and fertile soil for the farmers of the area. August brings **Tor-tor Mangalahat Harbo**, the ritual ceremony of the Lake Toba Batak tribe, when buffaloes are slaughtered and offerings are made at Sianjur Mula-Mula – the indigenous land of the Toba Batak. The **Basyafa Pilgrimage** also occurs in Sumatra around this time, when thousands of pilgrims visit the

grave of Syech Burhanddin located just south of Pariaman and carnivals, religious ceremonies and prayers are held. An interesting celebration in October is the **Belang Festival** celebrated in the Kai Islands which symbolizes the zeal of the villagers in fighting attacks from the sea. A *belang* (boat) from the main museum, is taken down and used for the

Whirls, twirls, and trances in Kalimantan.

celebration. Then, after the ceremonies, a procession is held to return the boat to the musuem once again.

During the year, there are many other reasons for celebration: Anniversaries of the founding of cities, births and deaths of famous heroes, feasts and festivities to appease spirits and events that highlight the traditions and cultures of Indonesia. Each island and area has its own special schedule, and visitors are usually welcomed and encouraged – to take part in the celebrations.

The anniversary of the founding of

Children's Day festival in Denpasar.

East Kalimantan is *January 9*, so you will find many festivities in cities such as Samarinda and Banjarmasin at this time. *January 31* is the anniversary of Sidoarjo in East Java, the town known locally for its *bandeng* (milkfish) *batik* crafts and *kerpok* (prawn cracker). At the end of January, many areas also "close the New Year," with special celebrations known as **Menulude** in Sulawesi. The festivities include all-night music and dancing, as well as the preparation of special cakes for the feast. Hila Village in Ambon, the Moluccas, holds a similar celebration lasting for most of the month and ending with a special beach or forest feast that includes *sago* (the area's special sweet potato) and traditional "*badendang*" where they sing until dawn. *April 17* is the anniversary of the west Lombok regency. In Mataram celebrations are held to gather those living in the area and encourage public participation in local development. Also in Ambon **ANZAC Day** is celebrated on *April 25*. This special holiday commemorates the Australians and other Allied forces who lost their lives in WWII. On this day celebrations are held to recognize and honour those killed in battle.

Batari Dewi Saraswati, the Goddess of Learning and Knowledge, is celebrated in Bali on *May 2*, or **Saraswati Day**. During this holiday, no reading or writing is allowed, and all books are given to the goddess for her blessings. In Mandor, west Kalimantan, the annual **Makam Juang Mandor Pilgrimage** is held on *June 28* in memory of the death of more

than 21,000 people during the 1942-1944 Javanese occupation. *July 14* is the anniversary of the founding of Manado. In Sulawesi the festivities include cultural performances and music staged on the city's open-air stage.

Every Saturday during October, mass wedding ceremonies are held in south Sumatra following the pepper harvest season. Central Sulawesi also celebrates the end of the harvest with mass marriage ceremonies near Tentena, along with feasts, ceremonies and *modero* and *maende* dancing. October is the main month, for celebrations, particularly on the northern islands. *October 10* marks the anniversary of Bitung in north Sulawesi and *October 23* of Pontianak, west Kalimantan.

Madura Island's Sumenep regency marks the anniversary of its beginnings and the arrival of Aria Wirajaya of the former Singosari kingdom *on October 31*. Also in Sulawesi, the Minihasa regency celebrates its birthday on the first day of November, with traditional dances and performances that last for an entire week. Due to the holiday season, many areas hold Tourism Weeks during the time before the new year.

It is an excellent time in which to get information on the celebrations taking place within the archipelago. Just stop by at the Indonesian Tourism Office in your own country and ask about the events. Or, pick up a free **Calendar of Events** available from the Indonesian Tourist Offices in Jakarta or Denpasar – as it is colourful, detailed and free!

I n the light of the moon, the Prambanan temple walls glow with life, the dimness of the night fading out all sense of colour along the ornately carved walls. Cool and silent, the night air is scented with the fragrance of incense, and led by the soft sound of the *gamelan* orchestra. In the centre of the complex is a stage onto which a band of dancers dressed as monkeys leap. Costumes of bright, tangled fur and perky tails whirl, ankle-bells jangle as they hop from one bare foot to the other in a comical yet intricate portrayal of the **Ramayana** ballet.

The precision of dance is seen in the coordination between body movements, music and costume.

145

Performing Arts

Stories Spun Over Time

The hero is the dashing Prince Rama, an incarnation of the Hindu god Vishnu, who was fated by the gods to kill Rawana, the evil king. Banished from the palace with his beautiful wife Sita, Rama heads for the forest, where Sita is kidnapped by the evil king. In his search for Sita, Rama enlists the help of the monkey god Hanuman, and monkey king. Their band of Sugriwa the

The Music of Moonlight

A gamelan band, distinctly Indonesian.

It was first used to summon the gods to a meeting on Java's Mount Lawu, or so the tradition of *gamelan* music tells. Now, the sacred *gamel* (hammer) is used for equally powerful means – to accompany *wayang* (puppet) and ballet performances. The large 40 to 80 piece orchestras, contain instruments of varied origins most of them comprised of percussion and strings.

The Sundanese *calung* (a set of bamboo tubes played with padded *panakol* hammers, bamboo flutes and reed pipes) may have come from India, while the huge bronze drums probably originated in Vietnam. The introduction of xylophones, chimes and string instruments add a gentle, flowing rhythm of notes that flutters around the main heartbeat tempo. Though the music may seem unpredictable and impromptu, it has been endlessly practiced and each long piece is played without stopping from beginning to end. Mistakes made are regarded as part of the learning process and are corrected with each session. The bronze slats of the *saron* (small to medium sized metallophone) are tapped with mallets to sound the soft melody, several different instruments intertwining it with texture and rhythm. The quickened waves of the *bonangs* (bronze kettle)

supporting the tinkling main tune. Human voices are another instrument that add emotion and feeling to the piece; no words are spoken, but rather a simple note is carried throughout the melody, rising and falling in tone and volume according to the part of the story. A note from the huge, suspended *ageng gong* marks the end of each melody, but it is the drummer who is in control of the orchestra's cues. It is his signal of rhythm that allows the musicians to find the correct pace for the story, or to change a musical combination of compositions. In the *gamelan*, only a basic outline of music is used, played by the *saron* and *slentem* (metallphone with bamboo resonator) while other instruments add a vibrance to it. The drummer also signals the entrance and the end of these elaborating notes throughout the melody and changes within them to accompany the puppet master's or dancers' interpretation of a particular story. Performances of the *gamelan* orchestra can be enjoyed every week at the Kraton, or Sultan's Palace in Yogyakarta – a magical, historical place that captures the feeling of the country with its royal setting and regal musicians. Other cities in Java often have shortened performances, and schools and professional groups are usually willing to let visitors sit in on a practice.

A flute player from Borneo.

monkeys eventually go to war with Rawana and rescue Sita from his hold. Yogyakarta is the most enchanting stage for this epic where every month the ballet is performed over four nights at the Prambanan Temple by the light of the full moon. It is absolutely magical; the costumes are both bright and flowing, the air crisp, the music haunting, effectively weaving a spell that will capture you in the beauty and passion of Indonesian culture.

While the **Ramayana** recounts the Ulysses-like adventures of Rama, the **Mahabharata** tells the story of an important war that took place in India c. 14 BC. It is about the struggle for power between the Kurava and the Pandawa brothers who eventually end up fighting for control of the country.

In the midst of the epic, a beautiful poem called the **Bhagavad Gita** is sung to the Pandawa soldier Arjuna by Krishna, who is both his advisor and another incarnation of the Hindu deity Vishnu. In the poem, the lyrics explain that the destiny of a warrior is confrontation rather than cowardice, and that death is not something to fear, as the soul will again be reborn.

Actually, both the **Ramayana** and the **Mahabharata** epics are derived from stories of India with names of the characters and locations changed when the stories were brought to Java with the onset of Hinduism. These stories have spread throughout the archipelago over the centuries. The same characters often appear in *wayang* (theatre puppet) per-

Ramayana is performed with variation from island to island.

formances and Balinese dances.

Shadows of the Night

The *wayang kulit* (shadow puppets) whirl in front of the stage, their movements smooth and rhythmic according to the sudden crash of gongs and bells emanating from the nearby orchestra. *Wayang* is the Indonesia word for "shadow", while *kulit* means "leather", thus, the characters of the *wayang kulit* are, literally, leather shadow puppets. Each figure is carved from the skin of the water buffalo with a thin knife and intricate chiseling to create fine, lace-like details, which are later painted with a mix of bright colours, gold highlights

Wayang kulit, shadow puppet play.

and black ink accentuations. Moveable arms are attached before the painting begins, then the *cempurit* (stick on which the puppet is mounted), is finally attached. Each puppet's face is different, as his or her character is reflected in the features and expressions painted by the various artists. *Halus* (noble characters), show elegance by elongated features, while *kasar* (vulgar persona) are easily recognized by their greatly exaggerated and often grotesque attributes. It is the *dalang* (puppet master), who brings these puppets to life before the large paper screen. Somehow, sitting cross-legged on a pillow for timeless all-night sessions, he manipulates the figures in an amazingly beautiful and life-like manner. Tilted slightly forward in front of

the screen, the characters can run, laugh, argue and fight, displaying a variety of animated emotions as they converse. The *dalang* is a diplomatic and charming leader of the performance, varying his voice to suit the puppet's character and mood, whilst weaving an atmosphere of passion, anger, friendship or forgiveness. Conversing at both the local and aristocratic levels of language, he spins impromptu stories of religion and history from the generalities of a well-loved script, whilst alternating between the neatly-lined puppets standing along both sides of the stage. The *dalang* also cues the *gamelan* orchestra to changes in format and tempo by various signals – the tapping of a *cempala*, (wooden mallet), or by using

Wayang golek, a performance of wooden dolls.

one of his characters to convey the message. It is the *kendang* (drum player), who signals to the *dalang* by changes in his or her tempo thus communicating the beginning and ending of each piece of music.

The Sundanese version is the *wayang golek* (three-dimensional wooden puppet shows that do not use the paper screen); they are most popular in the west Javan areas around Bandung, although you can find performances in Yogyakarta and even Bali. East Java's *wayang klitik* is also screenless, using flat wooden puppets to perform stories that recount legends of the Majapahit kingdom. In the central Javan dance dramas of *wayang orang* and *wayang topeng*, dancers emulate the movements of the puppets, though in *wayang topeng* masks are used to express the personalities of the different characters.

Movements of Legend

In Balinese dancing, every tilt of the hip, each hint of a smile, signals meaning. Movements are subtle, and slow, each performer conveying a separate message and mood, whilst weaving individual expressions into an enchanting musical drama. A maiden is captured in the story of the *legong,* a beautiful dance of grace and agility. The performers are two young dancers and the *condong* (attendant). Each dancer is dressed in tightly wrapped gold cloth, their fea-

Children are selected to train for the Legong, a dance of grace and agility.

tures are accentuated to highlight their natural beauty. The *condong* introduces the dancers, then allows the two to dance alone. Their movements depict love scenes and departure for battle.

Later, the *condong* reappears, having donned golden wings as the "Bird of all Fortunes", who brings the king a message of impending doom, signalling the end of the dance.

In the *baris* dance, male dancers act out the *legong* instead, using alterations in movement, energy and facial expression to convey the moods of a warrior preparing for battle. The *kebyar* which is another male dance places greater emphasis on the actions of each separate dancer, and in the *trompong* version the performer actually plays an instrument during the dance. Battles of good and evil define the well-known *kechak* dance, which uses a choir of men as a musical background rather than the *gamelan* orchestra. Chanting voices, fluttering fingers and flowing mass movements accompany this Balinese version of the **Ramayana** epic. In this dance, the bare-chested checkered saronged men move to the hypnotic rhythm of voices, in an unusual and exciting performance.

One of the most exciting Balinese dances is the *Barong and Rangda* ("kris dance"), in which the eternal struggle between good and evil is amusingly portrayed. *Barong Keket* personifies the good spirits in the mischevious form of a half-lion, half-dog being; with one man at the tail and one at the head. This long, four-legged creature comes to life

in a hilarious dance of snapping jaws and whirling tresses of fur. In the story, he protects a village from the evil witch *Rangda* (a terrifying creature with sharp, claw-like nails and a high, shivery shriek of a laugh). At first, *Barong Keket* plays the clown with his friend the nervous, chattering monkey, until the *Rangda* enters the scene.

The main characters, have no pity for a boy who is doomed to be sacrificed to *Rangda,* until God appears and makes the boy immortal. The battles between good and evil continue as characters change in and out of monster and animal form until *Rangda*'s powers become too strong; then only a duel of magic can save the village. *Krises* (wavy-bladed daggers) are drawn by the men for protection but *Rangda* uses her powers to make them turn to suicidally on themselves. In a trance, they run amok around the stage, rolling on the ground and foaming at the mouth to the wild sounds of the *gamelan* orchestra until the evil spirits are assuaged by a priest sprinkling holy water and the sacrifice of a chicken.

The *Sanghyang* dances are a combination of the *barong rangda* and the *legong,* where two young girls dance with their eyes closed in unison to the chanting of separate male and female *kechak* choirs. Known as the *Sanghyang Dedari*, this dance later developed into the *kechak*. Another version called the *Sanghyang Jaran* involves a young boy who rides a hobby horse through a ring of fire. In both versions, the dancers fall

The dramatic kechak dance, native to Bali performed at Pura Tanah Lot, with a central performance of Ramayana.

The barong (kris) dance, rather a
trance performance.

into a trance at the end, when a priest
blesses them with holy water and brings
them back to life.

Traditional dances of Indonesia either involve only a solo dancer, or are a
wild tangle of colour and movement
which even includes the audience. Traditional dances are hardly limited to the
popular entertainment found on Bali's
tourist circuit. Fortunately, for every
small village or town performance, each
culture is usually willing to allow visitors watch the show.

Songs of Sumatra

From Sumatra's Lake Toba region, the
musical Bataks bring song to life at

Tana Toraja dances in Sulawesi.

Jakarta's major bars and hotels. However, on their own island, you will find the more unique *sigalegale* performance. Using puppets carved from the wood of the *banyan* tree, these figures are life-size effigies of young Bataks dressed in their traditional costume of blue *sarong* (wraparound skirt-like attire) and red turban.

Resembling the Tana Toraja *tau-tau* (statues representing deceased persons) of the cliffside graves, the figures are set up in long boxes. The puppet master moves their limbs by employing a pulley to the accompaniment of the *gamelan*, drums and flutes. Performances are usually seen at weddings and funerals, when the *sigalegale* ceremony drives away evil spirits as spears are tossed at the puppet who dances on the grave of the dead.

However, if you want to enjoy more harmonious Batak song, visit the **Batak Cultural Centre** in Jalan Josep Sinaga on Prapat. During the week-long **Danau Toba Festival** each June, you can also hear them perform; or, try the Prapat Hotel (check the front desk to find out the dates and times of these interesting musical shows).

Also in Sumatra the dances of the Minangs are part of the tradition of the western region. There is the tari *payung*, (umbrella dance), which demonstrates a young man's love for a woman, and the amazing *tari lilin* (candle dance), in which young girls click castanets while simultaneously juggling candles attached to saucers, in a rhythmic style. The *pencak silat* is an aggressive form of self-defence practiced by young Minang boys to enable them to protect themselves. It is an exciting form of art, in which variations of the same theme result in dance-dramas displaying tension and skill in which tales of stalking tigers and battles are relayed.

The *randai* is derived from the *pencak silat*. It is a well-known group dance that is commonly performed at celebrations such as harvests and weddings; only men perform the parts, (even those of women characters), as they tell the story of a wicked woman who had to be driven away before she brought inevitable destruction to her village. The dance itself is performed in a circular fashion, with the characters alternately standing and sitting as the main characters play their roles in the centre. Sitted around the dancers, the chorus accompanies the story, while the *gamelan* orchestra adds flavour to the various moods of the tale.

Dances 'Round The Islands

In Lombok, the *Tandak Gerok* is an unusual and beautiful form of music in which the singers imitate the instruments of the *gamelan* orchestra. For a love story, there is the dance of the *gandrung*, while the *oncer* is an aggressive male war dance. The popular *cupak gerantang* dance also relates a romantic theme and can be seen anywhere on the island.

To highlight funeral ceremonies, those in Sulawesi's Tana Toraja add a form of simple, yet graceful dance accompanied by the beat of a drum – and the audience often rushes in to join the performer.

Various villages in Kalimantan, the Moluccas and Irian Jaya also have traditional music and dance performances. Try to talk to the locals or check with schools and tourist offices to find out what is scheduled and where and when the performances will be held.

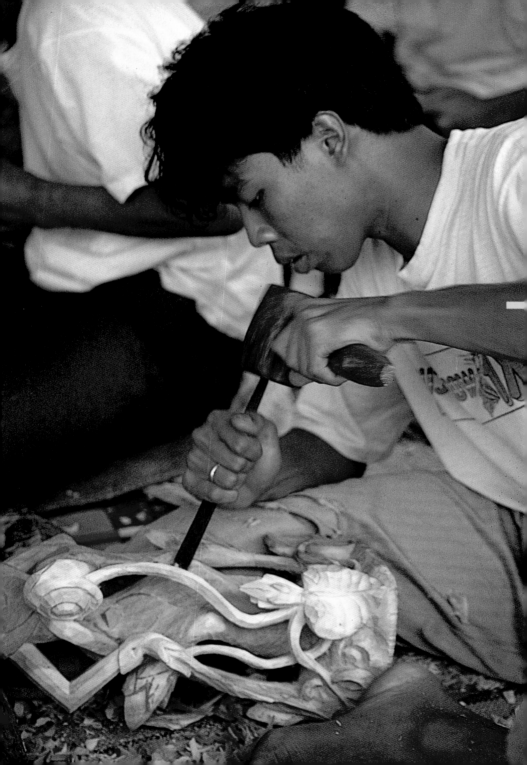

A carefully carved wooden figure smoothed to perfection, or a *batik* landscape painting carefully dabbled onto a thin sheet of silk... In Indonesia everyone is in some sense an artist, honing his or her craft not for the sake of tourism, but rather for the benefit of continuing their cultural tradition.

Handicrafts

157

Weapons of History

The Indonesians are master chisellers in wood.

In Indonesian tradition, weapons have always held a special place. Rather than mere tools of self-defence, they are also regarded as sources of divine protection which bear great magical powers. Passed on from father to son from generation to generation, these sacred heirlooms are often believed to allow the user to call on his ancestors for aid. One such weapon is the *kris,* or *keris,* as it is sometimes spelt. Taken from the word *iris* ("to cut"), this short knife resembles a curved blade dag-

Elderly ladies in Kalimantan have the time and patience for crafting, beading, basketry or weaving.

ger fashioned of either iron, nickel or steel. The blade is of a wavy, serpentine shape and takes the form of a *naga* (king cobra), when in motion, while the straight dagger resembles the reptile at rest. The number of curves in the blade can symbolize strength, passion, or a special legendary figure, while the design stamped on the blade often foretells the destiny of the one who wears it.

Images of Javanese mysticism or Hinduism are often carved into the wood of the hilt and the sheath in which the blade rests is often ornately designed. You can see the *kris* tucked into the back of the *sarong* (Malay skirt-like garment) of each member of Yogyakarta's Sultan's Palace, or in the uniform of those who play in the *gamelan* (percussion-type orchestra) orchestras on the south palace lawn. To the Javanese, the *kris* is far more than a blade, but rather an integral part of the island's culture, which is used in one's dress during ceremonial occasions. It is also an heirloom that according to *adat* (customary dictates) is presented by the father to the son when he reaches manhood.

Beads of Silver

From deep in the hills of Sumatra and Kalimantan, soft beads of silver are chiselled out of the earth using similiar techniques those from of sea trading days. Destined for small shops and factories, the precious metal is transported throughout the islands and delicately re-shaped into intricate artwork and jewellery. Good quality work is about 92.5 percent silver – lower grades of 50 percent or so (commonly found in inexpensive souvenir shops) will tarnish within a few months. The first step in the creation is hammering and firing; the process is then repeated then several times. The soft metal is then stamped, carved or shaped into the desired design, and temporary glue from what the Balinese call the "filling filling fruit" is used to attach small decorative stones and gems. Finally, the silver is cleaned and polished with sand to achieve the natural "white" hue of the lacy filigree style. One common technique is the "antique" colouring of jewellery and artwork by staining, this gives the silver a darker hue making it resemble items that have aged over the years.

Kota Gede in Yogyakarta is the central area for silver purchasing. Here beautiful jewellery, vases and intricate models of ships and carriages line the shelves of the stalls. Bali's southern area around Denpasar is crowded with silver workshops and stores; for an interesting day trip, informative tours to these silver workshops are available through agents and hotels in either city. South Kalimantan – particularly the Martapura area – has a thriving jewellery trade that makes use of the islands wealth of precious and semi-precious stones. Silver *salapah padusi* (boxes used to store betelnut), are found throughout the archipelago, though one of the most

popular places to find them is around Toraja in Sulawesi. Another prime area for silver is Bukittinggi in Western Sumatra, where the influences of the former Minangkabau kingdom of Pagaruyung are seen in the crafts of the many art centres that flourish around the city.

Sculptures of Wood and Stone

Honing a large monolithic block into a delightfully intricate piece of artwork takes not only imagination and time, but a great deal of talent as well. And, unarguably, the Balinese are some of the archipelago's most talented artists who, within a few weeks can carve a

Stone-carving is a speciality of the Balinese.

Young men engages themselves in carving with hibiscus wood or making paper-mache.

mere lump of wood into anything from a simple, smooth piece of fruit, to a detailed *wayang* (puppet) goddess carving. In Balinese carvings, one of four types of wood are commonly used: Ebony imported from Sumatra and Borneo, this wood is used to fashion dark, smooth sculptures as its hard composition makes the wood difficult to carve and therefore usually a bit more expensive; sweet-scented hibiscus wood from local forests is also quite hard and has the unique dual colouring of camel-white and milk-chocolate brown, it is often used to highlight the curves and intricate designs of a sculpture; sandalwood, imported from East Timor, is a common base for many carvings, most of which remain in an unpolished state;

crocodile wood so-named because of the scaly bark surrounding the trees is a less costly local product that is soft and easy to hone, sculptures fashioned are surprisingly smooth and white!; bare teak and mahogany are used by some artists, while others use vibrant or pastel oils to paint features on ordinary sculptures of shop wood instead. For works with a smooth, glossy finished tone, a fine polish is made from a unique combination of regular shoe polish and petrol; the white shoe polish is used for light-coloured sandy crocodile wood works and the brown polish for darker wood such as ebony and hibiscus.

Woodcarving is a natural Batak tradition and in the Sumatran region of Lake Toba, items are honed to suit both

After cutting out on leather,
wayang kulit pieces are painted.

everyday and traditional use.

Topeng (funeral dance masks) are carved to pledge the continued honour of descendents to the deceased, and *silaon na bolon* (paired figure for protection against evil) are made to resemble revered relatives who have passed away. A large part of Indonesian culture deals with magic, as do its carvings – wood-covered *pustasha* (magic books of formulas) and *tunggal panaluan* (magic wands) are believed to both protect the area and predict the future.

As for sculpture, the megaliths of Sumatra's highlands near the Pasemah Plateau are some of the most intriguing in the country. Believed to be from the Bronze Age, their design incorporates bas-relief carvings and curves depicting expressive battle scenes: men battling a snake, riding elephants and even a tiger greedily guarding a human head. The second type of sculpture is more primitive, and not as intricately carved often depicting groups of men squatting, cross-armed – which provides a significant historical clue to the culture of their times. In the central Kerinci area, in the town of Sungai Penuh, there is another interesting form of sculpture, that of the carved beams in the old mosque near the central square. Sculptures left behind by a legendary kingdom can be found by exploring the stunningly Tibetan-like valleys in the surrounding area. Nearby, Dusun Sungai Tetung, makes an interesting visit, village known for its beautiful woven baskets.

Brushes of Bali

Painting is a specialty of the Balinese, and works are categorized into one of four styles: "Traditional" motifs originate in small villages and depict detailed scenes of Balinese life, such as people, or dancing or harvesting; "Classical" works usually deal with the arts, paintings of characters from the **Ramayana** or of *wayang kulit* (leather shadow puppet) figures; unrestricted by traditional images, "modern" art often uses stationary figures such as tigers and bare-breasted women, painted in overtones of abstract, realist or expressionist styles one of the most prominent styles in recent years has been that of

Mural painting of Ramayana scenes are very popular, and saleable.

the "Young Artists School". The movement began in the 1970's when the Dutch painter Arie Smith came to Bali, together with several other prominent international artists, who made Ubud their permanent base. These other artists included American Antonio Blanco and the Dutch Hans Snel. Smith taught young artisit European Painting techniques which formed the basis of the movement, whilst subject matter, colours and composition were left to the boys own arrangements. Thus a new artistic tradition evolved.

Bali now attracts and nurtures artists fashion in a way similiar to Paris – thousands of art shops, studios and galleries line the roads around the Baluan and Ubud areas.

Museums & Academies

At the "**Puri Lukisan Museum**", there is an interesting display of island paintings dating back to the end of the 19th century, while the "**Neka Museum**" has an exhibition of works by well-known Indonesian and western artists. It is a fascinating area to visit, and day trips around various small galleries will reward the sightseer with display rooms full of traditional Balinese works as well as those executed in style of the "young artists". Yogyakarta's paintings are nearly as famous as the city's *batiks*, and students from all over the archipelago come to the city to study and practice their styles.

A Batik painting from Yogjakarta.

The **Indonesian Academy of Fine Arts (ASRI)** is probably the best-known institution, where commercial and graphic arts, painting, sculpture and design are all part of the educational curriculum. In the 1950s and 1960s, many professional Indonesian painters lived in the Yogyakarta area such as Hendra, Rusli and Saptohudoyo.

But it was probably the late impressionist Affandi (1906-1990) who reaped the most fame. Born in Cirebon, Affandi struggled for success in his craft throughout his youth, often taking rest and shelter beneath clusters of banana trees. Today, the memories of his hard work are symbolized by the banana-leaf shape of the roof on his home on Jalan Urip Sumoharjo, and in the two galleries housing his vast private collection.

Special Crafts of the Outer Areas

Pearls, shimmering shells and other sea ornaments are the decorative jewels accentuating the craftwork of Moluccas. A favourite style of framed artwork are the iridescent-shadowed white shells, placed on a soft black backing to bring out the finest sheen in the light. Jewellery such as *palau* (pins) and brooches of all animistic and geometric shapes are local specialities and small shells are strung onto necklaces and bracelets like beads.

Gold is another medium used in

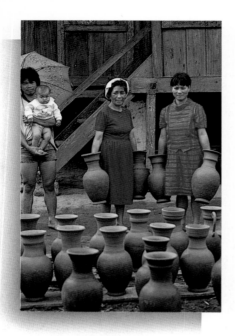

Pulutan pottery in Manadeo being prepared for decoration.

hold interiors and items of ornamental wear. The inner Dani tribes of Irian Jaya not only make use of simple shells feathers and bones in fashioning their jewellery, stones are also necessary in the crafting of *kapak* (axe blades), in which the black variety is second only to the harder blue stones, as the blue are effective in delicately honing the blade to the desired shape.

Cultural Centres

Most visitors to the islands want to learn about the various Indonesian handicrafts, particularly before they purchase a gift or souvenir. However, short holidays and business trip often limit these opportunities. Fortunately, there are several major centres where visitors can learn a lot about traditional crafts at one place and come away far more knowledgeable from this experience. In Bali, the **Werdhi Budaya Art Centre** is

ornate jewellery work on the islands, as it is a popular item with traders and tourists. An equally common – albeit simpler – craft involves cloves, the stems of which are stitched together to create the figures of sailors and intricate models of traditional ships. Craftware of the Sulawesi tribes incorporates a selection of natural fibres, made of silk and of traditionally woven threads – younger generations favour brilliant bracelets and small, beaded necklaces. Another unique addition is the use of carved stones and plant seeds found in designs for house-

Carving panels to be used for house decoration.

Waxing outlines on batik, the first step in the process.

the place to observe both performing and fine arts, as well as beautiful Balinese architecture. Designed in 1973 by Ida Bagus Tugur, who was also the architect for the National Art Gallery in Jakarta, this cultural centre offers three art galleries, several performing stages, seminar halls and exhibition spaces that feature various cultural programmes. Jakarta's "Taman Mini" or **Indonesia in Miniature Park** is the location of the **Museum of Indonesia**, where cultural exhibitions from all 27 island provinces are displayed. **Taman Ismail Marzuki (TIM)**, also known as the Jakarta Art Centre, is one of the best places to discover the cultures of the archipelago – an excellent way to learn about the fascinating crafts and varience in cul-

ture within this diverse country.

Woven Traditions: The Fabric of Life

Indonesian designs are known for their colourful beauty and diversity; which is not surprising considering the distance between the archipelago's islands and consequent development of local cultures reflected in the various fabric designs. *Batik* is the buzzword for the favourite designs – this style caught on in the central islands of Java and Bali but spread throughout the main tourist areas via clothing, handbags and *sarongs* (wrap-around skirt-like attire). Hardly an exclusively Indonesian technique,

Decorating the unwaxed spaces.

variations on the *batik* styles are found in many Southeast Asian countries. Interestingly enough some historians credit India with introducing the methods of artistry, while others believe that those in the major Javanese kingdoms developed the technique on their own. *Batik* means "to dot," and this effectively describes the process of design: wax is applied over areas of a cloth before being dyed to preserve the colour and design. After dying, the wax is peeled off in some areas to achieve a darker hue, and more wax painted on in other areas to sustain the most recent shade. The cloth is then dyed again – from the lightest colour to black – to produce an intricate design that can incorporate hundreds of different patterns and shades. The two methods of making *batik* designs are that of *batik tulis* and *batik cap*, or those of "written" and "stamped" *batik*, respectively. The former is designed by the artist, using traditional images of island scenes, animals and people, while the latter style is a repetitive stamp of a specific image, such as a bird or a fish – this later method is the authentic *batik* style. The materials used are usually cotton, rayon or silk; the latter is considered the best fabric and should always be dyed all the way through, on both sides. Probably the most well-known *batik* styles are the courtly flowers and elegant moon-lit landscapes which originate from the many schools and artistic masters living in the Yogyakarta area. Bali has its

*Ikat-weaving is a typical fabric throughout Indonesia;
styles vary with the region.*

own funky, free-hand designs, although traditional images are also popular, as are the Chinese-influenced Cirebon *batiks* and bright Maduran works.

Images of Ikat

Ikat weaving that originated with the proto-Malay peoples whose descendents now inhabit the eastern islands of the archipelago. This technique involves dying a design onto the threads prior to weaving them together; a complicated process that results in designs of incredibly intricate patterns. Dyes are made from local plants and earth minerals, which give them rich, rustic hues. The thread is usually a thick stiffened cotton

which is home-spun on special looms. The threads are then repeatedly dipped into the dyes to achieve the desired shades. After they are dyed these coloured threads are again woven together on a regular handloom to produce the final cloth. This process is similar to "tie-dying," in which the areas where the colour is to be preserved are *ikatted* (knotted) together. Ikat weaving requires great manual skill and also excellent mental foresight, as the artists must know which parts of the threads need to be dyed and in which colour, before they are woven into the final cloth.

Although *ikat* works can be found in areas from Kalimantan and Sulawesi all the way through Sumatra across to Timor, the best-known cloths are prob-

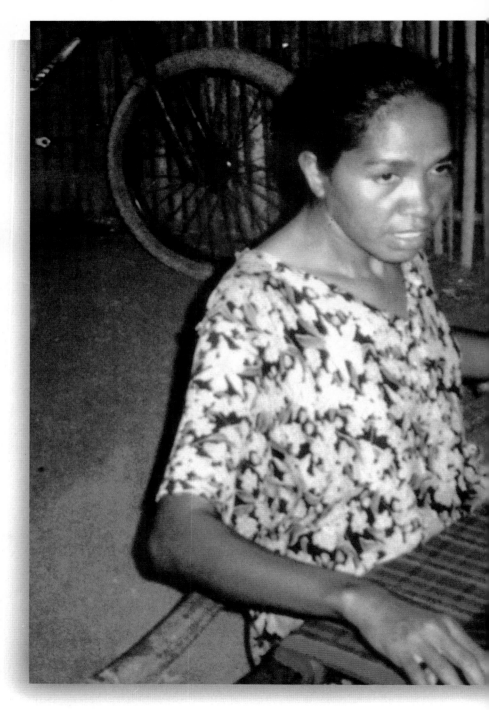

Ikat from Sumbawa, Flores and Nusa Tenggara are particularly well-known.

ably those of Nusa Tenggara, Flores and especially Sumba. They mostly employ geometric motifs such as hexagons, spirals and coats of arms, but more modern images have since come into style to cater to the tourist trade. Sumba *ikat* are of brilliant colours and a variety of life patterns which incorporate motifs such as snakes, spiders, deer, boats, dragons and even human forms. Sumbanese ikat cloth worn by men is known as a *hinggi*, while a woman's *sarong* (wrap-around, skirt-like attire) is called a *lau*.

Songket Styles

Songket cloth with its silver and gold threads can be found in Islamic-influenced areas, particularly in Kalimantan and west Sumatra where the Mataram kingdom once flourished. Found in scarves and particularly in *sarongs*, the weaving of this beautiful cloth can take several months. Common patterns are styles of flowers and geometric combinations, threads of real gold and silver are now rarely used. Kalimantan *songket* is used to make cloths and ornaments to decorate their longhouse manufacturing abodes.

The *doyo* technique originates from weaving for ceremonial rituals by the Tunjung Dayaks. Although once difficult to find, this type of cloth is now a treasured tourist souvenir. Another textile dying technique, called *sirangan*, is a unique feature of the southern part of the island.

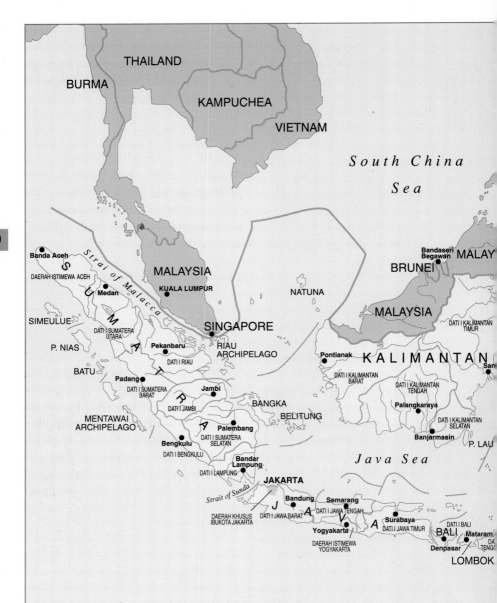

Java

The essence of Javanese culture resides within its spirits; the timeless deities which hide in its lush rice paddies and jagged mountains, who flit through tales of the past, their images imprinted in designs of the present and daily prayers of hope for the future.

These are the ghosts of brave Javanese warriors who for eons battled pirates and plunderers, the gods of the land who protested against the taming of their wild forests and tender fields. Now hidden in dark coastal caves and deep volcanoes, they are tucked into tradition, still worshipped for their wisdom in guiding the course of history to freedom – and feared for the natural forces that they control.

There is always an aura of mystery about the island; awe for its wondrous beauty mixed with a bit of sadness for past souls of lost time. But today, spread out from rugged coastlines to the ashen slopes of the central volcanoes, from modern metropolis to remote rainforest villages, it

Traditional Javanese dancer.

FEMALE HORNBILL, AND YOUNG BIRD.

at a village while a boat was being made watertight, I had the
good fortune to obtain a male, female, and young bird of one of
the large hornbills. I had sent my hunters to shoot, and while
I was at breakfast they returned, bringing me a fine large male,

*A sketch of a female hornbill with
its young hatchling.*

is the 118 million Javanese living on the
world's most densely-populated island
who are the keepers of their country's
history and culture.

Javanese Origins

According to legend, it is the *danjang*
(oldest spirit) who for eons guarded Java's
windy hills and lonely seas. Fearful of
those who arrived with the power to
tame the land, the spirits soon fled to the
powerful oceans and stark, smoking
volcano craters for refuge. However the
stories say, that man made an agreement – to share the island along with
the spirits and to use their wisdom to
advise them through life.

And so, while sailors and merchants
were making their way around the island of Java, it may have been the fear
of the spirits which at first kept them
away. Adventurers, too, only tramped
about the forest edges, gazed at mountains from afar, confining themselves to
the shoreline villages because of their
fear of what lay within the wild jungles.

King Sanjaya's 8th century domain
marked the first real reign of the land as
small villages flourished and grew closer
due to the binding effect of coastal trade.
Called "Mataram," the Hindu kingdom
rapidly spread its domain throughout
central Java, and provided an easy solution to the need for local control of crop
irrigation and the fertile *sawah* (wet rice)
farming.

As the tumbled remains of hun-

*A Hinduized past – statue of
Ganesha in the National Museum.*

dreds of temples scattered throughout the Dieng Plateau tell today, the beliefs and religion of Mataram were centred on the Hindu god Shiva. Dating back to around the 8th century, the earliest temples of the central plateaus were probably constructed by the house of Mataram. Many temples show an intermingling of Hinduism with the new religion – Buddhism.

And, while Hindu Mataram prospered, the Buddhist beliefs began to spread in Java as Mahayana Buddhism was introduced to the island. One of the best-known early Buddhist dynasties was the Shailendra empire, which was responsible for the construction of Borobudur c. AD 800.

Although these two very different religions were the basis for the largest kingdoms, they were not rivals and in fact seemed to flourish in co-existence. Only a few decades after the construction of Borobudur, the Hindu Prambanan temple was constructed while. As history does not record any signs of war, historians suggest that there was a resurgence of Hindu beliefs while Buddhism continued to be accepted by a large number. Because of the strength of both religions, the 8th-10th centuries were a time of growth for the first "Javanese," with the Shailendra and Mataram kingdoms expanding in influence, political structure and culture.

The Battles Begin

With the realization of the power and wealth surrounding the island, the fight for control soon began. Battles were waged between upcoming kingdoms, traders and tribes for landholdings, sea routes and individual freedom.

One of the most memorable characters of the time is young Prince Airlangga, son of a Javanese queen and Balinese king, who fled for his life to the forests during the turbulent times of the early 10th century. His meditation is chronicled in the famous Javanese poem **Arjuna Wiwaha** ("Arjuna's Temptation") which is popularly performed in shadow puppet performances. Later, he returned to rule the area around Surabaya and unite the lands of his ancestors in eastern Java.

After Airlangga's death, the land was once split again into the *Janggala* area east of the Brantas River and the *Kediri* area to the west. It was not long before the Kediri kingdom became the

Sanskrit found on Hindu vestiges.

stronger of the two, easily overpowering Janggala's struggling Singosari kingdom c. AD 1049.

Srivijaya & Singosari

The next century introduced the kingdoms of Sumatra, who were hungry for expansion of power and land. It was at this time that the house of Mataram finally crumbled, partly due to relentless attacks by the neighbouring island's Srivijaya empire – while the latter was engaged in numerous battles of its own, mainly against southern India's Chola kingdom.

A peasant named Ken Angrok, who in the name of Janggala's house of Singasari upset the Kediri lands by murdering their ruler and marrying his widow in the midst of overthrowing the kingdom soon joined this muddlesome fray.

This brutal and turbulent empire came to an end in the 13th century in a bid to unite the lands under the banner of Singosari. Although the empire lasted for a mere seven decades, it was a time of cultural enhancement and artistic expression, when the melding of religions into Shiva-Buddhism resulted in new the construction of temples and the evolution of sculptural styles.

But, the most infamous stories of power abuse are from the time of King Kertanegara, the last ruler of Singasari whose nefarious cruelty was known throughout Southeast Asia. Notorious for his maiming of the Chinese ambassador sent by ruler Kublai Khan to demand that Kertanagara submit to him, Kertanagara cut off the man's ears in an attack of furious melee. Two years later, when Kublai Khan's troops returned for revenge, they found Kertanegara had been previously murdered during a palace battle.

Majapahit Origins

With Kertanegara dead, Kublai Khan's Mongol troops had nowhere to turn, but Kertanegara's son-in-law, Prince Vijaya, soon solved that problem. In the civil war that ensued Kertanegara's death, Prince Vijaya ironically allied himself with the Mongol troops, defeating rival claimants, to the throne, like his uncle before him, refusing to go back with the Mongols to pay tribute to their ruler. Vijaya then founded the kingdom of Majapahit, Java's greatest kingdom.

The first Majapahit Prime Minister was Gajah Mada, whose vision it was to write the various "Indonesia" islands under one rule – the first time such a thought had crossed the mind of the leaders.

Under Gajah Mada (1331-1364), the empire took control of ports and trade routes to form the first commercial coastal empire. The other great kingdoms had traditionally been based inland, and had focussed their economies on land produce and agriculture.

The trading routes of his time extended through Burma, Cambodia, Siam and Vietnam. The land which came under Gajah Mada's rule is thought to have established many of the modern world's political boundaries as well. The cultural advances of the time opened the way for what is known as "Java's Golden Age."

On retrospect, Majapahit is considered the greatest kingdom of Hindu-Javanese times, although its scope included Java, Madura, and parts of Bali rather than the whole of the Indonesian archipelago. After Gajah Mada's premiership, but while still under his supervision, the second ruler, Hayam Wuruk (1350-1389) perpetuated the golden age of the kingdom.

However, with the death of Gajah Mada and the introduction of Islam, Majapahit soon fell into conflict over age-old disputes about the issues of religion and land. Eventually, the influence of Islam proved too strong to hold together traditional beliefs and power finally toppled as the kingdom was conquered by the Islamic resurgence of central Java's second dynasty of Mataram.

East Java & Sultan Agung

Islam defined Java's 15th and 16th centuries, as kingdoms based on Muslim beliefs soon began to take over the island, including west Java's Banten and eastern Mataram. It was a time of domination for the region which did not

A boat entering a Javanese river in the tranquil years of Javanese history.

allow for the melding of other religions, so the traditional Hindu-Buddhist domains left to establish new kingdoms in Bali and Java's mountainous Bromo-Tengger area.

In central and east Java, the kingdom of Mataram once again rose to dominate the land, using the guidance of Loro Kidul (Goddess of the Southern Seas), who is still used as a spiritual figure by the house of Mataram today. Ruled by the powerful Sultan Agung, the kingdom fought rivals in Palembang, Banjarmasin and Makassar but later failed in battles against Banten and Dutch Batavia.

A mystical figure of astounding military capabilities, Sultan Agung is often considered the greatest warrior of Indonesian history. The tomb marking his death in 1647 can still be seen at Imogiri in Koda Gede (near Yogyakarta), the former capital of the Mataram kingdom.

Another familiar famous figure of east Javanese history is King Joyoboyo, after whom Surabaya's *Joyoboyo* bus terminal is named. A bit of a soothsayer with a knack for predicting the future, his statements about a "yellow chicken" and "white buffalo" controlling the country were revived during the Dutch rule of the 1900s – and his prophecy that after the Dutch colonialists the *Ratu Adil* "Just Prince," would save the area by usurping power and ushering in a Golden Age kept Javanese hopes high during colonial days.

up of Bantenese inhabitants in 1673. In the centre a Javanese nobleman w
anshade, which was reserved for important members of society. On his right a C
t a "Moor": nis rather vague term was used to describe all people — Muslim
originally from countries which bordered on the Indian Ocean. from Bengal
from a sketch by J.P. Cortemünde).

*Meeting between a Chinaman and
a Batavian in the 17th century.*

Third Rise of Mataram

Sultan Mangkurat I succeeded Sultan
Agung. Unfortunately however, his empire, was one based on deceit and destruction. It was the cause of the crumbling of the Mataram empire during the
mid-1600s, when Mangkurat I moved
the palace to Plered amidst a milieu of
royal revolts and a kingdom rooted in
tyranny.

The Dutch took advantage of this
situation and eagerly followed the rising forces of rebellion throughout the
central and eastern areas of Java. In
1675, Prince Trunajaya led the defeat of
Madura and then made off for east
Java's Kediri kingdom with the plundered riches left behind by the toppled
kingdom of Mataram.

In revenge, Mangkurat's son
Mangkurat II allied himself with Dutch
forces to return and conquer Kediri in
the name of Mataram. Under
Mangkurat II, the Mataram capital
moved again, this time from Plered to
Kartasura (near Solo) and the Mataram
empire emerged yet again in the 18th
century – although this time amidst
much confusion.

And it was exactly this chaotic order which caused the First and Second
Javanese Wars of Succession, along with
the bloody Batavian Chinese massacre
of 1740. The Mataram kingdom was
once again defeated by the Madurese,
whose leader, Sultan Pakubuwano
(Mangkurat III's uncle) signed a treaty

*A Surabaya residence and a man
from Madura.*

The interior of a Dutch colonial house in Java.

in which the Dutch were granted numerous concessions in return for court rule.

A new Mataram court was founded at Surakarta in 1745, but the Third Javanese War of Succession tore any strongholds of loyalty apart. Thus making it easy for the Dutch to "divide and conquer" the warring rivals of Mataram, Surakarta and the Sultanate of Yogyakarta, which they soon split enabling an easy takeover.

the Madurese are intertwined with the realm of the Mataram kingdom and the dominating forces of the Dutch colonial government.

As with the central and eastern areas of Java, Sultan Agung's influence extended to Java's northern island of Madura, which he conquered in 1624. Under Madura's Cakraningrat princes, Sultan Agung formed a united leadership until the 18th century, during which time he continually battled with other reigning Javanese kingdom.

Interesting stories stem from the mischiefs of Madura's Prince Raden Trunojoyo, who defeated Mataram and ran off with the kingdom's treasures in 1677. Twenty-five years later, the Dutch took control of the eastern part of the island. Shortly after the First Javanese War of Succession between Madura's

Madura Island

To explain Madura's history, it is necessary to go back a hundred years, for

A colonial residence in Serang in the early 19th century.

The railway station in Tanjong Priok at the turn of the century.

Mangkurat III and his uncle, Pangeran Puger.

With the encouragement of Cakraningrat II, the reigning lord of West Madura, the Dutch began to support the Pangeran Puger. With their help, Mangkurat was exiled to the island of Sri Lanka and the Pangeran Puger took over central Java, creating a new sultanate – today's Yogyakarta – and taking the first title of Pakubuwana I.

In the process of settling power, Puger granted the Dutch control of Madura and other parts of Java via a treaty, while the Cakraningrats helped them put down rebellions in central Java that resulted in the gruesome 1740 Chinese massacre. In the following years,

Cakraningrat IV protested but failed to block a new deal by Pakubuwana II (the successor to Puger, Pakubuwana I) to give the Dutch full power over Madura.

Angry and frightened, Cakraningrat IV fled by ship to Banjarmasin but was robbed, betrayed and captured, before being exiled to the Cape of Good Hope in South Africa. After his disposal, Madura was split into four states, its men recruited for the Dutch colonial army and its salt became a highly prized item in Dutch trade.

West Java: Islam & Colonization

Overseas trade rather than agriculture

Ujung Kulon: A Place of Promise

Common palm civet cat.

Crouched in the southwest corner of Java, guarded by an arch of rain-swept peninsula between the Indian Ocean and the Sunda Strait, is a place where legendary creatures come to life in the hills and forest spirits play amidst shadows and light. Here, time stands still, each ridge and river is sacred and protected by the watchful eyes of the Tiger Spirit and is isolated from human life. Along each path, hidden footprints of man and beast mark journeys of strength and survival; within each secret cavern, old souls dance in a darkness that shimmers through the eyes of future generations in the quiet villages nearby.

This is Ujung Kulon, where the rare Javan rhino roams the low mountain ridges, where soft brown *banteng* (wild cattle) lift their heads and stare, startled and doe-eyed, as they graze next to clear, pebbled streams. Between thick jungle vines, macaques flash by, shrieking, while the heavy wings of hornbills pound a heartbeat in the air overhead. Through the scattered leaves of the lowlands, leopards silently stalk small pigs and deer, with soft and measured steps, each movement subtle, as if a flickering apparition of the imagination. Along the smooth beaches, wild dogs skip between long, rugged tracks of sea turtles, digging deep into the sandy outcrops in the hope of finding delicate soft white eggs for a nourishing meal.

Always, in Ujung Kulon, there is life. The question is, how to protect and preserve it. The land also shelters the "Sundanese" culture especially in the villages where images of Islam intermingle with traditional tales; it is a place where respect for the spirits is acknowledged with burning embers at "The Door" to the forest, and where shells of smoldering leaves mark hope within darkness at the Sanghyangsirah Caves. Fearful of the wrath of the angry Tiger Spirit, those who walk the twisted trails rest upon long plumes of palm to show that they are the descendants of the fisherman who once saved his life. Incense is lit between between tree roots, prayers of gratitude are softly chanted by sunrise and sunset, the aroma of cloves tainting the fresh forest air as wisps of smoke rise upwards to meet the clouds and the gods in a promise of good intentions.

But, at the last edge of a country charmed by smooth Western ways, the watchguard of spirits can no longer protect the land against the advancements of money and time. Now, it is not simply a matter of saving the saving species, but rather the integral challenge of honoring traditions spun over ages; a two-way glass that allows the modern world to look in and learn while enhancing the ways of the old ... preserving both the precious wildlife and human life within Ujung Kulon.

Walks and Wildlife

It was the rare Javan rhino that first sparked conservation concerns; once roaming the western half of the island, they came into conflict with human ambitions as villages spread and the need for land grew. As their forests were flattened for farming and housing, they retaliated unknowingly by damaging agricultural plantations so effectively that the Dutch colonial government offered a reward of 10 crowns for every animal destroyed. During the decades that followed, the rhinos retreated westwards, to an area of only 130,000 hectares for the 60 or so which now remain alive. But the rhino is not the only species that has been driven back by man's influence; the continuation of several endangered primates and cats, the rare wild dog, the more than 260 types of birds and thousands of plants, are also cradled within this land's last peninsular haven.

From **Taman Jaya**, the village on the park's northern border, a trail winds between rice paddies and thin dirt *jalans (walks)*, across two rivers and through a hazy mangrove swamp to the newly-built guard post at **Karang Ranjang** on the windier western side of the shore. Almost immediately life appears on all sides of the path; wild pigs and deer scampering through the thin shrubs, leaf monkeys peering down from long, slender vines that cross through the trees, the resounding whirr of hornbills' wings echoing through the air overhead. Start looking for prints in the soft ground – you may find two-toed hoof marks, as well as the light paw prints of small jungle cats.

Here the trail splits; a choice between the short, sunny trek north to **Cekok** and **Air Jeruk** or the shady path to the **Cibandawoh shelter**, where your guide may stop for a moment of silence to burn an offering of good will at "The Door" to the forest. Along the breezy beach, the sandy trail continues for several kilometres between the endless green waves of the Indian ocean and the thick, thorny coastal foliage to the **Ciujungkulon River** – these quiet hills are a prime rhino-spotting area, with a convenient camping site located near the water's edge. Several kilometres further, the beach walk ends as the trail cuts over high, jagged cliffs before rounding the bend between a long, rocky beach and a warm jungle pool to arrive at the **Cibunar shelter**. Surrounded by an endless chatter of birds and primates, this area is a popular place to watch wildlife (the tracks of leopards are often found along the shore between the sea and forest).

Across the peninsula, there is a short trek to the **Cidaon Grazing Ground**, where by dawn and dusk huge *banteng* (wild cattle) migrate

Bornean Gibbon.

slowly across the grassy field – the males are black and the females brown. Next to the stone shelter where boats from **Peucang** cross to pick up visitors to and from the island, the Ciujungkulon River flows slowly into the jungle; a silent journey by dugout will give you a glimpse of a sinewy snake sliding through the low branches or of a shy rusa deer drinking from a shallow pool hidden from the muddy banks. Rounding the bend to the lighthouse at **Tanjung Layar**, (also named "Java's First Point" from which the Dutch first sighted land after sailing from Africa's Cape of Good Hope), the coastal walk continues through fields of low, flowered vines to the serene sunsets and salty tidal pools of **Ciramea**. An evening walk along the beach is beautiful as huge ships bound for the Sunda Straits cross the horizon and, later, sea turtles crawl up from the waves – watch for deep burrows surrounded by long trenches where wild dogs and pigs have dug into their nests in

...Ujung Kulon: A Place of Promise

Chestnut-capped thrush.

a frantic search for the delicious soft eggs.

A wilder walk is towards the rugged southern coast, where the wind and waves never end, climbing over slippery rocks and running through unpredictable showers of rain to the dark, clifs and surging walls of water at **Sanghyangsirah**. Here, pilgrims trek from as far as Jakarta to bathe and meditate in the milky pools of the caverns where ancient spirits are believed to heal the bodies, hearts and minds of those who have faith in their powers. The dilapidated wooden shack at the edge of the shoreline is often crowded with trekkers, pilgrims and with birdwatchers who come to see the swifts which flit in and out of the mist hovering over the hills. There are usually several park officials around to keep a watchful eye on the area, as the swifts' nests are used in the preparation of the Chinese gourmet menu item "bird's nest soup", the caves of Sanghyangsirah and the islands beyond them have unfortunately also been known to attract numerous poachers.

The northern track from Cidaon follows the edge of the peninsula to **Cigenter**, the most popular grazing ground for spotting rhino. The trail first crosses through **Nyiur**, a swampland filled with bird life and colourful offshore reefs which is ideal for an afternoon swim. A canoe

trip up the Cigenter River to a stunning cascade of limestone waterfalls will be rewarded with a glimpse of larger wildlife; crocodiles are common, big cats have also been seen ... and this is the river where scientist Alain Compost shot his famous photographs of the Javan rhino. A forest trail parallels the riverbank for a distance and sometimes the huge *badak* (rhinoceros) tracks can be spotted; should you accidentally meet a rhino, advise the Sundanese villagers, climb a tree – or run behind it, as this supposedly confuses the animal, who does not like to run around trees.

As for the islands, **Handeuleum** is usually a stopover used for trips to Cigenter and beyond, while **Panaitan**'s smooth, tubular waves, wild jungle mountains and hidden caves with Hindu artefacts attract surfers and adventure-explorers. For pure relaxation, and for those short on time, **Peucang Island** is the answer.

Here, beautiful beaches, watersports and modern conveniences are coupled with vibrant wildlife ranging from wild pigs and screeching peacocks to giant monitor lizards and Javan rhino. A lovely two-hour trail winds through the damp forest to the island tip at **Karangcoping**, travelling between towering trees seemingly strangled by python-like buttress roots. Even on the neatly-trimmed lawn in front of the offices, wild deer graze in small groups while mischievous macaques play alongside; they have a liking for toothpaste and Tylenol, so keep your windows closed, tents zipped and valuables secure if you stay.

A few days is time enough to get a glimpse of the wildlife located within the park especially if you have only limited holiday time. However, for a more rewarding experience, one week to a month is recommended, both to get a true feel for the intertwining of culture and nature in the park and to gain an understanding of the aims and importance of one of the world's most valuable wildlife havens.

Space for all Species

Now, with the help of the WWF, more than two dozen hidden cameras have captured much of this wildlife in a continuing photo survey to monitor the movements and numbers of the species in Ujung Kulon. And, over the past century, there has been much improvement; comprising just one-fourth of Java's remaining 8 percent of original forest land, the area was declared a Natural Reserve in 1921 and a National Park in 1980. It was Indonesia's initial effort to protect the fragile biodiversity that was slowly slipping away.

However, the loss of habitat was not the only threat to wildlife; agricultural expansion, disease and poaching also played a large part in the disappearance of the species. And the rhino is only one of the animals at the risk of poaching in Ujung Kulon – dozens of mouse deer, reptiles and wild birds have been captured and killed for trade on the Southeast Asian black market.

But, for some, these traditions have been carried on over ages, these hunting and gathering practices sustained generations before the government stepped into the boundaries of Ujung Kulon. To catch fresh food from the sea, to hunt deer and pig, to build from forest materials are simple traditions for those who live off the land.

The government has even limited farms, homes and fields on the park border being exchanged for rupiah or less valuable property closer to modern developed areas. Now, with strict rules, strange officials and new western ways, a subtle sense of confusion has seeped into the simple life of the village, with a fine line of anger and betrayal lying beneath it.

And, herein lies the challenge: to protect the park and its people, to control the destruction of flora and fauna, to let visitors in to learn while neither offending old ways nor destroying the delicate balance of life within.

The Benefits of Wildlife Education

For Ujung Kulon, wildlife took top priority and is now monitored through research and regular census by conducted universities and conservation organizations worldwide. Park management programmes have improved the effectiveness of species protection, with local villagers trained as officers and as guards. Special education programs are now featured at local events, and public relations campaigns highlighting environmental protection can be found throughout west Javan schools. Promotion has reached an international level as well, with a doubling of the number of visitors to the area within the last decade.

Already the effects of the changes are visible; Peucang and Hendeuleum Islands have become resort stopovers for package trips to the park and the wilderness of **Panaitan Island** is no longer a surfers secret.

Along the road south of **Labuan**, five-star hotels are being constructed, while land is being bought from the locals without any explanations. In the forest, the incense of good intentions towards the spirits is often ignored, brand-new boots replace bare feet and tee shirts emblazoned with western cigarette advertisements are the most common village costume. As dirt roads turn into smooth pavement, as forests of coastline turn to golf courses and chic upscale resorts, as tourists arrive brashly toting new ways and ideas, the balance of concern has shifted from preservation of the traditional to promotion of the modern. The symbiosis between culture and wildlife may have been realized but at a cost of the traditions of the people.

Prosperous Chinese merchants in the early 20th century.

defined West Java's interests, and it was here that many of the island's cultural influences were first established. Though the impact of Islam was great, other influences such as Buddhism and Hinduism influenced the settlement residing at the port of Sunda Kelapa, where Jakarta stands today.

West Java's Islamic strength existed in the Muslim state of Demak. Demak was established along the northern coastline c. 1524, (today is still one of the few sultanates left in the country). Its most famous personality is General Sunan Gunung Jati, Demak's determined leader, who conquered the northern ports of Banten, Sunda Kelapa (Jakarta) and Cirebon during his illustrious reign.

Banten, became known as the "pepper port" as King Hasanuddin traded the commodity with Sumatra to open new routes of trade. In the early 1500s, the city was a trading stronghold of Arabs, Chinese and Indian merchants who used the Sunda Straits (after the fall of northern Melaka). Under Hasanuddin's son, Maulana Yusuf (c. 1579), Banten and the conquered Sunda lands of the Hindu Pajajaran kingdom grew in strength and power.

Amazingly, Banten remained independent of Mataram's power. However, with the arrival of the Dutch in 1600 the fight for independence began. The Dutch fought with the British, who also wanted to acquire Banten's strategic trading location, which resulted in the Dutch creation of "Batavia" in Jakarta's former port of Sunda Kelapa whilst they continued battling against the Islamic states (particularly Mataram, which by 1571 had established an independent trading network of its own through other European traders).

When civil war erupted in Mataram, the Dutch grabbed the advantage and by the end of the 17th century West Java had come under their control. Engaged in constant local battles, Mataram traded chunks of land in return for Dutch military help, granting central and east Javan territories as Dutch protectorates in the process.

By 1800, Java came under the Dutch, even though the small Mataram principalities lingered in the central areas of Yogyakata and Surakarta.

Yogyakarta's Past

Yogyakarta was founded by Hamengkubuwono I, the ruler of Mataram at the beginning of central Java's colonial era. It was formed along with its sister sultanate, Solo or Surakarta, as a result of a split within the Mataram empire. At first the city was a confusing mélange as it was caught between European influence and village rebellions.

However, the local hero Prince Diponegoro who started the Java War of 1825-30 managed to end the disputes once and for all. The Dutch blamed the sultanate of Yogyakarta for Diponegoro's outburst of rage, and used this as a pretext for annexing the outer district of Yogyakarta and Surakarta to bring them under their control.

Pakubuwana IV, the ruler of Yogyakarta at the time was understandably upset and fled to the southern seas for a spiritual consultation with the Goddess Loro Kidul, who was the traditional guide for the house of Mataram. However he was caught and brought back to Yogyakarta by the Dutch, before being exiled to Ambon in the Molucca Islands.

After Diponegoro's Java War, there was no longer room or power for Javanese aristocracy within the reigning colonial system, so the sultanate instead worked on developing the area's Javanese culture. For years, the small government was sheltered in the midst of the central mountains at the edge of Yogyakarta. However after Indonesian independence was declared, the city actually became the capital of the early Republic for a few years until the title was transferred back to Jakarta. Now, the Sultanate is still an autonomous Special Territory and enjoys provincial status within the Indonesian government.

A Capital History

However, since the 17th century, Jakarta has been the centre of control for both the bureaucratic government and for commercial businesses. Founded by Sultan Gunung Jati, the Muslim general

Dutchman Jan Pieterszoon Coen.

of Demak, Jakarta was the major port town of the Hindu Pajajran kingdom. The city's early trade contacts were in 1522 and with the Portuguese. They occured at the earliest settlements in the coastal port area of Sunda Kelapa at the mouth of the Ciliwung River. Later, in the midst of 17th-century British and Dutch wars for supremacy of the region, it was renamed Jayakarta, or "victorious."

In May, 1619, the Dutchman Jan Pieterszoon Coen literally blazed into town when he burned Jayakarta to the ground later rebuilding it as "Batavia," the capital and great port city of the Dutch East Indies, which under the command of General Marshall Daendals received a facelift that changed the look of the town to that of a more modern European city.

Batavia's trading influence expanded, as did its boundaries, attracting many Chinese merchants. However, the Chinese massacres of October 1740 incurred violence and fear within the new population, resulting in an exodus of Chinese to the "Glodok" area outside the city, which is now modern Jakarta's Chinatown.

Diseases spread through major epidemics in the mid-1700s, which cause fearful Dutch and Europeans to move their settlements further southwards away from the port. They constructed monuments such as the *Koningsplein* ("king's field,") now known as **Merdeka** (freedom) **Square** of 1818, the **Merdeka Palace** of 1879, and the stately Kebayoran Baru residential area of Dutch post-WWII.

When the Japanese took over after World War II, they renamed the city Jakarta, although the capital was moved to Yogyakarta when the Dutch returned after the war. In 1950, after independence was assured, control was returned to Jakarta, and "the mother city" became the final capital of the new, democratic Republic.

Tour of the Capital City

Sunda Kepala ... Jayakarta ... Batavia ... City of Victory ... The Mother City ...

Each of these names throughout history has meant Jakarta.

To some, it is a city of hope of freedom, beauty and joy. To others, it is one of history, full of culture and pride.

Ten million people more or less are crammed into the hot, dusty capital city, where taxis whisk past shining, air-conditioned skyscraper hotels and brillliant monuments while throngs of street vendors hawking fresh fruit and small goods shuffle on the broken brick streets below. At night, the streets are lined with small *warungs* (foodstalls) where hard wooden benches and tables are filled with hungry patrons while around them pounds the quickened beat of jazz dance music with a *gamelan* (percussion-type orchestra) flavour wafting from the posh hotel clubs along the main *jalans* (roads).

During the week, it can be a place of chaos, with traffic jammed five vehicles wide in two-lane roads, motorbikes whipping in-between vendors rolling their carts down the streets. However, the weekends are a lively retreat to the grassy fields near the monuments, with kites whirling, picnics spread on the ground beneath trees and young couples sitting, reading and quietly talking whilst basking in the shade on a long Sunday afternoon.

Moving To & Through the City

If you arrive via air into Jakarta from another island or international port, you will usually arrive via the **Sukarno-Hatta International Airport**, whose facilities were just renovated in 1992. Taxis are always available for the journey into the city, but a convenient airport bus stops outside the arrival terminals every half-hour from 0300 to 0000 hours and will drop passengers off at either **Blok M Shopping Centre**, **Gambir Railway Station** or **Grogol bus station** for about 3,000 rupiah.

If you arrive by train, there are four stations dotting the edges of the city: **Gambir** in the east, **Pasar Senen** even further in that direction, **Tanah Abang** in the west and the northern **Kota** station. If you arrive from other parts of the island, trains from Bandung and Yogyakarta drop you at Gambir, while those from Semarang arrive at **Pasar Senen**. From Merak and Sumatra, trains stop at **Tanah Abang**, while the expensive express trains to Surabaya and Yogyakarta arrive at **Kota** before turning around to make the same trip again.

Rail travel from Surabaya is either via Semarang or Yogyakarta depending on the train, so check your arrival point before you leave or you will find yourself in an unexpected area of the city.

Bus travellers will arrive at the new **K Rambutan Station** from the eastern cities of Bogor, Bandung, Banjar and most routes that run via these cities. Buses arriving at **Pulo Gadung** are from Cirebon along the coast, while **Grogol** is usually the Jakarta stop for those coming from the west. **Kalideres**, or "**Xderes**" station is the arrival and departure point

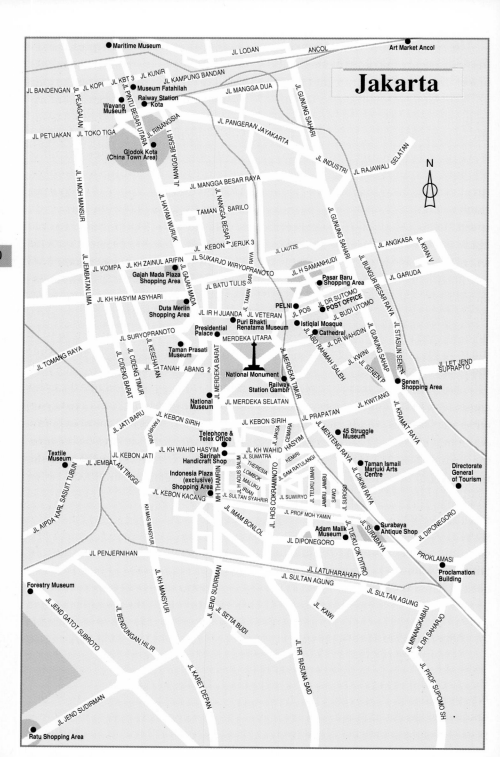

Jakarta

Maritime Museum

JL LODAN

ANCOL

Art Market Ancol

JL KOPI

JL KBT 3

JL KUNIR

JL KAMPUNG BANDAN

JL BANDENGAN

JL MANGGA DUA

JL GUNUNG SAHARI

Museum Fatahilah

Raiway Station
Kota

JL PINTU BESAR UTARA

JL PEJAGALAN

Wayang
Museum

JL PETUAKAN

JL TOKO TIGA

JL RINANGSIA

JL PANGERAN JAYAKARTA

JL INDUSTRI

JL RAJAWALI SELATAN

Glodok Kota
(China Town Area)

JL H MOH MANSUR

JL MANGGA BESAR 1

JL MANGGA BESAR RAYA

TAMAN SARILO

JL HAYAM WURUK

JL NANGGA BESAR 4

JL ANGKASA

JL KRAN V

JL KEBON JERUK 3

JL LAUTZE

JL KOMPA

JL KH ZAINUL ARIFIN

JL SUKARJO WIRYOPRANOTO

JL GUNUNG SAHARI

JL GARUDA

Gajah Mada Plaza
Shopping Area

JL BUNGUR BESAR RAYA

JL JEMBATAN LIMA

JL GAJAH MADA

JL BATU TULIS

JL H SAMANHUDI

Pasar Baru
Shopping Area

JL KH HASYIM ASYHARI

Duta Merlin
Shopping Area

JL IR H JUANDA

PELNI

JL DR SUTOMO
POST OFFICE

JL STASIUN SENEN

JL SURYOPRANOTO

JL VETERAN

JL POS

JL BUDI UTOMO

Presidential
Palace

Puri Bhakti
Renatama Museum

Istiqlal Mosque

JL ABD RAHMAH SALEH

JL TOMANG RAYA

Taman Prasati
Museum

MERDEKA UTARA

Cathedral

JL DR WAHIDIN

JL GUNUNG SAHAP

JL SURYOPRANOTO

TANAH ABANG 2

JL MERDEKA BARAT

National Monument

JL MERDEKA TIMUR

JL KWINI

JL SENEN P

Senen
Shopping Area

JL LET JEND
SUPRAPTO

JL CIDENG TIMUR

JL CIDENG BARAT

JL KESEHATAN

Railway
Station Gambir

National
Museum

JL MERDEKA SELATAN

JL KWITANG

JL KRAMAT RAYA

JL JATI BARU

JL KEBON SIRIH

JL KEBON SIRIH

JL PRAPATAN

Telephone &
Telex Office

45 Struggle
Museum

Textile
Museum

JL KEBON JATI

JL KH WAHID HASYIM

Sarinah
Handicraft Shop

JL SUMATRA

JL MENTENG RAYA

JL KH WAHID

JL JEMBATAN TINGGI

Indonesia Plaza
(exclusive)
Shopping Area

JL KEBON KACANG

THERESIA

LOMBOK

MALUKU

JL SAM RATULANGI

Taman Ismail
Marjuki Arts
Centre

Directorate
General
of Tourism

JL AIPDA KARL SASUIT TUBUN

MH THAMRIN

JL AGUS SALIM

JL SULTAN SYAHRIR

IRIAN

JL TEUKU UMAR

JL CIKINI RAYA

JL IMAM BONLOL

JL HOS COKRAMINOTO

JL PROF MOH YAMIN

SAWO

JAMBU

JL SUROSO

JL TUEKU CIK DITIRO

JL SURABAYA

Surabaya
Antique Shop

JL DIPONEGORO

JL PENJERNIHAN

KH MAS MANSYUR

Adam Malik
Museum

JL DIPONEGORO

PROKLAMASI

Forestry Museum

JL JEND GATOT SUBROTO

JL KH MANSYUR

JL BENDUNGAN HILIR

JL JEND SUDIRMAN

JL SETIA BUDI

JL LATUHARAHARY

JL SULTAN AGUNG

JL SULTAN AGUNG

Proclamation
Building

JL KAWI

JL MINANGKABAU

JL DR SAHARJO

JL PROF SUPOMO SH

JL KARET DEPAN

JL HR RASUNA SAID

JL JEND SUDIRMAN

Ratu Shopping Area

Playing football by the Monument.

A Quick Overview!

Although intimidating by map, in reality Jakarta is not such a confusing city. Taxis and buses are easy to find, and cheap costing less than US$5.00 to get from one end of the nearly 600-kilometre square city to the other in rush hour traffic. There is really no need to walk anywhere anyway, as the sidewalks are cracked and uneven, the air is hot and filled with a fine, ashen dust that settles into your pores and (air-conditioned) public transportation is always available and quite convenient.

The heart of the city is the **Kota** (centre) also known as the former Dutch settlement of Batavia. Near the Kali Besar Canal and Taman Fatahillah's cobblestone square, there is also the **Kota Railway Station** which connects this area to the rest of the city and the island. Adjoining this area, along Jalan Gajah Mada, is the area known as **Glodok**, or Jakarta's "Chinatown."

Sunda Kelapa is the harbour, where the majestic Makassar schooners tower over the docks that are scattered with pieces of plywood filling the air with the pungent scent of wood shavings. Nearby is **Pasar Ikan**, the morning market where thousands of shimmering fish wiggle along wide display shelves, the salty sea breeze accentuates the cries of their sellers.

The modern harbour for ships travelling to the other islands, and other parts of the world, is **Tanjung Priok** – a

for buses plying along Java's west coast, including the resorts and coastal towns of Merak, Anyer, Carita and Labuan, all the way down to the national park of Ujung Kulon.

If you travel via sea, your ship will arrive at **Tanjung Priok** harbour from other islands in the archipelago, as well as from countries such as Malaysia, Singapore and the Phillippines. Most common are ships belonging to the Pelni fleet, but if you are "ship-hopping" as crew or as a way to gain inexpensive adventure, the other port of call is **Sunda Kelapa**, the city's old harbour. Transportation by bus or taxi is available to both waterfront locations, and it is best to bargain for your onward tickets at the ship's offices here as well.

An aerial view of Jakarta's Jalan Sudirman.

few kilometres east of Sunda Kelapa, and near the **Ancol Dreamland Recreation Park**. Ancol has docks of its own from which ship's travel to the resort islands of Pulau Seribu. The park is also famed for its new entertainment facilities at Fantasy Land – an educational centre for science and technology that brings the history and culture of the world to life.

The **Monas Monument**, that huge, pencil-shaped structure that towers into the sky from mid-city, is perhaps Jakarta's most easily-spotted landmark. Kota, Glodok, Old Batavia, Sunda Kelapa, Pasar Ikan, Tanjung Priok and Ancol are all located north of the Monas Monument. In the surrounding central area are the museums and cultural facilities,

such as the **Istiqlal Mosque**, the **Presidential Palace**, the fair grounds and **Jalan Jaksa**, the cheap backpackers' accommodation area located close to the **Gambir railway station**. Jalan Thamrin South of the Monas stretches through the centre of the city for several kilometres, along which you will find all the large companies: hotels, travel and airline offices, banks, cinemas and the **Sarinah Department Store**.

The area around Sarinah is popular with visitors. Here is where you will see the huge golden arches of **McDonald's** restaurant or the brash automobile driving through the wall of the **Hard Rock Cafe** upstairs. Across from Sarinah, in the **Jakarta Theatre Building**, are the **Telecom International**

Timber being transported around Indonesia from Port Sunda.

Communications Offices from which you can make international phone calls, faxes, telexes and so on; across the hall is one of the busy but informative **Jakarta Tourism Offices**.

South of the city are the residential areas of **Jatinegara**, posh **Menteng** and **Kebayoran Baru**'s shopping area of **Blok M** near the **Cipete** suburbs. Buses and taxis are familiar with these areas but it is also good to give drivers a landmark, such as the Sarinah Department Store in the Jalan Jaksa area or Blok M if you are heading to the southern homes and shopping centres.

city, first, stop at the **Jakarta Tourist Office** (tel: 344 177) at the Jakarta Theatre Building on Jalan Thamrin which is, open Monday to Saturday, from 0900 to 1500 hours, depending on who is there and how many people are in the office. Alternatively the **Indonesia National Tourist Organization** (tel: 359 001) or Directorate General of Tourism is also a helpful centre for visitors at Jalan Kramat Raya 81. You find information at both locations; the staff of each office not only speak English fluently, but also exercise infinite patience with questions about addresses, bus routes, business hours and the like. Although the Jakarta Tourist Office is usually more convenient to visit, **INTO** provides details about activities and events

Museums and Monuments

When you arrive in the

A blast from the past – a traffic policeman in downtown Jakarta.

It's business as usual despite the monsoon weather.

Jakarta streets are well worn by becak, motorcycles and
Japanese people carriers.

MENJAGA KESEGARAN JASMANI

Murals meant to provide encouragemnt for a progressive society.

throughout the archipelago. Both have a variety of free publications that include brochures, maps and magazines – some helpful ones include the *Indonesia Travel Planner*, *Indonesia Map*, *Calendar of Events* and *Jakarta: Getting Around the City* for a basic overview.

If you are heading further abroad, the **Institute for Indonesia Tourism Studies** (tel: 334 898 / Lembaga Studi Pariwisata Indonesia) on Jalan Diponegoro 25 is an excellent place to find information – particularly about parks and cultural activities.

To visit the parks of Indonesia, you can also pick up permits on-site at the **PHPA** (Perlindungan Hutan dan Pelestarian Alam) or Directorate General of Forest Protection

and Nature Conservation offices of the various parks. However, information about activities and programmes, can be obtained through organizations such as the **World Wide Fund for Nature** (WWF) (tel: 720 3095) on Jalan Pela Raya 3, Gandaria Utara or the **Asia Foundation** (tel: 793 5533) on Jalan Darmawangsaraya 50 in Jakarta Selatan.

Jakarta's Many Monuments

To understand any city, first examine the meanings behind its monuments – and metropolitan Jakarta is replete with these:

First, there is the **National Monu-**

Children are brought to visit the Independence Monument where Sukarno stands on the left and Hatta on the right.

Walks Around Old Batavia

Interior of the History Museum, Jakarta.

Once the Hindu port of Sunda Kelapa, "Old Batavia," came into existence in the early 19th century when the then Governor-General Daendels demolished the original waterfront area. What he tore down was a classic piece of his own Dutch history – the area which the Europeans had called "*Kota*," (the city centre). Here Jan Pieterszoon Coen's fortress called the Kasteel stood guard, surrounded by a wide moat and thick, impenetrable defence walls against the cannon fire of unexpected invasions.

With his "modern" vision, Daendels ordered the area to be razed to the ground in his quest to renovate and rebuild a new "Batavia". Today, many of the original buildings are only contained within the cobbled sidewalks and alleys, but those that remain flavour the imagination with the Dutch presence in what was an important era to Jakarta's diverse history.

The centre of Old Batavia is the cobblestone square of **Taman Fatahillah**, located just one block east of the Ciliwung River's *Kali Besar* (Great Canal). Formerly a posh residential area, these streets are now lined with grand 19th-century houses built in the Dutch architectural style – where private owners can still sit and sip afternoon tea while gazing out over the facing canal.

At the head of Old Batavia is **Sunda Kelapa** – the grand docks where long rows of huge, bright Makassar schooners lie in anchor. These great ships have for centuries, sailed the trade routes of Indonesia; a bit of free time, and a talk with the captain of one of the boats could lead to an appointment as crew member and a lengthy stint as a mate on the high seas.

Near the entrance to the docks is the **Maritime Museum** – well worth a look, which boasts a pleasant restaurant – a nice place for a cool refreshing drink after a wander along the long harbour.

At the north end of the canal is the "**Chicken Market Bridge**", a Dutch construction which is an unmistakable landmark of the area. Close by

ment located in **Merdeka** (Freedom) **Square** in the city centre. Standing at 137 metres in height, it is capped with a 35-kilogramme flame of gold. An elevator located within takes visitors to a platform for stunning views of the city, while in the basement, the "Hall of Silence" is adjacent to a museum detail-ing the history of the country. This monument is representative of the ancient Hindu Javanese *lingga* (phallus) and *yoni* (vagina) of fertility, a modern-day symbol of national independence (perhaps also hinting at the virility of Sukarno, the leader who commissioned its construction!)

is **Toko Merah** (red shop), formerly the home of Dutch Governor General Van Imhoff, it is now the site of the Dharma Niaga company.

A classic sight in Old Batavia is **Geraja Sion**, (the Sion Church), where within a rather plain exterior are hidden stunning relics of Dutch times. Originally built for the Christian-converted "black Portuguese" slaves brought to the island from ports in India and Malaya, the church still has its original organ and old copper chandeliers. Most of the slaves brought over from abroad were Catholic, but they were freed when they joined the Dutch Reformed Church and were called *Mardijkers* (liberated ones). At the back of the church, is a graveyard, highlighted by the bronze tombstone of Governor-General Zwaardecroon, who humbly wished to be buried amongst "ordinary" people.

Around the Old Batavia area, there are quite a few museums, including the **Jakarta History Museum**, the **Wayang Museum**, the **Art Museum** and the intriguing **Si Jagur** (huge bronze cannon). Also called Taman Fatahillah, this artillery instrument is inscribed with the Latin phrase *ex me pasa renata sum* (out of myself I was reborn) – its end tapers into a clenched fist, a sexual symbol in the Indonesian cultural context. As stories go, childless women who believed they were barren visited the cannon regularly. Not only would they offer flowers before praying for fertility, but they would actually sit on the cannon for blessings and luck with their conception. After a while, the authorities tired of the antics surrounding the cannon, so they placed *Si Jagur* inside the museum – both to prevent damage and to counteract local

beliefs. Historically *Si Jagur* was actually a Portuguese cannon brought to Batavia as a war prize after the fall of Melaka in 1641. The fertility legend arose after the King of Sundra had an odd dream in which he heard the thundering of his strange new battle weapon. He told his Prime Minister Kyai Setomo to find a similar weapon as a replacement, threatening that if he did not, the penalty would be death.

The Prime Minister was worried, so he talked the situation over with his wife. However, the King was impatient, finally consumed with anger, he marched down to *Si Jagur*'s home to find the source of the problem .... where he found the couple transformed into two enormous cannons. The great Sultan Agung heard of the weapons and ordered the king to bring them to the Mataram court, but Si Agung (the male cannon) refused his request. Instead, still in the form of a man, he fled to Batavia at night but found the city gates locked and was thus unable to reach for safety.

The next morning, the citizens came across a strange sight; an enormous bronze cannon resting outside their boundary gates. In the Javanese manner, they declared it holy and gave it a paper umbrella for protection from the sun and named it *Kyai Jagur* (Mr Fertility).

For more details on walks around Old Batavia, you can find booklets at the Jakarta History Museum and the National Museum, which are available at reasonable prices. The most informative publications are probably ***The City Hall & Its Surroundings*** and ***Gereja Portugis***. Maps are available from tourist offices within the city.

Within sight of the National Monument is the rearing horseback **statue of Prince Diponegoro**, one of the republic's greatest heroes who launched the Java War against the Dutch in 1825. On Jalan Proklamasi towers the bronze **Sukarno-Hatta Monument** dedicated to the leaders who claimed Indonesia's independence in 1945, while at Lubang Buaya Memorial Park, the **Pancasila Sakti Monument** commemorates the seven heroes executed during the October coup of 1956.

Merdeka Palace which was constructed in 1794 is the official home of the President. During the British occupation of the city in 1812, it was purchased by Sir Thomas Stamford Raffles (the founder of Singapore). It later also functioned as the residence of successive Dutch Governor-Generals.

The **Park of Inscriptions** was formerly the Kebon Jahe cemetery, which was only restored in 1975. It is interesting to explore the grounds as famous figures such as Olivia Mariane Raffles, (the wife of Sir Thomas Stamford Raffles), Major General JHR Kohler and Major General AV Michiels have their final resting place here.

Also intriguing is the **National Archives Building**, found on Jalan Gajah Mada. It was built in 1760 by Governor-General Reinier de Klerk and later functioned for a short period during the early 1900s as the central location for the city's Department of Mining.

On Jalan Gatot Subroto, the **Parliament Building** is also worth a visit (if advance permission is granted). It is an attractive modern structure where the National Congress, or People's Consultative Assembly, meets at least once every five years.

Old Batavia

In Jakarta, there are also dozens of museums to explore, particularly around the cobblestone "old Batavia" area of **Fatahillah Square** which was restored by the Dutch in the mid-1700s. The area around the former Hindu port of Sunda Kelapa, was burned and refurbished by the city's leaders of the time, and today reveals some of the faded glamour and pride from the colonial era.

Probably the best-known museum in the area is the **National Museum**, with its brilliant white exterior and lush frontal gardens. Established in 1778 by the Dutch Batavia Association of Arts and Sciences, this cultural centre offers excellent displays of history, archaeology and religion, exhibiting important collections from international sites. Open daily from 0900 hours to 1530 hours, tours are available in English, German, French and Japanese, and every Sunday morning a special *gamelan* (percussion type orchestra) performance is featured.

Constructed in 1627, the **Jakarta Museum** at Fatahillah Square is a highlight of Old Batavia, where paintings, maps and antiques offer an opportunity to feel the flavour of life during the Dutch occupation of the country and the city.

The **Art Gallery and Ceramics Museum** is also in Fatahillah Square, it houses collections of works by Indonesia's most famous artists, as well as some of Southeast Asia's most valuable ceramic creations. One of the most interesting displays is located in the **Wayang Museum** in the Square nearby. Once an old Dutch church, the building now holds a fascinating variety of leather shadow puppets and colourful wooden models from Indonesia, China, Thailand and Malaysia. Instruments used in

The National Museum, Jakarta, is only one of many.

the *gamelan* orchestra are also placed out for viewing, and *wayang kulit* (shadow puppet) performances are featured every Sunday morning.

The **Textile Museum** is located a bit further away from the Square on Jalan Satsuit Tubun 4. Here, more than 300 types of *batik*, *ikat*, *songket* and other dyed and woven clothes are on display, with a workshop located on-site where visitors can view the process of *batik* making.

Just a short distance away, antique porcelains and paintings are featured

Borobudor

Each carving tells a story — stone reliefs in Yogyakarta, Jakarta.

It was a structure of one of the greatest empires, that of the Buddhist Shailendra, an incredible construction which broke ground AD 800.

Built stone by stone, day by day, the construction needed thousands of men. Although the initiative was that of a Buddhist dynasty, the influences were international; Indian architects, Asian workers and people from the surrounding Hindu kingdoms of the island of Java. The grand temple took decades to build, and not long after it was finished, the Sumatran kingdom of Srivijaya poured over the straits to trounce the earlier Shailendras. Then, for centuries, it was buried, silent and hidden in the central Java hills ... to be rediscovered by none other than Sir Thomas Stamford Raffles around 1814.

However, reconstruction only began in 1907 and for four years Dutchman Van Erp carried out the procedure. But, hundreds of years of erosion by natural forces, (including volcanoes, earthquakes and heavy rains), made Van Erp's efforts fruitless and the structure was ruined. In 1983, the United Nations completed a final 15-year restoration project through UNESCO, its cultural organization and brought the temple to a semblance of its former glory. The temple has since become a major tourist site.

A Tour of Borobudur

Outside the enormous structure, there are 72 *stupas* (bell-shaped stuctures), each with a solemn cross-legged statue of Buddha. Often seen in postcards and books, these bells and statues were originally meant to surround and enshrine a larger central figure of Buddha, which was never finished during the original process of construction. At the base of the temple, there are four long walls leading to four "galleries", which are set back from the edge of the structure in ascending order. The gallery walls are lined with ancient artwork which has somehow been preserved over time; more than 1,200

Magnificent sevenity – the Buddha surrounded by stone stupas in Borobudur.

decorative reliefs, nearly 1,500 figurative panels and about 500 cubbyholes each contain small seated statues of Buddha. Above these galleries, are the 72 *stupas* each with more large, seated Buddhas inside. It is also here that the large central sculpture stands as the pinnacle of the monument symbolising heaven.

Whilst walking through the temple, there are a few traditional Buddhist rules to follow, including the recommendation that visitors should proceed through the galleries looking to the right. By doing this, the panels and reliefs become clear revealing the Buddhist progression of human life. At the lowest level is "*Kamadhatu*", (the phase of Desires), which portrays the conflicting existence of love and hate, happiness and punishment and hope and hell. Up to the next gallery, stairs lead to the four second-level galleries of the "*Rupadhatu*" (the phase of form) which depicts Buddha's life.

On the third circular level there is a flat area of intriguing design located in an area of three rounded terraces. This is the highest level, surrounded by bare walls – rectangular on the outside but nearly circular within ... it depicts the transition from traditional Form to "*Arupadhatu*", (shapelessness – the highest level of existence). Here, at the top, the Buddhist concept of the abstract is contained, symbolizing the world of the "Unimaginable" and the acquisition of Eternal Redemption.

Temple Festivals

Borobudur is the world's largest Buddhist temple; it is thus a site of celebration for all Buddhsts the world over. One of the most famous festivals held at Borobudur each year is **Waicak Day**, to celebrate both Buddhist beliefs and the temple structure. Thousands of worshippers from Southeast Asia come to visit the temple at this time for the event; the height of the celebrations are the mass prayer sessions held by moonlight.

Fatillah Museum, Jakarta.

at the **Adam Malik Museum**, where the former Vice-President of Indonesia once resided.

Churches & Chinatown

For those who love battles, the **Satria Mandala Armed Forces Museum** at Jalan Gatot Subroto provides a good look at the function of the Army, with war planes and weapons from various countries and wars on exhibit. Traders and pirates are the highlights of the **Maritime Museum** at the Sunda Kelapa Harbour, which is set in two old Dutch East Indies warehouses with the former harbour master's tower nearby.

Religion has always been central to Indonesia's traditions, and reflections of the complete kaleidoscope of practises are found throughout Jakarta. Near Merdeka Square is the unmistakable dome of the **Istiqlal Mosque**, the main centre of Muslim worship for the city and possibly the largest mosque in Southeast Asia. Close to Fatahillah Park in "old Batavia," the 1693 **Sion Church**, or "Portuguese Church," has stunning interior architecture, and the 1879 **Saint Mary's Cathedral** near Banteng Square (restored in 1901), enjoys a favoured reputation as "the most beautiful church in town." Another good place to wander through is the **Glodok** area, otherwise known as Jakarta's "Chinatown," which is hidden along the border of Jalan Gajah Mada. Open markets and small shops,

Interior of an old church built during the Batavia years.

tiny alleys and charming cracked and colourful buildings make this area a photographer's paradise. Interesting sites in the area include the Chinese **Dharma Jaya Temple** built in 1650, (which is now the largest Buddhist temple in the city) the **Petak Sembilan Fish** **Market** south of Jalan Pancoran and the **Glodok Shopping Centre** and **Glodok Plaza** on Jalan Pinangsia near the train station – these are more modern, multi-storey complexes where you will be able to find unusual souvenirs and textiles. If you are into antiques, a walk through **Jalan Surabaya's** Antique Stalls will definitely be worth your time. Located in the suburb of Menteng, you can find all sorts of art and paintings, ceramics, porcelain, pottery, brass and furniture from international sources as well as a flea market where lucky prospectors often spot very valuable and unusual items.

Wildlife & Recreation

Jakarta also offers a number of educational and recreational activities that highlight the country's culture in natural settings.

Probably the best overview of the arts, including dance, music and written traditions, is the **Ismail Marzuki Cultural Centre (TIM)**, which is spread over more than eight hectares of land in Cikini. Named after the famous Jakarta musician, this centre houses art galleries, an art academy, libraries, exhibitions and a planetarium, as well as eight movie theatres. Surrounded by pleasant shops and cafés, TIM is also an excellent place for evening entertainment as you can see both Indonesian and Western performances of music, dance and drama. Check The *Jakarta Post* newspaper for daily arts schedules or ask at the Jakarta Tourist Office for a brochure. Also a popular recreational place is the **Taman Mini Indonesia Indah**, the 100-hectare amusement park/cultural centre/recreational area. The displays of the archipelago, such as

full-size traditional houses, a lagoon in which you can take a boat around the entire archipelago in miniature, an aviary, an orchid garden, cable cars, craft shops, displays and food from around the country's 27 provinces provide a true reflection of the national motto *Bhinneka Tunggal Ika,* or "Unity in Diversity".

Gateway to the Bali Pavilion at Taman Mini Indonesia, the 100-hectare park depicting the entire country in miniature.

Cultural performances are scheduled throughout the day, and the giant IMAX theatre specializes in fantastic three-dimensional, special-effect shows. Museums with exhibits from the various islands are scattered about the park; two of particular interest are the **Museum Komodo** and the **Museum Perangko** (stamp museum), a perfect excursion for philatelists. Plan to spend the entire day here, as the park is enormous - you can either walk or drive through. Wildlife enthusiasts should head for the **Ragunan Zoo** about 15

Memorial at Ancol Park, Jakarta.

kilometres south of the city. A huge hippopotamus pond, boating lake, Sumatran rhinoceros forest and children's playground are just a small part of this "garden of animals" that is jam-packed with species from all over the Indonesian archipelago – many of which are endangered and can not be seen in zoos anywhere else in the world.

The zoo is very crowded on Sundays and Public holidays. The enormous grounds with paths running everywhere can be a bit confusing at first especially as maps are hard to find. However, the office of **Sahabat Satwa** (Friends of the Zoo, tel: 780 6164), located on the second floor of the main office building will welcome you, stop in and say hello before walking around the grounds and you may get a "behind-the-scenes" tour, as well as a wealth of wildlife, park and conservationist–oriented information.

Other natural areas include the **Orchid Gardens** of Taman Mini, the lake and cycling trails of **Taman Ria Remaja Senayan Park** at Jalan Pintu VIII Senayan and the fruit orchards of the quaint **Condet village** in southern Jakarta. The most popular recreation park for weekend holiday makers may be **Jaya Ancol Dreamland** and its adjacent addition of **Fantasy Land**. North of the city at the Bay of Jakarta, the area shelters secluded beaches, man-made lagoons and marinas, which offer endless, opportunities for popular sports such as golf, bowling, swimming, fishing and boating. Restaurants, night-

Marketmen in Senen, a suburb in Jakarta.

clubs and an open-air theatre entertain visitors throughout the evening, while day tours and shows are held at the unique sea aquarium. Also located at Ancol is the **Pasar Seni art market** – one of the city's best places to purchase handicrafts and cultural souvenirs.

Pulau Seribu

Escape from the city on one the neighbouring islands. *Pulau* means "islands," while *Seribu* means "one thousand" and it seems as if there are truly a thousand sun-browned specks in the azure blues of Jakarta bay. Still relatively untouched by tourism, the Pulau Seribu Islands are a haven of golden beaches and tall coconut palms just a short boat ride north of Jakarta. They are also a favourite retreat of water nymphs from all corners of the globe, as the surrounding bays offer coral groves, colourful fish and vivid opportunities for skin and scuba diving.

The "Thousand Islands" are easy to reach as well; by boat or ferry from Jakarta's ports of Tanjung Priok or Pasar Ikan/Sunda Kelapa. The marina at Ancol Dreamland also has a special port for Pulau Seribu-destined yachts, motorboats and sailboats. Charter boats are easy to find here through most travel agencies in the city.

The most visited islands are the resorts of **Pulau Bidadari**, **Pulau Anyer**, **Pulau Laki**, **Pulau Putri** and **Pulau**

Tanjung. To reach the islands, you can even fly for 20 minutes to the Pulau Tanjung airstrip. Quiet bungalows and cottages, restaurants and facilities for marine activities are common on Pulau Putri and Pulau Pelangi. You will find cabins and fresh water on Pulau Air and Pulau Bidadari, while camping is a popular activity on Pulau Perak – just a day-trip from Pulau Putri – and there is diving camp on Pulau Papa Theo.

Two of the best contacts for trips to the islands are The Pulau Putri Paradise Company and Pulau Seribu Paradise (tel: 515 884) at Setia Budi Building Block C1 Jalan HR Rasun Said. Otherwise, contact local or national tourist offices.

Down the West Coast

Java's western coastline is a mixture of traditional villages and modern resorts; stark steel mills and production plants spilling out into small, busy market towns with large hotels lining the roads in between.

Located between Jakarta and the **Merak** ferry port are the ruins of **Banten**, the Islamic pepper trading port and the first landing point of the Dutch in the early 1600s. It is an interesting area to explore, with ruined walls and a Chinese temple set amongst the hills of Java's northern coastline.

Past the western town of Merak, traffic threads down the smoggy highway to the steel town of **Cilegon**, where

pubs and steakhouses show the presence of a definitively western population of workers. However as you head southwards, the highway thins after the ominous steel mills and power plants into a sweet-scented coastal road that runs between lush hills and a sandy shoreline. There are two areas stretched into sprawling resorts, the northern coast

The Krakatau Volcano is constantly monitored by the international scientific community.

along **Anyer** and the central **Carita** area. Anyer's hotels are luxurious, often filled with business conventions and sporting events, while Carita is more of a "getaway" area with charming beachside bungalows and wonderful sunset views.

Krakatau Volcano

Off the quiet west of Java coastline lies the shadow of **Anak Krakatau**, the "child" of the volcano which exploded in 1883 and ravaged the area's villages

Bogor: Gardens and Safaris

Sixty kilometres south of Jakarta lie the cool, clean resort areas near Bogor. Surrounded by a ring of higher mountain peaks, the city sits 290 metres above sea level; a beautiful short journey through curving hills, tea plantations and winding roads. Often cloud-covered and misty, the town itself is nicknamed the "city of rain," as the area boasts around 325 thunderstorms each year – the highest annual rainfall on the island.

From AD 12 to 16 , this area was the capital of the Pajajaran Kingdom, and was later also an important Dutch hill station. Discovered by Governor General Van Imhoff discovered in 1745, the Dutch found the site strategically located between the mountains and village valleys, close to the capital city but still central to Java's inner hideaways.

Bogor's cool mountain climate and remote location prompted Van Imhoff to eventually build his own large country estate there. He named it **Buitenzorg**, meaning "without a care". However, it sadly remained unused for years. In 1811, however, it did house an honoured guest when Sir Thomas Stamford Raffles stayed at the estate during the British occupation. Also known as the **Presidential Palace** or the **Bogor Palace**, Buitenzorg became the traditional residence for the Dutch Governor- Generals of the Dutch East Indies, until around 1942. Although the original building was destroyed in an earthquake in the 1580s, the palace which replaced it in 1856 was just as (if not more) glamorous, a centre of politics and parties for the aristocratic Dutch and their high-class colleagues.

The building is now found in the northwest corner of the Botanical Gardens. It was once the temporary home for Indonesia's first president, Sukarno. Empty of residents today, the building instead houses a lovely collection of paintings by great Indonesian artists ... and even a few works by Sukarno himself, as well as his private art collection of about 220 paintings and 150 sculptures.

This former home of Sukarno is south of the gardens, where the **Batu Tulis** shrine and 1533 stone inscriptions are located. It was said that Sukarno believed the area was a place of mystical powers and thus chose the location for his home. However, it is not open for public viewing, so contact the Head of Protocol at the Istana Negara on Jalan Veteran in Jakarta, if you are interested, as they may be able to arrange a tour if given about a week's notice.

However the international attraction of Bogor, is the beautiful **Kebun Raya**, or **Botanical Gardens**. Originally the inspiration of Sir Thomas Stamford Raffles, the gardens were

with tidal waves and ashen skies. Felt worldwide, its effects were vividly coloured sunsets and great tremors beneath the land, causing the death of more than 30,000 Javanese and Sundanese who made their homes along the water's edge.

Anak Krakatau was borne of an explosion in 1930 and is actually the sunken cauldra of what remained of the

The strong but delicate water lily in the Botanical Gardens.

designed by Professor Reinhardt and several assistants from Kew Gardens before being opened by the Dutch in 1817.

More than 15,000 species of plants and trees grow within the 100-plus hectares of gorgeous grounds, where deer and small mammals roam freely amongst the foliage. These include more than 400 types of palm trees and close to 3,000 varieties of orchids, including the rare black variety. Visitors will also find the large *Rafflesia*, the Victoria Regis water lily from Mauritius, many species of bamboo and hundreds of other specimens from all over the world. A special library of rare botanical volumes can also be examined by visitors.

The Botanical Gardens are also renowned for the early Dutch research of cash crops during the "cultivation period" of the early 19th century. Here, tea, rubber, coffee, tobacco, and quinine, have been tested for their adaptability to the area's environmental conditions.

Adjacent to the museum is the **Bogor Zoo**, where a wide collection of native and international species can be seen. Near the entrance, there is a monument in memory of Sir Stamford Raffles' wife, Olivia, who died in the area in 1814 and was buried in Old Batavia.

For animal lovers, there is also the **Safari Park** at Cisarua, just a few kilometres away from Bogor. In the hills of this drive-through park, lions, tigers, giraffes, and zebras bring Africa to the archipelago; the offices for the Centre for the Reproduction of Endangered Wildlife, are also located here.

original volcano. Now, the area is included within the Krakatau Scientific Reserve and is regularly watched and studied by the international scientific community. Today, Krakatau is once again glowing with life, as by night the crimson glow of flowing lava can be seen around its upper edges. Boat trips can be organized fairly easily through the Carita Tourism office and the

Krakatau Beach Hotel along the main road, about 10 kilometres south of Anyer. With old newspaper clippings and maps of the area adorning its walls, the Krakatau Beach Hotel is a particularly good source of information about the volcano, as is the **Krakatau Museum** located across the street.

Lazy Labuan

Labuan is the main town on the western coast, where supplies are bought for journeys north to the resorts or south to the national park of Ujung Kulon. Here, the offices of the **PHPA** Park officials, the **World Wide Fund for Nature** (in the same building) and **PT Wanawisata Travel** are excellent sources of information about trips to Krakatau and **Ujung Kulon**.

South of Labuan is the town of Sumur, the coastline here is now being developed into an enormous golf resort. Destined to have several greens, including a "mountain" golf course and a "beach" golf course, international hotels and a large marina, the resort is slowly taking over the village area and flattening the rainforests in the process of conversion to what could become the next popular area for tourism in Indonesia.

Ujung Kulon

Amidst the open coastal forest and lush

Rainforest respite.

mountains of Java's southwestern peninsula lies **Ujung Kulon National Park**, the haven of the last Javan rhino.

It is a wild land of rugged coastlines and waves that smash against sheer cliffs, a land of rainforest and arid lowland terrain. Wild pigs, deer, leaf monkeys, macaques and reptiles are commonly seen along the easy hiking trails, while wild dogs and large leopards can be sighted along the beaches after dusk. Reefs surround the park's offshore islands of Peucang, Handeuleum and Panaitan, where bright bays and tremendous waves attract surfers and divers to an underwater haven.

After picking up a permit in Labuan, head south for Sumur, and beyond the small coastal villages with their raised wood homes.

Taman Jaya is the beautiful bayside village where the one-room PHPA, Wanawisata travel and WWF for Nature offices are located in the middle of mountains and tall palm groves. From here, the main nature trail begins, skirting around the peninsula and over to the central grazing grounds; it is also possible to begin trekking from one of the parks' off shore islands.

There are guesthouses in Taman Jaya and on the Peucang and Hendeuleum Islands, and boats can be hired to ply between these areas, or even all the way down from Labuan. Many of Ujung Kulon's innovative conservation efforts has been used as a prototype for other country parks. (See box XXX).

Traditional musical tastes are appeased at the "**Gong Foundary**" on Jalan Pancasan 17. It is fascinating to watch the careful construction of beautiful *gamelan* (percussion-type orchestra) instruments: made by an ancient method, they are honed by heating the metal on a bed of hot coals, which is then beaten when white-hot until it achieves the correct pitch when played. These are rough instruments, used in Javanese musical combinations and *wayang kulit* (shadow puppet) performances, hewn from an alloy of iron, copper and brass.

Pristine Puncak Pass

Winding roads between Bogor and Jakarta take travellers through some of Java's most scenic panoramas. One of the most beautiful routes is via the **Puncak Pass**, standing at 2,900 metres above sea level it is the highest point of the Jakarta-Bandung road.

This thin highway threads through the lush, leafy tea plantations that tumble down the broad mountain slopes, only the yellow and blue hats of harvesters remaining visible above the thick crops like round, blossoming flowers. Along the road, chalets and bungalows nestle close to the edge between cliff and highway, glimpses through the misty hillsides revealing a panorama that spills out through stunning valleys and plummeting peaks.

Within this area are many pleasant trails and short tours; **Cisuara** is just 10 kilometres from Bogor, a tranquil area of walks and waterfalls. An interesting day trip from Bogor is the **Gunung Mas** tea plantation, which offers a free tour of the factory and a taste of the area's most consumed drink. Nearby is the beautiful **Telaga Warna**, or "lake of many colours;" much like the island of Flores' Keli Mutu scenery, the waters here are iridescent reflecting crimson, blue, jade and aquamarine depending on the changing light of the day.

Just over the Puncak pass is **Cibodas**, where the 80-hectare **botanic gardens** built in 1860 offer, a close-up view of

The Presidential Palace at Bogor.

temperate vegetation in an extension of Bogor's Kebun Raya.

A walk through the gardens takes trekkers all the way to the active **Gunung Gede volcano**, as the park is located along the twin slopes of **Gunung Gede** and **Gunung Parango**.

At 2,958 metres, the Gunung Gede volcano is windy and exciting, and on a clear day you can supposedly see all the way to Jakarta and Java's southern coastline. Trails also lead to the **Cibureum Waterfall**, as well as through gorges and dangerous, foggy cliff ledges. Al-

hot springs, as well as the summer **Presidential Palace** located just five kilometres after the Cibodas turnoff.

There are more hot springs near **Cisolok**. Gold and silver mines are found around **Cikotok** as the Puncak Pass winds closer to the summit. At 1,500 metres, the pass cuts across a mysterious place – a chilly, misty area in the hills that evokes a soulful sort of melancholy and an eerie feeling that ancient deities are looking over your shoulder. This is a wonderful area for hiking; particularly near **Lembang**, 16 kilometres north towards the mountain of **Tangkuban Perahu** which literally mean "the overturned perahu". Here, a visit to the planetarium, formally known as the Astronomical Observatory can be made by special request after a quick visit to the Director of the Department of Astronomy at the Institute of Technology of Bandung (ITB), located at Jalan Ganeca 10. Five kilometres east of Lembang are the hot springs of **Maribaya** – thermal spas, gardens, waterfalls and lovely river gorge hiking trails. Also close by are the **Ciatur Hot Springs**, just eight kilometres from Tangkuban Perahu, and neverending tea and clove plantations.

North of Bandung near Purwakarta is the **Jatiluhur Lake** and dam which is a popular resort for watersports. The village itself was built by the French in preparation for the construction of the huge dam, and is now also the site of Indonesia's ITT satellite station. Nearby trekking is available around the **Juanda National Park**, where open forests, rush-

though a permit is needed, fortunately the PHPA office is conveniently located just outside the botanical gardens.

Along the way to Bandung, near the small mountain town of **Cipanas** – which literally means "hot" – the road is dotted with fruit and vegetable stands which offer cool drinks and sometimes pony rides. Cipanas, also boasts several

Tea plantations in Java.

in the **Ciatur Hot Springs'** natural mineral baths is a soothing way to relieve travel stress.

Another active volcano is that of **Gunung Papandayan** – one of the country's most lively mountains. Formed in 1772, it erupted again in the early 1980s along with **Gunung Galunggung** located nearby. Another peak is **Gunung Telagabodas**, where a bubbly crater lake spews splashes of sulphur. Villages and tea plantations lining the road to Garut are located below these summits.

Garut was also a Dutch hill station, and is an excellent base for hiking to the area's hot springs and volcanoes, as well as a beautiful area to relax amidst lush, sloping rice fields and tea plantations. Famous for its *dodol*, (sticky-rice) made with sweet coconut milk wrapped

ing waterfalls, rapid rivers and stunning mountain scenery add to the relaxing atmosphere. The air here is cool and crisp in the mornings, the wind often frosted with mountain clouds which could be mistaken for the sulphurous smoke emanating from the surrounding volcanoes and hot springs.

Here, the Tankuban Perahu volcano is easily accessible – it is the only active volcano in Indonesia accessible by automobile right up to the rim of its crater! The best time to visit is in the early morning, to escape both the strong sunlight and the crowds. A dip

Gunung Gede – profile of the ruin.

reaches the coast, it passes **Cibadak** and **Pasar Jumbat**, where hot springs and the volcano crater of **Kawa**

in a small strip of bamboo leaf, the town is also close to **Kampung Naga** (dragon village), where you will find traditional attap houses.

Seventeen kilometres north of Garut is the only ancient Hindu temple in West Java. Even older than the Borobudur and Dieng Plateau temple complex, it is called **Candi Cangkuang**. Traces of Hindu, Muslim, megalithic and neolithic influence have been found within the design, and the structure was recently reconstructed in 1976. In the area is the village of **Tasikmalaya**, a cultural centre of *batik*, paper umbrellas, embroidery and rattan creations.

Ratu (Pelabuhan Ratu) volcanic crater, lie along the island's southern edge.

A fishing town just 90 kilometres south of Bogor, Pelabuhan Ratu means "Harbour of the Queen." Indeed, it is the royal residence of the spirit of Loro Kidul, the goddess whom all Javanese revere as a guide of the historically powerful

Spirits of the Southern Coast

The southern road is one of kingdoms and legends, for here the mountain spirits meet Loro Kidul, the Goddess of the Southern Seas. Treks lead across jagged coastal cliffs and sweeping beaches to serene fishing villages, past the central **Lokapurna** area. Before the road

Waterfall at Gede – Pangrango
National Park.

Walking on the volcano rim.

wear green, as it is her favourite colour.

The influence and power of Loro Kidul is commemorated at the

Mataram dynasty and of the modern Yogyakarta sultanate. Pelabuhan Ratu is also a popular seaside resort, where visitors can camp and explore rocky cliffs, rugged gorges and deep natural caves. Deserted and lonely, the coastline is a beautiful and wild place in which to spend endless wandering days.

Swimmers are warned against the strength of Loro Kidul's spells, as she often lures victims into depths to work for her underwater domain. Many drownings have occurred in these dangerous waters, including that of the Bulgarian Ambassador . Be warned: Do not

famous **Sea Festival**, which takes place at **Pantai Karang**. This beautiful area formed from volcanic explosions and thick pools of lava is made up of warm, shallow waves and tidal pools. It is believed that Loro Kidul once leaped from these cliffs into the ocean, to recapture her lost beauty and youth. Today, offerings of flower petals and buffalo heads are thrown every spring into the Sea. Beliefs are incorporated into local life, and even the resort hotels are not ready to relinquish legendary tradition in favour of modern rationalism. At the **Samudra Beach Hotel**, a room has been reserved for Loro Kidul; visitors can communicate and give offerings to number 318 through a medium who

Culture, history and religion around every corner.

An overview of Borobudur, one of Java's most important heritage.

can sense her presence.

Fortunately, only spirits of nature reside at the **Pangandaran Reserve**, a lovely resort and fishing village stretched along 530 acres of southern coastland. The game reserve at **Pananjung Pangandaran** shelters *banteng* (wild cattle), civets, monkeys, hornbills and pythons, with idyllic trekking through teak forests and smooth limestone caves.

Further east along the coastline, down through the hills 27 kilometres south of Yogyakarta, are the sweeping black sand dunes and rough cliffs of the sacred **Parangkusumo**. This is where Loro Kidul met her lover Senopati, a 16th century Mataram ruler, and they journeyed together to her underwater palace for three days of love making

and battle strategy. Today, the sultans of Yogyakarta's palace still make offerings here, as Loro Kidul is said to stand guard over all of Senopati's Mataram successors and heirs. Like Pangandaran, the waters make for dangerous swimming, but many come to meditate in the caves west of **Parangtritis**, or at the black-sand coves of **Baron**, **Kukup and Saman**.

Islamic North Coast

To the north, the coastal areas are also quiet, although here the influence of religion takes precedence over nature. At the border of central and west Java, the port of **Cirebon** was once the site of

Sultan Agung's mighty Islamic sultanate. Today, it is a quiet, unhurried seaport where a *charuban* (mixture) of Javanese, Sundanese and Chinese cultures define the language and customs. Founded by Sunan Gunung Jati, one of first Islamic *wali* (priests), of Demak in the early 16th century, the independent sultanate was later the subject of a dispute between the kingdoms of Banten and Mataram. The port was eventually sold to the Dutch in a treaty in 1705 which made Cirebon into a protectorate ruled by three sultans. The sultans turned Cirebon into an opulent trading city which attracted the attention of a new Chinese community.

Two traditional palaces replete with sultans *et al* remain in Cirebon, although they now exercise scant power and instead work towards preserving and practicing traditions. The oldest is the **Kesepuhan Keraton** (palace), built in 1527. Later, in 1681, the **Kanoman Keraton** was constructed and later still the **Kacirebonan Keraton** was built in 1839.

The city has an old-world feeling of ancient times; and indeed, little has changed since the 13th and 14th centuries. You can return to these ancient times by viewing treasures such as collections of *kris* (wavy-bladed daggers) weapons, court jewellery and costumes and beautifully carved carriages inside these palace museums.

When you visit Kesepuhan, look at the walls, as they are embedded with ceramic plates which were brought to the island by Chinese traders.

Outside, you will find the famous **Astana Gunung Jati**, the grave of Gunung Jati the most revered of Cirebon kings and the first *wali* (Priest or missionary) of Islam. His peaceful tomb and ancient mosque are highly worshipped and are considered one of holiest places in Indonesia and the site for annual Indonesian Muslim pilgrimages.

The Mesjid Agung mosque is another of the holiest points on Java, and seven pilrimages to this place are said equal one traditional pilgrimage is Mecca. It is rumoured that of the four main pillars, one was created by Sunan Kalijaga, an original apostle of Islam The Mausoleum of Sunda Kalijaga is also located nearby.

Cirebon has several cultural interests; one of them is *batik* fabric, which is found in the **Trusmi** village to the west of the city and the **Indramayu** village along the north coast. The Cirebon *Tari Topeng* ("masked dance") is also unique to the area; it can often be seen in villages or special performances conducted by art centres in the city.

Bandung, Java's Paris

Bandung is a cool, cosmopolitan city settled amidst subtle mountain slopes and fertile tea plantations in the midst of Parahyangan, the "Valley of the Gods". At one time, the valley in which it lay was a lake. Now, it is graced with green highlands, bamboo forests and misty volcanoes. Plantation homes line the hills where hired workers stay during the week, venturing by train into the city only for weekend visits to families and friends.

With a population of about 1.5 million, Bandung is the capital of West Java province and, somewhat surprisingly, Indonesia's third-largest city. It is often called *Kota Kembang* (city of flowers), referring to the beauty of both its gardens and its women. The majority of the population are of proud Sundanese heritage. Bandung is also a central hub, where the wooden *wayang golek* (imitation by human actors of the movements of the shadow puppets) puppets and special Sundanese flutes can be seen and heard everywhere. It is also an educational centre, where the Institute of Technology for Bandung, (ITB), is located. This is the most revered institute for science education in the country, if not in all of Southeast Asia.

Bandung was founded in the late 19th century as a Dutch garrison town, where the Europeans resided alongside about 90,000 Sundanese, Chinese and other Southeast Asians. For decades, Bandung's comfortable café society has deemed it the arty "Paris of the East." This ambience was derived from the Dutch, who used the area as a relaxing resort and built holiday bungalows to accommodate their weekend society flings with other members of the aristocracy. The social club of the time was the *Societeit Concordia,* now located in the central **Freedom Building**, (*Gedung*

Merdeka). These society parties flourished until the arrival of the Japanese, but after WWII, the Dutch returned to Indonesia to try to claim back their former colony. At this point, history is coloured with nationalistic ventures; the city decided it would rather burn to the ground than return to Dutch control. Thus, on 11 July, 1946 the Bandung residents fled to the mountains while they watched their city burned to the ground. It was at this time that the song "Halo, Halo Bandung" was composed to commemorate the event, and it is still a special melody sung by students and nationalist supporters today.

By 1962 Bandung had aspirations of being the capital city. This is particularly so after she played host to the first Afro-Asian Conference in 1955: From the 18-24 April 1955, 29 developing countries came together, with visiting leaders that included Nehru, Indira Gandhi, Gamal Abdel Nassar of Egypt and Prime Minister Foreign Minister Chou En Lai of China. The meeting was the basis for the first international non-aligned movement, and the event provided the core for familiar values such as "Bandung Spirit" and the "Ten Principles of Bandung."

Just 187 kilometres east of Jakarta, Bandung is still used as a pleasant getaway for workers and expatriates who reside within the capital. With clean air, a comfortable setting and a relaxed pace of life, it is a city that lends a "European" atmosphere to the young-at-heart way of life.

Bandung is also noted for scientific research and business ventures. Not only is the area known for textiles (60 percent of Indonesia's textiles are produced here) and tea, but it also boasts one of the largest quinine factories in the world (which supplies 90 percent of international demands).

The artistic status of Bandung is evidenced in its architectural styles. Buildings are structured in both modern and colonial styles, but the most intriguing are the *art deco* designs; (it is one of three cities in the world with a settlement of tropical *art deco* buildings). These artistic expressions began with private houses and hotels, the traditions expanding between 1920 to 1940. Fortunately,many of the buildings belonging to this era can still be seen along Bandung's wide streets today.

The **Savoy Homann Panghgar Heritage Hotel** in the middle of Jalan Asia Afrika, is a good example of the *art deco* style. In fact some of the original furniture is still intact. Also, opposite the Homann, the **Grange Hotel Preanger** has been renovated (into a teacher's college, no less) and elegantly graces over the town. Or visit the **Villa Isola**, with its curving terraces and ornate designs.

Along Jalan Asia Africa you will find the **Tourism Office**, or the **Bandung Visitor's Information Centre**, while the **West Java Regional Tourist Office** is on Jalan Braga in the Gedung Merdeka Building. Maps of the city and lists of cultural events are easy to find, as are ideas for walking and touring the surrounding mountain areas.

For those interested in the land, you can find interesting exhibits at the **Geological Museum** on Jalan Diponegoro 57, which is located in the former headquarters of the Dutch Geological service. Finds here include a skull of the famous "Java man," (*pithecanthropus erectus*), as well as a collection of geological finds from the surrounding lands.

You can view the film of the Asia-Afrika conference at the Freedom Building, it highlights the meetings between Sukarno, Chou En-Lai, Ho Chi Minh Nasser and other Third World leaders of the 1950s. Southwest of the city on Jalan Ottista is the **West Java Cultural Museum** that focuses on the traditions of the Sundanese, while the **Army Museum** at Jalan Lembong 38 concentrates on the 1948 to 1962 Darul Islam rebellion.

Perhaps Bandung's best-known establishment is the **Bandung Institute of Technology (ITB)**, which is located on Jalan Ganeca. With its unique *Minangkabau* (Indo-European) architecture, it is an unmistakable sight. Opened in 1920, the institute was the first Dutch-founded university for Indonesians. The institute is also known as the best scientific university in the country well known for its research. It is equally famed for its fine arts schools and local galleries. The school's most famous student was probably Indonesia's Sukarno, who studied civil engineering here until 1925. It was also here that Sukarno's Bandung Study

Club was formed, which rapidly grew into the Indonesian Nationalist Party (PNI).

Also famous here is the **Institute Pasteur**, now called Bio Farma, which researches and produces vaccines against smallpox, and serums for rabies. Modern industries such as travel and telecommunications are also represented by the Industri Pesawat Terbang Nasional (IPTN) which produces small and medium-size aircraft and PT Inti, the centre of the country's international communications.

Bandung is not only industrially successfully but it is also a beautiful city. In the surrounding countryside, volcanic peaks, green plantations and clear, rushing rivers, provide the perfect setting. The city contains a string of parks and gardens, and the open-hearted hospitality of the people adds to its pleasantness.

Just a walk away from the ITB is the **Bandung Zoo**, located along Jalan Taman Sari. Other walks in the area are through the hills of Dago, where the **Dago Tea House** offers a lovely sunset view and a stroll to the waterfalls behind or along the nearby Cikapundung River. Three kilometres further is the **Gua Pakar Cave**, where the Japanese stored ammunition during WWII.

For those who prefer city walks, shopping is a popular Bandung pastime, and one of the best overview locales is the **Parahyangan Plaza** south of the main square. **Jalan Braga** is the high-class browser's haven, while the fashion industry is found at the colourful and youth-oriented **Cihampelas** markets.

There is a popular puppet factory where you can watch the 81 characters of the wooden *wayang golek* (imitations by human actors of the movements of the shadow puppets) puppets being carved - called **Cupu Manik** located near the square on *Gang* (alley) *Haji*. Along the narrow streets off Jalan Pangarang, are crowded markets specialising in cottage industries, where you will find all sorts of beautiful Sundanese wooden characters, masks and *wayang golek* puppets.

The backpackers' area is near the railway station, where most of the budget hotels, *losmen* (rooms to let) and guesthouses are found. North of the city is the wooded **Dago** area, where hills and walking trails wind amidst the popular **Bandung Giri Gahana Golf and County Club** and the **Panorama Panghegar Golf Course**.

Eating in Bandung is always a treat, as local Sundanese food is both good fasting and nutritious. The smooth, clear skin of the residents is largely due to their diet – fresh fruit and vegetables are always included in meals. Special dishes include *ikan mas* (goldfish), *ikan mas goreng* (fried goldfish), *ikan mas pepes* (goldfish wrapped in in banana leaves) and *sayur asem* (vegetable soup). *Krupuk* (crackers) and preserved fruits are common, while fresh tropical offerings include avocados, bananas, papayas, mandarin oranges, rambutans and the

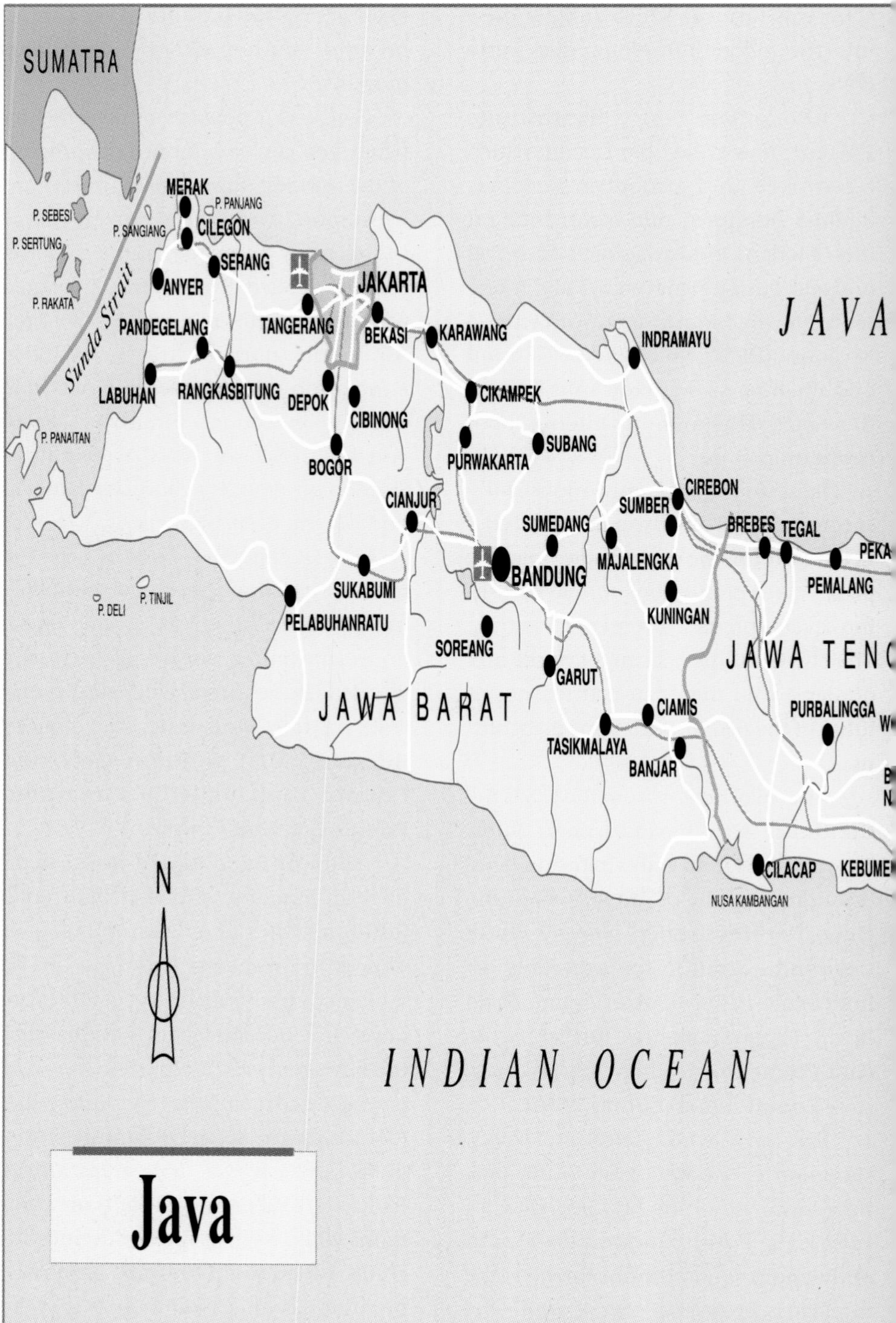
SUMATRA
MERAK
P. PANJANG
P. SEBESI
P. SANGIANG
CILEGON
P. SERTUNG
SERANG
ANYER
JAKARTA
P. RAKATA
Sunda Strait
PANDEGELANG
TANGERANG
BEKASI
KARAWANG
INDRAMAYU
JAVA
LABUHAN
RANGKASBITUNG
DEPOK
CIKAMPEK
CIBINONG
P. PANAITAN
SUBANG
BOGOR
PURWAKARTA
CIREBON
CIANJUR
SUMBER
SUMEDANG
BREBES
TEGAL
MAJALENGKA
PEKA
BANDUNG
PEMALANG
SUKABUMI
P. TINJIL
P. DELI
PELABUHANRATU
KUNINGAN
SOREANG
JAWA TENG
GARUT
JAWA BARAT
CIAMIS
PURBALINGGA
TASIKMALAYA
BANJAR
CILACAP
KEBUME
NUSA KAMBANGAN
N
INDIAN OCEAN

Java

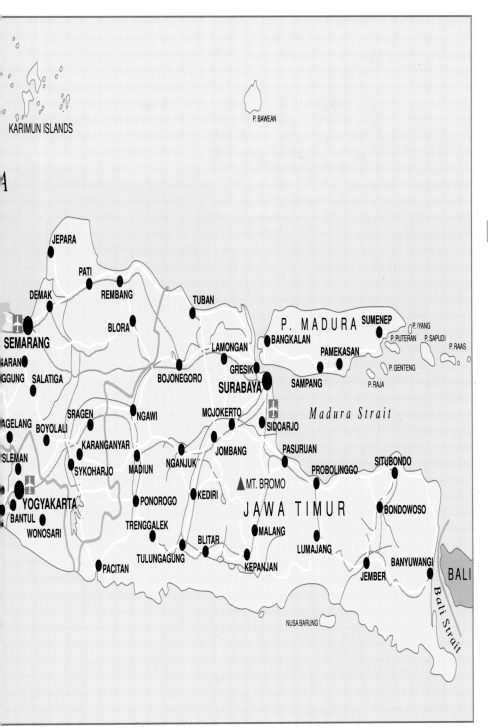

KARIMUN ISLANDS

P. BAWEAN

JEPARA

PATI

DEMAK

REMBANG

TUBAN

BLORA

P. MADURA

SUMENEP

P. IYANG

P. PUTERAN   P. SAPUDI

P. RAAS

SEMARANG

BANGKALAN

LAMONGAN

PAMEKASAN

GRESIK

P. GENTENG

ARANG

GGUNG

SALATIGA

BOJONEGORO

SURABAYA

SAMPANG

P. RAJA

SRAGEN

NGAWI

MOJOKERTO

Madura Strait

AGELANG

BOYOLALI

SIDOARJO

KARANGANYAR

JOMBANG

PASURUAN

SLEMAN

SYKOHARJO

MADIUN

NGANJUK

PROBOLINGGO

SITUBONDO

MT. BROMO

YOGYAKARTA

PONOROGO

KEDIRI

JAWA TIMUR

BANTUL

BONDOWOSO

WONOSARI

TRENGGALEK

MALANG

BLITAR

LUMAJANG

TULUNGAGUNG

BANYUWANGI

PACITAN

KEPANJAN

JEMBER

BALI

NUSA BARUNG

Bali Strait

"love it or hate it" durians.

After dining, catch cultural performances at the **Yayasan Pusat Kebudayaan Theatre** (YPK) on Jalan Naripan 7. At the **Panghegar Hotel**, there are often special *wayang golek* puppet shows and Sundanese dances.

In the southern area of the city, the **ASKI-Bandung**, or **Kokar-Konservatori Karawitan** at Jalan Buah Batu 212, is a school specializing in traditional Sundanese arts, music, dancing and *pencak silat* (self-defence). Another location for viewing traditional movements is the **Bamboo Workshop** on Jalan Padasuka, where you can sometimes see the unusual *angklung* (hollow bamboo which produces a xylophone sound). Bandung is also a major city for the sport of ram fighting every Sunday morning in **Cilimus**, near Ledeng to the north. It is an exciting event, a gathering of colour, confusion and noise with wild cheers and ringing gongs, a bit like a Spanish bullfight crowd. Many villages also hold ram and cock fights as well. Visit the Tourist Office or just ask around among the locals for more details.

Central Java

The Yogyakarta region of Indonesia is a rich and beautiful land of many cultural attractions. This was the land of the great Mataram Empire whose wealth is still displayed today in an enormous collection of artefacts. Religion has also had a decisive influence in this fertile region. Hindu, Buddhist and Muslim temples dot the landscape among the rice fields.

Yogyakarta

Yogyakarta (which means "prosperity

Ancient ruins preserved in Prambanan, Yogyakarta.

without war") was a sultanate founded by Prince Mangkubumi in 1755 after a land dispute with his brother, the Susuhunan of Surakarta. A rebel prince who returned to the former Mataram dynasty and constructed the **Keraton** (palace) at Yogyakarta, he then took the title of sultan and **Hameng-kubuwono** ("the universe on the lap of the king,") a name which all of his successors had to use.

After the Mataram empire was split into Surakarta and Yogya, the city grew into a powerful Javanese state and a symbol of resistance to Dutch colonial rule. Between 1946 and 1949, it was the capital of the Indonesian Republic, and it was during this time that the palace was given to the new Gajah Mada University, which opened in 1946.

Later, during the Dutch occupation in 1949, the palace was also the link between the city and guerillas as the sultan locked himself in his room and allowed the rebels to use the building as their headquarters. Sultan Hamengkubuwono IX then acted as vice president of the country until his death in March 1978. After his funeral in 1988, Prince Bangkubumi – the oldest of his 16 sons – became Hamengkubuwono X in a spectacular ceremony.

Today, Yogya (as it is often called) is a semi-autonomous territory which enjoys a sultanate status. Situated in the cool climes at the foot of the active Merapi volcano, it is home to a population of about 3 million. Turtledoves are the city's symbol as many residents keep the birds for the enjoyment and peace they are rumoured to bring. Also known as the "cradle of Javanese culture," Yogya and the surrounding temple areas are bathed in solemn beauty, and are a magical area of colourful crafts, wild dance performances and long-told legends.

City Culture

Festivals are part of Yogya's cultural tradition, the palace being the central area for the celebrations. In fact, three main palace festivals with parades and traditional court dress are held each year; floats of flower petals and *gunungan* (cakes of sticky rice) accompany the colourful processions that march to the traditional melodies of *gamelan* (percussion type orchestra)music and prayers. Yogyakarta is also an excellent arts centre, with beautiful displays of silver, *batik* and paintings displayed along the walls of the shops and schools.

Orientation is fairly easy; just remember that the long walls of the **keraton** (palace) are south of the city, while **Jalan Malioboro** is the central road linking the old and the new areas. Along this wide street are the main shopping and dining areas, as well as the **Tourist Office** (Jalan Malioboro 16). South of the city is **Kota Gede**, the first capital of Mataram where the royal cemetery of **Imogiri** and **Sultan Agung's tomb** rests on the hillside – an area of fine silverwork today. To the northeast across the plateau lies the magnificent **Prambanan temples** and to the northwest **Borobudur**.

The *keraton,* lies at the heart of the "old city". It is surprisingly large (within its walls live more than 25,000 people). Colourful, it has mosques, shops, trees, gardens, art centres and schools. Two sacred banyan trees introduce the *alun-alun utara* (northern keraton square) where lingering remains of the battles from feudal Javanese times remain. In the centre of the palace are the oldest buildings, constructed between 1755-

56, with wide courtyards, bright pavilions and sunny hallways which add to the structure's dignified beauty and serenity.

One of the most photographed sites is the *Bangsal Kencono* ("Golden Pavillion") reception hall, where teak columns run smoothly up to a beautifully designed upper covering. Styled as a sort of bandstand in a European motif, its stained-glass windows cast a colourful light on the weekly *gamelan* (percussion-type orchestra) practice sessions performed by the sultan's staff. A wonderful museum inside the palace, exhibits colonial paintings and collections of various items from the sultanate. Also included are numerous of the sultan's personal items; *wayang* (leather) puppets, artwork, clothing, books, gifts and heirlooms. Other featured items are *gamelan* instruments, royal carriages, an enormous gong and hundreds of photos and portraits of the royal family tree and various celebrations.

Alun-alun selatan (the south square) is known as the located in the "back yard" of the palace area. The layout of these structures follow the natural features of the land, with the commemorative column and palace lying in a direct line with Mount Merapi.

West of the palace is **Taman Sari**, the "Fragrant Garden," also known as the Water Castle or Water Palace – a small **bird market** marks the entrance. Designed by a Portuguese architect from Dutch Batavia, it was built between 1758 and 1765, although the former

pools, waterways and palaces stand in tumbled ruins today. The sultan supposedly had the architect executed so that he would not give away the location of the ruler's "pleasure rooms". Although no traces are left today, you can still see the ornate structures hidden beneath the vines and shadows. An 1985 earthquake in 1985 caused even more damage to the Water Palace, but it is still an intriguing area to explore.

Keraton Crafts

The key to looking for crafts in Yogyakarta is – initially to look without buying as prices though at first exhorbitant will be reduced after a casual cup of tea and a free demonstration. *Batik* could be Yogya's most and stylish creation. Galleries proliferate in this area and visitors are often followed by dozens of students anxious to show off their talents and make a quick sale. To get an idea of colour, design and value, try the **Balai Penelitian Kerajinan dan Batik** (Batik and Handicraft Research Centre) at Jalan Kusumanegara 2, where English-speaking artists will show potential buyers and students around the displays of hand-painted and *cap* (block)-printed works.

Ask the Tourism Office for ideas, or just shop around, at galleries, workshops and *batik* displays. Some tips: Look at framed works by holding them up in front of the light to check for a phenomenal glow that awakens vibrant colours.

Batik designs vary from region to region.

Make sure that if you want a quality purchase of either silk or cloth, that it has been painted through on both sides and not just filled "colouring book" style.

Also, for a general overview, try the Academy of Fine Arts (ASRI), or the less expensive galleries along **Jalan Wates** and near the Water Palace. Allow plenty of time, as most vendors are quite friendly and want to show you their wares. *Batik* courses are even available, but check around; the ***Batik* Research Centre** recommends some schools more than others and has some of its own as well.

Leatherwork is a popular craft in the *keraton* area, and you can also (see a selection of *wayang* (puppet) characters here. South of Yogya, in the village of **Kasongan**, unique earthenware and pottery designs are created.

However, silver has gained fame in the Yogyakarta area, particularly the crafts of **Kota Gede**, just five kilometres from the central city. Although the silver is from Kalimantan or Sumatra, the creations are local; delicate filagree designs of jewellery, and models of ships and *becak* (trishaws). Most of the shops are found near the grave of Senopati, while the main street is lined with silver workshops where you can observe silversmiths at work.

Museums of Yogyakarta

Yogyakarta offers some of the best and extensive collections of art and artefacts with displays that often pre-date the settlement of the Javan islands. The **Sono Budoyo Museum** is at the main palace square which houses works of Javanese, Madurese, Balinese, Chinese and other Southeast Asian works of art. Here Statues, puppets, paintings and carvings, are found in various displays that add flavour to your knowledge of the crafts and performances offered by the city. A favourite of locals and visitors alike is the **Diponegoro Museum and Monument**, built to honour Prince Diponegoro, the eldest son of Sultan Hamengkubuwono III.

Diponegoro is famed for his instigation of the five-year Java War, and the building is a reconstruction of his home, which the Dutch burned in 1825 – including the hole in the wall from the punch Diponegoro threw to escape during the fight. Today, a collection of the Prince's belongings and heirlooms are displayed within the museum.

At Jalan Sultan Agung 22 is the **Biology Museum**, where there is a good display of stuffed animals and plants. You will find memoirs of the Indonesian Revolution at Jalan Kol Sugiyono's **Army Museum**, which houses weapons, uniforms and equipment used during the revolution, as well as a biography of President Suharto's successes in Yogyakarta's Diponegoro Division.

Palace Performances

To get a glimpse of Yogyakarta's magical dances and plays, the main place to go is the **KONRI/Conservatory of Classical Dance** on Jalan Agus Salim near the *keraton*. The **ASTI/Academy of Dance** on Jalan Colombo is also open to visitors, while a private school at Jalan Singosaren 9 and studio at Padepokan show off the works of Kussudiharjo, Indonesia's leading choreographer. Classes for international students are possible.

One of the most beautiful dances found in the archipelago is the *Ramayana* ballet performed by moonlight at the ghostly site of the **Prambanan temple**, 17 kilometres from the city. Held outside, by the light of the full moon, the performance combines the talents of more than 100 dancers in an extended four-part ballet held over a weekend, once a month.

At the *keraton*, all-night *wayang kulit* (shadow puppet) performances are also held once a month. It is a fun, laughter and music-filled play that attracts a large local audience and runs until the first light of dawn.

Shorter performances can be seen at the **Yogyakarta Craft Centre** and the **Arjuna Plaza Hotel**. For wooden *wayang golek* (imitations by human actors of the movements of the shadow puppets) performances, try the **Agastya Art Institute**.

Try to eat your dinner and shop at Jalan Malioboro. The area is beautiful, cool and open all night; Take a *becak* (trishaw) ride through the city and alley ways, as a romantic end to your day.

Temple Shadows & Ruins

Along the road which stretches towards Solo through Java's vast central plains, temple ruins tell of the island's greatest ages of religion and culture. Seventeen kilometres from Yogyakarta on this eastern road, travellers first find the solemn Hindu temples of the **Prambanan** village. Constructed between AD 8 and 10, they are oddly intermingled with Buddhist temples (one of them being **Borobudur**), each with architectural trends that lean towards shared design traditions.

With the dynastic wars of the ancient empires, many effigies were torn apart and left decrepit among the hills. Eventually, the remnants of the Buddhist Shailendras and Hindu Sanjayas of the old Mataram empire moved to east Java and left these remains to be crumbled by an earthquake in the 16th century and plundered by adventurers in later days.

One of the stories behind the Prambanan kingdom is the legend of Loro Jonggrang. Known as the "slender virgin," she was the daughter of King Prabu Baka, who was killed in battle by the Bandung Bandawasa. King Boko's son, Bandung Bondowoso wanted to marry Loro Jonggrang, who was the daughter of a Prambanan ruler but she decided to trick him, into accepting the proposal on the condition that in one night he would build her a thousand temples. With the help of an army of gnomes, Bondowoso completed the task – but, to his horror, when he counted the temples at dawn he discovered there were only 999! Bondowoso then cursed Loro Jonggrang and she changed into a statue which still stands today in the inner hall of the Temple of Loro Jonggrang – also known as "The Thousand Temples."

Built 50 years after Borobudur, the Prambanan complex was probably erected around the 9th century to celebrate the resurgence of Hinduism in Java. In 1937 reconstruction efforts were made on more than 200 of the temples, which can be viewed today including:

Shiva Mahadeva – the largest of the buildings, dedicated to the Hindu god Shiva is a gorgeous temple that towers over 45 metres high. This structure is known locally as the Loro Jonggrang Temple, it is surrounded with scenes of heaven and the **Ramayana** carved into the gallery walls. In the main chamber is a four-armed statue of Shiva sitting upon a large lotus petal.

Also in the main chamber is a jolly, bearded figure of the divine teacher Agastya, and Ganesha, Shiva's elephant-headed son. The figure of Durga is also present and is believed to represent Loro Jonggrang, the "slender virgin" herself.

Next to the Shiva temple are the smaller temples of **Brama** and **Vishnu**, the former incorporates final scenes from the **Ramayana** and a four-headed Brahma statue. In the Vishnu Temple, scenes from the **Mahabharata** epic are depicted, along with a four-armed image of Vishnu the preserver.

The **Nandi Temple** is a small shrine situated near the Shiva Temple, which showcases a beautiful statue of Nandi, the bull (Shiva's vehicle).

The **Sewu Temples** are grouped in the northern area just a few kilometres from Prambanan. These are the **Thousand Temples** dating from c. AD 850. They feature a large central Buddhist temple ringed by 240 guard structures and four sanctuaries, each located at the points of the compass.

Two kilometres east of Sewu are the **Plaosan Temples**, constructed around the same time as Prambanan. On the rugged Gunung Kidul hills lies the **Ratu Boko Palace**, part of the southern temple group, where the 9th-century **Palace of the Eternal Lord** is a beautiful Hindu complex of pools and water fountains, that offer a stunning vista of the Prambanan plains.

To the west is the **Kalasan Temple**, one of the oldest Buddhist temples on the Prambanan plains, which boasts the added feature of an AD 778 Sanskrit inscription. Old paintings and remnants of statues (reputedly bronze) can also be seen here. However, more commonly spotted are the numerous bats which hang from the inner chambers.

Around the **Sari Temple**, in the midst of a lovely palm grove, there are several sculptured reliefs. Perhaps the final Prambanan plains construction was that of the **Sambisari Temple** possibly built by Mataram – discovered by a local farmer in the mid-1960s, it still lies amidst volcanic ash six metres below fields and offers sights of the Agastya, Ganesh and Durga images.

Along the Dieng Plateau

Known as "beautiful-amazing," the land of the Dieng Plateau is also the local "abode of the gods". With ruins scattered about the misted plains, jagged volcanoes smouldering above the shadowed land, it has the edge of remoteness captured by a lonely, wind-swept beach.

The holy waters of the Spring of Youth near the Serayu River is a quiet area for long, pondering walks, while the beautiful **Telaga Warna**'s multicoloured lake shines with the hues of sunlight. Nearby, the **Sikidang Crater** bubbles with mud pools and rushing springs from sulphurous slits in the ground. The holy **Cave of Semar**, the ancestor of all spirits, is the site for local meditation, although President Suharto has also come there for spiritual guidance.

Along the Dieng Plateau, the Hindu temples built sometime between the 8th and 12th centuries are among the oldest on the island. Most of the 400 or so temples are now abandoned and overgrown. However five main temples remain, connected by raised walkways along the central plains, with a museum located south of the plateau.

Amidst some of the most beautiful scenery in the Dieng, the 9th-century

Surakarta Keraton, Solo.

Gedung Songo temples are scattered amongst the misted foothills. The setting is moody and mystical, with smouldering clouds and steep ravines. Below, the vista sweeps over Mount Merapi and Mount Merbabau all the way to the Rawa Pening Lake and into the clouds.

Solo or Surakarta

The god Allah is believed to have decreed in a prophecy to Pakubuwano II, the ruler of Solo, that his city would become great and prosperous, and so it

Life in Solo today is still slow and steady.

is that central Java's royal city grew up from the small village of Solo, to the great centre of culture and royal life which it is today.

Located on the west bank of the Bengawan Solo River, Solo is also known as Surakarta. It is a peaceful, quiet place, with narrow streets and quaint homes, where crafts are common and culture is held in high regard.

Jalan Slamet Riyadi the main road runs through the city, with the palace near the east end and a small shopping area in the north towards the railway station. The **Tourist Office** is at Jalan Slamet Riyadi 235, with the **Radya Pustaka Museum** of musical instruments and puppets located conveniently next door.

At the **Surakarta *Keraton***, (palace), sacred banyan trees greet you at the entrance, while the *Nyai Setomo* cannon is the sexual match of Si Jagur at Old Batavia, Jakarta.

In the courtyard, marble statues and stained glass adorn the buildings, and a museum and art gallery that contain Dutch carriages and beautiful carvings are nearby. In the courtyard is also a special tower built in 1782, used for meetings with Loro Kidul, Goddess of the Southern Seas.

In the centre of the city lies the **Mankunegaran *Keraton***, (palace) which was the second ruling house, constructed in 1757. Athough the Prince and Princess of Mangkunegara still live in the palace, it is open for viewing, and its highlights include a ceremonial hall with the Javanese zodiac spread across the ceiling and beautiful *gamelan* (percussion-type orchestra) sets called *Kyai Kanyet Mesem* ("drifting in smiles"). There is also an interesting museum housing collections from the personal items of Mangkunegara VII, which include jewellery, costumes, portraits, and a valuable library.

Pasar Klewer, the *batik* market, is a two-storey "hanging market" with hundreds of cloths to examine. However, if you are shopping for something unique, it does not take much more than a casual look to spot the differences in style that make the valued "Solo batik" different from other designs seen throughout the archipelago.

East of Solo

The area of ancient remains fifteen kilometres east of Solo, is **Sangiran**, where the original "Java Man" was discovered in 1936. At the same site is a small museum with exhibits of bones, mammoths and fossils. A bit further on, in a cold mountain setting, the 15th-century **Sukuh Temple** is set on the slopes of Mount Lawu and combines many odd, erotic images imbibing the area with a unique aura of passion and mysticism.

Nearly 3,000 metres high, the peak of **Mount Merapi** volcano, ("fire mountain"), lies only 50 kilometres east of Solo.

Near Semarang, going north, the

port of **Demak** was the capital of the first Islamic state on Java, founded by "Jin Bun", (Raden Patah), the first sultan of Demak and a Muslim hero who defeated Majapahit in the late 1400s.

The only Javan city to retain an Arabic name, **Kudus** ("*al-Quds*" or holy) was founded by the Muslim Saint Sunan Kudus. Known as an Islamic holy city and a place of pilgrimage, it retains a

The lines on the volcano sides of Mount Bromo are more pronounced at sunset.

Middle Eastern ambience and is filled with traditional buildings of carved and decorated wood. This area is the centre for *kretek* (clove cigarette production), for companies such as Djarum®.

In fact, the aromatic *kretek* smokes were invented in Kudus, and the area now is responsible for the 25 percent of the country's production.

Mayong was the birthplace of women's rights activist Raden Ajeng Kartini. Kartini was a well-known writer who published her works in the volume entitled ***Through Darkness to Light*** and

Mount Bromo

A desolate, moonlit landscape before sunrise, the cool mist melting into sulphurous smoke, ashen seas of sand swirling up into the dim twilight. Gradually a crimson line appears across the horizon, bright like a thin cut of blood on taut, blackened skin, spliting open the day and casting warmth onto the grim panorama of craters and mountains below.

Mount Bromo is the ruler of central Java's high mountain ranges and the island's most wistful area, a lonely landscape carved into craggy peaks and shallow craters with a sandy sea tossed in-between. Hiking is rather cold, and can be tough, either by sturdy horse or by foot, footholds can not grip the slippery volcanic ash layered along the steep slopes ... and no marks are left along the dry, barren trail for future followers seeking the way!

An air of murky volcanic ash disseminates a greying tinge, the harsh strength of the growing sunlight casting an apocalyptic feeling about the land. A crater within a crater, Bromo is one of four peaks which formed within the caldera of an ancient Tengger volcano.

This an area of great legend, it is believed that the volcano was carved from the half-shell of a coconut by a love-struck ogre vying for a young woman's love. Challenged to carve a great well by dawn, he was foiled by her father who made the cock crow early, in anger the ogre threw the shell upside down to form Bromo's neighbouring swell of **Mount Batok**. The trench which is believed to have been dug from the earth by the ogre is known as the **Slippery Sand Sea**.

But, the mountainsides are hardly deserted. Rather, they are the home of the Tenggerese and the Javans who moved eastwards during the influence of the Majapahit empire and began to cultivate the fertile sides of the mountain slopes. Bromo then became a place for both religious and festive traditions which are still carried out today, particularly during the **Kasodo Festival** held around January each year, when a parade of Tenggerese toss offerings into the crater at sunrise.

Trekking the Mount Bromo area requires much supplies and sometimes, horse-back transportation

The best view of Bromo is at early sunrise, while the air is still cool, and is a pleasant departure from the morning darkness. From the east Javan town of **Probolinggo,** travellers head for the village of **Ngadisari** and often continue onwards towards **Ceoro Lawang** which is located at the rim of the crater. Before dawn, it is a three kilometre-long walk to the crater wall and across the Sand Sea to Bromo. Begin the trek at 3 am from Ngadisari, and at 4 am from Cemoro Lawang as sunrise is at 5 am. The chilly winds make a jacket a necessity, as is a good torch and sturdy walking shoes to ascend the 246-step climb up to Bromo across the plains.

Another option for reaching the rim is via **Ngadas** on the Tengger crater's southern rim less popular paths and lovely scenery make this route a bit more special. From **Malang** or **Surabaya,** the first leg of the journey is to **Blimbing** and **Tumpang.** Then it is on to **Gubug Klakah,** from where you can walk the 13 kilometres to Ngadas and three hours (eight kilometres) to Cemoro Lawang across the crater – or on to **Mount Semarau,** the highest mountain in Java.

Also known as Mahameru (Great Mountain), Mount Semaru is the most sacred mountain amongst the Javanese Hindus and is also believed to be the father of Bali's sacred "Mother" peak of **Mount Agung.** A lakeside village at 2,200 metres, with the trek winding up to more than 3,600 metre scan be found via **Rano Dani.** Another 12 kilometres route, by way of the Tengger Sand Sea from Mount Bromo, before descending towards the open grassland and thin forests of **Mount Ayek-Ayek** makes for breathtaking views of the **Ranu Kumbolo** crater lake at 2,400 metres. It is just a 10 kilometres hike from Rano Dani to Kumbolo.

The best time to hike in the Bromo area is during the dry season, from April to November. For information and permits, stop in at the PHPA (Park) office at Ngadas.

opened a school for young girls living in the area. A monument built here commemorates her, and special ceremo-

nies are held on her birthday on April 21 which is known as Kartini Day. **Mantingan** is the site of the memorial tomb dedicated to Kartini, as well as that of Ratu Kalinyamat, the great warrior-queen of Jepara. Ratu Kalinyamat even battled against Portugese Melaka although she was unsuccessful, she still managed to frighten the male troops! Also close to the area is **Jepara,** perhaps the best-known woodcarving centre on the island.

East Coast

Eastern Java is a real treat for those seeking the mystery of the undiscovered. A scenic and agricultural land, it has hardly been encroached upon by the tourist trade. However, the populations is surprisingly large several million people being concentrated in a few cities. Attractions range from temples to bull fights.

Central Cities and Temples

On the banks of the river Brantas lies the cosmopolitan town of **Malang,** a cool, clean student town with a definitely European flavour. Established at the end of the 18th century by the Dutch, this city is said to be the place where coffee was first introduced to Java.

However, once in the surrounding hills, the scenery returns to ancient times. The slopes and plateaus are dotted with temples and ruins the central **Singosari Temples** date back to the dynasties of the 1300s, while the crumbled courtyards at **Panataran** date back to c. AD 1200. At **Wendit**, there are hill resorts and gardens at Purwodadi, as well as the tomb of the "wise man" of Mount Kawi – the tourist office at Jalan Tugu 1 provides useful information on the area.

Surabaya

Surabaya the capital of east Java, is a city of more than two million, a main shipping port as well as a base for the Indonesian navy.

Hot, dry, crumbled, faded, it is still interesting to explore. The **Tourist Office** for **East Java** can be found on Jalan Pemuda 118 – it's a good source of information, with an English-speaking staff and lots of maps and brochures. A favourite site is the **Surabaya Zoo**, located along the main street of Jalan Diponegoro, which houses one of the largest collection of species in Southeast Asia. A good display, with large cages, wide paths an excellent aviary, an island where the Sumatran rhino grazes where boats cruise around, and there is a clean nocturnal house and a pool for the *dugong* "mermaid". Admission is cheap – but try not to visit on Sundays or public holidays unless you enjoy being an exhibit yourself among the masses!

Also of interest in Surabaya are the **MPU Tantular Archaeological Museum** and the **THR People's Amuse-ment Park** located just east of town. At the latter, the atmosphere is carnival-like, with rides, music bands, theatres and cultural performances.

Joko Dolong, the "fat boy" statue in the city centre was constructed in 1289 to commemorate King Kartenagara, king of the Singosari empire. **Tanjung Perak Harbour**, several kilometres north of the city, has ships that sail all over the archipelago and Southeast Asia.

The port of **Gresik** located nearby is also a popular port, as well as the site for the **Tomb of Sunun Giri**, the first *wali songo* (apostle) of Islam. To view old *pinisi* (ships), take a walk over the harbour, or for lovely hillside scenery, try the nearby resorts of **Tretes**, with its waterfalls and climbs to **Mount Arjuno** and **Welirang**. During the dry season, this is the site of the East Java Ballet Festival, and you can also tour the ancient 14th century Hindu **Jawi Temple** here.

For a visit back in time to Java's "Golden Age," take a trip to **Trowulan**, the former capital of the Majapahit empire which lies 60 kilometres west of Surabaya. Its ruins are now scattered about the area, but there is plenty to see, including the **Trowulun Museum**, the **Tikus Temple** and the **Pendopo Agung** open-air pavillion.

Madura Island

Just a few kilometres across the channel

The government is actively designating more territory for preservaton and national parks.

April and October and are complete with music, parades and festivities. The great finale of the competitions, called *Kerapan*, is sponsored by the government and held in the stadium of **Pamekasan**, the capital of Madura Island.

The old royal cemetery of the Cakraningrat family is located in **Arosbaya**, an eastern coastal town with terraced hills and jagged ravines. Close by is the town of **Tanjung Bumi**, where you can find the famous Madura *batik*, as well as see the traditional *perahu* (a swift strong sailing boat) at Siring-Kemuning beach.

Sumenep, an interesting town near Pamekasan, has a royal palace and a museum, the **Asta Tinggi Royal Cemetery** and the amusement park of **Taman Sari**.

from Surabaya via ferry is Java's large outer island of Madura. Covering about 5,000 square kilometres, this area is home to about three million proud Madurese, who are famed for their bull fights and races.

The competition began as a contest held between farming families in which bulls were raced down the plowed rows of the fields. Today, huge bulls are covered with ornamental decorations, with "gladiator"-style riders sitting on each animal's back, charging down a 50-metre track in front of a crowd to create a Spanish carnival-like atmosphere.

Most of the races are held between

Parks of East Java

Within the tall, dry forests and plains of eastern Java roam the last large animals of the archipelago's western islands, now confined to the rounded peninsulas and low mountain areas.

Tigers, which have been extinct in Bali for decades, may still survive in the flat eastern jungles of Java. Black and brown *banteng* (wild cattle) graze in the savannahs, while several species of primates scream from the trees. Alas, there are no elephants or rhino, but birdlife abounds, with the wings of hornbills whirring above and smaller birds flitting through the trees in flashes of colour.

Grouped within in the **Baluran** area are three east Javan parks: **Alas Purwo**, **Baluran** and **Mehru Betiri**. Accessible from Banyuwangi, the journey north to the Balurans parks takes only a half-hour or so by bus or *bemo* (a small three or four wheeled covered vehicle); travellers are dropped off at the PHPA office just outside the park to pick up permits and maps.

A small museum there displays a collection of fossils, animal bones and pictures of wildlife within the park area. The gravel road next to it leads 12 kilometres to the northeast into the Baluran grounds, where huge, chalet-like guesthouses, an office and kitchen area offer modern comforts – a generator provides electricity from sunset until about midnight.

The parkland is beautiful, a stunning combination of jagged mountains, soft beaches and wide stretches of savannah similar to the African plains. *Banteng* (wild cattle) graze here, and big

cats have been seen roaming the hills; their cries can sometimes be heard after dark. In the mornings, the park is a cacophony of primate shrieks and bird whistles, with monkeys, wild pigs and peacocks mischeviously scampering over the grounds.

Hiking trails climb over the forested mountains and wander along the central plains. Two watchtowers offer dusk and dawn views of swampy watering holes, where large game are often spotted in the cool wallows. To the south, the journeys to Alas Purwo and Mehru Betiri are a bit more difficult. From Banyuwangi, the minibus route involves several transfers and lots of local stops – plan to take a whole day for your trip.

Within the smooth southeastern peninsula of the island is the park of **Alas Purwo**, with sandy beaches and widespread jungle carpeted with enormous dry leaves. It is here that several of the last Javan tiger are reputed to roam; if not, leopards can be spotted prowling the wide beaches every night.

There are also guesthouses here, and a watchtower looking out over a rough savannah and out to the mountains beyond. Herds of *banteng* (wild cattle), wild deer and pigs graze side-by-side, but after sunrise the air is stifling – it is thus best to arrive before dawn or come back in the late afternoon.

The PHPA office for Alas Purwo is some distance from the park; about 20 kilometres by motorbike shared with one of the officers, so you can not carry too much baggage along. At the office, there is an informative museum, as well as information on special areas designated for resorts and marine activities in the park.

The huge waves that batter the peninsula are also famed among the surfing community, and sportsmen from Australia make the pilgrimage each year to catch the waves.

To get to **Mehru Betiri**, head for the village of **Rajegwesi** on the southern coast, the last stop before heading into the thick rainforest that absolutely covers the mountain territory here. It seems as if everything is covered in green, glistening with alternate showers of dew and rain, the scent fresh and clean ... and you can sense the presence of large leopards and tigers peering curiously at you from within the leaves. This is also a stunning area of rocky beaches and rolling waves, with bays so clear that you can see fish moving beneath the jade surface. Rugged trails lead along the tumbled coastlines to hidden beaches and coves, while inland there are two watchtowers that offer a view of the mountainous land and grazing grounds below.

The PHPA office is about four kilometres outside Rajekwesi and just inside the border is a dusty museum filled with maps, trails and published results from research studies. One of the most popular stops at this park is at the remote coastal resort of **Sukamade**, famed for its rare species of turtles that come up to the shore to lay their eggs in the soft sand.

The Last Eastern Edge

A quiet break from your tour of Java journey is the north coast's **Pasir Putih Beach** resort area, a combination of convenient modern features with a relaxed pace of life. Here, you will find open-air restaurants, sailboats and white sand situated just a few hours between Surabaya and the east coast ferry to Bali – a popular bus stopover on trips to and from the big cities of both islands.

The legend of the River Banyuwangi is well-known. A man named Patih Sidapaksa had a beautiful wife belonging to the lower caste, his mother was unhappy about the union. So, she sent her son to Mount Ijien on a long and dangerous journey to search for the bud of a magic flower. When he returned, both his wife and small baby had died after being tossed into the River Banyuwangi by his mother, he ran there to find only two small flowers embracing one another. The river has always been fragrant – for *banyu* means "water" and *wangi*, "sweet-smelling."

The last stop in Java is the town of **Banyuwangi**, where the railway ends and eastern park permits for Baluran, Alas Purwo, Mehru Betiri and Bromo are obtained. From here, *bemos* will whisk you to the ferry port of **Ketepang** in ten minutes, where the ferry to Bali continues in its journey towards the east, while travellers travelling westwards will find smooth going at the train terminal and busy bus station.

Ramayana performed at Yogyakarta.

Ancient inscriptions call the island "the first Java," as did the explorer Marco Polo, who during his stay at the northern tip of Aceh in the 13th century referred to this fascinating jungle island as Java Minor.

The two islands were once attached, although they are now separated by the narrow Sunda Strait in which the volcanic island of Anak Krakatau from the Sanskrit word *karkata* (crab) stands silent guard. Geographically placed to the north of the Straits of Malacca, both Sumatra and Java remained as trading satellites long after the geographical separation of their mountainous lands.

However, Sumatra could never be mistaken for Java. Within its rugged terrain and cool, lakeside valleys there are sheltered diverse pockets of culture, magical wilderness and definitively different customs which have grown upwards and

Sumatra

247

A Bukitinggi woman.

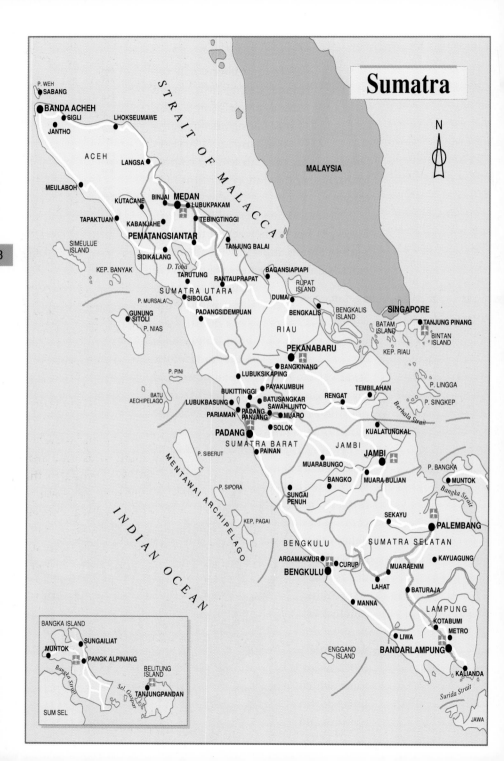

Sumatra

SUMATRA

248

P. WEH
● SABANG
● BANDA ACHEH
● SIGLI
● JANTHO
● LHOKSEUMAWE

STRAIT OF MALACCA

ACEH

● LANGSA

MALAYSIA

● MEULABOH

● KUTACANE
● BINJAI ● MEDAN
● LUBUKPAKAM
TAPAKTUAN ● ● KABANJAHE
● TEBINGTINGGI
PEMATANGSIANTAR
● TANJUNG BALAI

SIMEULUE
ISLAND

KEP. BANYAK
● SIDIKALANG
D. Toba
● TARUTUNG
● RANTAUPRAPAT
● BAGANSIAPIAPI

SUMATRA UTARA
P. MURSALA ● SIBOLGA
RUPAT
ISLAND
● DUMAI
● PADANGSIDEMPUAN
● BENGKALIS
BENGKALIS
ISLAND

GUNUNG
● SITOLI
P. NIAS

SINGAPORE

RIAU

BATAM
ISLAND
● TANJUNG PINANG

BINTAN
ISLAND

PEKANABARU
KEP. RIAU

P. PINI
● BANGKINANG
● LUBUKSIKAPING

BATU
AECHIPELAGO
● BUKITTINGGI
● PAYAKUMBUH

P. LINGGA

● LUBUKBASUNG
● BATUSANGKAR
● SAWAHLUNTO
● TEMBILAHAN
● RENGAT

P. SINGKEP

● PARIAMAN
PADANG
PANJANG ● MUARO
● PADANG
● SOLOK

Berhala Strait

● KUALATUNGKAL

SUMATRA BARAT
● PAINAN

P. SIBERUT

JAMBI

● MUARABUNGO
● JAMBI

P. BANGKA

P. SIPORA

● BANGKO
● MUARA BULIAN
● MUNTOK

Bangka Strait

KEP. PAGAI
● SUNGAI
PENUH

● SEKAYU
● PALEMBANG

SUMATRA SELATAN

BENGKULU
● ARGAMAKMUR
● CURUP
● MUARAENIM
● KAYUAGUNG

● BENGKULU
● LAHAT
● BATURAJA

● MANNA
LAMPUNG

● KOTABUMI
● LIWA
● METRO

ENGGANO
ISLAND
● BANDARLAMPUNG

● KALIANDA

INDIAN OCEAN

MENTAWAI ARCHIPELAGO

Surida Strait

JAWA

N

BANGKA ISLAND
● SUNGAILIAT
● MUNTOK
● PANGK ALPINANG

Bangka Strait
BELITUNG
ISLAND
Sel. Gaspar
● TANJUNGPANDAN

SUM SEL

apart from those of its sister island.

Religious Rivalries

Their most marked difference was religion. Both Hinduism and Buddhism were carried along the trading routes in the 7th century. For almost 600 years, Sumatra was a central trading force in Southeast Asia, until the Hindu kingdom of Majapahit turned against it resulting in the notorious *Majapahit-Srivijaya* rivalries in which the Javan kingdom of Majapahit emerged victorious. The powerful Srivijayan empire was Buddhist. This empire settled near Palembang in the south central mountains.

Ironically this rivalry led to the growth of the Malay peninsula as an area of great trading power, as the Srivijayan prince Parameswara fled to the new port of Melaka to escape attack. Later, this area fell to the Portuguese, who journey to the east in search of "gold, gospel and glory."

Religion was a key factor resulting in the differences between Sumatran cultures. Many Srivijayans still adhered to Buddhism whilst after Srivijaya's fall, others embraced the new-found beliefs of Islam which arrived on their shores via rich Arab traders. However not everyone converted; along the south and west coasts earlier religious beliefs remained strong; a Buddhist monk colony flourished around the Palembang area, whilst the central mountains cultures

Topless candi at the Buddhist Muara Takus Ruins.

remained steeped in local practices and rituals.

From Aceh, the religious influence worked its way southwards and then through Java and far beyond to the outer island. Even today, the power of Islam is clearly reflected in the beliefs and behaviour of the Acehnese, and the grand sight of the lovely **Baiturrahman Mosque** whic focuses the city of Banda Aceh around Islam.

Attraction of Wealth

Sumatra has always had an abundance of natural resources that were long awaiting discovery by merchants travelling from the New World.

Sumatran coastline.

Rich in coal, tin, and aluminum (bauxite), as well as timber, rubber, tea, cacao and coffee, this island's unexplored natural wealth attracted traders. Today, its natural resources are still being tapped, as the eastern areas hold substantial reserves of oil and natural gas. Gold also provided a glittering magnet to the area, in fact the Sumatran gold mines are one of the world's most productive small industries.

Historical annals reveal that the Italians first reached Sumatra when the Italian explorer Ludorico de Varthema (who named Sumatra) arrived in 1505. However, it was the Portuguese who put up the first port and established a clear connection to Europe on the island thereby becoming the first benefactors of trading profits from Sumatra.

Later, the Dutch gained a foothold. They were drawn to Sumatra by rumours of spices and mineral wealth. Sumatra was also a strategic base for control of the busy Melaka and Sunda straits, the main trading routes for merchants plying the sea between Asia, India, Europe and Africa.

Unfortunately, Dutch control was often threatened. Not only was their rivalry with the British further heightened during the Napoleonic Wars, but the Dutch also found enemies among the Sumatrans as well. After taking Palembang and Jambi in the early 1800s, they came head-to-head with the Islam revival efforts that were going on in the area. These efforts were encompassed within the *Paderi* movement which was centred in the Minangkabau highlands. By siding with the traditionalists, the Dutch were able to put out the last fires of violence and revolt in the central districts and easily control the area.

The Dutch settled their colonial differences with the British, in "The London Treaty," which gave the Dutch control over all British possessions in Sumatra in exchange for their holdings in Singapore and India.

However, the resurgence of Dutch rule was not happily accepted by many of the Sumatran people and the Acehnese and the Batak resistance forces fought violent battles until the early 20th century.

Wild & Wonderful

As the world's fourth largest island, the nearly 2,000-kilometre length of mountainous land shelters an incredible diversity of wildlife wonders and natural parks.

Only Greenland, New Guinea and Borneo are larger, and none hold such a variety of species. There are nearly 200 types of mammals – 20 of which are endemic and found only on Sumatra; including five primates, the Sumatran *kelinci* (rabbit), the Sumatran weasel and several branches of bat life … as well as the rare, whistling, red-haired Sumatran rhino.

Once, the Javan rhino also roamed the forests of Sumatra, but since the last confirmed shooting in 1928 the species is now sadly confined to Java's lingering south-western peninsula of Ujung Kulon and the Nam Kat Tien reserve in Vietnam. Sumatra was also once home to leopards which were found in nearby Java. This member of the cat family adapts easily to any environment and it is still not known why the species disappeared from the island.

The *Rafflesia arnoldi*, the world's largest flower is mostly found within Sumatra's wild jungles. Sumatran's describe it vividly as – "the Devil's betel box", or "the Stinking Corpse lily" – as its fleshy orange petals burst through the forest floor in a great vision of colour whilst exuding a stench similar to that of rotting meat. A parasitic plant with no leaves, stem or roots, it only grows on the host *tetrastigma* vine. The buds from

The Sumatran Rhino

The tiny, shy and sweet Sumatran rhino can be seen wandering along the trails of the thick central forests. No larger than a strong pony, this rare *Dicerorhinus sumatrensis* is a direct descendent of the prehistoric Woolly Rhinocerous which roamed the earth almost 40 million years ago.

However, today's species is small, unagressive, and even friendly (in captivity). It is a congenial animal whose long, low whistling song is more like the call of a forest bird than a sound emanating from a mammal. Two horns, tassels of red hair on its ears, torso and tail, and its Sumatran habitat mark the differences between this rhino and its rare Javan cousin. Expertly camouflaged by the brilliant rainforest green, they are still difficult to spot in the jungle, although their preferred lowland paths and well-known swampy wallows make them easy for poachers to find. They are pursued by poachers as their horns are essential additives to Asian folk medicines and fever tonics (not aphrodesiacs). In fact, numbers have fallen to 700 in the wild and are also declining in zoos. Not only are the horns used, but other body parts are well-known ingredients in folk medicine which have been the main motive for hunting the animal and causing the population to rapidly decrease.

The timber industry has not helped, either, as the forest hills now tumble down in massive landslides as trees are felled and burned. Pushed further and further into the disappearing central areas, conservationists wonder just how much longer their land (and their species) will be able to survive the stress and the changes of man's encroachment into their world.

Since 1985, captive breeding programs have been started in zoos throughout Indonesia, Europe and North America to prevent their disappearance. The Ragunan Zoo in Jakarta, ran a programme that successfully resulted in a recent pregnancy, and both the San Diego Zoo and the Cincinnati Zoo in the United States boast a well-matched pair.

In Cincinnati, the Center for the Reproduction of Endangered Wildlife (CREW) has embarked on a reproductive research programme. The programme involves international students and experts in the scientific fields who gather to work on world issues dealing with endangered species. Other projects concentrate on the development of new techniques for the propagation and preservation of rare plant and animal species with the aim of creating an "ark" for the future of life in our world.

this plant can grow up to nearly a metre wide and take almost half a year to bloom, while the flowers only last for a week.

Apart from the **Batang Palupuh** reserve, the *Rafflesia* is also common to the **Kerinci-Seblat National Park**, along with the striking *anaphalis javanica,* (Javan edelweiss) of the area's upper elevations. Only found on volcanoes, this tall plant grows to a height of four metres, with white flowers and fine white hair that gives it a ghostly presence as it ascends on the bare volcanic cone of **Mount Kerinci.**

Sumatra's 600 species of bird life are second only to the variety of Irian Jaya's aviary world, and include the loud, colourful-billed *buceros rhinoceros* (rhinocerous hornbill) and large Argus pheasant. Within the island's waters life is valued as well, for here the rare *golden arowana* ("dragon fish"), the world's most expensive aquarium highlight is found.

The distribution of animals may be explained by the volcano at **Toba**, which in prehistory exploded into a fiery mass that created the crater Lake Toba. During the eruption, the peak threw out

A Sumatran tiger, no longer to be found wandering on the island.

kilometres of volcanic ash, which spread a broad barrier between the north and south ends of the islands, preventing species of animals on either end from intermingling with one another and encouraging them to develop an adaptation to the different environment.

Parks & Activities

With the expanse of wild hills, lowland swamps and stunning coastal areas, Sumatra's park system has come about through the settlement and development of the island.

North of Medan, **Gunung Leuser** may seem a recent establishment but, it

is in fact one of Indonesia's oldest national parks, covering an area of about 8,000 square kilometres along the Bukit Barisan range south of Aceh. The stunning forests feature a smooth combination of montane and equatorial landscape that is home to well-known wildlife such as elephants, the Sumatran rhino and tiger, clouded leopards, tapir, and sun bears. Leuser is also the haven of primates, including gibbons, macaques and the playful *orang-utan*, while almost 500 bird species flit through the nearby skies.

Sumatra's largest park is **Kerinci-Seblat**, lying at the centre of the island. The most dominant feature here is the powerful

Sumatra's sprawling areas make a natural habitat for a vast number of tropical and migrant birds.

The brilliant reds of the Jxora colour many of the towns and villages.

Gunung Kerinci volcano, which is still bare from its last eruption in 1934. At 3,800 metres, it is the highest Indonesian mountain outside of Irian Jaya.

Sprawling over the provinces of Jambi, Bengkulu, and West and South Sumatra, Kerinci-Seblat encircles a 345 kilometre strip of the **Bukit Barisan Range** parallel to Sumatra's west coast. The total area is almost 15,000 square kilometres encompassing varying altitudes and habitats, which include lowland forests, alpine vegetation and the highest freshwater swamp forests in western Indonesia.

Lake Toba was formed nearly 75,000 years ago, as a result of the volcanic explosion of the Toba volcano.

Now, at about 100 kilometres long and 31 kilometres wide, the crater lake at Toba is the largest lake in Southeast Asia, while the central island of **Samosir** is larger than the island state of Singapore. Toba at more than 450 metres is also the world's deepest lake, and historians note that the explosion causing these land formations was probably the most powerful volcanic eruption to ever take place in the world.

On the south-eastern edge of the island, just half a day from Java's ferry ports, is the **Way Kambas Elephant Reserve** and training centre, (*Pusat Latihan Gajah*) in Lampung province. Declared a reserve in 1937, it is one of the oldest in the archi-

Sumatra's landscape boasts many colourful tropical species of floras.

Samosir Island in Lake Toba.

pelago, encompassing a small area of about 1,500 square kilometres of swampy lowlands and freshwater marshes. Primates are the most common wildlife in the area which also includes siamangs, gibbons and several types of playful macaques.

More than 300 elephants live in **Way Kambas**, where they are enrolled in a "training programme" to help prevent the protected species from damaging area farms. "Wild, angry elephants" is a rumour gone rampant within the province which has in past decades resulted in battles between villagers and the animals.

However, now with pride in their local involvement in the programme, the park's twice-daily training classes

and rides are a major tourist attraction which has created educational and profitable opportunities for the area.

The marvelous **Mentawi islands** once connected to Sumatra by a thin bridge of land, have since been separated by a deep trench of ocean that runs more than 2,000 metres in depth.

This occurrence half a million years ago isolated a number of species on the island and allowing them to develop their own idiosyncrasies to form an endemic Mentawai population of cats, squirrels, birds, insects and reptiles. Perhaps the most unusual are the monkeys, which include the *bilou* (black gibbon), the Mentawai macaque, as well as the monogamous long-tailed *joja*, and the pig-tailed *simakobu* (langur), which

Elephants are trained to work in the cultivated areas.

is believed to be related to Kalimantan's proboscis monkey.

A Journey Through Sumatra

Although 20 percent of Indonesia's population resides on Sumatra, each city and cultural area is surprisingly different.

Covering nearly 475,000 square kilometres, the island is split up into eight provinces that can hold up to 40 million people. Travel between these areas is difficult, at best. This difficulty in communication has separated cultures and religions by boundaries of geography and even language resulting in the diversity that richly defines each area.

Across the Sunda Strait, where the Panjang or Bakauheni ferry terminals lie on Sumatra's eastern edge, you will find **Lampung**, the first and flattest of Sumatra's eight provinces.

Lined with dormant volcanoes like Gunung Raya, Gunung Seminung and Gunung Sekincau, the marshy coastline faces Java's western port of Merak and the famous caldera of **Anak Krakatau**. It is accessible by boat via the seaside village of Canti. The area's capital, **Bandar Lampung**, boasts the **Monument to the Krakatau Eruption**, as well as the interesting **Museum of Lampung** on Jalan Umar and demonstrations of the unique *tapis* weaving style.

The occasional slithering in a tree may be that of the Sumatran snake.

Lampung & Palembang

From Lampung, once the centre of pepper trade with the Dutch, the road winds north with parallel train tracks all the way to the port of Palembang. Along the way, is the sunny **Merak Belantung Beach** just 40 kilometres outside the city and the ancient Chinese, Polynesian and Hindu-Buddhist relics of the **Pugung Archaeological Site** at the village of Pugung Raharjo.

Try not to miss the **Way Kambas Reserve and Elephant Training Centre** just two hours away from Bandar Lampung; or, try to sail along the beautiful natural path of the **Way Kanan River** before moving on to the northern city of Palembang.

Centuries ago, **Palembang** was the centre of the Buddhist *Srivijaya* kingdom and later grew into one of the archipelago's most important ports for the Chinese and the Dutch.

Located on the Musi River 80 kilometres inland from the China Sea, this town now thrives on trade which brings in more than one-third of Indonesia's national income.

Palembang is Indonesia's richest city and Sumatra's second largest. It is mostly an industrial oil town with more than one million residents (slightly less than Medan). In Palembang you can find floating Musi River markets, a **State Museum**, an old Dutch fort and a beautiful central mosque. Check with the

European vessels ventured to Sumatra in the early 19th century.

Tourist Office at the **Museum Sultan Machmud Badaruddin II**, or the **South Sumatra Regional Government Tourist Office** on Jalan Bay Salim 200 for what to see and do.

The areas outside of the city are probably the most interesting. You can embark on short day-trip explorations to villages scattered with the ornately carved and decorated **Limas traditional houses**, the 16th century tombs of the **Ki Kede Ing Suro ancient cemetery** or the beautiful 90-metre **Tenang Waterfall** and nature area.

Offshore islands are an easy getaway from Palembang as well, such as **Kamero Island**, just 40 kilometres away with bare beaches and Buddhist temples, or an overnight voyage to the re-

sorts on **Bangka** and **Belitung** islands.

Directly north of Lampung and South Sumatra are the islands of the **Riau Archipelago**, which are the second gateway for travellers to Sumatra. Nestled between Indonesia, Singapore and Malaysia, these islands were where the basis of the Malay language was formed – in fact, *Butanul Katibin*, the first book on Malay grammer, was written and published in the islands in 1857.

The largest and most familiar islands are **Binten**, **Lingga** and **Singkep**, which are each close to 1,000 hectares in size. On Binten, the busy port of **Tanjung Pinang** is just a two-hour jaunt by boat from Singapore, while **Batam Island** is just 20 kilometres away. Both are popular places for weekend getaways

Mainstreet of the town of Palembang.

as well as for fast and easy visa renewals for those holidaying in other parts of Southeast Asia.

The capital of **Pekanbaru** is also interesting. Located more than 150 kilometres up the Siak River, the surrounding land shelters the **Palace of the Sultan of Siak** and its museum, relics of the 16th century Siak Seri Inderapura sultanate which ruled as late as 1946 and the Buddhist temple near the **Muara Takus village**, believed to have been built by the Srivijayan empire in the 9th or 10th century.

From Pekanbaru, the **Kerumutan Nature Reserve** can be reached in a day's boat trip from the city. There are also numerous deserted areas to explore around the Riau Archipelago.

Central Explorations

The western trail from the ferry terminal leads first through wide fields and lines of raised wooden homes. Here, the sun yields a softer light than Java's searing light, the air is scented with the sweet pollen of fragrant white flowers that bloom everywhere. Suddenly, everything is clean, the air clear and quiet; pure peace after the hustle of Malaysia or the chaos of west Java located just on the other side of the Sunda Strait.

Lubuklinggau is the first stop, at the fork between Palembang and Bengkulu; a small town of modern products mixed with Indonesian customs, and often *losmen* (rooms to let) lit by

A typical crowded street bazaar.

cake) is flipped on round grills and the beaches are filled with laughing locals. Particularly beautiful is the time of the **Tabot Festival**, when parades of colourful, towering floats are carried by darkness and tossed into the sea in a gathering of glorious excitement to satisfy the spirits.

Founded by the British in 1695 with the noted presence of Sir Thomas Stamford Raffles, Bengkulu's **Benteng** (Fort) **Marlborough** stands by the water, as does the quiet **Bengkulu Beach**. On Jalan Pembangunan PD Harapan, the **Bengkulu Museum** is an interesting stop, and it is also possible to see **Sukarno's House** where he was exiled within the city for three years, until 1941. Graves and megaliths are scattered throughout the **Pasemeh High-**

candlelight. Heading northwest to the province of **Bengkulu** is one of the most beautiful rides of the archipelago, through twisted, misty mountain roads that wind through thick jungle foliage, where the imagination runs wild with thoughts of fiery tigers or red-haired Sumatran rhinos peering from the leaves. A wide coastal city of solemn mosques and sparkling waves, Bengkulu has a definite aura of spirits, and of Islam; a presence felt in the afternoon rains and the prayers chanted daily at dusk and dawn.

By day, business runs smoothly, while by night some of the country's best seafood *warungs* (food stalls) sizzle with giant prawns and crabs along the main road, crisp *martabak* (stuffed pan-

Weaving sarong cloth.

Christian Missionaries set up posts in Bintan Island in early 19th century.

lands near Bengkulu, while the island of **Enggano** lies across the bay from the village of Malakoni.

But, this is wild tiger and rhino country - as the stunning coastal road smoothly parallels the sunset along low hills and rubber plantations until it dives inwards towards the massive mountains of the central Bukit Barisan Range.

Muko Muko village makes for a nice stop over between Bengkulu and Padang on the seaside road, or a rest midway through the rough journey to the Kerinci-Seblat National Park from either city. A quiet town with wavering electricity, a bland, timeless beach and cows wandering through the streets, Muko Muko is a serene "waiting place" for gathering energy, that somehow seems an ageless pause in time.

Kerinci Jungles

For the road to Kerinci, be prepared; this is one of the hardest, rough-and-tumble journeys ever made by vehicle, and the urge to get out and walk may flicker more than once through the mind. To **Sungai Penuh** (the base city for treks in the park), the one-lane gravel "highway" trip is a test of nerves, patience and automotive knowledge as the bus will burst a tyre, blow an engine, lose a wheel/piece of luggage/passenger – or a combination of all three. The destination, however, is well-worth the journey.

The port of Belawan through which much of Sumatra's produce is exported overseas.

If you arrive at dawn, be prepared for a stunning sight; huge, jagged mountains sloping downwards towards cool, flattened plains that spill out over the land in an uncanny resemblance to the plateaus of Tibet. The air, too, is chilly, for you are in the midst of mountains, such as the bare, grey cone of Sumatra's highest peak, **Gunung Kerinci**.

And, from Sungai Penuh – a flat, grey Muslim market town with unescapable charm – the journey to **Kerinci-Seblat National Park** is quite easy.

Many options for day trips and trekking are available through Eco-Rural Travel which is operated in conjunction with the World Wide Fund for Nature (WWF), who are in the process of creating programmes to integrate the interests of culture, trekking and tourism. These opportunities include hikes to the cold summit of **Gunung Kerinci**, treks to **Lake Tujuh** in the central mountains, or day trips to the **Kayo Aro** tea plantation or the nearby **hot springs**.

North of Kerinci, is the highway to Padang – yes, unless you fly, you have to first take that rough road back to Muko Muko.

However once out of the mountains, the journey is along a rugged western coastline not unlike that of New Zealand's South Island, or South Africa's Cape of Good Hope, or even that of North America's Highway 1 in California, filled with sunsets, palm trees, jagged cliffs and thundering waves that brings you into the port city.

Jet-ski on Batam Island, the new resort island.

The early years of Padang's development.

Padang and the West

In the middle of beaches and mountains, cultivation and culture, **Padang** is an interesting stop on any traveller's Indonesian itinerary.

And, indeed, many do stop here, for the city is a halfway mark on the west coast, as well as the capital of the West Sumatran province and the island's third-largest city. A major port on the archipelago, ships here enjoy easy access to Pacific merchant routes, such as India, Africa, the Middle East, and the rest of Southeast Asia.

Close to Padang, are wide stretches of beach and forest, whilst within the city are several museums and an en-lightening **Cultural Centre**. At the port, small boats from the Muara River Harbour or Teluk Bayur can be hired to the islands of **Pulau Pisang Besar**, **Pulau Sikoai**, **Pulau Padang** and **Pulau Bintangur**.

Bungkus Beach is inland and approximately 22 kilometres from the city – even closer, at four kilometres south, is the village of **Air Manis**, where hiking, swimming and boating activities provide one with a lovely view of the harbour.

From Padang, the road splits in two directions: north, along the coast all the way to Banda Aceh, or the more popular inland route through Bukittinggi to Medan. This road cuts through thick jungle between seascapes and the

Padang men with typical head protection.

Singgalang and **Merapi** volcanoes, close to the **Lembah Anai Nature Reserve** (filled with wild orchids and the *Rafflesia* flower), as well as the nearby **Lake Singarak** and **Lake Maninjau**.

Minangkabau Highlands

This is the heart of Minangkabau territory, the tribe of matrilineal traditions and Islamic beliefs whose insignias are based on the buffalo. Minangkabau, in fact, means, "the buffalo wins" in reference to a contest with a former kingdom of Java from which the weaker, younger but craftier Sumatran tribe came out victorious.

Among the four million Minang-kabau are some of the friendliest people in the country – and, interestingly, the society is based on and dominated by female action.

Family heritage is traced through the women, and it is to them that inheritance is given, with all the Minang-kabau's identifying with the ancestors of their mother. Matrilineal clan groups are termed *suku*, of which there are several in each village. In turn, each *suku* is split into a *paruik*, which stands for the entire line of descendants from a single great-grandmother.

Since inheritance is given through the women, so all property, such as family houses and rice paddies, belong to the women; men may manage them, but women are the ones who bestow

Regular town transportation in the Padang area.

property rights to their children. This contrasts with Islamic law, which states that two-thirds of a parent's estate is divided among sons and one-third to the daughters. However, the Minangkabau, do not seem to have trouble with sharing.

Beautiful Bukittinggi

With its volcanic surroundings and ornate central square clock, **Bukittinggi** is a peaceful mountain resort sitting in the heart of the Sumatran highlands. An area of undeniable natural beauty, the town is in the centre of the **Tandikat**, **Singgalang** and **Merapi** volcanoes, with the **Ngrai Sianok** canyon separating it

by 12 kilometres from **Kota Gadang**, the village known for its delicate filagree silverwork and colourful hand-embroidery. In the centre of this city which was formerly called "Fort de Kock" by the Dutch is the actual **Fort de Kock**, built during the Padri Wars of the 1820s and 1830s. For historians, the **Military Museum** standing next to the Minang Hotel may be of interest.

Nature lovers may prefer the nearby **Panorama Park** and the **Japanese Caves** ... or perhaps the **Taman Hutan Raya Bung Hatta Botanical Gardens** and the hilltop **Taman Bundokandung Museum and Zoo**. An amusing site situated nearby is the **Equator Monument**.

Although no physical line has been

Padang's interesting architecture among the wooden houses.

drawn it is always fun to jump over the border. Bukittinggi's mountainous location makes for plenty of outdoor activities in the area, these include the wildlife and waterfalls of the **Harau** and **Anai Valleys**, the **Ngalau Indah Caves** and the lakes of **Solok**, **Diatas** and **Dibawah**, along the road from Padang. At a distance of 64 kilometres, the **Rimba Panti Nature Reserve** is the best place on the island for spotting the rare *Rafflesia* flower as well as many species of wildlife.

Local villages provide a spot of cultural experience: **Pandai Sikat** for woven cloths and ornaments, **Payakumbuh** for basketry and **Padang Panjang** for a look at the national institute, which highlights the music and dance of the Minangkabau culture.

Above Kerinci but before Medan, the province of **Jambi** is on the east coast along the Straits of Melaka. The city of the same name is the province's capital and sits at the edge of the Batanghari – Sumatra's longest river, which runs more than 150 kilometres down from the sea.

Entrenched in centuries of trade and under the control of Java's Majapahit kingdom, Sultan Muhammad Nakhruddin and the Dutch EIC, this area combines the cultures of India, China, Arabia, Malaysia, Java, and various indigenous tribes – including the Kubu, a tribe of nomadic forest dwellers believed to be among the first Malay immigrants to the island.

Yet another alternative means of getting about.

Medan to Toba

The former site of great battles between the sultanates of Aceh and Deli, **Medan** – meaning "field" – is now Sumatra's largest city and busiest port. Sprawling out in the dusty heat over the coast, the **Mesjid Raya**, or **Great Mosque** and the **Palace of the Sultan of Deli** reflect Medan's history, while the harbour of **Belawan** better reflects the variety of heritage collected in the city's cultural stew.

A bit of a callous, Chinese-run, expatriate town, Medan is filled with as many taverns and seedy clubs as it is with temples and historical markings. There is the **Museum Bukit Barisan** on Jalan H Ainul Arifin 8, and the nearby **Parisada Hindu Dharma Temple** or the **Taman Ria** amusement park's fair-like atmosphere for play. **Taman Margasawata**, Medan's zoo, is located along Jalan Sisingamangaraja, with a **Crocodile Farm** at Asam Kumbang just five kilometres from the city.

However for a true glimpse of nature, head for the **Bukit Lawang Orang-hutan Rehabilitation Centre** just a two-hour ride from the city, where a programme by the WWF has preserved, protected and released a number of formerly captive animals into the wild since 1973.

Gunung Leuser National Park is close by, as is the **Great Bukit Barisan Forest Park** of the Karo highlands, which

The Minangkerbau roofs dominate architecture, even though many are constructed with zinc nowadays.

since 1916 was known as the *"Arboretum tongkoh-Berastagi'* and only in 1989 was its name changed to **Forest Park.**

Lake Toba Legends

South of Medan are two of Indonesia's most popular areas for tourism and surfing, those of **Lake Toba** and **Samosir Island.** The main resorts are in the town of **Parapat**, four hours from **Medan,** or in the villages of **Tomok, Tuk-tuk, Ambarita** and **Sialiagan** on **Samosir Island.** Here, boating, fishing, sunbathing and other watersports are the main activities – pleasurable pursuits to be enjoyed in this quiet setting of placid waters and offshore islands.

Among the Sumatrans who live in the area, it is said that

Lake Toba came into existence due to the fate of a fisherman who reeled in a magical catch. This catch contained a female fish who told the man to keep her in his rice field so that his crops would be plentiful – but only if the fisherman came to feed her every day and told no one from where she came. In the Indonesian way, the fish turned into a woman who bore him a son, but one day the farmer let it slip that his wife had come from the sea. In her anger, legend says the fish-wife split the Sumatran sky with terrible storms that

A Sumatran lady after gathering fruits.

Lake Toba environs.

filled up the Toba valley, then dived into the waters where she still lives today.

The area of **Tapanuli** is the land of the Batak culture, the centre of which is on Samosir Island. Today, there are six main Batak groups, and six million Bataks, who enjoy a diversity of language and customs which vary between each line of heritage. More than half of the Bataks live in the highlands surrounding Lake Toba.

It is said that Batak history began with the arrival of Si Raja Batak, the legendary ancestor of the tribes, who came down from a volcano on the shores of Lake Toba. However, historians mark the Batak origins as from the Philippine Islands and Borneo, c. AD 2007 - 1007.

In former times, the Batak languages were distinguished by three distinct groupings: the Simalungun, the Karo and Pakpak, and thirdly the Toba, Angkola and Mandailing. The society was similarily divided : inherited ranks of nobility, commoners, and slaves. Power rested only in the hands of the *rajas (prince, lord or king)* and married men, and was centred within patrilineal societies which traced their heritage back to one forefather.

Division is still a common form in Batak life; for instance, in architecture. Like Sulawesi's Toraja clans, the Batak homes are built above the ground on three levels – to symbolize the lower "underworld," the current life and the heavens. At first, influenced by Hindu-

An elderly lady from Lake Toba area.

Modernised Sumatran chalets.

Buddhist religious beliefs, the Batak culture recognizes certain beings within each of these worlds: a seven-tiered upper world of deities, a human "middle" dwelling and the ghost and demon-inhabited underworld. The highest god is Mula Jadi Na Bolon, (the Creator), even today and ancestral spirits are still greatly respected in the practices of modern Bataks.

Although the Mandailing, Angkola and Karo cultures have converted to Islam and currently consider themselves more Malay than Indonesian, the influence of Christianity has led to a conversion rate that makes the Toba region the largest Christian area in the country.

Not only are the Bataks rice farmers, but they also farm maize, yams, potatoes, vegetables, coffee, cinnamon, coconut and sugar. Livestock including cattle is also raised for profit, and in the home structural system, the animals stay beneath the house while families live on the "earth" level inside and sacred ancestral heirlooms hang beneath the eaves.

The Myth of Fierce Aceh

As early as the sixth century, the Chinese were exploring Sumatra's northern tip of "Po-Li" (as they called it), as were the Arabs, who brought Islam with them some 300 years later. The explorer Marco Polo visited Aceh in AD 1292, where he told of six trading ports and a

Sumatran ladies in western-style dress.

strange spotted "unicorn" kept at the Banda Aceh palace.

A series of powerful sultanates reigned until the death of Sultan Iskandar Thani in the mid-1600s. Then, for 200 years trade and power struggles raged between the Acehnese, the Dutch and the British.

In the 1824 London Treaty, the Dutch received control ... and the subsequent Aceh War that raged from 1873 to 1942 was the longest fight in the history of Holland, one which imprinted the "fierce Acehnese" reputation on the people of the area.

On the way along the east coast is the **Gunung Leuser National Park**, the site of the great **Gunung Leuser** volcano and home of many endangered species – including the Sumatran rhino, tiger and orang-utan.

The powerful **Alas River** of white-water rafting fame, runs through the park as well as a research station which is the centre for studies conducted on the indigenous species of plant and animal life, only found within this part of the island. Also on this route is the city of **Lhokseumawe**, a major commercial centre for products such as liquified natural gas (LNG), minerals and cement, where the **Samudera Pasai grave-yard** marks the burial place of *Malikussakeh,* the king of the island's first Islamic empire. Further on is the **Takengon Resort** near **Lake Laut Tawar**, which offers caves, cliffs and hot springs for adventurous exploration.

There is always room along Sumatra's long coastlines and beaches.

Beaches & Coasts

This coastal route is gorgeous and hilly with curving roads lined with palm forests and a wide horizon. At night, the journey along the smooth highway is often made through misty rainstorms. By day, the landscape is lush and fertile, reflecting the humid climate of this equatorial area. **Banda Aceh** is the regional capital, located at the northern tip of the Sumatran island along the **Krueng Aceh** (Aceh River). Mirroring the province's strong Islamic beliefs is the beautiful central **Baiturrahman Grand Mosque**; burned down at the start of the Aceh War, it was rebuilt in 1875 and is

after Indonesia's 1945 Declaration of Independence.

One of the most interesting sites is the **Syiah Kuala Grave**, two kilometres from the city, where the most powerful Muslim "*Ulama*," (religious scholars) Teungku Syiah Kuala, was buried at the mouth of the Krueng Aceh. The **Indra Patra Fortress** and **Gunongan** and **Pinto Khop** monuments were constructed during the 16th century rule of Sultan Iskandar Muda, while the **Kerkhof** (churchyard) graves of more than 2,000 Dutch soldiers balances the number of Muslim relics found in the same area. The beaches around Banda Aceh are beautiful, moody, wind-swept and with high waves, afternoon rainstorms and brilliant sunsets that are the crowning glory of the archipelago.

Ujong Bate, **Lam Puuk** and **Lhok Nga** are just a *bemo* (small covered vehicle) ride from the city. **Sabang Island**, across the channel an hour away by ferry, is a well-known resort for locals, holidaymakers and divers. Its colourful and impressive coral gardens around the island are one of the country's best kept secrets.

Contrary to popular belief, the Acehnese are the most polite, friendly, giving and caring people on the island, if not in the entire country. Single women, do not fear; these people are wonderful, helpful and giving – just dress modestly and be as kind as you would have them be to you and you will have the most incredible experience of their unique culture, learning and life.

the central feature of the city's pride and culture. The museums are filled with relics of history, such as the **Museum Negeri Aceh (Aceh State Musem)**, where in 1914 a clock was brought as a gift from the Emperor of China by the great Admiral Cheng Ho. The **Museum Cut Nyak Dhien** commemorates the memory of the heroine, Cut Nyak Dhien from the Aceh War. It, too, was burned down during the war but was rebuilt

Tthe largest island of the Indonesian archipelago for centuries, Borneo has been the subject of confusion in power and trade. Currently on the map, the lower two-thirds of the island belong to Indonesia under the name of Kalimantan, while the upper third is split into Malaysia's provinces of Sabah, Sarawak and the sultanate of Brunei.

Kalimantan

277

Nipah swampland among meandering rivers in Kalimantan.

Trade Conflicts

Although Hindu and Sanskrit relics from the early fourth century AD have been unearthed from within the wilds of south Kalimantan, the first large settlements began as resting points for passing traders.

Nestled conveniently between the South Pacific, Southeast Asia and the Spice Islands, the huge island of Borneo began to burst with port cities around the coastal areas. With the advancement of Islam, the sultanates of Kutai and Banjarmasin grew into popular ports around the 16th century.

Then, the major fight for trade began between the Dutch and the Brit-

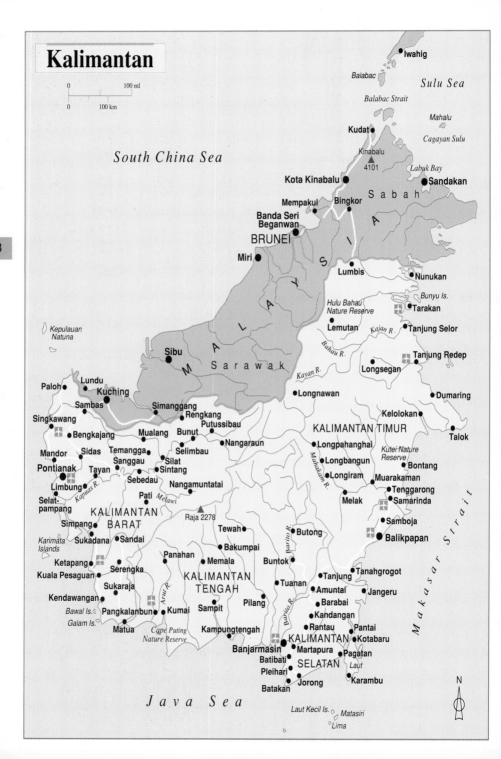

Kalimantan

0   100 ml
0   100 km

Iwahig

Balabac

Sulu Sea

Balabac Strait

Mahalu

Cagayan Sulu

Kudat

Kinabalu
▲ 4101

South China Sea

Kota Kinabalu

Labuk Bay

Sandakan

S a b a h

Mempakul   Bingkor

Banda Seri
Beganwan

BRUNEI

Miri

Lumbis

Nunukan

Bunyu Is.

*Hulu Bahau
Nature Reserve*

Tarakan

Lemutan

Kajan R.

Tanjung Selor

Bahau R.

Sibu

S a r a w a k

Kayan R.

Tanjung Redep

Longsegan

M
A
L
A
Y
S
I
A

Longnawan

Dumaring

Paloh   Lundu

Kelolokan

Kuching

KALIMANTAN TIMUR

Sambas

Talok

Singkawang

Simanggang   Rengkang

Putussibau

Bengkajang   Mualang   Bunut

Nangaraun

Longpahanghai

Mandor   Sidas   Temangga   Selimbau

Longbangun

*Kutei Nature
Reserve*

Bontang

Pontianak   Tayan   Sanggau   Silat
Sintang

Longiram

Muarakaman

Kapuas R.

Sebedau

Tenggarong

Limbung

Nangamuntatai

Melawi

Melak

Samarinda

Selat-
pampang

Pati

KALIMANTAN
BARAT

▲ Raja 2278

Simpang

Samboja

*Karimata
Islands*

Sukadana   Sandai

Tewah

Butong

Balikpapan

Ketapang

Panahan

Barito R.

Tanahgrogot

Serengka

Memala

Buntok

Kuala Pesaguan

Sukaraja

KALIMANTAN
TENGAH

Tuanan

Tanjung

Jangeru

Kendawangan

Aru R.

Pilang

Amuntai

Bawal Is.

Pangkalanbun   Kumai

Sampit

Barabai

Galam Is.

Matua

*Cape Puting
Nature Reserve*

Kampungtengah

Kandangan

Rantau

Pantai

KALIMANTAN

Kotabaru

Banjarmasin   Martapura

Pagatan

Batibati

SELATAN

Laut

Pleihari

Karambu

Batakan   Jorong

Makasar Strait

J a v a   S e a

Laut Kecil Is.   *Matasiri*

Lima

N

ish, who both wanted a monopoly over Banjarmasin's pepper trade. Feeling threatened by the dominance of the British presence, Banjarmasin's sultanate rebelled against them in 1701, but the British regained control of the area for the next seven years.

Undaunted by the British presence, the Dutch vyed for dominance of the island to add to their growing colonial power.

The British, who already controlled the areas of Java and Sumatra, wanted to maintain their rule over the area and its routes of trade, which again led to a conflict between the two powers. During this time, piracy along the coasts was nearly out of control, yet the Dutch managed to regain control. Their domain, via various treaties, extended along parts of south and west Kalimantan, including control of part of the protesting Banjarmasin sultanate.

Brash Young Brooke

It was the arrival of a brash young Englishman named James Brooke in 1838 that changed the destiny of the land.

Almost single-handedly, Brooke and his ship halted a rebellion against the Brunei sultanate by the inland tribes– and for his actions, in 1841 he was gratefully granted power over northern Kuching.

Once in power, Brooke built his own "white Rajah" dynasty which kept

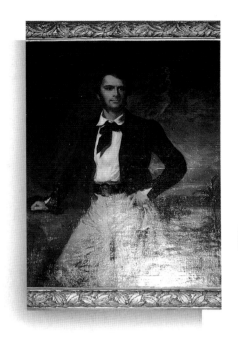

Portrait of James Brooke.

a constant watch over the inland tribes. His influence also extended through custom and trade, both inside and out of the island, as he put an end to the practice of headhunting within the jungles and eliminated the terrifying Borneo pirate trade from Kalimantan's coastal routes.

At this point, the Dutch again took action to maintain control of the island, for the threat of new European powers encroaching upon their territory suddenly became very real.

Soon, their growing commercial trade included minerals from new central mines, and more treaties were signed between the local governments to secure greater power over the land for the Europeans.

Polynesian-style canoes amongst Chinese junks in the early 19th century.

Border Beginnings

Today, the island of Borneo is split into four sections: Indonesia's territory known as Kalimantan, and Malaysia's states of Sabah, Sarawak and the sultanate of Brunei. Originally, the area now known as "Kalimantan" was divided as a result of Dutch-British disputes, into dual control of the area.

This division came about as a result of a series of incidents. First was the continuing Dutch conflict with the Banjarmasin sultanate that resulted in a four-year war during the late 1850s. To fuel the fire, the Brooke family gave their own British government control of their large northern domain, which is now known as "Sarawak".

"Sabah", once part of the larger Brunei sultanate, merged under the domain of the British North Borneo Company in the early 1900s. Caught for a time in a fierce rebellion headed by the Sabah leader Mat Salleh, the British finally gained control of the area until 1963, when Sabah joined Sarawak, Brunei and the rest of the Malay Peninsula to create the new nation of "Malaysia" separating these lands from the lower two-thirds of Indonesia's "Kalimantan".

Guerrilla warfare continued along the border of the two countries, particularly during the *Konfrontasi* (when Suharto threatened Malaysia with military intervention) in the 1970s. What did not add to the happiness of the inner tribes was the exploitation of new-found oil and mineral mines by the Dutch and British in the form of the Royal Dutch Shell Company.

Today, Kalimantan is split into four regional areas: East Kalimantan (Kalimantan Timur, or Kal-Tim for short), Central Kalimantan, South Kalimantan and West Kalimantan. Easy to remember, but difficult to travel between. Thus, the atmosphere of the coastal cities and cultural traditions of the mountain tribes can be surprisingly different in each area.

Barely touched until the 20th century, Borneo is the huge island just above Java and the largest in the archipelago, the lower two-thirds of which comprise Indonesia's territory of Kalimantan. An enormous mass of emerald jungle threaded by rivers of golden brown, Kalimantan is dotted with oil-based cities on the fringes of its larger waterways, which provide the only access to the delightful and sometimes dangerous interior jungles.

For those who dare to explore this secret forest world, an experience of oddity and enchantment awaits. Stretching 300 metres through the forest and across the river edges, the roughly-hewn Dayak longhouses are distinctive giants. However, the natives who share these shelters are of slight frame and quiet voice; a culture whose whorls of tribal tattoos mark their deep spiritual beliefs and whose lengthened earlobes hung with sparkling metal bangles are the ancient markings of beauty. Thin

Rainforests in Java.

riverboats glide through the tepid waters between villages like vessels crossing over to Hades, tangled vines and branches on either side reaching over to pull the unsuspecting traveller within.

Kalimantan's forests are also the playground of animals whose presence in the real world is rare and endangered. The button-eyed *orangutan* is friendly and mischievious, as it moves slowly through the frailest branches like sparks of fire through the trees. Special sanctuaries are reserved to preserve and protect the animals which still remain, as well as to rehabilitate those who have previously been held captive as pets or sold on the black market. Best-known is the *orangutan* research center at **Camp Leakey**, located at **Tanjung Puting Na-**

Checking on rainforest preservation sites.

tional Park up the Sekonyer River near Kumai, for details on visiting, write to Dr Birute Galdikas, who founded the programme, c/o the Orangutan Research & Conservation Project, Tanjung Puting National Park, Central Kalimantan, Indonesia for details.

Another primate special to Kalimantan is the unusual *proboscis monkey,* whose bulbous nose, rounded belly and red faces give this shy character a sweet aura of cheerful humour. Rather cheekily this monkey was given the Indonesian nickname *belanda* ("Dutch monkey"), for its resemblance to members of the former colonial government. Close to the eastern port of Banjarmasin, reserves on **Pulau Kaget** and **Pulau Kambang** are good spots for sighting this gentle creature. A boat journey could provide a true close-up view of these monkeys for, as the best swimmers of all primates, they often climb aboard in search of treats.

Centres of Culture

Wide seas separate these three unique areas of the archipelago, each with markedly different cultures. However, although these groups of humans evolved in completely different settings of climate and terrain, there are still many parallels in terms of customs between the thousands of tribes into which they have branched over the centuries.

In Kalimantan, the term *Dayak* is a

Communal living in the longhouses.

word used to distinguish non-Islamic tribes from the Muslim peoples. It was first used in reference to the indigenous and converted Kutai and Banjar tribes. Another name commonly used for the Dayak groups is *orang gunung* (mountain people), a reference to their jungle-dwelling habits that accelerated as they were pushed further into the interior by the growing trade ports, timber harvesting and slowly spreading religious movements of an encroaching modern world.

Thriving on the produce of the land, most tribes practice slash-and-burn farming techniques that force a nomadic way of life, each time the fertility of the soil is used to its limits. Other tribes are simply "hunter-gatherers" that live from day-to-day on the surrounding wildlife,

such as the wandering *Punan* (or *Penan*, as they are known in Malaysia's Sabah and Sarawak areas).

One of the most unique features of the Dayak tribes are their *lamin* (longhouses) which are the centre of life for the farming and river communities. Also known as *balai* in the south and *betang* in the central areas of Kalimantan, the longhouses are often more than 200 metres long yet only one room wide, guardian statues often stand in front to protect against evil spirits, bad fortune and diseases.

These enormous, raised structures accommodate many families inside, while an outer verandah running the length of the building is the scene of craftwork, cooking, meetings and tribal

Longhouse tribal leaders in a ceremony.

ceremonies. Found along riverbanks, groups of *lamin* (longhouses) form the core of permanent villages, while more mobile cultures often break down and move their longhouses after each season of slash-and-burn farming.

Transmigration

Overpopulation on the main islands of Java and Bali has led to efforts in transmigration, or moving people from these areas to less populated lands.

Originally, the idea was focused on spreading the population of Indonesia more evenly throughout the islands, particularly to severely underpopulated areas such as Kalimantan and Irian

Jaya. The country's second largest province, Kalimantan only holds around six million people – compared with Java's crushing 180 million or so – while Irian Jaya is home to a minute 1.2 million.

However, transmigration programmes are not the only way to redistribute population. South Sulawesi's Bugis have been crossing the strait between the islands in cultural waves for nearly five centuries. Now settled in East Kalimantan near Banjarmasin and Samarinda, the Bugis are often joined by more relatives and friends who also arrive in search of a more adventurous and profitable existence.

However in government-sponsored transmigration programmes, East Kalimantan has absorbed only a small

Administering to rid a villager of her ills.

amount of the country's targeted goal of movement.

Besides smoothing out the population distribution, economic factors have since come to play in transmigration schemes. Developing untapped land and resources through careful, environment-conscious plans could be the solution that links cultural preservation with economic profit and a better life in these traditionally hidden areas.

Modern Mining

However, as the rumours of resources within these remote lands spread throughout trading circles, myths quickly evaporated into modern quests for money in many of these forest areas.

Starting with the Dutch, Kalimantan's wealth was discovered in the southern and eastern hills, where coal mining efforts split the surface of the land as early as the 1840s. Soon afterwards, the well-known Shell Transport & Trading Company was formed in London to begin the drilling of oil. Expansion by way of a 1907 merger with the Royal Dutch Company for the Exploitation of Petroleum Sources in the Netherlands Indies led to the formation of the new Royal Dutch Shell, a business whose power drew "black gold" resources from North America through Europe and Southeast Asia. Balikpapan is now the main centre for this lucrative industry, although the ports of Pontianak and Banjarmasin are equally important in the centralization of production for the earth's liquid riches.

From the land, Kalimantan's diamonds are world-renowned, and the mines are one of the main attractions to investors in the area. Semi-precious stones are also glittering attractions, as are metals of gold, brass, iron and the delicate silver for which the intricate *filigree* crafts are created througout the islands.

Agriculture & Orchids

The land especially in Kalimantan, is rich; rubber, copra, coffee and tin are all common produce.

Further afield, however, are the orchids of the upper islands. The prizes of the forest, these natural beauties grow wild throughout the jungles of Kalimantan, where more than 3,000 species wind through the shadows to add a hint of extra colour to the deep greens of plant life.

Particularly elusive is the *bualagna pandurata* (rare black orchid), whose subtle presence can be seen at the **Kersik Luway Reserve** of East Kalimantan. **Melak** which is also in the east, shelters an orchid forest of more than 5,000 acres – with nearly 30 species including the beautiful black orchids.

Kalimantan's western Ketapang regency holds the **Gunung Palung National Park** and the **Singkawang Nature Reserve**, where the unusual

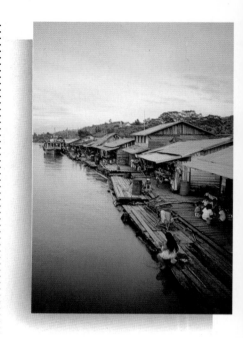

A typical floating village.

Rafflesia flower is found. Hectares of wild forest are also protected in the areas of Baning and Kelam in the Sintang regency, while the **Bentuang Karimun Nature Reserve** near Lake Sentarum is a quiet area for observing rainforest treasures.

Special Sporting Adventures

Kalimantan is the adventurer's fantasy; wild rivers, thick jungle, rugged mountains and hidden tribes can transport an explorer back in time. The Mahakam River is both for travel and rafting, depending on the traveller's willingness to take a chance on the waters. For trekking, the rich, trailless rainforest has

Candle dance performance by village girls.

Port Cities in Power

often turned an impulsive walk into disaster and many a well-planned journey into a rewarding memory of life at the very basic limits of endurance and knowledge.

The rapids of the Amandit River are quickly gaining fame with whitewater rafters, both for the beautiful scenery on its shores and the varying grades of danger that accommodate adventurers of whatever experiences. Starting at Meratus and travelling through Loksado to meet the rushing Barito River, this trip is a thrilling journey over the heartland of Kalimantan – made even more spine-tingling by the adventurous rubber rafts and bamboo boats used for the journey.

Oil has long been the slick base of the provinces' ports and towns; perhaps the most popular stopover being that of **Balikpapan**. At the edge of the central eastern coastline, this city is dominated by refineries and expatriate suburbs: the hub of the oil trade.

Because of its location, Balikpapan hardly has an "Indonesian" feel to it. Rather, the city is filled with familiar western automobiles, hotels and goods brought by those employed by the rich companies who use this city as their base for trade. Along the rugged walkways near the water's edge, enormous

Dragonflies, like many other insect life abound.

Shifting location of an oil well in Kalimantan.

An oil rig out at sea off Borneo.

tankers plunge through the straits between Japan, Southeast Asia, Indonesia, India and beyond. Cruise ships also make this port a common stopping point for passengers who want to take advantage of the modern products and services available here in the midst of a very Asian voyage.

Travel along the road for two hours and you will reach the quieter port of **Samarinda**, a well-known Mahakam River gateway to the interior, where timber is the main product. It is a city with a slight Muslim atmosphere, as the presence of the Islam-converted Banjar and Kutai cultures is clear, as is, oddly enough, a Chinese temple that reflects the influx of completely different traditions.

Its proximity to the rivers has given Samarinda a more visible industry for traditional cultures, seen in the various "cottage" or local artist crafts of nearby **Samarinda Seberang**. Here, the unique *doyo* (wraparounds) of the Tunjung Dayaks are woven from the leaves of the *doyo* tree. Also special to East Kalimantan are the beautiful Samarinda-style *sarongs* (wrap-around skirts) and ornaments whose colours and patterns reflect the cultures of the area.

The sounds of thousands of saws buzz through the sunlight from the huge mills around nearby **Tenggerong**, a canal town which was once the centre for the sultanate of Kutai. The tourist office here is not only place to find details on the nearby **Kutai Nature Re-**

Riverine domestic chores.

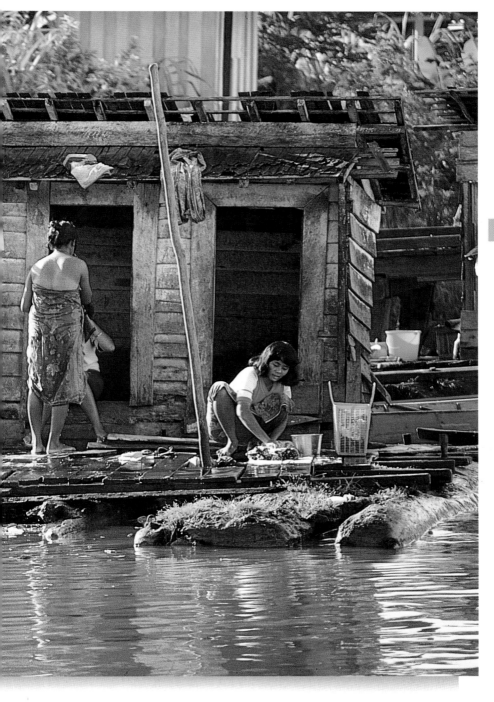

The wide-brimmed hat is typical worn to provide maximum shade.

serve, but also an ideal base for day trips to the wood-felling factories that offer one a unique understanding of the relationship between nature and the needs of the modern world.

South Kalimantan's most popular port is the "Venice of the East", or the intricate waterways which form the network of **Banjarmasin**.

Located on the Barito and Martapura rivers, this city is a hub for trading lumber, rattan, rubber, ironwood and meranti. *Pasar terapung* (floating markets), are a daily feature in the area between the Barito and Kuin rivers – get there early, as 5 am is the start of bargaining hours. Take a walk along the lines of houses and shops which sway along the wooden platforms of the float-

ing villages bobbing gently near the Trisakti harbour.

Just 45 kilometres away is **Cempaka**, a centre for diamonds and gold, where traditional digging is still accomplished with simple equipment –and the workers are neck-deep in sludge. **Martapura** is also a centre for crafts and jewellery, where it is common to find treasures such as uncut semi-precious gemstones, colourful beads and intricate silver creations.

West Kalimantan's capital city of **Pontianak** is the major port of the Kapuas river, where a mixture of modern life, beach resort and traditional cultures make this a curious mix of a variety of influences. The **Equator Monument** is an interesting site, as the

Helmeted hornbill, one of the several types of the hornbills to be found in Borneo.

city sits directly on the earth's dividing line. Another unique feature in Pontianak are the lively floating markets between the Kapuas and Landak bridges near the centre of town.

River Roads

Most international ports are based on ocean trade, but Kalimantan has the double blessing of being an island based on a network of rivers. Except for air travel, the rivers are the roads of the jungle, carrying goods, communication and passengers between forest and coastal areas.

East Kalimantan's cities of Banjarmasin and Samarinda are gateways to the interior, settled on the banks of the Kayan and Makaham Rivers. In South Kalimantan, "the province of a thousand rivers", the Barito River forms a wide major highway which extends up through Central Kalimantan with the Kahayan River, the other inland trade route. Finally, along the west coast from Pontianak's busy port are the lengthy Kapuas and Melawi waterways.

Along these rivers ply vessels of every shape and size imaginable, from sturdy, chugging ferries and sparkling speedboats to *taxi sunggai* (river taxi), battered houseboats and rough wooden dugouts manned by only one oarsman. Upon them goods are carried: petrol, animals and even relatives from other islands whose curiosity and longing have

Daily chores under the hot sun and a large hat.

led them to experience this lengthy jungle journey.

Entering the Central Areas

From Pontianak, there is a traditional longhouse at the village of **Saham**, where more than 250 Dayaks practice their traditional way of life. East Kalimantan is the gateway to the central areas where a true reflection of traditional tribal cultures is better seen and experienced.

In the eastern area, the settlement of **Tanjung Isuy** is an interesting place to begin your lesson in Dayak culture. Here, a longhouse of the Benuaq Dayaks has been opened for tourists, where it is not only possible to stay overnight, but to observe traditional dances, medicinal practices and music as well.

At **Muara Ancalong** and **Muara Wahuau**, traditional dances of the Kanyah Dayak are often performed, and crafts are sometimes available for viewing and purchase.

Along the Mahakam River, **Mancong** and **Muara Muntai** are two villages on the way to Lake Jempeng; longhouses are located close to both areas and usually offer tours and traditional entertainment. In fact, most villages along the riverbanks offer simple and friendly accommodation for visitors, making a leisurely trip up through the central areas an enjoyable and educational experience.

An afternoon breather for this camouflaged bird.

For the Mahakam River, **Melak** is usually the end of the line, although adventurers can travel further fairly easily with a bit of patience and bargaining.

The **Belayan River** trip to **Tabang** is a pretty journey made from Samarinda by longboat (three days). An unusual trip could be along the **Kayan River** to **Tarakan**, on the border of Sabah, Malaysia. Here, all sorts of vessels are available to ports throughout Indonesia and Malaysia.

The **Barito River** is a well-travelled route that takes tourists and traders all the way up from Banjarmasin through **Muara Teweh** in the central areas. From here, a two-week trek can lead to East Kalimantan's **Long Iram** village and then by boat again down the Mahakam to Samarinda. **Pangkalan Bun**, accessible by air or boat from Banjarmasin or Pontianak, is the start for journeys to the national park of Tanjung Puting and the Camp Leakey Orang-utan Research Centre.

In the western region, the **Kapuas River** – the country's longest – offers adventures for about 1,000 kilometres until its end at **Putussibau**. However before this, there are thousands of travel options branching off into the **Sintang** and **Melawai** rivers, through exciting river rapids and alongside great Dayak villages by simply jumping from boat to boat – allow lots of time, for the schedules are unpredictable ... but the total adventure is thoroughly worthwhile.

Bali

Before there was life there was Bali. Once believed to be the centre of the universe, a land of rare flowers and perfumed sky, Bali was banished from Java by legends older than time itself.

In the anger of a father casting away his mischievous son, a king led his young prince to the waters at the narrowest point of the land. As the son disappeared over the eastern horizon, the king drew his finger in a thin line across the sand ... and now the narrow, shallow strait between the two islands marks the permanent line of grief drawn between the two islands.

In truth, Bali was once connected to the land mass of Java but broke away during the plate movements of plate-tectonics. Still, to the Balinese, this tiny island is their only world, fringed by the northern Bali Sea and pock-marked by the dangerously volcanic **Gunung**

Bali always beckons a golden welcome.

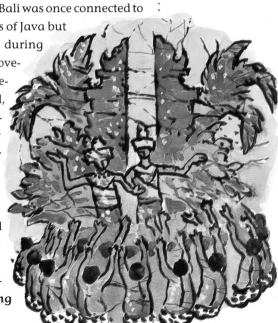

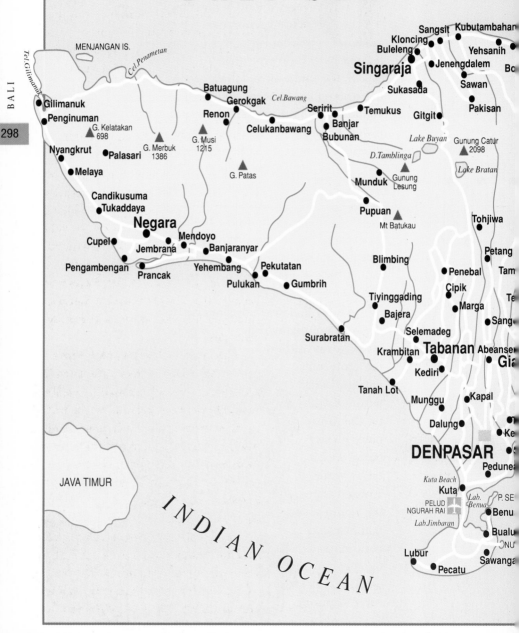

BALI SEA

MENJANGAN IS.

Cel.Penametan

Tel.Gilimanuk

Sangsit
Kubutambahan
Kloncing
Buleleng
Yehsanih
Singaraja
Jenengdalem
Bo
Sukasada
Sawan
Batuagung
Gerokgak
Cel.Bawang
Seririt
Temukus
Pakisan
Gilimanuk
Renon
Gitgit
Penginuman
Banjar
G. Kelatakan
Celukanbawang
Bubunan
698
Lake Buyan
Gunung Catur
G. Merbuk
G. Musi
2098
1386
1215
D.Tamblinga
Nyangkrut
Palasari
Lake Bratan
Melaya
G. Patas
Munduk
Gunung
Lesung
Candikusuma
Pupuan
Tohjiwa
Tukaddaya
Mt Batukau
Negara
Petang
Mendoyo
Cupel
Banjaranyar
Blimbing
Tam
Jembrana
Penebal
Pengambengan
Yehembang
Pekutatan
Cipik
Prancak
Te
Pulukan
Gumbrih
Tiyinggading
Marga
Bajera
Sang
Selemadeg
Surabratan
Tabanan
Abeanse
Krambitan
Gia
Kediri
Tanah Lot
Munggu
Kapal
Dalung
Ke
DENPASAR
S
Pedune
Kuta Beach
Kuta
Lab.
P. SE
PELUD
Benua
NGURAH RAI
Benu
Lab.Jimbaran
Bualu
NU
Lubur
Sawanga
Pecatu

JAVA TIMUR

INDIAN OCEAN

Bali

ula

N

Trunyan

BATUR
717

Kubu

Lake Batur

Culik ● Amed

Besakih G. AGUNG
3142

G. SERAYA
1174

sut Buyan

Budakeling

Selat Babandem ● Seraya

Rendang

ngli ● Sidemen Tenganan **Karangasem**

Selat Manggis **Amlapura**

● Sengkidu

ngkung Dawan *Lab.Amuk*

● Padang

Gunaksa *Tel.Padang*

● Kusamba

Negari

UNG STRAIT

NUSA LEMBONGAN

Jungbatu ● Toyapakeh

mbongan ● Sampalan

NUSA ● Sekti

CENINGAN Penida ● Tulad

NUSA
PENIDA

Agung, the sacred "Mother" volcano, otherwise known as the "navel of the world".

It is also the mythical land borne on the back of a giant turtle, and there it rests to float along within the universe. It is believed that when the turtle groans, the skies thunder, when it moves, the earth quakes; and when it cries, the rains fall.

Movements Across Time

The histories of Bali and Java have always been intertwined, embraced by similar cultures and religions that have only recently evolved of their own volition. Writings dating back to the nineth century have been recorded on the island, along with artefacts of metal and even the fields in which *sawah* (wet rice) traditions have slowly evolved over the centuries.

Two hundred years later, crownprince Airlangga brought the islands together while fleeing from raids on the Javanese kingdom in Surabaya. In fact, his father was a Balinese king while his mother was from Java, and when he went to reclaim the territory of his ancestors some decades later Airlangga established an undesirable link between these two islands.

Rulers of Java's Singasari dynasty and the Majapahit kingdom came and went throughout the years, although the violent ruler Kertanagara's dominance of Bali in the late 1200s led to

The old Royal Palace gate in Ubud.

more than 200 years of conflict between the two islands.

However, in the early 1300s, the Pejeng Dynasty near Ubud gained power under the mysterious supernaturally empowered leader Dalem Bedaulu, until Gajah Madas's Majapahit forces managed to regain dominance on the smaller island.

During Majapahit's rule of Java, the centre of Bali's kingly power moved from the Ubud area to Gelgel near Klungkung, while many artists emigrated over the straits to the smaller island. And, once again, Bali itself began to gain power, both in terms of land area and religion, as it took over Lombok and parts of Sumbawa, while expanding Balinese beliefs under the well-

known priest, Nirantha.

The Intrusion of the Europeans

At first, the Dutch Colonists were only interested in profit and trade; thus, Bali was left to expand its kingdoms alone and once again move its centre of power from Gelgel to Klungkung.

But, the Dutch eventually decided that they wanted to control Bali as well. So, they used the "divide and conquer" methods which had been successfully used in Java to coerce the Balinese into confusion and eventually submit to their power.

From the time they arrived in 1600 to the first actual battle that was fought in 1846, Dutch holdings had grown strong. The Dutch already had control of the north and a "reason" for conflict – arguments over salvaging Dutch shipwrecks in the north. They used this "reason"(though the Balinese were actually within their reef rights) as an excuse to land their troops on the island.

The infamous conflict between the Dutch and Balinese occurred in 1906 almost two years after the dispute of rights to the looted Chinese shipwreck off Sanur and the increase of Dutch forces. The threat of battle was imminent, and for the people of Badung it seemed hopeless, surrender was out of the question, as was capture and punishment. There was only one noble way out, that of a *puputan* (a royal, and suicidal, fight to the death).

It was an ominous day, the Balinese seemed fated and their hopes had slowly died. In Badung, Denpasar, Pemecutan, Tabanan and Klungkung, the Balinese marched out dressed in their finests only to be gunned down to their death.

More than 4,000 Balinese were murdered on that day, the aristocracy were eliminated and the Dutch took

The ancient parliament at Klungkung.

control of the island.

Although blessed with fertile lands and cheerful, friendly spirits, Bali has not been lucky; a decade later **Gunung Batur** exploded within the island's central mountains, with steam and lava swallowing the Lake Batur area causing the loss of thousands of homes, 2,500 temples and nearly 1,500 lives.

A rice farmer plows on in the traditional methods.

Just half a century later the sacred Gunung Agung exploded in an erup-

Temple Tales

Shrines and temples are the island's roads to the gods, avenues of worship and wishes through which the Balinese routinely express gratitude and requests for advice or forgiveness.

Each home in Bali has a *sanggah* (small house temple) in its yard. Shrines for the gods are sometimes made of stone, red brick, with black palm fibre and *alang-alang* (palm grass), although the increasing cost of materials has led to the popularization of concrete and zinc.

In fact, the housing compound is thought of as the body of a man, with the temple or shrine at the *kaja* (head), facing towards the direction of the mountains which are believed to be the home of the gods. Comprising the "navel" are the central rooms for sleeping and living, while the opening in the gate is the reproductive area and the kitchen and granaries form the legs. Facing the *kelod* (the direction of the sea and evil spirits), are the animal shelters such as pig styes and the places where rubbish is burned.

The Balinese also have a temple in the *sanggah gede* (mother yard), linked to the *pura batur* (ancestral temple). Within this ancestral temple is an important *kawitan* (family shrine), which is not only an expression of past heritage, but one of present being as well. It represents an identifiable mark which allows each Balinese to identify with a position and role in the family and in society.

The temples are always central to the life of a Balinese.

There are even more temples outside the family home — those of the village, three in all, each of differing significance and ceremony. In the centre of the *desa* (village) is the *puri desa* (village temple), with the *puri puseh* (navel temple), and *pura dalem* (temple of the dead) usually located nearby.

In the temple system, there is also a hierarchy of structures that are used for worship and ceremony throughout the Balinese year. Irrigation temples are found throughout the rice fields, while old regional temples are larger and more important than those of the village and family.

Most sacred of all, are the temples which encompass the whole of Bali, such as the stunning Besakih complex which stands in the central southern area of the island.

tion killing thousands of Balinese. Furthermore, after Suharto's takeover of the government, thousands more were killed in an anti-Communist purge.

Today, thousands more are lost to the flood of drugs and drinking that trample through Bali in the tourist season.

Bringing offerings to the sea.

Balinese Beauty

But, Bali is a gorgeous place; a glance at its lush terraces and forested mountains always turn into a gaze.

In fact, according to legend, Bali was a dry, barren island that stretched out into flat, humble plains. When Islamic influence overtook Java's kingdoms, the Hindu gods moved eastward to Bali, creating the mountains as their own lofty dwellings.

On Bali, there are four major mountains of which the highest is **Gunung Agung** (the place of honour) in the east with **Gunung Abang**, **Gunung Batukau** in the central region, **Gunung Batur** in the north and the smooth plateau of **Bukit Peninsula** to the south.

Gunung Batur is the subject of ancient Balinese stories, which centre around the helpful giant Kbo Iwo who assisted the villagers with their construction work as long as they could feed him until he was full. Being a giant, this was quite difficult for the villagers, so they tricked Kbo Iwo into digging a huge well – then, when he fell asleep, they rolled him in and buried him alive. The well water splashed out into **Lake Batur**, and the part of Kbo Iwo which sticks out of the top of the well is said to be Gunung Batur.

Now, Lake Batur is a peaceful place within the new ten-kilometre crater which it blesses with good irrigation, and village settlements are located only

A natural at Kuta Beach.

on the "safe" side of the waters. To see Batur in its full glory it is best to start in the early morning for an inspiring start to the day.

In the village of Batur itself greet the **Puru Ulun Daru Temple** through the morning mist. The temple once lay at the foot of the volcano but was destroyed by an eruption, only in 1927 did the brave people of the village lay the foundations for the temple to be rebuilt. The goal was to complete 285 shrines and work is nearing its completion. The temple contains a gold bell, presented by the king of the Singaraja dynasty.

At the top of the steep Bukit Jambul Hill is probably the most important temple in Bali, the incredible **Besakih temple** within the volcanic cone of Gunung

Agung. This is the holiest temple in Bali, the mother temple of all temples, and every year a pilgrimage is made to toss wealth and offerings into the fiery pit. Besakih is not just one temple but a series of approximately 30 temples within a complex in which nearly every god in Balinese religion is honoured. The temples are situated alongside the seven hillside terraces of the Gunung Agung volcano. Built around 1007, in the 15th century it was the state temple of the Gelgel-Klungkung dynasty. The temple is dedicated to Siwa the "destroyer" of the Hindu faith.

On the shores of Lake Batur lies the village of **Trunyan**, a delightful village with a Polynesian influence, the inhabitants are non-caste and claim to be Bali

Piled high with offerings, Balinese maidens make their way
to the village temple.

Aga (original Balinese). This is probably the only place in Bali where cremation is not practiced, the dead being left to disintegrate in a wired off field.

Just south of Lake Batur, a huge vista opens out from the village of **Penelokan** "the place to look". The panorama is beautiful, at the summit is the highest temple in Bali, **Pura Penusilan** from which you can see North Bali and the mountains of East Java.

Bali is an island of contrasts, where fertile rice fields give way to dry mountain peaks, and lush rainforest melts into rough grassy plains. Stories tell that on these plains is the legendary city of Pulaki, which was made invisible by the great Wahu Rahu of Java while fleeing the city Gelgel. He did this to save his daughter from the power of the kingdom's evil ruler.

Across the arid limestone peninsula of Tafelhoek, or **Bukit**, where cliffs rise from the sea to the fascinating **Temple of Ulu Watu**. Ulu Watu is one of the holiest temples in Bali.

The rocks on which the structure was built are believed to be the ship of the Dewi Danu, goddess of the waters, who was turned to stone in yet another Balinese legend. It was at this temple that the 16 century priest Nirartha attained *moksa* (a form of deliverance from this life).

Actually, despite the beauty of their coastline the Balinese actually dislike the sea, for their animistic religion imparts the belief that, as the gods are

Funerals are prepared with elaborate cremation pyres and ceremony.

sacred to the peaks of the mountains, malevolent spirits lie in the forests and lonely beaches. Thus are derived the tales of *Djero Gede Metjaling*, the fanged giant of Nusa Penida Island, and other demons who have inevitably led to a dislike for eating seafood or for swimming among the Balinese.

Be warned: do not go out after dark, either, for fear of the *leyaks* (mischievous spirits) who live under the banyan trees and have powers that can make human beings turn wild. However, it is good luck, to carry a *jim* (a little man who magically takes money from other people's pockets and puts it in your own pocket).

The island of **Nusa Penida** to the east of Denpasar in the Bandung Straits is the home of yet another monster, *Ratu Gede Macaling*, destroyer of evil and helper of the good. There is a temple, **Dalem Pentaan Peed** dedicated to Ratu Gede on the northern coast. Another large temple complex, **Pura Batu Medau**, also lies on the northern coast.

Geologically Nusa Penida is a rough and rocky place of a rectangular shape.

Terraced paddy fields beautify the Balinese landscapes.

The islands of **Nusa Ceningan** and **Nusa Lembongan** lie off Nusa Penida's north-west coast, the latter of which is extremely popular with surfers.

Accomodation at Nusa Penida is restricted to **Samplan**, again on the northern coast. Here there is a govern-ment resthouse, where rooms are avail-able for renting and a number of *warungs* (food-stalls), be warned this is not a luxury destination but the scenery makes it worthwhile. To reach Nusa Penida and Nusa Lembongan, take the ferry from Kusamba on mainland Bali, where

A celebration at Besakih, mother of temples.

boats exit regularly, a less frequent service can be taken from Kuta Beach.

Cycles of Life

The shining eyes of a Balinese child reflect the souls of their ancestors, whose spirits live through succeeding generations. This belief in an everlasting cycle of life that runs through all beings, is an indispensable concept in the Balinese belief system.

Within each person's mind and heart is not one but many souls, preserving the past, sharing the future and urging a respect for life and the gods.

The birth of a child marks a relative's return; the recurrence of an ancestral soul that again wishes for life. And so, the family will bind the baby to the earth, perhaps by finding the ancestor's identity through a *balian taksu* (medium). They will grant any wishes this soul might have so that unhappiness will not encourage it to leave the earth again.

On the baby's 105th day of life, it is brought to the shrine for the first time. On this day, ancestral wishes for special sacrifices or performances will be granted; but more importantly, the baby's status as a living being is confirmed at this time. Names of the child are given by his or her position of birth; in fact, only four titles are used by 95 percent of the population which are part of the common *sudra* (servant or

gods, which involves an intricate preparation of *jejaitan* (small palm-leaf strip baskets filled with delicate petals of flowers and incense). Other *banten* (offerings) to the spirits include *sesamuhan* (rice dough biscuits), moulded and carefully decorated with fruit, rice, coconuts, or bits of meat. They are often shaped into effigies of animals, plants or people.

Death and cremation do not end the cycle of life but simply continue it with a procession of bright noise and colour.

Wildly decorated funeral towers are built to carry the body, feasts and parades march merrily down the streets in a crazy, whirling procession to confuse the soul from returning to the world. The next of kin will then ritually bring the soul out to the sea, where it is believed to ascend to the mountains and the world of the ancestors.

Traditionally cremation is necessary to free the soul from its physical confines so that it may return to the realm of the gods or to the life of another child.

Tour of the Emerald Island

Temples are scattered all over the island; small shrines within homes and *losmen* (rooms to let) complexes, tucked into alleys, on the shelves of small *tokos* (stores selling goods), even on the rough gravel roadsides to appease the demons. Larger temples may charge an admis-

slave) class. Regardless of whether the child is a female or male, the first child is called "*Wayan*", the second "*Made*" the third "*Nyoman*" and the fourth "*Ketut*", then with the fifth child the cycle again begins with "*Wayan*". Thus, each Balinese shares his or her first name with more than a million others on the island – surnames, of course, are not the same.

Throughout life, each person has responsibilities to the self and society – and part of keeping the favour of the gods is to always act within the boundaries of religion and family life. Troubles are brought on only by neglect or defiance of duty, and *balian taksu* (mediums) are often used for consultations regarding sickness or disasters that one is unable to explain.

Everyday offerings are made to the

Blessed Beaches

Beauty by the beach.

Rumours abound about the decadence of **Kuta**'s southern stretch of beaches, where deep massages, drinking contests and nude sunbathing are all a standard part of a sun-lit afternoon.

True – do not be too shocked – but there is also a feeling of freedom here; a true escape from work and life's rigours where, not that you would want to ... but, you could do just about anything you like short of breaking the law; play until dawn, sleep in until noon, sunbathe in the nude with an early afternoon drink and a good, trashy novel. Then, at sundown, see a haunting performance of Balinese spirits before starting the cycle again until the end of the holiday.

Kuta is quite westernized, but it is cheap and fun, with decent western food for those who can not stomach the often spicy Indonesian palate. Inexpensive crafts and clothing are stuffed into the street shops. Pubs and hotels offer shortened cultural fare and standard cocktails – try finding these on any of the other Muslim islands! Modern facilities cater mostly to the backpacking crowd, although larger hotel chains do good business along the posh, more expensive beachfront areas.

Sanur is just a step up from Kuta, for those

sion fee of 100 to 1,000 rupiah or so depending on how well they can attract tourists. Proper attire is *always* required; no shorts or risqué tops, knees covered —

often a simple *sarong* (waist wraparound skirt) is provided.

South of Sanur, on **Serangan Island**, the shrines at **Pura Sakenan** (the

Macho surfer watching the waves.

who like a little more sanity, and an escape from the 24-hour craziness of the former tourist area. Across the bay are the quiet islands of **Nusa Penida** and **Nusa Lembongan**, where snorkelling and surfing are a nice change from the more popular areas.

The "newest" resort in Bali is **Nusa Dua**, the up-class hotel area of the "two islands" of the Bukit Peninsula close to the airport. Two hours west are the beaches of **Gilimanuk** and the national park of **Bali Barat**, while eastern journeys leave travellers on the shores of the pleasant **Padang Bai** harbour at the edge of the Lombok Strait, where colourful sailboats speckle the waters by day and candles sparkle behind the hills at night.

On the calmer north coast, are strings of black-sand beaches along the area surrounding **Singaraja**, where the calm waters host a brilliant array of colourful coral. **Yeh Sanih**, just 15 kilometres away, is an area of hot springs, bright gardens and fertile rice terraces leading to the village of **Tulumban**, with its excellent watersport facilities such as windsurfing, and snorkeling to the sunken WWII American *SS Liberty* ship sunk just 50 metres from the shore.

temple of Sakenan) can be seen ... as well as the large turtles fattened by the southern Balinese for feasts, which lend their name to this "Turtle Island". The turtles are eaten in such dishes as *sate* and *lawar*. For epicures, turtle eggs are recommended, best when fresh.

At low tide, it is easy to walk from

Whorls and convulations on the Bangli temple decorations.

Pura Tanah Lot, a place of frequent homage.

Benoa Harbour across the bay to view the *candi* (pyramidal shrines). Every year two festivals highlight the temple with huge *barong landung* (puppets) being one of the central ceremonial attractions.

Denpasar the capital and largest city in Bali means "north of the market", and it is indeed a bustling town. There are many things to see in this town which many tourists use as a base to exploring the whole island. Most tours start from **Puputan Square** named after the 1906 suicidal battle where many residents lost their lives. The main street **Jalan Gajah Mada** with yet more shops and restaurants and **Jalan Veteran** with its many handicraft shops are the places to buy your souvenirs.

Markets & More

The market of **Pasar Badung** sells assortments of wickerwork, fruits and vegetables provides opportunities for a real cultural experience. At the northwest corner of Puputan Square presides the **statue of the god Guru**, showing himself as master of north, south, east and west. Meanwhile in the **Kokar** (Conseavatory of Performing Arts) one can watch live dancing and the intriguing *gamelan* orchestra at practice. The **Werdi Budaya Art Centre** is on **Jalan Nusa Indah** and is the site for the annual Bali festival. The Denpasar shrine of Bali's supreme God Sanghyang Widi shines with white coral, its **Pura Jagatnatha** temple stands next to the Bali Museum in Denpasar. The temple is rather modern in appearance and contains statues of representations of the *naga* (serpents) and the famous *padasana* (throne), illustrating Sanghyang Widi's rule over the entire world. A short way down the road from the Pura Jagatnatha, is the **Bali Museum**, with its excellent collection of Balinese art ranging from prehistoric to contemporary times.

Puri Pemecuta, the former home of the raja of Bandung, was destroyed in

Gunung Batur at dawn.

the 1907 *puputan*, but has been rebuilt and is now a hotel designed in accordance with the former palace. Other hotels include the Natour Bali Hotel – which was built in the 1930s – the Artha, Dharma Wisata and Pendawa hotels.

Between Denpasar and Ubud is **Batubulan**, the centre of stone carvings where many of the island's scowling yet friendly-faced temple "guardians" are carved. Batubulan is

Lake Bratan.

also the centre of the colourful but somewhat gaudy spectacle of the *barong* dance. *Barong* means tall and this refers to the tallness of the puppets which are ornately attired. The puppets are believed to have special powers to exorcize evil and are kept for sacred reasons inside the temple complex.

Nearby is **Puri Puseh**, and the Pura Gaduh **temple of Blahbatuh**, which is believed to date from before the time of the Javanese on Bali and contains a representation of Kebo Iwa; the last king of the Bedulu empire who was eventually killed by Gajah Mada of the Majapahit kingdom. The hilltop **Pura Bukit Dharma** temple is between Kutri and Klungkung ... and a wander through the Ubud hillsides will take you

Ramayana artfully expressed on wood.

to hundreds of crumbled relics of ancient times.

Culture Around Every Corner

Just a few kilometres north of Batubulan, the small town of **Celcuk** is the centre for the silver trade. Here you can loiter in the streets watching silversmiths fashioning their trade. The unique elegant filagree style is an excellent buy here. Continuing north you will reach the small town of **Sukawati**, whose *wayang kulit* (puppet shows) are renowned throughout Bali. **Mas**, is famous for its woodcarvings made known internationally by the great carver, Illa Bagus Tilem.

A typical Balinese stone carved god.

Garuda-winged lion carved into the elaborate door panels.

Goa Gajah is the "elephant cave" on the road to Gianyar, a Hindu-Buddhist temple area with several open structures, bathing pools and flowing fountains. The atmosphere outside is peaceful, one of holiness and worship, while inside the small cave it is surprisingly humid and dry.

Beyond the main complex is a lovely stream that bubbles under a wooden bridge, and further on are steep stone steps leading to another complex and a large, lily-covered pond. For this popular tourist attraction, dress properly; otherwise, *sarongs* (waist wrap-around skirt) are available for rental at the door.

Yeh Pulu is a beautiful hill area filled with rock carvings and relics just a

The remainder of Arjuna painted by Bonnet, at the Neka Museum.

kilometre or so from Goa Gajah. Continuing northwards, **Bedulu** village marks the former site of the powerful Dalem Bedulu the last king of the Pejeng dynasty who were eventually defeated by Java's Gajah Mada in 1340s.

Still further along the road is **Pura Kebo Edan**, otherwise known as the "crazy buffalo" temple where a statue of Bima (one of the five Pandawa brothers of the **Mahabharata** epic) is particularly well-endowed.

The **Pura Penataran Sasih** temple is in nearby **Pejeng**, the resting place of the great bronze drum known as the "Moon of Pejeng" which according to legend fell to earth in an explosion when a group of thieves tried to put out its light. The drum is the largest drum in the world and dates from the bronze

Vivid painting of a dancer.

The drama of the Ramayana story is performed frequently for visitors.

Barong dancer with a "kris".

A Gamelan band.

The Balinese remain devoted to their beliefs in gods and spirits.

age. Also in Pejeng visit the **Archaeological Museum** which contains some 14th century Hindu antiquities.

At the great crater of **Gunung Kawi** is Bali's oldest and largest structure of worship, smack in the middle of the fertile volcanic valley. The temple dates back to AD1150 and contains royal tombs, a hermitage and monastry. Ten *candis* (shrines) are scattered in the area, supposedly carved out from the land by the powerful ruler Kebo Iwa. It is not quite clear which kings are honoured here but this area is right at the heart of the ancient Pejeng kingdom.

Further up the road are the temple and holy springs of **Tirta Empul** which are believed to have the power of immortality.

More Temples

Just before you reach the beautiful Besakih temple is the town of **Klungkung**, the former seat of Bali's most powerful dynasty, the Gelgel kingdom. Special 500-year-old Kamasan paintings, unique *wayang* (leather) puppets and original architectural styles distinguish this area from the rest of the island. A visit to the **Kerta Gosa Hall of Justice** and the adjacent **Floating Palace**, or Bale Kambang, is well worthwhile. The Kerta is an excellent example of the Klungkung style of painting and architecture.

Goa Lawah is a large bat cave just beyond Kusamba, the tunnels of which

Buffalo racing, a dusty sport in Makepung.

Children's Day in Denpasar, the capital city.

Horse carriages provide taxi-rides in Denpasar city.

Street life in the city.

are said to lead all the way to Besakih Temple. Rounding the road through Amlapura to the end of the eastern road lies **Puri Agung Karangasem**, the palace of the 17th-century Karangasem kingdom, and the **Water Palace of Tirta Gangga** which has a public swimming pool.

Near Bangli (capital of a kingdom descended from the early Gelgel dynasty) is the state temple of **Pura Kehen** (the temple of the dead), Bali's second-largest temple which contains a collection of historical records inscribed on bronze plates. The **Pura Dalem Penuggekan** (temple of the dead) also on the way to Gianyar is a fine example of its kind. From here, the great Besakih temple and the Gunung Agung volcano area are both accessible, and there are several small and clean *losmen* (rooms to let) in the Bangli-Kintamani area close by.

In south-west Bali at the crossroads of Kediri a small track leading to the sea will bring you to the **Temple of Tanah Lot**, the beautiful temple of postcard fame. Here dusk and dawn reign equally in a beautiful setting. Also in the area are the beautifully sculptured temples of **Pura Sadat** (in Kapal) which honours the spirit of Ratu Sakti Jayengrati and **Pura Dalam** (in Lukluk) where there are excellent examples of detailed sculpture, as well as Mengwi's **Pura Taman Ayun** which was built for the Mengwi principality in 1634 as a broken branch from the Gelgel kingdom.

Natural Wonders

It is a gentle, fertile heartland where **Gunung Agung** and the smooth crater surface of **Lake Batur** encircle the chilly "Abode of the Gods". Along the roads and settled back into the hills, the misty villages of **Batur** and **Kintamani** flow over the landscape, colourful markets and temples splashing the moody landscape with brightness.

Gunung Agung the "navel of the world" is the home of the deities worshipped at the holy temple of Pura Besakih. In 1963 the gods expressed their anger at some offence in an awesome eruption killing hundreds of the local inhabitants after being dormant for several centurie. Many contemporary people saw this eruption as an apocalyptic sign.

At the lofty village of Penulisan a bend in the road leads to **Pura Tegeh Koripan**, which at 1,745 metres is Bali's highest temple, with sweeping views out to the coast of the island.

From the village of **Kedisan** and the **Tirtha** hot springs, several trails wind up the slopes of **Gunung Batur** all the way to the rim – and even into the crater. Nestled along the shore of **Lake Batur**, Kedisan is a lovely little village from which you can hire a boat to the hot springs before ascending the mountain summit. Along the eastern ridge, **Gunung Bratan** is a quicker climb through lush rice paddies, waterfalls and orchid gardens to a quiet lake where the temple of **Ulu Danu**, dedicated to *Dewi Danu* the goddess of the waters, rests on a small offshore island.

To the west is the "coconut shell" of **Gunung Batukau** and **Gunung Pura Luhur**, where the state temple of Tabanan and shrines for the lakes **Bratan**, **Buyan** and **Tamblingan** are hidden within the mountain slopes.

On Bali's east coast, just a few kilometres from the ferry port of Gilimanuk, the **Bali Barat National Park** is a natural area shelter for the rare *jalak putih* (Bali Starling). Also known as the "Rothchild's Mynah", this rare bird is part of a breeding program administered by international zoos and the PHPA (Directorate General of Forest Conservation Park) office in Cekik – from where you can pick up a permit to visit the area. Macaques play merrily along the smooth road leading into the park, and hiking the trails will lead to sightings of wild pigs, deer, buffalo and many species of colourful forest birds.

Crafts & Culture

If you can head into the city of Denpasar, it is a good chance for you to gain an invaluable overview of Balinese culture, starting at the series of buildings and courtyards comprising the **Bali Museum** and its **Pura Jagatnatha** temple, dedicated to Sanghyang Widi, the highest god. For a look at the various performing arts, head for **Kokar**, (the Conservatory of the Performing Arts) and the **Academy of Indonesian Dance** located at the same site.

The arts complex of **Abiankapas** in east Denpasar holds exhibitions of woodcarvings, paintings and dance, while the **Sanggraha Kriya Hasta** art centre and shop in Tohpati near Sanur offers a fascinating display of imaginative island offerings.

Once the centre of power for the Dutch and the islands of Nusa Tenggara, **Singaraja** is both a centre for island culture and the silverwork trade. Particularly interesting is the **Gedong Kirtya** historical library, which protects Balinese *lontar* (Palm leaf writings) some of which date to more than 3,000 years old.

Also head to Celuk for silver. Here, you can watch artists at work and buy excellent quality jewellery – do not believe the "Japanese" prices on the items as they are for quick shoppers; start the bargaining at one-third of that price.

Mas is the woodcarving centre, where carved wooden pillars and statues scent the area with sandalwood and teak, while the sound of chisels and hammers chip away happily into the day. For smooth, intricate carvings of stone, **Batubulan** is the place where it is most popularly made. You will know that you're near the area by the statues lined up along the roadside. *Batu* means "stone," and *bulan* signifies "month," or "moon." This is an area where the spirits are especially strong as faces of good and evil are carefully honed from hunks of sandstone and other materials for the use of temples and homes around the island.

Cool & Quiet Ubud

And, of course, there is cool, quiet **Ubud** the peaceful home of painters, where soft colours and images of the new "Young Artist" styles mix with the splashy battle and life scenes that dominate traditional works. Many famous artists have emigrated to this area from Europe, Australia and America; much like one of the western art centres, this relaxing, creative town is a pleasant escape from the noisy beach areas.

Ubud is affectionately known as the "Paris of the East", the side walk cafés and art shops rather reminiscent of Montmartre. You can visit the homes of Walter Spies and Rudolf Bonnet and the galleries in the homes of contemporary Hans Snel and Antonio Blanco, where you may even here their personal anecdotes of time gone by.

On the road heading west after the Camuan Bridge, visit the **Neka Museum** a must for all lovers of Balinese, Indonesian and European art. For a better selection of pure Balinese art, head for the **Pura Lukisan Museum**, in its beautiful hilltop surroundings it is supremely informative, detailing the progress of modern Balinese art movements.

As an important cultural and tourist centre, Ubud has no shortage of places to stay, ranging from the pricey Amandari Hotel to the budget Melati Cottage. **Hans Snel's Garden** and the **Café Lotus** are two popular day places to lounge away an afternoon under the hot sun.

Southern Bali

Besides spirits and temples, the southern towns of Bali have very much to offer. Denpasar, Kuta and Sanur, have grown into world famous resorts, much to the surprise of the locals who along with other Indonesiam nationals gather to watch the spectacle of "beach fun" and also to make good capital out of the tourist trade.

To control the influence of tourism in Bali, the government has limited hotel centres to the south; at Denpasar, Sanur, Kuta and Nusa Dua on the Bukit peninsula. According to Balinese legend evil spirits reside in these coastal areas whereas benevolent spirits watch over the interior land. The ideas of "beach resorts" are thus rather novel to the Balinese who traditionally have always detached themselves from this dangerous realm.

Infamous Kuta Beach

In **Kuta**, the goddess of the sea, is supposed to claim one victim a year on **Kuta Beach** which may vindicate the local's fear. However the stakes to be made selling *sarongs* and cold drinks on the beach to rich expatriates and holidaymakers are just too good for these poor people to avoid.

Kuta, which is famous for its excellent surfing area, hotels, beach and western holiday life, was inaugurated as a resort by Keful Tantri, an Englishwoman who built a house on Kuta Beach which she called Kuta Beach Hotel. This hotel had few guests and it was not really until the 1960's that beach life really took off. At this point the locals began to cash in and opened up their own homes "Bed & Breakfast" style. Nowadays beach life has become a tradition and Kuta is one of the world's most popular resorts. This is evidenced by the presence of a number of large hotels which include Kartika, Plaza Bali and the Oberoi. The beautiful sea's water remains warm after dusk encouraging the all night parties which are so popular with western tourists. Beer gardens and western restaurants selling "soul" food are extremely popular here. However, local culture is heavily promoted in the hundreds of boutiques (many selling Balinese beachware) that line the streets. Nightlife is also hot here with nightmarkets, discos, bars and restaurants. Kuta has the added advantage of being situated near the airport.

Scintillating Sanur

Sanur, a few kilometres north from Kuta, is a city famous for its painters and orchestras. Two popular attractions are the *Arja* (opera of courtly romances) and *wayang kulit* (puppet) shows. Rather similar to Ubud, Sanur has throughout the twentieth century become a focus for the development of art.

Le Mayeur a Belgian artist came to live here nurturing the influence of western techniques in Sanur, his house which has been taken over by the Indonesian government is now open to the public. There are a large number of hotels here but due to a government ruling that no hotel can be higher than a coconut palm the hotels are less obtrusive than in other resorts. The largest hotels here are the Hotel Bali Beach with its Bali Seaside Cottage Wing, the Bali Hyatt and the Sanur Beach. Sites include a spectacular coral pyramid in the sea and a selection of nightclubs.

Magic of the Island

Wherever you are in Bali, remember the belief that the spirits are watching, waiting, lurking in the mountain folds and shadows of the night.

These spirits are integrated into the life of the Balinese people, and to be aware of this important aspect is to have an understanding their way of life.

There are good spirits, who will entrance you with the beauty of the island landscape, and place you in awe of the mountains and power of the sea. They will introduce you to the Balinese people, to their special way of life, and give you a glimpse of the frightening netherworld in fiery dances and wild musical interludes.

One is to believe that they will guide you about the island in a leisurely way, showing you the importance of pleasure, of letting time linger, and of the close bonds between past and future of families and friends.

An understanding of its history will give tremendous insight into the culture on the island and the practices and psyche of its people. As Bali is physically beautiful so the Balinese are gentle and warm...enough to leave one with a special feeling for the island that endures long after a visit, and perhaps to lure one back again.

Travel east through Indonesia ... through the crowded traffic and temple splendour of Java ... through Bali's incense-perfumed Hindu magic and mystery ... over the windy Lombok Strait ...... and you will find the legendary islands of Nusa Tenggara.

It is a far different world from that of the west, for the Nusa Tenggara (southeast islands) are the dry, parched counterparts of modern Indonesia whose dusty soil and rugged hills make evident their position across the Asian-Australian flora and fauna division of the Wallace Line. Here, there is a deeper, more solemn beauty; Gunung Rinjani a towering silhouette standing at the edge of the horizon, the gem-coloured jewels of Keli Mutu's crater lakes, the slithering dragons of Komodo, or the stunning *ikat* cloth patterns woven throughout history.

Little English is spoken here, and *Bahasa Indonesia* is often the second language to more common dialects that flit through market conversations. Cus-

A Lombok man is happy to welcome a visitor, though not always in English.

Nusa Tenggara

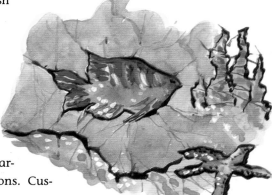

Lombok

N

LOMBOK STRAIT

to Bali (Lembar-Padangbai)

Amburamb

Tanjung

Gili Air Is.

Trawangan Is.

Pamenang

L O

Pusuk

Batu Bolong

Lingsar   Surana

Ampenan   Cakranegara

Mataram   Narmada

Pagutan

Sukarare

G. Pengsong

Pujung

Praya

Lembar

Labuhanpon

Plambi

Se

Batugendang
Pt.

Blongas

Sara Pt.

Bayan

Sajang

Lawang Is.

Sulat Is.

Lake
ura
Anak

G. Rinjani
▲3726

Sembulan

Panjang Is.

M B O K

Sapit

to Sumbawa
(Labuhan Lombok-Alas)

Labuan
Lombok

Belang Is.

Tetebatu

Pringgabaya

ALAS

Kotaraja

Masbagik

Kopang

STRAIT

Tapir Beru

SA TENGGARA BARAT

Labuhanhaji

Genti

Balat
Pt.

Tallwang

Jareweh

Sunut

Ringgit
Pt.

ngkulan
Pt.

Amat
Pt.

Sumbawa

toms here are more strict, but the culture more friendly, more caring than the other islands of the archipelago.

There are smiles all round in the shops and street stands and inquisitive grins and shy greetings that turn a stranger into an immediate friend.

Each one of the main islands are surprisingly different, both in traditional practices, culture and religion. Lombok and Sumbawa, just a stone's throw from Hindu Bali, retain the feel of West Java's strong Islamic faith. Komodo, Timor and Sumba shelter a mix of religions and animism, whilst Flores and Roti profess strong Christian and Catholic beliefs.

Sharing the Past

Without the scent of spices to lure traders from the west, Nusa Tenggara remained a string of lonely islands throughout most of Indonesia's history.

A few cultures wandered their way across the wide straits. The rugged terrain did not help; Lombok's lush, grassy palm forests and plains tumbled into the steep cliffs of Sumbawa and Flores' winding mountain trails were overgrown with petals.

Some civilizations spread out along the coastlines in villages like Bima, Sape, Labuhanbajo and Maumere, while others dared to cross the mountains to settle in the cooler plains.

Javanese traders were probably among the first outsiders to reach the islands, and it was Sumbawa and Sumba which they touched –- probably in the form of the Majapahit empire. Various agricultural advances may have been introduced at this time, but most significant was the advent of by Islam with the arrival of Sulawesi's Makassarese, who took over these islands in the mid-16th century.

In Lombok, both Hindu and Muslim influence surround Mataram, the capital of Nusa Tenggara, where Bali's crown prince Karang Asem resided at the beginning of the 18th century. Later, this Lombok town merged with the nearby port of Ampenan on the island's western coast to form Cakranegara, the province's largest modern-day settlement .

The temple **Pura Lingsar** between Cakra and Narmada reflects both Hinduism and Islam; built in 1714, it is a reminder of peace between Bali's Hindu cultures and the Sasak peoples settled on Lombok island. Eleven kilometres east of Mataram, King Karang Asem's **Taman Narmada** (temple gardens), were constructed c. 1727 as a place of worship to the god Shiva – legend has it that Narmada represents Gunung Rinjani and its crater lake, Segara Anakan, to which an annual pilgrimage is made up the mountainside to the gods who are appeased by throwing offerings of valuables into the waters.

At the end of the century, the West arrived in the form of the Dutch, who decided that although no riches could be reaped from the land it might be a good idea to set up trading posts. These posts were seldom used, until pirate activity precipitated further action in the area.

However, pirates were not the only spur beneath the Dutch saddle, for in the early 1800s the greedy race for colonization was rapidly heating the trading routes. Early conflicts with the nearby Balinese were further heightened over accusations of sabotaging offshore shipwrecks. Thus resulting in the Dutch attack on Bali in the mid-1800s.

The Balinese enjoyed dominant status over their eastern neighbors, as technically they had inherited control of Lombok from Sumbawa. Fighting continued between Bali and Sumbawa until nearly 1815, when Gunung Tambora erupted and wiped out most of the population and agriculture on the latter island.

As for Lombok, the island was eventually separated into four different kingdoms that maintained very different relations with ruling Bali. In the western areas, there was a peaceful blending of culture and religion between the Balinese and the local Sasak people, but in the east constant friction led to a flickering status of control that left Lombok with little power.

Unhappy with the Balinese rulership, the residents of Lombok conveniently looked to the Dutch for assistance when the time came to rebel in 1891. Seizing the opportunity, the Dutch sent out troops to conquer Bali, then in a sly move, added Lombok to their cache as well.

This was the time of the Balinese *puputan* (suicidal fight to the death) with the Dutch, who were led by General Van der Vetter. The **Pura** (Temple) **Agung Gunung Sari** Temple, now stands on the Gunung Sari mountain to commemorate the heroic fight of the Balinese leader Anak Agung Nengah and those who died with him on November 22, 1894.

The next Dutch target was Flores, which they conceived as a possible site for the slave trade. The Dutch, however, found Flores' waters to be filled with sabotaged wrecks and a thriving Portuguese missionary establishment that involved thousands of Florinese.

In the mid-1800s, the Dutch sent several exploratory fleets to deal with the wrecks and the local cultures, but it was not until the early 1900s that the Dutch completely took over the island. In 1908, the Dutch held direct control over Sumbawa, as a result of their inter-

The frangipani leads the flora in Lombok.

vention in a potential war between the three conflicting western areas of the island.

Since the 1500s, the Portuguese had been in Timor and Sumba, where they were involved in the profitable sandalwood trade (especially on Timor). Neglected by the economically depressed Portuguese after WWI and caught between the Australians and the Japanese during WWII, Timor suffered from both severe poverty and violent guerrilla warfare.

When the Republic of Indonesia declared independence in 1945 the western half of Timor was swept under the realm of the archipelago's government, while the eastern half still remains in the hands of the Portuguese today – and

the fighting continues.

Fabric of the East

Images of the islands' histories have been captured within their woven cultures, and of the archipelago's traditional threads the *ikat* works of Nusa Tenggara are probably the best-known. Although the *ikats* executed on each island differ in terms of style and motif, the method is usually the same, involving the *ikatting* (knotting) of thin, naturally dyed hand-spun threads into an intricate design.

Usually, the robust threads used in *ikat* are spun from cotton, although now factory-made synthetics are often used

A rice farming community.

in the design. Threads are lightly dipped into the dyes to create softer hues, to achieve stronger colours – the thread has to be repeatedly reimmersed.

To create certain colours, dyes are created from the earth's natural hues; these include various minerals that add rich browns, bright indigo, sharp orange and yellows and deep shadows of grey to the patterns. The bark of the *kombu* tree is used to achieve the most valued rust colour used in the designs, while other unique shades are made by dipping the threads in a variety of colours. Throughout Nusa Tenggara, *ikat* fabrics can be found at markets and in family homes, in the forms of *sarongs* (waist wrap-around skirt), *parilonjong* (burial blankets), panels and most com-

monly the *selimut* (blanket). The best-known *ikats* come from Sumba and Flores, although each area has its own original pattern and motifs.

Lombok

Lombok is a very green land of rich lushness which is evident even on first sight. The air is moist and thick filled with the freshness of endless sea breezes and flashing summer storms that rejuvenate the thick flora of the island.

Paradise Found

If you push past Bali's frenzied tourist

The solemn stillness of Gunung Ringani, Lombok's great volcano.

trade, past the crowded beaches, busy roads and crowded shops, you may find part of Lombok lingering somewhere behind amidst the central hills and terraced rice fields.

Lombok is more untouched than Bali because of the influence of the latter on the tourist trade. It is a quieter place, a haven to escape the heated crowds and shopping pressures, where the greatest pleasure is to simply relax by the seaside and listen to the wind whipping through the long palm leaves.

On Lombok, the thick coastal rice

est peak: **Gunung Rinjani** which over-looks Nusa Tenggara at more than 3,700 metres in height. Hot springs and odd-shaped craters add a spiritual aura to the slopes, where each year thousands of Balinese make the *pekelan* (ceremonial pilgrimage) during the full moon to throw gifts of gold jewellery into the silent waters of the lake.

In between, nestled in the valleys, are the Sasak villages of **Sembalun Bumbung** and **Sembalun Lawang**, where the Hindu-Javanese heritage is hinted at and it is claimed that a Majapahit ruler is buried in the vicinity. Whatever the case, the area provides a cool retreat from the beaches and is a place where long walks and camp outings are the best ways to enjoy the incredible surrounding mountain scenery.

Bright coral reefs ring the islands offering many things to see beneath the seas; one of the most brilliant areas to view is around the area of the southern *gili* (islands). Crisp, white beaches mark **Gili Air**, the first of these flat, serene islands; **Gili Meno** and **Gili Trawangan** are just a wave's jump away by motorboat, and all offer peaceful ambience and perfect snorkeling or diving .

fields slope upwards into steep inner hills covered with what remains of the jungle rainforest on the eastern side of the Wallace Line. Fields of coffee, cloves, *kapok* (cotton) line the roadsides and valleys, as do crops of spicy *lombok* (chillies) which gave the island their name.

Just 80 kilometres wide, Lombok folds into the archipelago's second-high-

Sasaks and Wetu Telu

Born of Malay heritage, the Sasaks comprise more than 80 per cent of Lombok's population, adding a unique flavour of blended Islam and animism to the archipelago's culture.

In the early 17th century, records show that Sasak princes ruled the island's scattered kingdoms, which fought for power with the Makasarese of Sulawesi before eventually retaining control.

However, the Balinese entered the picture and four main kingdoms emerged from the fighting. The island of Mataram emerged dominant. During this time, the Sasaks siphoned Balinese Hinduism into their own culture, integrating the western island's festivals, shrines and agricultural techniques into their customs. Even the government changed with Balinese rule, as traditional village chiefs were eliminated and the *rajas* (aristocrats) of Bali were instead allowed to run the area.

For the most part, the Sasaks were a culture of the land, practicing agriculture that was interwoven with animist beliefs and spiritual worship. Most of them are currently congregated in the central and eastern areas closer to Islamic Sumbawa – officially, they are Muslim, but aspects of Balinese Hinduism and animism are closely interwoven with their faith.

One of the most interesting practices of the Sasaks is their *Wetu Telu* religion, which is found only on Lombok island. Centred on an interchanging and arguable trinity of beliefs – *wetu* (result) and *telu* (the three cardinal rules of life – obeying God, community leaders and parents) – could refer to Islam, Hinduism and animism, or thousands of alternative explanations of well-known religious triads.

Wetu Telu is centred in the local, unwritten customs, or codes of *adat* (customs), by which rites of marriage, ownership, death and so on are followed. And, those who are born into *wetu telu* must remain there; those who are not cannot covert, either. Like the Balinese, a caste system is also incorporated into this Sasak society, and violations of *adat*, known as *maliq*, are punishable by illness, bad fortune and even death.

Today, although Islam is the predominant religion of the Sasaks, about 30 per cent of the island follows the *Wetu Telu* religion – and some practices differ greatly from those practised in devout orthodox.

Muslim areas of other islands. For instance, the Sasaks do not observe the traditional Muslim fasting period of *Ramandan,* nor do they make the *haj* or *haji* (pilgrimage to Mecca) or pray five times a day or observe a pork taboo. In fact, with the exception of Bali, it is difficult to find pork on any of the other islands.

Blood Sports

Football it is not, but battle it certainly is, for on Lombok, one-to-one "blood sport" fighting is a popular form of physical entertainment.

Performed to the sound of the *gamelan* (percussion-type orchestra), the form of *peresehan* (fighting) takes place between two men, each one armed with a rattan stave. *Lanca* is another type of battle that instead uses the knees as weapons.

Beautifully costumed in colourful sashes and turbans that provide magical powers, the men go around, only with shields of buffalo hide for protection. If part of the costume falls off, it is immediately replaced, and the battle begins again.

But this first fight is just a simple demonstration; the crowd gets into the action as well, as staves are passed to onlookers, who are then chosen as future contestants. Three rounds is time enough for battle, which leaves the loser bleeding or exhausted. However, everyone winner and loser alike usually receives some sort of prize to compensate for gain or loss of pride.

Across the Island

Though small, Lombok is a fascinating island that is a blend of Balinese charm and Muslim moodiness. Temples, mosques, offerings and animistic art are all part of the fascinating sights, while the land itself is a stunning combination of the wild Asian tropics and rich rainforests settling southwards to dry, Australian desert-like plains.

Eastwards from Bali, the four-hour ferry ride leaves the docks at **Padangbai** to cross the shallow, choppy waves of the Lombok Strait. Dolphins often leap alongside as the vessel chugs through

the waters between low hills out to wider waters, Gunung Rinjani often casts a distant shadow on a clear day.

Closer to Lombok's port of Ampenan-Mataram, bamboo fishing platforms stand on thin stilts in the turquoise bay, bright sailboats often thread in and out of the surf beyond them and along the beaches. At the boundary of Lombok, small *bemos* (small covered vehicle) wait to whisk travellers down to the beaches or to the main minibus station at the city centre just a few kilometres away.

Just a note: **Ampenan** is the port, **Sweta** is the central bus station, **Mataram** is the administrative capital of the entire western Nusa Tenggara, and **Cakranegara** is the commercial centre. Better known as **Cakranegara**, the shopping area has a surprising number of Chinese faces. The Chinese first arrived as workers for the Dutch but remained to carry on successful business interests. The Balinese also make a noticeable presence in this area as well, but the available craftwork definitely belongs to Lombok.

Weaving factories at **Sukarare** south of Cakra make an interesting day trip, for they provide an insight into just how complicated the *ikat* process really is. Ampenan's Museum on Jalan Banjar Tiler Negara is full of intriguing masks and baskets that provide a basic idea of what might be worth purchasing in the markets.

Temples are common in the area's hills, including **Pura Meru**, the largest

Weaving in Lombok.

one on the island. Built in 1720, it is now located just off the main road and has three differernt courtyards, as well as more than 30 shrines situated inside. In June, a festival is held to celebrate the structure, which is supposedly a symbol of the universe commemorating the Hindu gods Brama, Shiva and Vishnu.

The Sea Temple of **Pura Segara** is just north of the Ampenan port, while the **Taman Narmada** pleasure gardens of King Anak Agung are 11 kilometres north of Mataram. Seven kilometres further on is **Pura Lingsar**, the Hindu-Muslim shrine that symbolizes the harmony of both religions and the peace between the islands of Bali and Lombok.

A mixture of religious influences can also be seen in the gardens of **Taman Mayura**, where statues and a large, shimmering pond covered with water lilies mark the place where the Balinese Royal Court once presided. Also known as the **Mayura Water Palace**, this structure built in 1744 is located in Cakra, just beyond the main market.

Best of the Beaches

Good things seem to come in threes for Lombok. First, there are the triad of villages of **Sengkol**, **Pujut** and **Rambitan** that line the road to Kuta Beach. These villages are valued for their traditional houses and cultures and quiet ways of life that have not yet been disturbed by the growing influence of tourism. **Kuta Beach** is nothing like Bali's resort of the same name; rather, this clean, deserted stretch of connecting bays is a lovely place to spend several days of nomadic retreat. It is also a special place for island festivities, as each year in February or March (the 19th day of the tenth month of the Sasak lunar calendar) when the Nyale fish come to the ocean's surface, young men and women compete in *pantun* (rhyming games), frolicking on the beach in a teasing effort at turning friendships into more serious commitments.

Facing the crimson sunset beyond Gunung Agung, just nine kilometres from Mataram is **Batu Bolong Beach** a beautiful sea bathing area. Here, a hollow rock provides a stunning view over the Lombok Strait to Bali – it is said that the temple here was built as a reminder of virgins who were once sacrificed at the site ... and of the sharks that still inhabit the waters! And then there is **Senggigi Beach** of travel brochure fame, just a kilometre or so up the road. A popular tourist retreat but nevertheless a lovely one, with unlimited snorkeling and diving opportunities around the offshore coral reefs.

Sumbawa

A shimmering crimson sunset behind and to the west; ahead a pale, full moon lights the rugged mountainous land. It is dusk and there is a brisk ocean breeze

In Sumbawa there is a blend of Balinese charm and moodiness.

... this is the day's last Lombok-Sumbawa ferry crossing.

It is a journey that takes just two hours across the channel to **Poto Tano**, where waiting *bemos* (small covered vehicle) swoop down for customers at the ferry port. Going east, it is best to bargain for bus tickets right on the ferry, as there is always "room for one more", usually at a greatly reduced price.

In western Sumbawa, the land could be mistaken for Lombok, as could the people themselves, who probably share the same heritage but crossed over the thin strait some years before. Now a quiet, reflective place, the island marks the beginning of "Outback" Indonesia, an area through which few outsiders pass and where customs have been

The Sasaks are a happy folk.

little affected by an unknown modern world.

A narrow, hilly road winds its way from the port to the village of **Taliwang**, a former vassal state of an ancient kingdom centred in the city of Sumbawa Besar. Nearby is **Lake Taliwang**, and the tiny sea settlement of **Potobatu**, where idyllic stretches of beach and hidden caves offer a quiet escape just a hop away from the busy western islands.

A second ferry port is **Labuan Alas**, *labuan* meaning "port" .and the word *alas* meaning "forest". A centre of timber trade and fishing villages raised from the water on stilts, this charming area is another of western Sumbawa's quiet hideaways where time is enriched by the simple ways of life.

Around the northern coastal road are the small towns of **Utan** and **Badas**, while above the shore lie the large **Pulau Moyo**. Surrounded by peaceful coral reefs and dotted with small, charming villages, two-thirds of this lovely natural area is a wildlife reserve in which the central mountain of Moyo slopes down to wide savannah and thin forest filled with wild pig, deer, cattle and brightly coloured bird life.

The main western town is **Sumbawa Besar**, or "big Sumbawa", which is the first introduction to the truly Muslim feeling of the island.

Formerly the seat of the Sumbawanese sultante, the **Dalem Loka**, or Sultan's Palace is a raised, ramshackle remnant of former days of glory which

A cemetery clearing in the forest.

was somewhat restored in the early 1980s. Also interesting is its imitation situated on Jalan Merdeka, where you will also find the government head-quarters for the western half of the is-land. However, Islam is not the only prominent religion in this city, as the **Pura Agung Girinatha** Balinese Hindu Temple and *banjar* near Jalan Yos Su-darso exemplify the differences in cus-tom.

Sumbawa Besar is a good spot for an overview of island artwork, best seen at the **Kantor Departemen Perindu-strian (Small Industries Department)**, on Jalan Garuda. Here, you'll find the beautiful *songket* (cloth interwoven with gold), also found in ceremonial shawls and *sarongs* (waist wrap-around skirt),

as well as other crafts offered for sale. Permits to visit the parks can be ob-tained at the PHPA Park Office located just down the street.

Surprising in their languid beauty, central Sumbawa's **Dompu Plains** spill out over the central island. Fringed by coral coastline and palm trees, they gently encircle the central mountains where **Gunung Tambora** looks over the mellow landscape that was once flooded with heated ash and steaming lava dur-ing one of the archipelago's largest erup-tions. Along the southern coast are some of the world's best surfing waves, and Australian sports camps are annually set up around the **Huu village** area.

In the highlands, the *Dou Donggo* (mountain people), have settled into

The ferry point from Sumba to Komodo.

the hills, speaking their own dialect and practising a mixture of animism, Islam and Christianity. Recognized by their black costumes, their culture is centred around the village of **Mbawa** in the southern part of Gunung Soromandi and *uma leme* (traditional houses) can

be seen along the Dompu-Bima road.

Cilacai is the village from which most trekkers begin the three-day **Gunung Tambora** climb. It is no longer a mean feat since the fantastic and disastrous 1815 explosion nearly melted the surrounding land. The ascent is stun-

is left of the great Bima sultanate. **Dara**, a village just two kilometres from town, is said to be the actual core of the kingdom, which was converted to Islam when overtaken by the Makassarese of Sulawesi in the early 17th century.

Now, Bima is very Islamic, and the people a bit more reserved than the Banda Aceh of Nusa Tenggara. This is also the island's port city, where *pelni* (ships) dock enroute to and from Lombok, Flores and other islands, while ferries to Komodo sometimes depart from the village of **Raba** a few kilometres further on.

However, for Komodo and Flores, the usual exit point is from **Pelabuhan Sape**, the busy docks of the port town of Sape on the eastern tip. Beautifully set in the surrounding hills of gold and green grass, the villages are decidedly Muslim and moody, with swirling clouds, gleaming Islamic domes and hidden graveyards tucked into small valleys, the pastel headstones always facing the direction of Mecca.

At night the town is active with food stalls lining the roads, special crafts created along front verandahs, while bell-fringed, horse-drawn carts known as **Ben-Hurs** (in reference to the Charlton Heston movie of the same name) clatter and jingle through the rough gravel *jalans* (walkways). It seems that everyone is a talented musician as young boys who are local guides by day strut through the streets strumming and singing lonely ballads throughout the darkness.

ning, leading up through ashen slopes to the 2,820-metre peak of the crater rim inside which is hidden a lovely lake. The surrounding panorama extends across the western horizon as far as Lombok's Gunung Rinjani.

Continuing on the northern road is the central city of **Bima**, where the former **Sultan's Palace** and **Museum** is all that

Komodo, land of the dragons.

Sape is also a centre for traditional threads. From below the shade of their raised wooden homes, women work patiently over long looms in the age-old *ikat* weaving process.

Small festivals stated here are fun to watch: the May onion-braiding cel-ebrations are only one of the pungent harvest parties, where the laughing and feasting that accompanies the work of the merry front-yard gatherings will often last until dawn.

Two kilometres east are the docks for the ferries; take a *Ben-Hur* (horse-

fishing boats or village *perahu* (sailing boats) from Kampung Komodo, which demand another 1,000 rupiah or so to get you from the bay to the docks at the park shoreline.

Flowers & Dragons

Riptides and whirlpools of the wild waters surrounding the island did not stop explorers from reaching Komodo – nor did the four-metre, 150-kilogramme lizards which lumber through the long grasses of the dry, lonely hills. Actually, Komodo is not such a desolate place now. It is more a day-trip for "dragon hunters" keen to see the gruesome weekly goat sacrifice or a pretty bay for posh boating parties to enjoy the sun. To really get a feel for the island, the best thing to do is stay there for a while.

Contrary to tourist gossip, there is plenty to do and see, for the island is a fascinating flora and fauna experience ripe for trekking and exploration. It is also a hangout for scientists, and visitors often get to bump into crews from the BBC, Japanese television, international zoos, nature publications, conservation organizations or America's Smithsonian Institution.

Upon arrival, travellers march up the long dock to the office of the PHPA, where each person registers for a permit with name, address, passport number and intended length of stay. Accommodation is inexpensive and clean, in huge wooden bungalows raised above ground

drawn cart) just for the thrill of the ride. Schedules often change so first check with locals before planning the trip; some ferries chug out the ten-hour journey to Labuhanbajo, Flores, without first stopping in Komodo Island. Those which usually leave around 8 am, twice a week, take about six hours – dropping passengers off mid-channel into ricketty

Nosing around, komodo dragons on the prowl.

just beyond the central grounds, where it is common to see deer and lizards by day, while wild pigs storm through the brush after dark – close your cabin doors, as they are often curious and might explore the interior in search of rubbish.

Below, a quiet restaurant serves filling, albeit bland Indonesian dishes. Bring your own food as a supplement or take the short, adventurous climb around the rocky corner of the island to Kampung Komodo (Komodo village). Komodo village is a tiny, picturesque fishing settlement of colourful boats and warped wooden homes raised on stilts from the sandy ground. Here are small *tokos* (stores) selling water, fried bananas, crackers and a few other basic items.

Beware, as you can only walk the coast at low tide, usually at mid-morning; rent a boat from one of the villagers and snorkle amongst the reefs before heading back to the park, before returning the vessel to the village the next day.

To sight the dragons, you will need a guide, who can be hired at negotiable prices and most can speak English, although ideally you should also have a basic knowledge of *Bahasa Indonesia,* or a good dictionary with you. Walks, through the arid rainforest or up over the longer, steep mountain trails for stunning views of the other side of the island are fairly easy.

If you are cheerful and friendly, your guide will be extremely helpful in relating island stories and legends as well as pointing out the vast variety of wildlife, from the enormous 10-centimetre spiders that string webs of gold across the path to the great lizards which lumber suddenly out of the bush and are pushed away by the neck with a forked walking stick.

Across the sandy trail it is two kilometres to the "dragons' lair" where the weekly goat sacrifice is made – an interesting but canned sort of show. It is mostly done to thrill the throng of daily tourists with the savage display of several dozen lizards tearing the animal (and sometimes one another) from limb to limb in a great pit that resembles an ancient Roman lion-fighting arena.

If you stay on the island, it is better to explore the area with a quiet group so that you can really observe the dragons without the pushiness for pictures and bloodthirsty cheers of the tourist crowd. Get to know a guide and you could walk the area with him at night – a thrilling, frightening trek that completely immerses the senses in the sounds, scents and feelings of the jungle wilds of Komodo.

The dragons are best seen in the dry, sunny seasons from May to September, athough mid-way through they mate and then remain hidden to guard their new eggs.

To move on to Flores, the fishing boat leaves around noon from the Komodo dock and waits, sometimes for hours, in the middle of the bay until the ferry arrives to pick up passengers to Labuhanbajo.

Flores

Shaped a bit like a long fish chasing after the prey of Komodo and Rinca, Flores is an island of sweet scents and soft sunlight with flowers overflowing the twisted mountain trails.

These are the two images that in fact define the island; the rugged mountains and the abundance of blooms. So difficult is the dry, grassy terrain that the road winds in a ribbon twice as long as the distance of the island, flowing through grey, balding mountains and over sheer cliffs that tumble down to lush rice fields and low forests, glimpses of wide coastlines and the blue ocean horizon can occasionally be seen over the edges.

From the west, the ferry arrives at the fishing village of **Labuhanbajo**, where colourful boats make easy passage for snorkeling expeditions to the surrounding reefs. Friendly faces, helpful young guides and an excellent English-speaking tourist office along the main road make a stay here quite pleasant, as does the availability of clean *losmen* (rooms to let) that are inexpensive and include breakfast, fresh goods are also available at the local market.

Travel in Flores can not be hurried, buses usually only run in the morning, and only for certain day jaunts, unlike the long Javan and Sumatran overnight cross-island hauls. As the road pushes eastwards, it rises up through the mountains along an exciting (and often terri-

Volcano Nusat in Flores.

fying) thin strip of highway on which two vehicles can barely pass one another, but often do. Best views are enjoyed while going east, sit on the left-hand side; do not under any circumstances sit here if you have a fear of heights, for often the bus clings to the curves with just centimetres left before sheer drop-offs that fall hundreds of metres through the treetops below.

Four hours from Labuhanbajo is the cool mountain town of **Ruteng**, heartland of the black *sarong*-wearing Manggarai hill peple. Although Christi-

on a boat for other coastal villages, or even other islands. Then, the road stretches leisurely through dormant volcanoes, plunging valleys and cool masses of clouds all the way to **Bajawa**, the small hill town that is central to the Ngada cuture.

Gunung Inerie

Fourteen active volcanoes line the landscape of Flores, and **Gunung Inerie**, near Bajawa, is one of them. For mountain explorations and day trips to the Ngada villages and tombs, Bajawa is a good base – as is **Bena**, the small village right at the base of the Inerie volcano.

There are around 60,000 Ngada people living in the Bajawa plateau area, identified by their *ngadhu* and *bhaga* structures of small, thatched-roof houses with three-metre, umbrella-like poles jutting up from them. The *ngadhu* (male) and *bhaga* (female) are representative of the continuing presence of ancestors, and their traditions are annually celebrated in a festival held around the end of the year in the village of Bena. Villages for viewing traditional houses, customs, buffalo sacrifices and beautiful *ikat* weaving include **Boawae**, **Langa**, **Wogo** and also **Soa** where there is also a good market and a short trek to an area of hot springs.

The town of **Ende** is one of the largest ports in Flores where large ships dock during trips to southern Sumba and Timor. A dry, dusty, heated area

anity has caught on throughout the island – about 85 per cent of the Florinese are Catholic – this area has a strong Muslim feel, and a beautiful setting at the base of formidable, mist-cloaked mountains.

Reo is a valley town at the banks of an estuary flowing out to the sea, and its port of **Kedindi** is a possible place to hop

Shipbuilding has been influenced by the Buginese.

seemingly dropped onto the coast at the foot of the **Io** and **Meja Volcanoes**, **Ende** is a "tailor city," with an abundance of woven crafts and excellent samples of *ikat*, as well as interesting hikes and pretty beaches on which to while away the hours if you are waiting for sea or land transportation to other islands of the archipelago.

Keli Mutu

Most visitors to Ende arrive enroute to or from **Keli Mutu**, the tri-coloured gems of crater lakes that lie 1,600 metres up the pine-forested slopes of the volcano by the same name. Cool and serene, this area is one of Indonesia's most beautiful attractions, especially by the crisp light of dawn – stay all day and watch the colours change with the sun.

Access to Keli Mutu is easy via Ende, but it is best to start from the closer village of **Moni** instead. If the weather lets you down, the lively market here provides cheer, and the nearby village of **Wolowona** provides an interesting glimpse of *ikat* weaving traditions.

Maumere and **Larantuka** are the eastern towns of the island, the first a popular port for ships to the upper islands of Moluccas, Sulawesi and Kalimantan, while the latter is a smaller fishing town where travellers often jump out to the straggling **Solor and Alor Archipelagos**. This area is excellent for watersports and a favourite of snorkellers and divers. Once a crossroads for trade with the Portuguese and Dutch, the Christian influence is strong and evident in the many crosses and Catholic churches about each town.

Animism can however still be found on Flores, a mysterious belief that is congruous with the beauty of the landscape and its people.

Timor

Despite the conflict among the Portuguese, the government and the settlements of the rest of Indonesia, the western half of Timor is open to travellers.

It resembles Australia; rocky and mountainous, dry and rough, with the high peaks of the central range standing more than 3,000 metres high. In the wet season, valleys are flooded and cool plateau are lush with bushland life. However, more often seen are the arid landscapes of eucalyptus and acacias shattered by cracked riverbeds.

Kupang is the main western city, popular with travellers from Australia due to the cheap flights from Darwin. Its citizens are a mix of every heritage from Dutch and Portuguese to Southeast Asian. The original tribe was the Helong, who now live in various villages on **Semau Island**; this is rather an entertaining tourist stop for the area, with beaches, hot springs and barbecues organized on day trips by local pubs and establishments.

A dry, hilly city of markets and crafts, **Kupang** is actually quite interesting for those who are able to stay several days. The **Museum NTT** on Jalan Perintis Kemerdekaan has informational displays on art and artefacts, while **Lasiana Beach** or **Monkey Island** are places for relaxing away the day. Lots of details about activities, the surrounding area and nearby islands are available from the main **Tourist Office** located on Jalan Sukarno.

Waterlilies blossom in Flores.

Soe

The road to **Soe** is like travelling through Australia's flat, western lands; cool hills, wide fields and dry, parched foliage make images of marsupials such as wallabies and kangaroos cross one's mind. On the way, the Camplong area holds some interesting possibilities for exploration – forests for hiking, caves for climbing and even a small, man-made lake for a refreshing pause along the journey.

Soe is a bit of an expatriate town, lined with traditional *loe* (bee-hive) houses. Crafts such as weaving and carpets are popular buys here, and two of the best village markets are found in the villages of **Niki Niki** and **Ayotupas**, about 30 kilometres away.

Atambua

At the border of East and West Timor is the town of **Atambua**. Take care, as

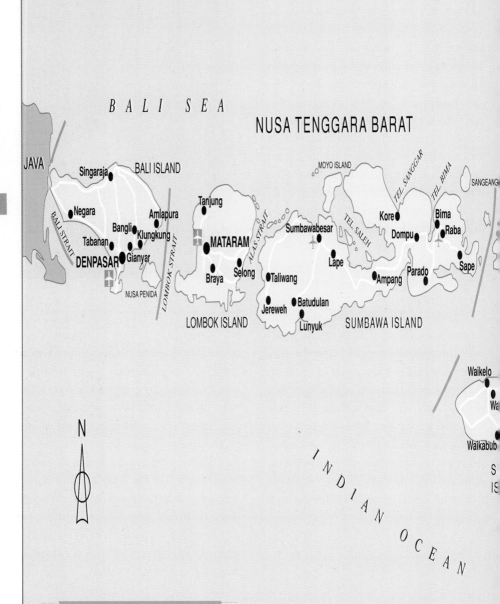

BALI SEA

NUSA TENGGARA BARAT

JAVA

Singaraja

BALI ISLAND

MOYO ISLAND

TEL. SANGGAR

SANGEANG

BALI STRAIT

Negara

Amlapura

Bangli

Klungkung

Tabanan

TEL. BIMA

Kore

Bima

Tanjung

Dompu

Raba

DENPASAR

Gianyar

LOMBOK STRAIT

MATARAM

ALAS STRAIT

Sumbawabesar

TEL. SALEH

Sape

NUSA PENIDA

Braya

Selong

Lape

Parado

Taliwang

Ampang

LOMBOK ISLAND

Jereweh

Batudulan

SUMBAWA ISLAND

Lunyuk

Waikelo

Wa

N

Waikabub

S
IS

I N D I A N   O C E A N

Nusa Tenggara

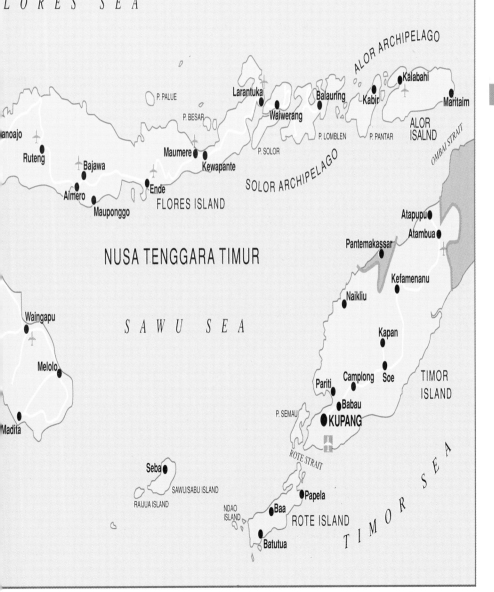

visitors usually can not venture much further than here.

Permits are rarely given (*do not* say you are a journalist, government official, communications personnel or anyone even remotely connected with the media or power).

But if you do get through by some stroke of luck (good or bad), Maliana and the coastal town of **Maubara** have decent accommodation and food, as well as battle relics that are a testament to the continuing violence in the area.

Once the Portuguese capital of Timor, **Dili** is a surprisingly modern town, but one where foreigners are eerily kept under the close watch of the military.

Continuing eastwards – passports are suddenly snatched and scrutinized at various checkpoints along the way – it is four hours to the hillside colonial town of **Baukau**, with its pleasant beaches and swimming areas at the base of the slopes, then onto the forts and palm forests of **Tutuala** and **Vikeke** ... if you dare go that far.

Roti & Sawu

Perhaps an adventure to the little-visited islands of **Roti** and **Sawu** would be an easier Timorese journey from Kupang. With their strong *jungitiu* (animistic beliefs), these islands hold dangers of the imagination more than physical fears and are perhaps a wiser gamble of time. You decide.

Sumba

Heading in from the west, Sumba's hills seem low and dry, a parched collection of shaven off shrubs and simple ripples of far-off gold across the wide ocean surface. This is a brilliant and mysterious island where patterns of *ikat* cloth are woven into images that linger somewhere between past history and unseen spirits. No one knows about the heritage of the Sumbanese. Perhaps they came by ladder from the heavens, or across the great seas by boat, in the form of the legendery ancestor *Umbu Walu Sasar*. Possibly Malaysian and Melanesian, the religion is *marapu* (a form of animism which centre around the spiritual forces of both the gods and the ancestors).

Traditional village homes are rectangular-shaped and thatch-roofed, raised one or two metres above the ground. Before building the homes, offerings are made to please those watching over the dwelling, and decorations of animal jaw bones and horns are hung above the doorways as reminders of past sacrifices to maintain a good relationship with the spirits.

Kateda (spirit stone), are found at the head of the village, near the entrance to discourage visitation from bad spirits. Village tombs, laid out in the central square, are also near the *kateda*, and in former days the *andung* (skull tree) from which the heads of slain enemies were hung could also be found here. Today the images are only seen in the designs made by *ikat* weaving.

Famous for its strong horses and beautiful blankets, Sumba is still not a popular place for visitors. Which makes it all the better, say the adventurous, who often spend weeks on the island exploring small towns, outer hills and beaches while indulging in a good dose of language practice. The usual port of entry is the town of Waingapu, located on the northern side of the island. By air, it is a quick leap from Kupang, or Denpasar. The port is popular for ships crossing between Timor, Flores, Lombok and the other southern islands.

Waingapu

By dawn, **Waingapu** is a charming town of wide eyed people and solemn smiles, where pink sunrises glow against the smooth silver bays surrounding the quiet town. Markets and blankets are popular fare, and there are several centres at which to watch *ikat* weavers at work, but one of the most entertaining options is to simply sit with the locals and talk about life on the island.

Bondokodi

At Sumba's western tip lies the small coastal town of **Bondokodi**; often known as just "Kodi," it is an area with lovely beaches and breathtaking tropical scenery. Tombs are an addition to the sand and surf around the area of **Anakalang**,

where you will find interesting local markets, tombs and the **Departemen Kebudayaan** (Cultural Department) at the village of Matakakeri. Also famous is the **Anakalang festival of Purung Takadonga**, the mass-marriage ceremony held during the full moon every other year.

West Sumba

West Sumba is also the site of the fascinating *Pasola* (ceremonial "battles") in which two horsemen duel until blood stains the field. Usually held around February or March, these contests are interwoven with the traditions of planting each season. The battles begin at dawn, the time of the arrival of the *nyale* (sea worm), which is believed to predict the bounty of the harvest.

Melolo, Baing & Nggongi

Travelling along the southeast road, buses wind through small villages with bright piles of thread lying out to dry in the sun, then through the hills and graveyards to **Melolo, Baing** and up across the rugged mountain roads to **Nggongi**. Tombs and weaving centres are the main features of easygoing Rende, which is about 70 kilometres from Waingapu. Further on, the villages of **Mangilli, Pau** and **Umabara** offer much of the same, with locals who are just as open and friendly!

I
t is a land shaped like a star, where coral-ringed coasts lead to stark, shocking central cliffs and lush rice paddies that lie in steep, staggered layers along the hills. A place where the largest animal is no bigger than a dog, where more than a hundred isolated offshore islands await paradise seekers and effigies of the dead stare out from the sheer rock walls in the middle of this island.

A hot, dry expanse of land that resembles Australia's rough inner ranges more than the lush rainforests which spread throughout the archipelago's lower islands. Yet, palm forests line the thin beaches around each point of the star, and thick groves of papaya and banana crowd the coastline all the way to the central mountains, where the shrubbery winds up and around the narrow, hair-pin curves of the mountains leading to the hidden sites of Sulawesi's

Sulawesi

359

■ ■ ■ ■ ■ ■ ■

Young man from North Sulawesi.

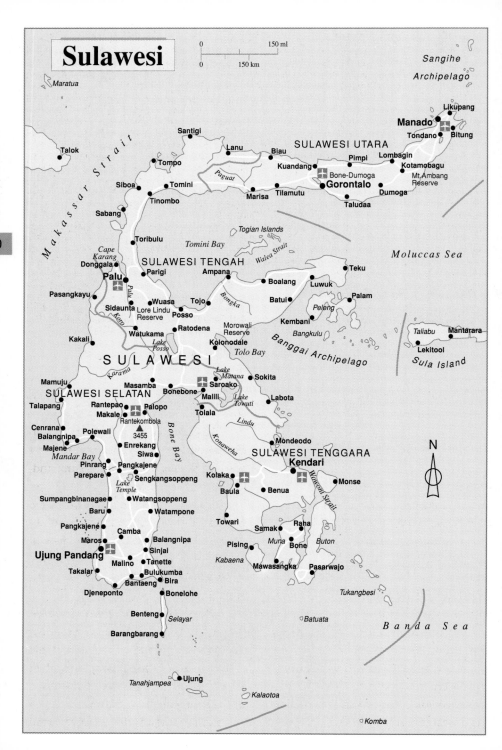

Sulawesi

0   150 ml

0   150 km

Maratua

Sangihe
Archipelago

Talok

Makassar Strait

Santigi

Tompo
Lanu
Biau

Siboa
Tomini

Tinombo
Paguat
Marisa
Tilamutu

Sabang

SULAWESI UTARA

Pimpi
Lombagin
Likupang

Manado
Tondano
Bitung

Kuandang
Bone-Dumoga
Kotamobagu

Gorontalo
Dumoga
Mt.Ambang
Reserve

Taludaa

Toribulu

Togian Islands

Tomini Bay

SULAWESI TENGAH

Walea Strait

Moluccas Sea

Cape Karang

Donggala
Palu
Parigi
Ampana
Teku

Pasangkayu
Boalang
Luwuk
Palam

Sidaunta
Wuasa
Tojo
Batui
Peleng

Pulu
Lore Lindu Reserve
Posso
Bongka

Kakali
Watukama
Ratodena
Kembani
Bangkulu

Morowali Reserve
Taliabu
Mantarara

Kona
Lake Posso
Kolonodale
Banggai Archipelago
Lekitool

Karama
SULAWESI
Tolo Bay
Sula Island

Mamuju
Lake Matana
Sokita

Masamba
Saroako
Bonebone

SULAWESI SELATAN
Malili
Labota

Talapang
Rantepao
Palopo
Lake Towuti

Cenrana
Makale
Tolala
Lindu

Balangnipa
Polewali
Rantekombola
▲
3455

Majene
Enrekang
Mondeodo

Mandar Bay
Siwa
SULAWESI TENGGARA

Pinrang
Pangkajene
Kendari

Parepare
Sengkangsoppeng
Kolaka
Monse

Lake Temple
Bone Bay
Baula
Benua

Sumpangbinanagae
Watangsoppeng

Baru
Watampone
Towari
Samak
Raha

Pangkajene
Camba
Pising
Bone
Buton

Maros
Balangnipa
Muna

Ujung Pandang
Sinjai
Kabaena
Mawasangka
Pasarwajo

Takalar
Malino
Tanette

Bantaeng
Bulukumba

Djeneponto
Bira

Bonelohe

Benteng
Selayar
Batuata

Barangbarang

Banda Sea

Tanahjampea
Ujung

Kalaotoa

Komba

N

Harvest over, bambooing being floated down river to be sold.

secret tribal ceremonies.

Sea Gypsies & Spices

Hidden corners and caves, open seas and wild waves ... these are the legendary haunts of the *orang laut* (sea gypsies) of Sulawesi, who were the Bugis and the Makassarese. Both races traversed the waters of the Indonesian archipelago for centuries, both to trade with the neighbouring islands and to plunder the passing ships carrying goods from India, Asia and Africa.

According to legend they may have come from the south to settle in the coastal regions; the Makassarese to the south-western arm of the star while the aggressive Bugis to the north through the Gulf of Bone.

Other stories tell of the Banjar boat-dwelling people who lived on their vessels in the seas and swamps surrounding the thin land areas.

However when the Bugis and the Makassarese arrived, they pushed other earlier cultures inland, namely the elusive Toraja tribes who now live in the heart of the star to the steep mountain territory.

Settled into the pockets of land between the vast central landscape, the Toraja tribes remained reclusive. Little is known about their past save for their fiery conflicts with the aggressive Bugis of the southern sea territories.

In fact, *toraja* is the Buginese word

Bamboo cutting in Toraja.

for "people of the mountains", and when not in conflict, the Bugis traded goods such as porcelain and textiles for the famous Toraja coffee.

For a time, the Javanese dynasties held power over the central area, as did the Sultanate of Ternate. In the early 1600s, the first Europeans (the Portuguese and the Spanish) wandered into the strangely shaped new island.

But, both were purged from the islands when the Dutch swept away the Ternate sultanate in the late 16th century.

Sulawesi's lush and unspoiled terrain.

Roundabout Religion

However, what the sultanate did leave behind, was a strong sense of Islam, which was soon tightly bound around the culture of the sea-faring tribes. At that time, the most powerful Makassarese kingdom of Gowa (where Ujung Pandang, formerly Makassar is today); was perhaps only rivaled by the Bugis eastern empire at Bone. During the mid-15th century, Gowa was the leader in trade and in battle, aggressively top-

After a padi harvest.

pling Bone just as the influence of Islam began to spread throughout the southern arm of the island.

Toraja's protective hideaways helped it escape traumatic adaptations to new customs – as did their natural enjoyment of pork and the notorious *tuak* (rice wine). However, the continuing flow of missionaries throughout the area during WW1 and WWII led to a majority of Christian followers, although strong beliefs in Islam and animism are still interwoven into the culture and there is strong protection of many ancient sacred burial customs.

To the north, the Minihasan tribes had already been the subject of Portuguese Franciscan attentions for nearly a century, while Jesuit priests were doing missionary work in the Sangir-Talaud islands. Christianity caught on in the Minihasa areas in particular, where in the early 1820s a group of Calvinist missionaries spread their influence throughout Moluccas and to Manado.

An interesting note is that this Western-based adaptation of culture led to an underlying comraderie with the

Sandy shores of south Sulawesi.

Dutch troops who were soon to arrive. In fact, the close identity with the Dutch led to the subtle isolation of the Minihasans from other cultures throughout the archipelago, who nicknamed them *anjing Belanda,* ("Dutch dogs") in derogatory reference to their willing col-

laboration with the Europeans, against the rest of the country.

Efforts Thwarted

During this time, the trade routes were

slick with swift shipping lanes that led north through the Philippines to the South Pacific and southwards all the way to Australia. Timor's sandalwood was a rich attraction, while Moluccas' spices kept sailing suitors close to the many Sulawesi coasts.

In the first decade of the 17th century, the Dutch found their way to the island, where they encountered strong opposition to their presence and forces. In fact, the kingdom of Gowa worked against them with other European powers to keep them from gaining a monopoly over the spice trade. However what Gowa did not count on, was a battle of protest from one of Sulawesi's greatest heroes, the Bugis prince Arung Palakka, who in 1660 marched more than 10,000 Bone Bugis into the territory.

Although the fight was bound to be unsuccessful, they quickly became allies of the crafty Dutch merchants, who granted them permission to settle into their port of Batavia (Jakarta) — and three years later encouraged them to return and rise against the Makassarese, resulting in the Bugis returning to power in the 1667 Treaty of Bungaya. Later, the Dutch made their way into Toraja-land, where they staunched the rebellion to take control of the central areas as well.

Similarities in Dissatisfaction

The Dutch presence dominated the islands until WWII, bringing both religious and commercial influence with them. Christianity continued to spread within the northern and central areas, although Islam was still a strong influence among the southern Makassarese. Tasty Toraja coffee was actually a European introduction, and once out of their mountain hideaways the Torajas added the Balinese-style *sawah* (wet-rice) steppe cultivation to their culture.

Many Minihasans actually served in Dutch troops during the wars, and the feeling of betrayal and misuse by the Indonesian government quickly grew throughout the islands. In 1959, during the Permesta Rebellion which coincided with a similar rebellion in Sumatra, demands for better education, more power and even the reallocation of funds were made to the central government.

The result was the eventual decla-

Upcountry in Manado.

ration of Minihasa as a separate state of North Sulawesi in mid 1959. Both Sulawesi and Sumatra, were suspected of using arms from the United States to fuel their rebellion.

Later, major cities on both islands were bombed and the hope of US aid quickly faded. In 1961, the rebel forces were finally and permanently extinguished. In southern Sulawesi, violent forces under the leadership of Kahar Muzakar, an ambitious local from the Luwu area confronted the central government. Previously involved in youth organizations who fought against the Dutch in WW II, Muzakar now gathered some guerrilla forces and used the momentum gained by West Java's separatist Dar Islam state to fight against the central Javanese government until his death during the conflict, in 1966.

Wealth in Wild Corners

Since the 1970s, Sulawesi has looked inwards for power, gaining in economy and education along with the other outer islands of Indonesia.

Mining projects have introduced investment by international corporations into the nickel industry, while the northern areas are filled with gold. Petroleum fields have recently been discovered and oil wells have been found in the eastern arm of the island. Natural gas reserves have increased the value of the Lake Tempe area, and Buton island

Sulawesi wildlife is relatively undisturbed.

holds the largest deposits of natural asphalt in Asia.

Although the island boasts of stunning natural beauty, unfortunately except for European treks to Toraja in the centre and the divers' Manado reefs, few areas have been explored by tourists. From the mountainous inland terrain, Gunung Rantemalio looks out over the northern territory from a height of 3,450 metres and the remnants of several extinct volcanoes have created a lush, fertile land in the southern area.

Still, the land to the north is alive, particularly in the Minihasa region, where the brooding smoke of several volcanoes whispers against the sky. In Sulawesi, there are 11 active volcanoes: one more than in Sumatra's lively Bukit Barisan range, and second only to Java, where 17 peaks still smoke with unmeasured fury.

Sulawesi also boasts of some of the world's largest cave systems, mostly around the area between Lake Towuti and Lake Matana. And, although the island's shape eliminates the possibility of long rivers – save for the Lariang at 200 kilometres in length – there are 13 large bodies of water, including Lake Towuti and Lake Posso, which spill out over the land as the second and third largest lakes in the archipelago.

Because of its shape, Sulawesi has more coastline relative to its land mass than any of Indonesia's other major islands. Including the adjacent islands, this land mass totals more than 227,000

Bawean Hog deer, endemic in Sulawesi.

square kilometres in area, with a majority of virgin beaches – known nesting areas for four species of sea turtle.

More than 100 small offshore islands are strung among the colourful world of coral reefs. Although the Manado and Bunaken areas are popular with underwater sports lovers, even richer are the Togian Islands in the Tomini Bay area, where the shores contain fringing, barrer and atoll formations, a kaleidoscope of all of the major coral reef environments.

Species of Sulawesi

Like Sumatra and Kalimantan, Sulawesi shelters an incredible diversity of species. However, its geographic position on the eastern side of the Wallace Line gives them distinctly Australian characteristics.

With 127 native mammals on the island, 79 (or 62 percent) are endemic – in contrast to the lesser 18 percent of endemic animals on the entire island of Borneo across the western strait. The bird life is also rich, of non-migratory aves, 34 percent are endemic – except for New Guinea, this is the highest percentage of species in all of Asia.

Rather than big cats such as the leopard and tiger, or large hoofed mammals like the rhino, there are instead a variety of unusual indigenous smaller species. The largest mammal is the shy *anoa*, a small buffalo no larger than a

Ujung Pandang, Sulawesi's port for many trading vessels.

dog, and the striking, grey-wrinkled *babirusa*, a wiggling, burrowing pig with frightening tusks that curve upwards from its cheeks and nearly into the skin of its snout. Primates and smaller mammals are relatively visible in the forests of Sulawesi. On the island, there are four species of black or brown tailless macaques, in addition to the thick-furred bear and dwarf cuscus. The tiny, round-eyed *tarsier* whose sticky fingers help it to leap from tree to tree can sometimes be spotted as well.

Estuarine crocodiles are no longer as common to the area as they were in the past, but Sulawesi is still home to the world's largest snake, the reticulated python, which stretches to a record ten metres and has been known to swallow

a grown man!

Of the 88 endemic bird species, the most unusual is perhaps the Maleo bird, which buries its eggs beneath huge mounds of dirt and twigs, the heat of the hill's thickness keeping them warm within. Flashes of colour between vines and leaves reveal the dark green Purple Bearded Bee-eater darting by ... or the Red-knobbed Hornbill, the Finch-billed Starling or any of the varieties of mynah that find refuge on the island.

Changing Face of Ujung Pandang

Ujung Pandang is one of those odd cities from which people establish highly

Walking to the market near Rantepao area.

variable impressions. Arriving hot and tired, in the searing central hours of the day can be a crass introduction – while sailing in to the chilly docks at dawn, amidst a stunning pink sunrise and the sound of early prayers and ship's horns is a wonderful welcome to one of Indonesia's most unusual cities.

Always a popular port city, Ujung Pandang was once known as Makassar, (headquarter of the Makassar kingdom) an international centre for trade and the steadfast home of the Muslim seafaring Bugis. In the harbour, in the north-west area of the city, several magnificent Bugis *pinisi* ships are usually lined up at the docks of **Paotere Harbour**. However, Jakarta's line of kilometres of Bugis ships docked at Tanjung Priok provide a much more stunning display.

A note about the *pinisi:* they are usually constructed as three-masted *perahu* (wooden sailing boat) that stretch nearly ten metres wide in the centre, with ample space for cargo, bunks and a charcoal cooking fire in the "mess" area.

The form originated in the days of the Romans and Phoenicians, the idea for the ships' structure was probably introduced to the Bugis by the Portuguese. Traditional boat building can often be seen in the Bugis and Makassarese villages near **Banta Eng**, about 125 kilometres from Ujung Pandang on the south coast.

Ujung Pandang, or Makassar as it

Sharing a meal at Batu Toraja.

was then known, was also the seat of the powerful Sultanate of Gowa and later a base for Dutch control of the seas. The influence of both rulerships can be seen in **Fort Rotterdam**, which stands near the harbour. It was originally built by members of Gowa's sultanate c. 1545, before being seized and rebuilt by the Dutch in the late 1660s after the Treaty of Bungaya was signed. The Dutch, particularly the Dutch commander Admiral Cornelis Speelman found the fortress provided a good supply of water, and sheltered ships that harboured from the wind. Now also known as Benteng (or Fort) Ujung Pandang, this enormous building also houses the **Conservatory of Dance and Music**, the **Historical and Archeological Institute** which was once used by the Dutch as a prison and **The National Archives**.

Jalan Diponegoro is the final resting place of the hero, Prince Diponegoro who was exiled to Sulawesi for the last 26 years of his life by the Dutch. **The Diponegoro Tomb and Monument** commemorates his bravery and leadership during the Java War of 1825 against the Dutch and has recently been declared an Indonesian national heritage site.

More relics from Gowa are found at the **Tomb of Sultan Hasanuddin**, or **Makam Hasanuddin**, who ruled the powerful kingdom during the 17th century. A heavenly deity is said to have descended to earth at the site of the nearby **Tomanurung Stone**, where for years the successive kings of Gowa were crowned.

At **Sungguminasa**, just 11 kilometres outside of Ujung Pandang, is the **Museum Ballalompoa**, the former residence of the Sultan of Gowa. The palace is a stunning raised wooden structure similar to the Makassarese palaces of Bima and Sumbawa. Special royal treasures are available for viewing upon request.

Naturalist Alfred Russel Wallace made his presence known through his butterfly collections at **Bantimurung**, a lovely park just 45 kilometres from Ujung Pandang. Here, beautiful waterfalls and limestone cliffs lead to hidden crevices and caves.

Just a few kilometres before Bantimurung are the **Gua** (caves) **of Gua Leang Leang** where you can see paintings and handprints etched in ochre along the rough walls.

Closer to town and tucked into Jalan Mochtar Lufti is the **Clara Bundt Orchid Garden**, with its well-known flower plantation and collection of giant clams and other intriguing shells. Admission is free but check with the **Tourist Office** at Jalan Andi Pangerant Petta Rani (tel: 21142), as it is a bit out of the way, to find out about opening hours.

Small **Selayar Island**, south of Ujung Pandang, is a Muslim island famous for its rough "Selayar cloth" of blue and white patterns. The island has a long history of cotton production. The Buton language is spoken on this isolated island and since the 1930s Christianity has grown with the inception of the Mahdi Akbar movement which the Muslim community is trying to ban, the movement has found refuge with the support of the local small Hindu community.

In the northern part of Selayar there are good beaches and a modern hotel in the main town of **Benteng**. Also in Benteng is the **Don Son Drum**, an intricate artefact excavated in the 17th century which is decorated with frogs. It is not quite known what the drum was used for.

Touring the Central Areas

A day's trip to Torajaland winds over a flat, coastal road; between thick rice fields and sharp limestone cliffs that represent lumps above the landscape on one side and smooth bays filled with fishing platforms and ricketty wooden docks on the other.

Once the sun is up, the air can be stifling, but the scenery is well worth the price of the heat. Houses along the roadside are raised from the ground, often a few are clumped together close to the busy street, with wide rice paddies encircled with sheer cliffs jutting out behind. Thatched or corrugated tin roofs are sloped and raised to a point in the centre, with small decorations such as bows or horns carefully attached to the small summit below the eaves.

Parepare is the city that marks the last stop for petrol, as well as the en-

A Toraja house with its roof ends flanging outwards.

trance to the stunning mountains of central Sulawesi. Parepare is the second largest port in southern Sulawesi, after Ujung Pandang and has an efficent freight service which runs regularly. Continuing out of Parepare across a wide river, the thin road suddenly begins winding upwards in a series of shocking hair-pin curves. Groves of papaya and banana trees plunge hundreds of metres down the cliffs on one side of the highway.

Close to this route lies Watampone (or Bone), the former kingdom of the Bone culture. Bone was historically a staunch Bugis state, but in 1610-11 it accepted Islam. After a series of rebellions the people allied with the Dutch in the mid-17th century and retained con-

siderable authority within the Dutch government. About 40 kilometres further on, near **Uloe**, is **Gua Mampu**, the largest cave in southern Sulawesi, where small rock formations mysteriously shaped like humans and animals make one wonder whether they were once live characters from the stories now passed on about them.

Tales of Toraja

Toraja is a land of cliffside graves and coffee plantations, woodcarving and elaborate funeral celebrations. To understand the culture, it is imperative to first grasp the concept of *adat* (village tradition), which is the basis for architecture, religion, ceremony and celebrations of life and death. (See box on pages 376-77).

In the southwest central region are the Sa'dan Toraja near the river Sa'dan, in the area of Makale and Rantepao. A third smaller in size than the island of Bali, their territory is marked by crops of cloves and pepper, rice, cassava and corn and, of course, the imposing bull-headed *tongkonan* (bull-headed) homes.

The *tongkonan* are the family "seats", or special Toraja houses which according to legend were brought down from the heavens by the ancestors. However, modern explanations state that the *tongkonan* were founded by the woman *Lai' Ambun ri Kesu,* (Lady Morning Mist of Kesu), built on the Kesu mountain. Most of the traditional Toraja houses are built on the slopes to represent the "lofty" position of the ancestors, although some are now situated on the plains as well.

Within these homes, each space has a representation of the *rapu* (family group), and the beliefs followed by the Toraja. Beneath the house is the "underworld," while the living area is the "earth" and the roof above points to the upper world of the gods, the triangular gable represents the place where the soul supposedly leaves the house.

Direction is also important in structure, as *Puya* (the realm of the dead), is south of *Tanatoraja* (Torajaland) and the western sunset also signifies death. Thus, the deceased are laid out and funeral rites are performed in the rooms of the western area. Eastern sunrise denotes life, so the kitchen and living areas are located in this direction. Homes always face north and east in the direction of the realm of the gods.

Decorations of *tongkonan* (family seats) are made with buffalo horns from funeral feasts – the more piled up at the front of the home, the higher the status of the house and the family inside. In former Toraja society, there were in fact four classes: the lower slaves, the freemen, nobility and finally the *Puang* (princes) that ruled the three small "states" in the area.

The buffalo is the most important animal in Toraja life, being used to symbolize the strength of headhunters and the fertility of the many rice fields. Once popular, headhunting and sacrifice of slaves and prisoners at royal funeral ceremonies are customs that have long since disappeared. Since the introduction of Christianity, pigs and buffalo are now slaughtered for food instead.

Chickens are also symbolic; many long-necked carvings adorn the front of the *tongkonan,* (family seat) symbolizing the mythical Lando Kollong ("she with the long neck") of legend. In addition to buffaloes, chickens are part of the funeral ceremonies, not only as the carriers of souls to the other world but also in the bloody sport of cockfighting introduced by the Bugis several centuries ago.

A similar "game" among the Toraja is *sisemba* (a kick-fighting sport). This is

Festivals for the Dead

*Wooden effigies at Londa, seated theatre-like,
watching people watching them.*

Aluk To Dolo is the ancestral religion of the Toraja, otherwise known as "the rites of the people of the old days." The ritual ceremonies that celebrate the dead are at the very core of this religion – practices which honour those who have passed on and stand guard over those living in the current world.

Style of Celebration

There are many styles of festivals, from the *sang bongi* (one-night festival) for common citizens, to the *pitung bongi* (week-long celebration) for those of higher status. Those of *Puang* (princely orders), are given special honour with a *dirapa'i*, (a lengthy funeral that includes a rest period and takes place in two stages lasting a month).

Darkness means death, and so at the funeral the relatives of the deceased don black *sarongs* (waistwrap around skirt), scarves, shirts or head-

dresses. The exception is the ceremony for a *Puang* whose relatives wear white during the final funeral stages, which is what the Toraja believe is the colour of princely blood.

Special village artists carve the *tau-tau* (effigy made of wood and painted and clothed to resemble the dead) Not everyone is entitled to a *tau-tau* – or can afford one. Carvings are expensive, particularly those of jackwood, which are revered as of the highest quality and value, and are reserved for the richest and most powerful members of the societal ranks.

Hidden in a large wooden *saringan* (container or coffin), the deceased is placed on a central platform during the ceremony. As it can take weeks or months to gather the mourners from the various corners of the Indonesian archipelago, the body is wrapped and embalmed first to preserve the physical form. It will stay in the home with the family, and is often offered food just as if the person were still alive.

At the start of the funeral ceremony, the *matundan* (gong) rings a deep sound through the forest; literally, the word means "to be woken from sleep" for the celebration. Relatives who arrive contribute their share of pigs, buffalo and chicken for sacrifice and each payment is recorded aloud by the central speaker for all present to listen and respect the donor.

A Festival Visit

Funeral parties in (Tanatoraja) are amazing; a riot of sound and colour that is enjoyed – in fact revered – to a surprising degree by all who attend. Word of a person's death is spread with the tentative date of the ceremony for all relatives and well-wishers who plan to attend and donate towards the lavish celebration. Before the ceremony begins, rows and rows of bamboo platforms are constructed, food is cooked, animals are gathered and carvings are made in preparation for the enormous festival.

On the day of the feast, the guests arrive to sit, laugh, smoke, drink coffee and eat peanuts, upon the fragile platforms. Food is passed around by the women, who might sit barefoot below, stirring huge oil cans of rice and kettles of boiling water for coffee, drinking t*uak* (rice wine) and chewing betelnut. The central pavilion contains the body and sometimes a photo of the deceased. Rituals are conducted to send the soul to *puya* (the afterworld) and the body is followed by a procession of veiled women and men beating drums. All are dressed in black.

The stench of raw meat is everywhere. It hangs from trees, along poles, and is chewed by men and stirred into spicy dishes in the makeshift kitchen area ... or is thrown down from the tree platform where the main speaker, or funeral announcer, stands shouting or talking into a modern megaphone. With a flourish, he tosses out chunks of bloody flesh to indicate who has given how much to honour the deceased, while below pigs tethered upside-down to long bamboo poles squeal in fear as boys carry them to their death at the chopping block.

Through the crowd, the deep sound of the gong reverberates in the air as the relatives, march slowly around the central arena. Men first, then women follow, often in matching dresses and scarves that lend an ethereal presence to the chaos of the children's shouting and animals' bellowing. After they circle the area several times they sit down for a while and chat with relatives and friends, then the gong sounds and off they go again for a repeat performance.

Then, the bulls are brought out and, abruptly, stabbed in the throat with a spear. Blood suddenly gushes everywhere as the animal screams in fear, eyes rolling, slowly lowering its tone and legs to the ground as the spirit of strength leaves it and it accepts the fate of the otherworld, where supposedly the deceased Toraja will ride it to the heavenly lands.

Even before it is dead, young boys circle the animal and shove wide tubes of bamboo into its throat to collect blood. The pride in their eyes as they take on this bloody duty is a measure of its importance, both to their sense of honour and responsibility to the family and their ancestors.

The most important sacrificial animal of the Toraja is the buffalo which plays a part in countless myths. The buffalo horns are the emblem of headhunters. Warriors look upon the strong brave bulls as their examples, the buffalo is judged by posture and size, shape of the horns (preferably pointed and sickle-shaped like the moon), and by colour. Pitch black is highly praised, but spotted buffalos found virtually only in Tanatoraja usually cost more. The most expensive are the white buffaloes spotted like a plover's egg. As spots are associated with abundance such as grains of rice stars in the sky, completely white buffalos are worth nothing as the Toraja believe that they were born blind.

The feast continues with more marching, more food, more laughter, and more sacrifice, of more often than 30 buffalos for one celebration. For the Toraja, life is endless; ancestors watch over time and inhabit the presence of others ... keeping within their elaborate and frenzied funeral ceremonies a sense of tradition and beauty which has remained uncrushed by Christian missionaries.

After the sacrificial slayings, chieftains pose beside the head of a buffalo.

a test of endurance between two opponents in which the use of the hands is not allowed. There is plenty to see and do in Toraja, and the area is surprisingly quiet, even considering the influx of European tourists particularly during the July to August ceremonial season. The **Tourist Office** (located just before you reach Rantepao) will have a list of dates for celebrations and ceremonies that take place throughout the year.

Rantepao & Beyond

Rantepao itself is an interesting place; the centre of tourist accommodations, there is no lack of places to stay although the town is very dusty and the road potholed. A market in the middle of town is a lively centre where both food and cattle

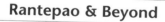

Buffalo trade at Rantepao market.

are sold. Hundreds of Buffalo take over the roads as they are led to the market to be haggled over. The market is surrounded by craft shops and small restaurants, and minibuses can take you just about anywhere in the mountains and valleys that you would like to travel to. Car and drivers are easily available for hire from the larger hotels.

Short trips from Rantepao are to **Lemo**, just a few kilometres off the main road south to Makale, where the famous (funeral effigies) stare out from cliffside graves. This is an odd and awe-

Festival day at Palawa.

some place, life-size carvings looking out over lush rice fields and sombre, rugged mountains from forest-topped cliffs. Sadly most of the original *tau-tau* (funeral effigies) were stolen in the 1980s and sold on the international art market. In 1988 these effigies were replaced by the government. Get there early, just after sunrise, for the best light and the coolest temperatures. This is a popular tourist spot and souvenir and parking facilities are provided.

Londa may be the most famous site of the *tau-tau* (funeral effigies) which are designed to protect the dead. Here balconies of them are located close to the ground for easy viewing. Below, are small caves filled with bones and coffins, which can be viewed by hiring a

kerosene lamp at the entrance that provides an eerie sort of tour. As these effigies face west, the best lighting in which to enjoy them is late afternoon.

Other areas for *tau-tau* (funeral effigies) viewing are at **Palatokke**, about six kilometres from Rantepao. At **Suaya** (25km from Rantepao) the *tau-tau* are rarely visited but are packed into galleries for easy viewing, the local church is worth a visit too. Nearby **Tampangallo** also has *tau-tau* but as this is a rather remote destination you may need to hire a guide which can be done from the village. Hot springs are found throughout the area in the rice paddies and along the trails, with a natural pool for swimming at **Tilanga**, as well as natural bathing areas at **Makula** 20 kilome-

Plying the islands in small craft.

tres east of Makale and **Sarambu Sikore** close to the waterfall at **Mamullu Mountain**. If you are travelling in the area during the off-season, there are still many funerals and ceremonies to attend in one of the traditional villages such as **Marante**, **Nanggala** or **Lempo** all located within 30 kilometres of Rantepao. The woodcarving area is around **Kete Kesu**, while weaving can be seen in **Sadan**.

Alternatives for accommodation to Rantepao are in Makale and Palopo – the Rantepao Tourism Office has an excellent map listing the details and distances of all the above areas.

Makale is the administrative capital of Tanatoraja and lies 17 km south of Rantepao. The town is expanding and its administrative and medical facilities are improving, to encourage tourists the government decreed that every building on the main road running through the town should be built with a Torja motif. Like Rantepao Makale has a lively bustling market. **Palopo** is the main town in Luwo lying in a beautiful mountainous setting. The mosque of **Mesjid Kuno Batupassi** was built in 1603 it faces the wrong direction – away from Mecca – the interior has thus been rearranged. Ferries run from Palopo to Luwuk and other islands.

Up & Around the Island

Home of the rebel Kahar Muzakar who

Tomohon Volcano, Manado.

fought the government in the 1950s, the Southeast point of Sulawesi's star is one of emotional intensity and geographical contrast.

In **Kendari** the largest town of southeast Sulawesi there are more than half a million Sulawesians, of whom nearly 250,000 belong to the Tolaki culture. The indigenous inhabitants of southeast Sulawesi, the Tolaki name means "brave people," possibly referring to conflicts with the Buginese, Dutch and the influx of foreigners who have flooded the area during the last century.

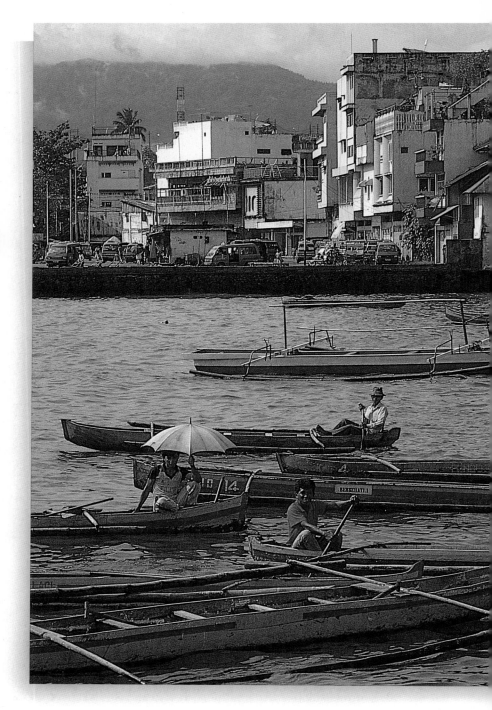

Boating in Manado, North Sulawesi.

Today Kendari is a prospering town and administrative centre. Kendari's golf course is well kept by Indonesian standards, and an early morning game is a pleasant form of relaxation on arrival from the nearby airport. Kendari is also well known for its silverwork in the uniquely Indonesian filagree style.

Settled near to the string of villages that encircle the Kendari area, the Tolaki people's customs are strict and frown on marriage with other tribes. Thus, elopement has become a common occurrence, for instance, between a Tolaki and a Buginese, which is against the traditional *adat* (customs) of the area.

Further north, the scenery along the road to Saroako following the Larona River is stunning, **Saroako** is well known for its nickel plant while mining companies control most of **Malili**. Malili has a developed port constructed by PT Inco in the late 1960s for the processing of the locally mined nickel utilizing the latest technology. The nickel processing plant is open to visitors. Across the bay to the southwest is the former pirate hideout and slave trading centre of **Buton Island**, where the delightful hilly town of **Bau Bau** provides a breather for cruise ship passengers and the crossroads for cargo shipments throughout the archipelago. Along the docks, young boys dive into the clear turquoise waters for coins, while many of the older islanders address visitors in Dutch, reflecting the former influence of these colonists on the area. The people on Butan speak the language of Wolio which used to be spoken by the Buton Sultanate. On the small island of **Bulopeway** near Malili there are lovely beaches and boating facilities.

Southeast of Kendari is the island of **Muna**, famous for its horses. These horses can be seen both alive and in the paintings of the caves of **Raha** on Muna. Muna is an Islamic island, where the practice of horse fighting is still popular after many years. Reasonable accomodation can be found in the main town of **Raha**, but a knowledge of **Bahasa Indonesia** will prove invaluable in this remote region. Through the heart of the star, near the central town of Palopo, are the jungle areas surrounding the 32,000 hectare **Lake Posso**. On the lakeshores are the quiet settlements of **Pendolo** at the southern edge of the lake and **Tentena**, while **Posso** is the port at the crossroads for catching buses and ships either back to Ujung Pandang or north towards Manado. **Posso** is a small town where the Dutch influence is revealed in the architectural style, there are also a large number of restaurants and hotels. Lake Posso's environs are lushly vegetated and cultivated with corn and coffee. The locals believe that Lake Posso is the second clearest lake in the world.

The capital of this area is **Palu**, a major Bugis port town full of markets and endless possibilities for jumping ship to Moluccas and the outer islands. Palu was a nostalgic place for the Dutch, the flat environs being reminiscent of the Netherlands. The **Provincial Mu-**

Clear seas around Manado make for ideal snorkelling.

A marketplace in north Sulawesi.

Little boy lost among the pumpkins.

seum is worth visiting in Palu an informative introduction to the area, found on Jalan Sapiri. On **Jalan Professor Muhammed Yahmin** the *Gedung Olah Seri* is the venue for local dance performances, go to the tourist information office on Jalan Cik Ditiro for details. Once the bureaucratic centre of the Dutch, **Donggala** is now a peaceful harbour town next to long, peaceful beaches – an ideal area for breaking up a long and tedious Ujung Pandang-Manado journey. About half a kilometre north of Donggala the beach at **Tanjung Karang** is beautiful but a small amount is charged to swim.

The central and northern areas contain Sulawesi's wilds, including the national park of **Dumoga-Bone**, home of the endangered *anoa* and *babirusa*. Near Bitung in the north peninsula, the **Tangkoko Batungas Nature Reserve** is also home to these special species, as well as the large maleo bird and kilometres of pristine coral coastline.

Manado & Minihasa

Northern Sulawesi is a different world; a bit like the northern islands of Moluccas, with a definite South Pacific tropical feel. Less tribal than the central areas, less pressured than the southern cities, this palm-forest, coral-coast peninsula is a relaxing retreat that invites exploration of both land and sea.

Here, the Minihasans are the major culture, who were impressively converted to christianity during the Dutch occupation. However, there are still traces of animistic belief in the practices of the *tonaas* (traditional priest) who still perform ceremonies and healing rituals, or the "Festivals of Merit" which help to gauge the talents of candidates and the outcome of various local elections. The Minahasans are particularly well known for their singing ability and group dancing which takes the form of the *Maengket* and *Marambak* where songs are sung by way of accompaniment as the group dances. Sometimes known as *orang Manado* (people of Manado), the Minihasans are actually comprised of eight different ethnic groups, each with its own regional language. Both culture and expression contain a mixture of various influences, comprising Malay, Dutch, Portuguese, Spanish and the cultures of various nearby islands.

Monuments for the Dead

One of the most interesting features of Minihasa society are the monuments made for the dead. Graveyards have spectacular constructions of tombstones that border on the outrageous. Shaped like trucks, boats and cloves, they boast of the family's riches, while the *waruga* (mausoleums) stand as testament to great Minihasans and can be seen amidst the graves or in family yards.

Although **Manado** is the largest city in northern Sulawesi, it is more a collection of monuments than of culture. Set against an awesome backdrop of volcanoes it has been designated an official tourist destination. To find the **Toar Lumimuut Monument** (on Jalan Yos Sudarso) representing the original Minihasan ancestors Lumimuut and Taor, the **Monument to the Worang Battalion** (Jalan Sam Ratulangi) remembering the fight for independence against the Dutch, the later **Monument of the Allied Forces** (Jalan Sarapung) commemorating the defeat of Japan in World War II, and the **Monument of Ibu Walenda Maramis**, a leader of women's rights in Indonesia (Jalan Yos Sudarso), try the **Tourist Office** near the Immigration Office near Jalan Eddy Gogola. Manado was influenced by the Dutch for several centuries and the Christian religion predominates here, manifest in 266 church and the strict formality with which Sunday worship is observed. The **Ranotano market** on the outskirts of the town is a good place to gain an insight into the Minahasan lifestyle.

From Manado boat trips run to the islands of Bunaken and Manada Tua, which now form part of a government marine reserve. **Bunaken Island** is surrounded by beautitul coral reefs breathing with a whole host of marine life, this is a most impressive diving location. Equipment fan be hired for snorkeling and scuba diving in a number of shops in Manado. The best tip is to follow travel agency trips or diving agencies (try the Nusantana Diving Club) to view these infamous coral reefs. There are also good underwater sights near the **Manado Tua Island** and the dormant rise of the **Mantehage Volcano.**

Other idyllic destinations from Manado are **Tasik Ria** and **Tana Wangko,** with their beaches, palm trees, and coconuts. Along the road to the **Airmadidi Hot Springs** are the *waruga* (Minahasan Sarcophagus), while at **Tondano** and **Tomohon** there are several large Japanese caves to explore. Tondano is the birthplace of Dr Sam Ratulanga a nationalist leader educated in Switzerland, there is a large monument to him. Sacred stones mark the site of **Batu Pinabetengan,** or literally translated the "stone of the division of land", where the Minihasan territory was divided and eventually unified by agreements made between the tribal leaders.

Gorontolo is the second largest city in northern Sulawesi. The city has a pleasant harbor area and a good range of shops. Gorontolo is renowned for its *krawang* embroidery which is sold in profundance. The *bendi*, (a horse drawn vehicle) is the indigenous method of transportation. At the upper edge of Indonesia lie the **Sangir-Talaud Islands**, which highlight the area's continuing active volcanic chain. Legends here tell of men and women possessed by spirits, supernatural occurrences and ceremonial sacrifice practices and magic – though the area is now mostly Christian. Few travellers make it up to this area, but it is possible by air or boat from Manado ... a wonderfully remote place to explore and snorkel from.

The history of the Moluccas (also known as the Spice Island) is as much a fractured puzzle as the shapes of the thousand islands themselves. Scattered across the northern area between the shadows of Sulawesi and Irian Jaya, the Moluccas is a mixture of culture, history and heritage from the surrounding Asian and Melanesian ways of life.

Settled into the "Ring of Fire" that encompasses one of the world's largest volcanic belts, more than 70 eruptions have occurred in the area during the past four centuries. Flora and fauna are also a mixture: a blend of the Asian and Australian species separated by the imaginary but very plausible boundary of the Wallace Line that runs up the strait between Kalimantan and Sulawesi.

Set in fertile volcanic soils the Moluccas is known for its growing of spices and lush vegetation.

Looking Glass to the Past

Borne of the land named *Mi-li-ku* found in the writings of the Chinese Tang Dynasty, the

Moluccas

391

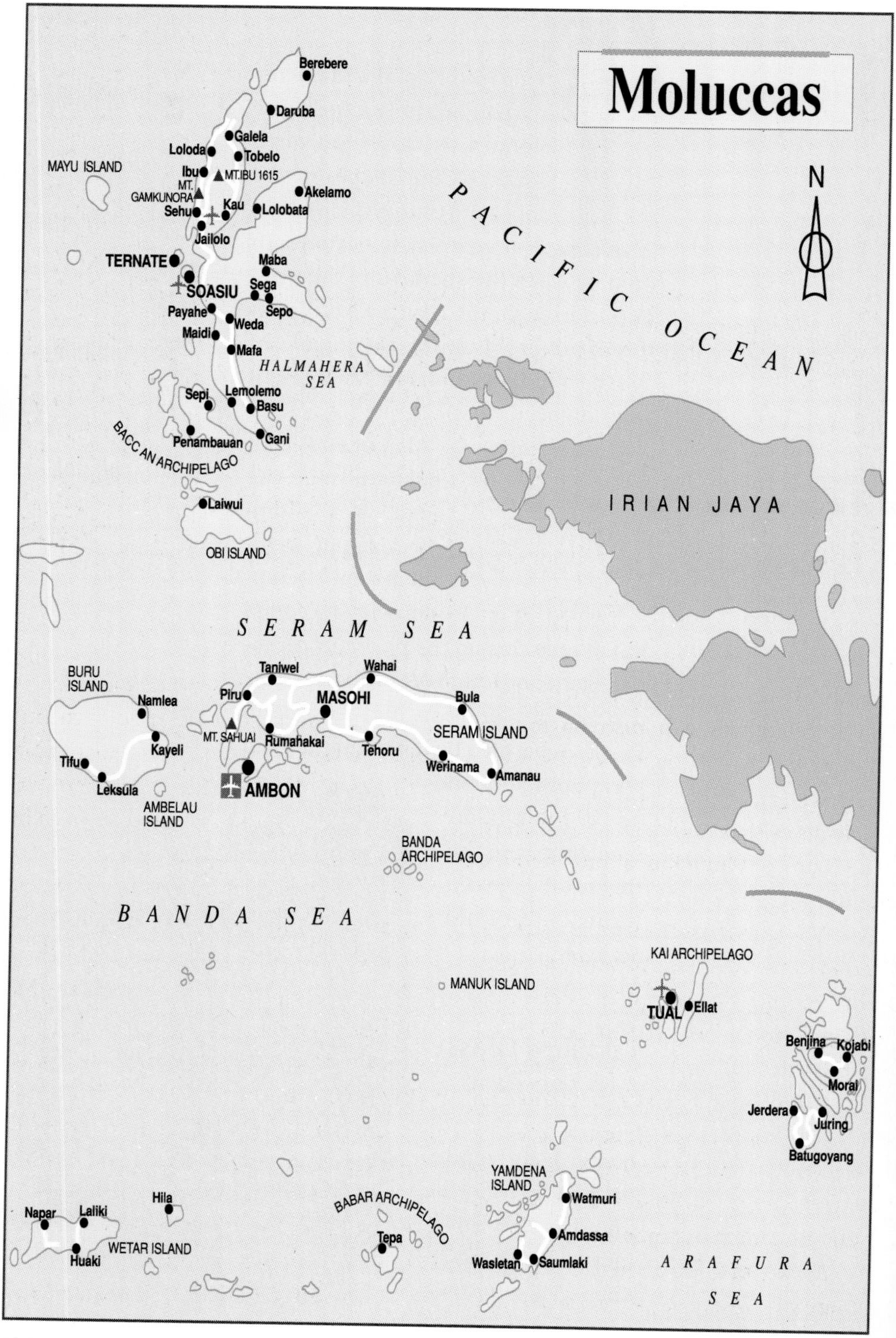

Moluccas

N

MAYU ISLAND

Berebere
Daruba
Galela
Loloda
Tobelo
Ibu
MT. IBU 1615
MT. GAMKUNORA
Akelamo
Sehu
Kau
Lolobata
Jailolo
TERNATE
Maba
SOASIU
Sega
Payahe
Sepo
Weda
Maidi
Mafa
HALMAHERA SEA
Sepi
Lemolemo
Basu
Penambauan
Gani
BACC AN ARCHIPELAGO
Laiwui
OBI ISLAND

PACIFIC OCEAN

IRIAN JAYA

SERAM SEA

BURU ISLAND
Namlea
Taniwel
Wahai
Piru
MASOHI
Bula
Kayeli
MT. SAHUAI
Rumahakai
SERAM ISLAND
Tifu
Tehoru
Leksula
Werinama
Amanau
AMBELAU ISLAND
AMBON

BANDA ARCHIPELAGO

BANDA SEA

MANUK ISLAND

KAI ARCHIPELAGO
TUAL
Ellat

Benjina
Kojabi
Moral
Jerdera
Juring
Batugoyang

Napar
Laliki
Hila
YAMDENA ISLAND
Watmuri
Huaki
WETAR ISLAND
BABAR ARCHIPELAGO
Tepa
Amdassa
Wasletan
Saumlaki
ARAFURA SEA

Fishing boats anchored for the day.

identity of the area was formed c. AD 7. Later references can also be found; Moluccas is called *Maloko* in the Javanese writings of the 14th century and *Moluquo* by the Portuguese, who entered the "Land of Many Kings" only about a century later.

Whether these foreign names referred to the island of Ambon's popular port of call, or Ternate, Tidore and Banda, three of the more popular spice islands, is unclear from these records. One certain fact, however, is the reason for these islands' attraction to traders, namely the availability of spices for accentuating food, preserving goods and other uses such as embalming.

Spices, of course, are the riches of Moluccas, where clove, nutmeg and other spices drew merchants from around the globe. Also unique to the area are sago and cassava, which take the place of rice as starchy staples for nutritional fillers in both the islands and the province of Irian Jaya.

Who let out the secret of the Spice Islands? Nicoli de Conti, an explorer who returned to Europe around 1440 to boast of his new-found wealth in the archipelago. Although maps were hardly an accurate means of direction in those times, an explorer and merchant sailor named Fra Maura sketched a map of the world based on de Conti's observances ... and it was not long until the journey to Moluccas became the vision of European traders.

In 1509, the "white Bengalis" ar-

Natives carrying a sedan chair outside the ruins of a Christian church.

rived with the straight forward goal of simply overtaking the Spice Islands for their own purpose of trade. These people were the Portuguese, who arrived to find, that the industry was under Muslim control but with the swift caputure of Melaka in 1511 and the establishment of the first fort on Ternate, the tables were suddenly turned in the favour of Portuguese.

Clove Trade

Ternate and Tidore were the centres for cloves, where crops were produced and traded with merchants from all over the world. Fighting with the Muslim-run islands continued through the end of the century, when the unsuccessful Portuguese moved on to Seram's port of Ambon to again try to gain control.

A second effort to control the spice trade came with the arrival of the Dutch who, in 1599, brought an armed fleet to the islands under the command of Jacob Van Neck. The cloves with which they returned fuelled the fire of greed, and in 1602 the Dutch East India Company was formed at great cost to the local island communities, where the Dutch *Hongi* (expeditions to maintain the monopoly) resulted in the destruction and deaths of thousands of homes and villagers. In the mid-1600s, the Dutch finally maintained stable control, and later the British showed their presence occupying the islands during the Napo-

The Malay quarter in the early 19th century.

leonic Wars. The Dutch bounced back in 1814 but the local reaction was far from enthusiastic.

Thomas Matulessy - "Pattimura"

One of the most significant revolts against the Dutch rule was led by Thomas Matulessy, known to the Ambonese as *"Pattimura"* (the generous hearted one). Pattimura who was a Sergeant Major in the British militia during the Napoleonic Wars led a strong fight against the re-establishment of Dutch control from the island of Saparua east of Seram.

Matulessy's rebellion in 1817 led to his status as one of Indonesia's national heroes, and today the name *"Pattimura"* graces many of Ambon's main areas. His likeness is depicted in a monument in the city centre and one of the main streets bears his title. Also, Ambon's army unit and university recognize his name, lest his leadership and bravery be forgotten by upcoming generations.

It was not until 1863 that the forced cultivation of spices was discontinued in the islands, but revolts rocketed through the area for the next 50 years during Indonesia's wars for independence. In April of 1950, the area was declared *Republik Maluku Selatan* (The Republic of the South Moluccas or RMS). However, jungle fighting continued between the Indonesian troops and those

Water taxis waiting a fare.

of the *RMS* even through the 1970s.

Today, though, the islands are for the most part peaceful, they are still centres of trade and increasingly havens for naturalists, cultural seekers and holidaymakers as well.

Aves of the East

Birds are the gifts of the gods to the eastern islands of Moluccas, where lorikeets, parikeets and the red-crested cockatoo make the rugged forests their homes. More than 22 varieties of parrots flutter throughout the skies, along with the beautiful birds of paradise seen in the forests of Aru island. The flightless cassowary with its slick, velvety feathers

fine as human hair and bright wrinkled skin seemingly painted to resemble tribal markings of crimson, lavender and powder blue roams the ground. The **Manusela National Park** in the centre of Seram, Moluccas's second-largest island, is a beautiful secluded area for trekking and wildlife watching. Although often rainy, the bird variety is colourful and lively and the area itself remote enough so that few other tourists are seen.

Ambon

Best known to the Australians as the finish line of the annual Darwin-Ambon Yacht Race, this port city on Ambon Island is the provincial capital of the

War Cemetery in Ambon.

Moluccas. Remnants of fortresses and battle sites speckle the island, and hillside cemeteries lead down to the sea. Culture is a refreshing mixture of Melanesian, Indian and Asian, with the spicy aroma of *warungs* (food stalls) mixed with scenes of colourful craftwork and glittering offerings from the sea.

Aura of Ambon

At the cultural crossroads for centuries, the atmosphere is open and friendly, with a definitly Christian feel. However, mosques are tucked into corners between the wide streets to be solemnly heard at dawn, noon and dusk. Many words stem from Portuguese – in fact, some of the older islanders speak Dutch –- and the music has a slight Spanish flavour in some of the ballads and pieces with a faster tempo.

Yet, the city is as Indonesian as its brilliant *becak* (trishaw) teams, which flood the streets with uniform colours depending on the day of the week. Crowded into alleys while they await customers, they are a lively bunch, always ready with smiles and friendly greetings. A *becak* ride around the central area is inexpensive and a fun, breezy way to get a feel for the city.

Monuments & Memories

The history of the dominance of the

Ambon, a quiet town.

Spice Islands by various peoples is evident in its many forts, whose remains are crumbled throughout the steep islands hills. Built by the Portuguese in 1575, **Fort Victoria** has moved from the coastline to the waterfront due to a recent development project and is now surrounded by the park gardens of **Taman Victoria**. Statues, shells and stones are the evidence of the spice trade that fills for the **Siwalima Museum** located just a few kilometres by *bemo* (small covered vehicle) from Amahusu village.

For a bit of history, the **Pattimura Monument** stands at the edge of the central sports field where teenagers are often spotted playing lively football and other sports games. The **Australian War**

The endless beaches around the islands.

Cemetery is an easy two-kilometre trip by *bemo* (small covered vehicle) to the suburb of Tantui, where soldiers from all nations worldwide have been buried. Just down the road is also the **Indonesian Heroes Cemetery** where those killed in the skirmishes against the Moluccas rebels are buried.

One interesting monument is the **Martha Christina Tiahahu Memorial** which is set on the hill overlooking the city. In the fight against the Dutch led by Pattimura, Tiahahu was captured with her father; he was executed while she was sentenced to exile in Java, but her grief for him led her to starve to death in a statement of protest. Tiahahu was buried at sea, but the memorial still stands to commemorate her valiant action for her country.

Seaside Resorts & Villages

For a dip into culture, there is the **Karang Panjang Village**, where traditional crafts, dances and ceremonies are often performed for visitors. However, with brilliant hillside views of the bay and winding coastal roads, a wander around the island by foot, *bemo* or car is an interesting way to investigate the area's various cultures–and get some good exercise at the same time.

Around Ambon and Seram Island are stunning beaches and coral groves that make for a relaxing afternoon swim. Bungalows are inexpensive and easy to get to by minibus or taxi; most have

quiet, private facilities that provide an easygoing holiday or well needed break from travel. Particularly recommended are the beaches at **Latuhalat** and **Namalatu**, around the other side of the island, where snorkelling and scuba diving have drawn a quiet tourist trade. Popular with local tourists is Natsepa Beach less crowded is **Toisapau** across

Clove craftsman in Ambon.

the Baguala Bay. The beautiful, coral-fringed island of **Pombo** has a nice coral reef, get there by *bemo* (small covered vehicle) from Ambon to the Tulehu village wharf, where a speedboat can easily transport you there.

Waai is another water paradise graced with a submerged ocean cave and a spring filled with sacred carp and eels. Nature lovers can try **Liang**'s rainforests where they will find orchids and insects and good hiking conditions, **Halong** on Ambon's south bay is also an interesting place to visit, familiar to

Australians, it is the site of the end to the annual Darwin-Ambon Yacht Race.

Ambon's **tourist office** has to be the best in the country as far as friendliness, helpfulness and availability of information is concerned. Conveniently located in *Kantor Gubernor* (the governor's office) near the harbour and main minibus station, it is a logical starting place for finding out what is available to see and do around the islands.

Ternate & Tidore

A miniature replica of Sulawesi, Ternate and Tidore lies just above the largest Moluccas island of Seram, a night's sail each way between Ambon and Manado. Long-forgotten after the spice trading times, these small islands offer a quieter alternative to the hustling ports of Ambon and Banda ... a bit of peace and a picture of Moluccas former profit and piracy days.

Twins & Rivals

For decades, kings controlled the clove trade on the twin islands of Ternate and Tidore, which had been long-time rivals in trade. However, without their own merchant ships, they depended on the outside world for their goods.

No strangers to domination, the Dutch immediately keyed in on the possible profits and pitted Tidore against Ternate by gaining a spice monopoly on the latter island. Unfortunately for them, the reigning Sultan Ullah and his son Sultan Said were not keen on the Dutch presence and managed to eject them from the island about 50 years later. Hard-headed as ever, the Dutch ignored the insult and went on expanding throughout the islands, even building a fort on Tidore after being thrown out of the area. The Spanish also had holdings in the two tiny islands, but both powers soon moved their interests in cloves to that of nutmeg and mace, grown primarily on the southern islands of Banda, Ambon and Seram. By the early 1800s, interest in Ternate and Tidore was fading quickly as the European colonies established their own more convenient and hospitable spice plantations closer to home.

Wrecks & Relics

Most of the Moluccas has been washed with the flood of Christian missionaries. However, Ternate and Tidore still take strength in strict Muslim ways. Ruins of every culture are found near the town of **Ternate** – Dutch, Portuguese and Spanish forts and relics, as well as the main museum, which was once a sultan's palace. Wrecks of ships and aeroplanes are also scattered throughout the bays, as this area was a strategic air base for both the Allies and the Japanese during WWII. Rusted weapons and ammunition are often found in the foliage while dozens of historical relics dot the is-

Some in Ambon perch their homes very close to the sea.

lands, including the 13th century **Gamlamo Fortress**, the **Toloko Fortress** erected by Admiral d'Albequerque in 1512, the **Kayu Merah Fortress** built in 1518, the 1522 **Santo Pedro Fortress** and the **Oranje Fortress** erected by Madeliede around 1607, now occupied by Indonesian police and army, but open to the public. Influences of Islam can also be seen in the 1234 **Ternate Sultanate** *Kedaton* (Sultan's palace) with its ornate harems, which is now a museum, and the **Ternate Sultanate Mosque** that dates back to the 13th century.

Courses of Nature & Culture

Surprisingly, Ternate is surrounded by

natural wonders – flora such as sago, coconut, cloves, nutmeg and orchids, while fauna includes the beautiful double-tailed birds of paradise, the *angang* (year bird), Maleo bird and dozens of parrots and cockatoos. Dominated by rugged mountains and sloping valleys, the island was the perfect pirate and soldier hideout during many historical eras.

About four kilometres from town grows the oldest clove tree in the world, which is believed to be nearly 400 years old. Huge in size, this great tree produces upwards of 600 kilograms of cloves in only one harvest – a reflection of the glory of former trading days in the islands.

The **Gunung Gamalama** is one of

the Moluccas' many volcanoes – and one which erupted as early as 1737 ... and as recently as 1987. Standing at more than 1,700 metres in height, this mountain has three crater pools settled into its slopes and is an excellent area for hiking and viewing the panorama of the island. **Batu Angus** (burnt corner), a large stone formed by the earlier Gamalama eruption, is now the site of a Japanese war memorial from WWII. Two lakes add island beauty – **Lake Laguna and Lake Tolire** – located seven and 25 kilometres from town, respectively.

At Laguna, the effects of erosion can be seen in the sloping lake edges, while Tolire has an intriguing deep blue colour which is atypical of other inland waters.

Beaches are also common playgrounds along Ternate's edges, such as the **Sulamadaha Beach Resort** just 16 kilometres from town. Here, the sparkling black sand is a refreshing change from Moluccas more common white beaches; **Bastion Beach** is closer, only seven kilometres away.

The Moluccas is for those who are divers at heart, although anyone with curiosity enough to place one's face underwater is immediately immersed in a colourful new world of fins, fish and brilliant coral finds.

Within the waters surrounding the Moluccas more than 1,000 islands, a psychedelic mosiac of dappled reefs and gentle warm waves, embrace swimmers, snorkelers, skin and scuba divers of every age to engage their eyes with yet an-

other hidden side of Indonesia's beauty.

Cultural Changes

Music and dance in the northern Moluccas is slightly different from the southern areas, due to the influence of Islam and the oscillation of various Eu-

Children pumping for their baths from a covered well.

ropean powers that allowed different degrees of domination.

Palace dances are interwoven with traditional performances and ceremonies that reflect the lingering stronghold of sultanate days. Dance rituals can be celebrations of freedom or war,

and can include various styles of movement that incorporate mysticism or tell stories of heritage at the same time.

One of the classic mystical acts of Moluccas is the **Crazy Bamboo Dance**, which is difficult to find and only performed upon request, although some-

Young men of Ambon.

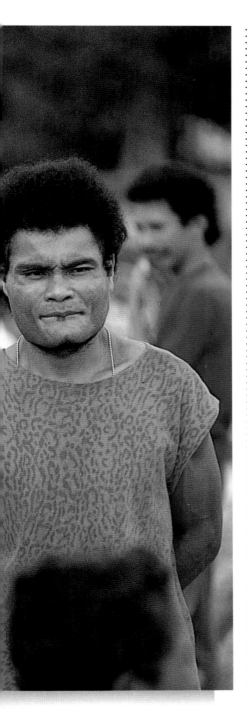

times it can be seen in the tourist areas around Ambon. As the Tourist Office brochure describes: " ... a group of seven strong men hold a bamboo and a magician puts magic into the bamboo three or four times, and the bamboo will be crazy. If you do not believe please come to Ambon and you will experience it directly". Enough said.

Moluccas Cultural Sites

Another amusing Moluccas cultural site of the Moluccas is that of the **Crown of the Sultan of Ternate**. Each year, the family of the sultan holds a "hair cutting" ceremony related to this ancient relic; the old hairs of the sultan are said to grow from the crown which is believed to be a repository of magical powers. Again, the brochure describes the site best: "It is said that women who want to have their hair long, come to Ternate and they will get it".

Crafts are always a reflection of culture, and the twin islands have their own styles to boast their talent. *Tikar* (braided crafts), are common, as is bamboo furniture and decoration. One interesting handicraft is the *saloi* (sieve), also known within the islands as *tohes*.

Stone jewellery is often seen on both women and men, and *kabilano* (betelnut boxes) are also popular market items. "Commander sticks" made of black wood, and artificial shields carved from various timber substances are used for battle.

Banda Islands

South of Ambon, three large islands ring the edge of one of the world's deepest seas, seven smaller land masses dotting the areas in-between. These are the islands of Banda, which have settled into more than 6,500 metres of deep ocean water in an international belt of fiery volcanoes that brings constant life to Indonesia's upper archipelago.

Banda, Banda-Neira and Gunung Api are the three larger islands, of which the bare **Gunung Api** (Fire Mountain) is probably the best known. Smoke from Api is evidence of its recent eruption in 1988 which shook the Moluccas area causing much devastation, and making Gunung Api one of the most fascinating and dangerous volcanoes in the country.

Banda and **Banda-Neira** are lush islands, covered with forests and nutmeg trees, while life around them teems within the seas. This is a diver's paradise – the sea gardens of the Moluccas – where 100-metre visibility and brilliant coral groves make ocean life easy to spot and to intermingle with. Clean, deserted beaches give the islands a wild romantic feel.

Sailors of Yore

Islam has always been a way of life for the Bandanese, with "gathering" practices the basis of land living that was often enhanced by the spice trade.

Nutmeg and mace were the popular produce, exchanged for supplies and worldly goods with visiting Arab, Asian and European ships. Settled beneath the main port of Ambon, as well as south of the Ternate and Tidore island duet, Banda encouraged an industry of its own based on its convenient location. In 1512, the Portuguese could have taken hold of the island but were lured away by the temptation of Tidore, the current centre for the blooming clove trade.

Some 80 years later the Dutch sailed into the area, but they were not the only ones who latched onto the southern Moluccas trading game. The Portuguese returned, then the British, and even the Spanish, as the rotation of merchants added rumour to the profiting cycles of trade. Eventually, the Dutch took hold of the islands under the command of Jan Pieterszoon Coen, who envisaged the area useful additon to the growing empire of the Dutch East Indies Company.

Coen's Cruelty

Some of the most violent rebellions occurred during this era between 1609 and 1619, when Coen's "penal expedition" nearly wiped out the entire population of **Banda** on Lontar Island. More than 2,000 Japanese and Javanese convicts were forced to work as slaves and porters for the 13 war vessels included in the expedition. A telling testament to

Happy schoolboys enjoy the benefits of improved education programmes.

the cruelty that was yet to come.

Later, the land was divided into *perken* (lots), *Perkeniers, as* the employees were termed, were forced to grow nutmeg and sell the crops at prices set by the Dutch, while the captured slaves laboured over the fields. It was a time of deep depression for those in the land; part of a bitter history for those forced into working for the system.

Relics of the Era

Remains of the farm houses can still be seen throughout the land, while the 1611 **Belgica Fort** constructed by Coen still towers against the mountainside setting. **Fort Nassau** still remains near the town , now restored from the crumbling structure which had been founded by the Portuguese in 1529 .

Rumah Pengasingan, or the house of exile of Sutan Sjahrir, is next to **Rumah Budaya**, Banda's museum. Sjahrir, one of Indonesia's early leaders along with Suharto and Mohammad Hatta, did not actually spend his time in this area, although the photos and relics of his life are intact and make for interesting viewing. However, the spirited leaders of the early Indonesian government did live in Banda for a while during the late 1930s, and so the **Residence of Hatta and Sjahrir** can still be viewed. Amusingly, the home is situated directly adjacent to the central town prison.

411

A land of ancient tribes running around in *horim* (penis sheath), with feathers in their hair, grass skirts swaying, bare breasts ... all of this can be experienced while walking down the main street of Wamena, a village in the central Baliem Valley. And beyond, in the beautiful forests, (snow-covered mountains and plumed and coloured wild birds fly in a heavenly world) where strange marsupials roam the thick jungle floors and rivers flow into places where humans have never been.

Youngsters from the "hot land rising from the sea".

The island of New Guinea is cleanly divided by a straight line through the centre – east is Papua New Guinea, while on the western half lies the Indonesian province of Irian Jaya. Though this area is the most recent acquisition for the country, it has survived a turbulent political history, and the province is still one of the world's last rainforest haven with special cultures and more than 600 species of birds.

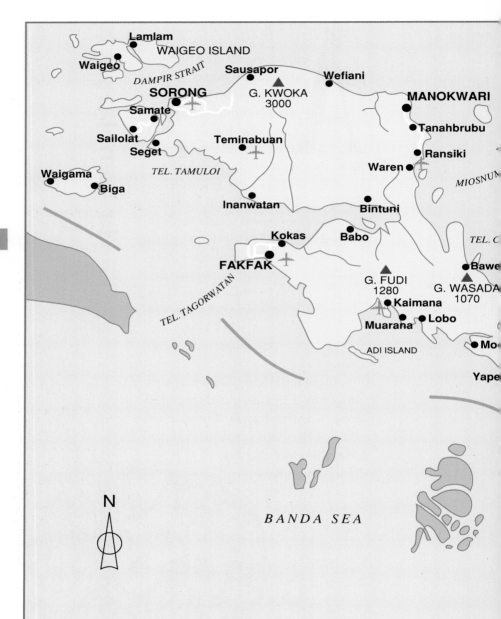

Lamlam
WAIGEO ISLAND
Waigeo
DAMPIR STRAIT
Sausapor
Wefiani
SORONG
G. KWOKA
3000
MANOKWARI
Samate
Tanahbrubu
Sailolat
Teminabuan
Ransiki
Seget
Waren
MIOSNUM
Waigama
TEL. TAMULOI
Biga
Inanwatan
Bintuni
Kokas
Babo
TEL. C
FAKFAK
Bawe
G. FUDI
1280
G. WASADA
1070
Kaimana
Muarana
Lobo
TEL. TAGORWATAN
ADI ISLAND
Mo
Yape

N

BANDA SEA

Irian Jaya

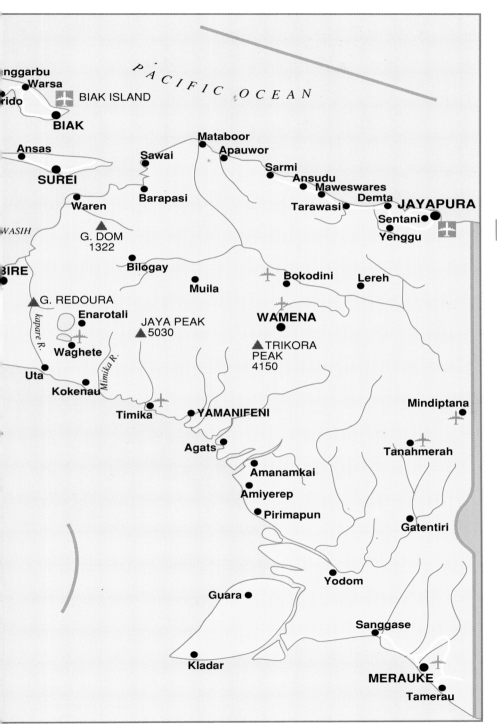

A gathering at Kurulu Pasar.

Enter, If You Dare

Truly, the tribes of Irian Jaya and Papua New Guinea resemble the dark-skinned, thick haired cultures of Africa. And so the area was named after the conti- nent's country of Guinea by the Dutch.

The slave trade was only the first abuse of the people living in this area, who probably arrived in the islands of Irian somewhere around 30,000 years ago. Islam and the Malay language arrived some time later with the traders, although there was no formal power until the Dutch took control of the large "bird's head" area in the mid-19th century.

About 50 years later, the Dutch took the western half of the island, while the British and German governments divided the eastern leftovers. In the early 20th century, the Australians jumped in to control the British territory before WWI and the German section afterwards, renaming IT the "Territory of Papua" and finally – after independence in 1975, it was named Papua New Guinea.

Independence, or Indonesia?

However, the border territory, has long been a battleground, between Papuan rebel forces and the Indonesian powers. It was Sukarno's efforts in 1960 that first challenged Dutch control as well as ignited Papuan anger. Pressure from the United States, due to fear of Soviet collaboration with Indonesia, forced the Dutch to back out of the territory in 1962. Thus, a year later, Indonesia took hold of the area.

The most important contract of the time was the "Act of Free Choice," in which the Indonesian government gave what they now called "West Irian" a few years to decide whether they wanted complete independence or to remain a part of the new Indonesian republic. The *msyawarah* (decision process), utilized a "consensus" of local elders. How-

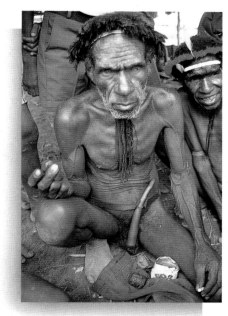

An elderly Irian man in Kurulu Pasar.

ever, when it was announced that West Irian would remain within the Republic of Indonesia, violent protests and battles were fought against the decision.

Areas along the border are still aflame with occasional disputes between Papuan guerrillas and the Indonesian government. In addition to arguments over boundaries and control, those in the area are concerned about forced efforts to bring in the "Indonesian" ways of life to the "Papuan" areas, as well as the growing effects of logging and destruction of the forests.

Now, the area is known as Irian Jaya; "*Irian*" meaning "hot land rising from the sea" and "*Jaya*" meaning "victory" in Indonesian. To those against Indonesian control, it is called West

Private property in Irian Jaya.

Papua New Guinea, but the shortened "West Papua" and "West Irian" titles are also occasionally heard. Until the identity of the area is firmly established and the disputes smoothed over with peace, the political side of life in the province is destined for mixed emotion and confusion between the will of the government and traditions of culture.

Jayapura

Most flights to Irian Jaya stopover in **Biak**, a quiet town at the crossroads between the South Pacific, Asia, and North America.

However, just a coral-fringed reef and a channel away lies **Jayapura**, the capital of Irian Jaya. Air traffic travels through the **Sentani airport** about 36 kilometres from town, while ocean vessels are common to the downtown waterfront area. In between, the land is lush and humid, lazily reminiscent of the Caribbean; low, rounded hills of thick palm trees and wide blue skies, with smooth, shining lakes lined with raised wooden homes nestled right up to their edges.

Jayapura is a surprisingly modern town; with only a few working phones, faxes and the like, but with plenty of Western products and stylish hotels with air conditioning. A "last stop" before the interior jungle trails, or prior to flying home after a holiday, Jayapura's mix of odd shops, open stalls and slow traffic is

Free port reclamation, Timika.

a delightful reconciliation between the confusion and noise of major Indonesian cities such as Jakarta or Medan and the efficient capitalism of nearby Singapore, Hong Kong and Los Angeles.

This is also one of Indonesia's most polite places – lots of "Hello Misters"but without the intrusive questioning that often follows inquiries in other islands. Many of Jayapura's residents are Indonesian Army families, and camouflage uniforms abound everywhere, as are the friendliest greetings and widest smiles towards Westerners within the archipelago. It is a simple place, with many hills and valleys to explore; an area of stunning beauty that is a step back from modern times. By day, beaches such as the serene **Base G** and **Hamadi**, along with the **Hamadi Market** and the central **Gedung Loka Budaya** or museum are worthwhile adventures, as is **Lake Sentani** and the crocodile farms closer to the airport.

Afternoons last until sundown when the city is closed for rest – but by night things liven up with bright shops and restaurants. A stroll by the waterfront near the Pelni ship office will take the wanderer to some of the most tasty food stalls in town.

Warning: Rumour has it that the only two people in Jayapura who are *not* carrying the malaria parasite in their blood are two Canadian expatriates. Everyone else has it, and mosquitoes are rife in the cities. Bring a net for sleeping under, bring mosquito coils to burn in

A typical home – round and wooden – Mapnouma.

your room, and above all, make sure that you are taking anti-malarial drugs of some kind properly on a regular basis. If not, you *will* get malaria here, so consider yourself warned.

Also, to reach the interior areas a *asurat jalan* (permit), is required for all visitors. You can pick this up at the main police station – plan for one to three days depending on the flow of work and the mood of the staff. Bring four black-and-white photographs (get them at **Happy Photo** on the main street), your passport and lots of patience. A winning

The Irian Jayans subsist on crops grown around their homes.

smile will help – and do not say you are a journalist or a member of the government!

Beauty of the Baliem Valley

Accessible only by air (and a fleet of shaky planes at that), the journey to Irian's inner **Baliem Valley** is an adventure of sheer joy and wonder.

Richard Archbold, an early 20th century explorer, was the first Westerner to discover the beauty of the area– and within it he found a civilization that was amazingly modern and friendly. These were the tribes grouped under the single name of "Dani", who lived in the highland and valley areas across the 120-kilometre expanse of land.

In addition to Baliem, there are three valleys in the interior of the New Guinea island: the **Asaro Valley**, the **Panai Lakes** area and the **Wahgi Valley**. Within the Baliem, the Grand Valley stretches more than sixteen kilometres in width as the Baliem River winds its way through the stunning Baliem Gorge out to the Arafura Sea. Mountains stud the landscape, tall enough to be covered in snow, including **Gunung Puncak Trikora** near Wamena and **Puncak Jayakesuma** (also known as Gunung "Jaya"and Mount Carstensz) – at over 5,000 metres, it is Irian's highest peak.

The fertile slopes of the mountains

One of the most common fruit, bananas.

settlement carved deep into the surrounding mountains, **Wamena** is the usual visitors starting point for walks in the area. The scenery is beautiful, both flying into the area and around the town, as the plane dips between clouds and below shadowy mountain peaks, yet high above endless kilometres of thick forest cover and enormous lakes that stretch into the hills.

In the tiny town, the conciseness of layout makes everything convenient – you can easily walk to the post office or bank, which are only a couple of blocks away. There are plenty of simple hotels in which to stay while planning a trip; a local market is a lively place to find crafts and food, while small festivals are often open to guests. After dark, though, everything is quiet but rises again with the sun and the roosters around 5 am each morning.

Walks Around Wamena

A centre for trade, tourism and culture,

are not only covered with natural flora, but with manmade provisions as well. Alongside the mountains of the highlands, the Amungme, Sempan and West Dani tribes have lived for more than 30,000 years, using these slopes as their farming areas. The fields are steep, but crops are amazingly successful in particular, the *ubi* (sweet potato) which replaces rice as the main staple of food here.

A cool, flattened valley

The people-laden walk heavy into the towns to sell their crops.

Tree kangaroo, reminiscent of its larger relative in nearby Australia.

Wamena is a convenient place to begin a journey of Irian Jaya, whether it consists of several short day trips or a few weeks spent in the mountains and wilds.

Day walks are a good introduction– in fact, you could spend a week doing different trails, such as the easy two-hour stroll through wide yellow fields and rounded thatch-home villages to **Sinatma**.

Two hours in a different direction takes you to the traditional village of **Pugima**. A walk along the main road leads to the saltwater wells near the village of **Hitigima**, and a few kilometres further to the **Kurima** and **Hitugi** villages.

One of the most intriguing villages is **Akima**, which is home to the infa-mous blackened, smoked *momi* (mummy), seen in just about every Irian publication – plan on tipping a few thousand rupiah for a peek at this gruesomely notorious site.

At **Jiwika** there is another mummy and an interesting Sunday market that makes the 15-kilometre journey a bit more worthwhile. On the way to the caves of **Wago Wago**, the village of **Pommo** boasts a mummy as well.

Treks & Wildlife

To the north, **Meagaima**, the **Wolo Valley** and **Lake Archbold** have some beautiful trekking areas that make civilization seem an entirely questionable

The Wildlife of Irian Jaya

Irian Puncak Jaya is the highest mountain peak in the country, towering into the clouds at more than 5,000 metres in height. Also known as **Gunung Jaya** and the Carstensz Pyramid, it is a slick glacial climb from which chilly air, wild winds and snow-covered slopes make this summit a challenge to even the most experienced mountain climbers.

The first successful attempt was in 1962 when a Dutch-supported expedition from Holland began from the Dani village of **Illaga** with 115 porters. The main members of the group included Heinrich Harrer of Austria, Bert Huizenga of Holland, Russell Kippax of Australia and Philip Temple of New Zealand.

For nearly four days they made their way through the thick inner jungles before reaching the Carstensz area named after a Dutch Sea Captain who was impressed by the place in the 17th century. Here, they set up a base camp and then the four main climbers plugged on with 11 others to reach the level called **Ngapalu** several days later.

At this point, Harrer, Huizenga, Kippax and Temple went on alone in the small hours of the morning on the 13th of February. In the worst weather conditions, they cut through snow and ice for nine hours to reach the height of the mountain – the first team in history to be victorious over this formidable summit.

Today, Puncak Jaya is known to climbers as one of the top seven peaks, and it is one of only three remaining tropical glaciers in the world. To prepare for the growing impact of tourism and to protect the culture of the more than 11,000 villagers who live within the Lorentz Reserve where Puncak Jaya is located, a new Information Centre is being established by the World Wide Fund for Nature.

Local guides are being trained for the Irian Jaya Guiding Association, educational conservation programs are being presented in area schools and a community cooperative is planned for the sale and distribution of traditional tribal crafts.

Alfred Russel Wallace, who proposed the

Mist on the Carstensz range.

Wallace Line division of flora and fauna between the east and west sectors of the archipelago, also sailed his way through the upper islands of Indonesia; his findings are published in the acclaimed *Malay Archipelago*.

Irian Jaya is truly a blissful land for birds, for it is the haven of more than 600 species - and around 50 types of "birds of paradise" found only in certain areas of this province. First seen in Europe in 1822 as treasures of skin and plumes reaped during Magellan's round-the-world voyage, myths about their mysterious beauty spread through the trade routes. One particularly amusing tale included the belief that these special aves remained in the sky – because, to highlight the beauty of their plumes, tribal traders always pulled off their legs and wings before the merchants ever saw them.

Since Irian Jaya (and even Moluccas) are across the faunal boundary of the Wallace line, the mammals are also of the Australian variety and include cuscus, bandicoots, tree kangaroos and wallabies. The insects are frighteningly large, as are the stunning butterflies of brilliant colours.

Reptiles such as monitor lizards and crocodiles take to the strong sun and fresh water, while in the surrounding seas some of the best underwater wildlife in the world slithers silently through the currents in the form of fishes, sharks, turtles and the rare *dugong* (a white, walrus-like mammal) sometimes mistaken for mermaids by tipsy pirates and sailors of yore. Motivated by profit and moved by adventure, Marco Polo and Magellan were among the first to travel through these unknown lands. Their curiosity led their fleets to discover new cultures and wildlife species, such as Magellan's "bird of paradise" plumes and Marco Polo's "unicorn" – probably the one-horned Javan rhino – which they introduced with a great aura of grandeur to the rapidly growing European and Asian worlds.

Irian Jaya's central Baliem Valley shelters the many tribes grouped under the common name of Dani peoples. Traditionally, their society is based on agriculture – mostly of tobacco, vegetables and the starchy *erom* (sweet potato) of which there are more than 60 varieties grown throughout the area. Men prepare and plow the soil, while women plant, harvest and weed during the times in-between. Settled into thatched, *honay* (rounded houses), each *kampung* (village) has many separate buildings for cooking, animals, men, women and larger structures where several families might live together.

Irian Jaya's southern coast is a remote escape for underwater adventure as well, as is the area between Biak and the main island.

However, trekking and walks around the central Wamena area are more popular, as the airfare is relatively inexpensive and the chance to travel back into the world of the *Dani* tribes is an adventure that most explorers are reluctant to miss.

Puncak Jaya, in the middle of the main island, is a mountaineer's Mecca, while parks such as **Lorentz** and **Manusela** provide excellent walking and wildlife viewing opportunities for those willing to "suffer" the remote areas' basic life style.

dream. West of Wamena, **Lake Habbema** is settled almost 3,500 metres above sea level on the way to **Gunung Trikora**, which rises upwards for 4,750 metres and promises excellent climbing and camping adventures.

Serious climbers make the annual pilgrimage to **Puncak Jakakesuma**, which towers more than 5,000 metres over the land.

A glacial peak, **Gunung Jaya** is so high that you can look out over the rugged landscape all the way to the ocean; get a permit, proper gear and a good health check before embarking on this strenuous journey.

The rather unusual glory of the cassowary.

For wildlife watchers and explorers, the interior also shelters species found nowhere else in the world–and the remoteness of the reserves within which they lie makes the trip there that much better.

By plane, one can reach the start-ing point for **Lorentz National Park**, where the World Wide Fund for Nature has invested in educational programmes for blending wildlife conservation and local culture with the growing influence of tourism – contact the office in Jayapura for information.

A wallaby in Timika.

At the very end of the line of the Indonesian archipelago, the **Rawa Biru Wasur Reserve** is a rough-and-tumble jeep drive from the eastern town of **Merauke** and a haven for parrots, cassowaries, marsupials, crocodiles and the elusive *dugongs* – marine mammals of the sea.

Permits are also required for these parks as well, so after picking up your *surat jalan* (travel permit), head for Jayapura's office of the PHPA. For details on walks and guides in the Wamena area, most travel agencies and *losmen*

Trial to Carstensz Base Camp.

(rooms to let) in Jayapura will be happy to provide information – or, when you arrive in Wamena, you will probably be greeted at the airport by a cheerful and knowledgeable young guide looking for hire.

Above the wide area of islands which outline the better-known areas of the archipelago, the sea and jungles of Indonesia's outer provinces still remain relatively unscathed by the influences of a 20th century world.

These are the areas which, for the most part, have only been settled in the

Hamadi Beach, Jayapura, for those who wish to dust off.

outer fringes. Here, around the edges and along the central shipping paths that wind between them, large port cities sprawl between rough coral reefs and wide, wild rivers. Civilization lingers at the edge of the thickest forests, but is not yet able to push its modern way through the deep, tightly protected paths of ancient cultures.

Modernization is slow in Irian Jaya, a mysterious land of unknown treasures of wildlife and anicent tribes. In Irian Jaya only of all Indonesia's islands will you find beauty truly unspoiled.

I

ndonesian cuisine is a celebration of the fruits of the land, accented with a world of flavours that "spice up" the taste. From restaurant to *warung* (stall) to small village kitchen, excellent but usually hot food, is available. A spoon of spicy-hot *sambal* (hot spicy chilli sauce), a pinch of salt; several drops of *kecap asin* (similar to soy sauce), and a little *kecap manis* (sweet sauce similar to molasses) balance the taste. Pungent, fresh *bawang* (onions), garlic, *jahe* (ginger) and red and green *lombok* (chilli peppers) are favoured accents to any meal prepared throughout the islands.

At the street *warungs* and local restaurants, small bottles of these flavourings and a dish of vinegar *acar* (pickled vegetables) will be at the table. Taste the food *first* before adding the accents, as blind mixing can result in some potent, even inedible combinations.

Watch out for the special *sambal* bowls of seedy crushed *lombok rawit* chillies; the red variety can be quite tame in

429

First to market, then a spiced-up meal.

For Indonesia, spice never runs out.

Bali and Java – but the green Sulawesi and Irian mix can set a tongue smoking in seconds. The most common cooking utensils are the *wok* (cast iron pan), in which the food sizzles over an open wood or kerosene fire, along with the boiling pots and the grill. The styles of cooking are:– *goreng* (fried or stirred in oil) *rebus* (boiled) and *bakar* (barbequing over an open fire). If you want extra hot sauce, ask for *pedas* (hot), *manis* (sweet) and *garam* (salt).

Rice & Noodles

When you arrive in the country, be prepared to eat *nasi* (rice) – and lots of it. Aside from the bland western offer-

ings, it is included in nearly every culinary offering from main meals even to snacks and sweets. But, there are so many varieties of dishes, that it soon becomes second nature to have a steaming plate of it for breakfast, or alongside an after-dark dinner.

The texture and quality of rice are usually perfect and, like baskets of bread that accompany food in most western restaurants, rice is the natural complement for any sweet or spicy meal. *Nasi putih* (white rice) without added side dishes or spices, is served simply steamed or plain and is always handy for slowing the inevitable uneasy stomach. Heaping plates of it accompany bowls of *sop* (clear soup with bits of meat and vegetables), and *soto* (soup with a stronger, meaty broth often filled with thin noodles and larger chunks of tomato, onions and greens). The soup is spooned over the rice, mixed with a few drops of *kecap manis* (sweet sauce), a dash of *sambal* (hot spicy chilli sauce) and a squeeze of lime for a fantastic and filling meal.

Nasi goreng (fried rice), is the most popular dish to be found anywhere in the islands, and probably the only one that tastes much the same wherever you order it. *Nasi goreng* is made by tossing cooked rice into the *wok*, spicy smoke spilling out from it as vegetables and sauces are chopped up and dabbled into the mix which is topped with a light *keropok* (prawn cracker) before being served up by steaming platefuls.

Other common rice dishes often served as the main fare are *nasi rames* (white rice with a mixed side dish of bits of various boiled, spicy vegetables), *nasi pecel* (rice served with a side of bean sprouts, cucumbers and leaves in sweet peanut sauce), *nasi rawon* (rice served with spicy onion-beef soup), *nasi gudeg* (rice served with pieces of chicken and jackfruit), and *nasi campur* (rice topped with a sample of almost everything from the kitchen).

Rice is also the central serving in *padang*-style (field style) meals where bowls of various meat and vegetable dishes are brought to the table for diners to chose their own meal. Ask for the cost first; as the usual procedure is that you pay for each item you eat, regardless of whether you finish the serving.

Indonesia fare, dressed up in 5-star style.

Varieties of *mie* (noodles) are the secondary basis of Indonesian food that can be a welcome relief from the endless servings of rice. Contained in a pack of, they come thick and wavy, and can be boiled up in less than a minute. In restaurants, you may find a spaghetti-type noodle served, such as in *bakso* (meatball soup), or the thin *bakmie* (rice-flour) noodles that add a lighter eastern texture to soups and fried dishes.

Delicious *mie goreng* (fried noodles) is served up with the same sauces and spices as *nasi goreng*, and is also a popular dish found just about anywhere in the islands. In the Moluccas islands and parts of Irian Jaya, *sago* is more common than rice (which tends to be rather bland in these areas). Similar to the

Bak mee goreng (fried noodles with shredded meat) is dependable and inexpensive everywhere.

potato, *sago* is a thick, starchy food extracted from the tree of the same name. It is usually served either chopped and boiled or fried along with the usual side dishes. However, in east Java, tasty *sago* chips flavoured with spicy ginger make for an unusual and sweet afternoon snack.

Main Fare

Along with their rice, most Indonesians enjoy meat and vegetables just as much as in the west, although perhaps to a less voracious degree. In restaurants, the portions are sometimes smaller than western expectations, but eaten slowly and supplemented with servings of noo-

dles and rice they prove to be a filling meal. However, the *warungs* (street stalls) will usually heap on the toppings for an inexpensive and spicier serving that is often impossible to finish. When browsing through the menu, keep in mind that *daging* means meat; *sapi* is beef, *ayam* is chicken, *telor* or *telur* are eggs, *babi* means pork and *kambing* is goat. Meat is usually chopped and fried, and is used to top different dishes, it is a bit tougher and less tasty than most western offerings. Some of the best seafood in the world is also found in the islands, and most restaurants include selections of *ikan*, (fish) – for example, *ikan bakar* (grilled fish), *ikan asin* (salted fish), ikan *laut (ocean fish) and ikan belut (eel).* In northern Sumatra and central Kalimantan, the huge size of the *udang* (prawns) is incredible; also available throughout the archipelago are *kepiting* (crab), *cumi-cumi* (squid), *udang karang* (lobster), oysters and tiny, tasty *kodok* (frog).

The best place to find *ikan bakar* is at Ambon's night market in the Moluccas, here enormous meaty fish, whole or half, are blackened and served with a cone-shaped loaf of sour dough bread. These servings are far too much for one person to consume, but they make excellent leftovers for the next day.

One of Indonesia's specialties is grilled meat on a stick, covered with sweet, spicy ingredients which is then dipped into a thick peanut sauce. Known as *satay*, or *sate*, it is a delicious change as a main meal, be it of chicken, beef, pork or goat meat. Ten sticks is the usual portion, served with a plate of hot white rice or *lontong* (rice packed into a tubular banana leaf and then steamed). The city nights are filled with entire streets boasting rows of *satay* stands that fill the air with the pungent aroma of meaty smoke wafting from open fires.

Martabak is a unique food which is common in central Sumatra, Java and Bali, though it can be found in most other islands as well. It is similar to an omelette, and consists of a scrambled egg mix of spices and vegetables fried on a round, flat grill and folded into a thin square, then cut into small pieces and dipped in hot sauce for a crispy snack – Bengkulu in Sumatra and Gilimanuk in Bali serve incredibly tasty *martabak* from their street stands.

There is no better way than the traditional open fire for satay.

Another tasty Indonesian invention is *bubur* (rice porridge), served thick and filled with chunks of seafood or chicken and topped with dried onions. Cooked in coconut milk, sweet versions are also a common afternoon treat : *bubur kacang* (porridge made with mung beans; *bubur hitam* (porridge with a dark, sweet syrup); and *bubur hijau* (porridge with a flavouring a bit like white chocolate but green in colour). Seasonal vegetables are served to accompany the meal in a number of different styles. *Sayur* is the usual term used, but you will find it is everything from boiled spinach-like leaves to *sayur kacang* with bean sprouts. *Kacang* is the word used for nearly every variety of "beans", including green beans, sprouts, red kidney

Gado-gado, a regular snack of mixed vegetable, slopped over with sweet peanut sauce.

beans, mung beans and peanuts. *Sayur-sayuran,* (vegetable soup spooned over rice) and *gado-gado* (a snack of mixed vegetables served hot or cold and slathered in sweet peanut sauce) are also popular vegetable accompaniments to any meal.

Cap cai (pronounced "chop chai") is a bland mix of stir-fried lettuce, tomatoes, onions, celery, carrots and other garden fare, usually served in enormous portions that can easily be eaten with rice or by itself, and it also makes a great side dish for spicy meals.

Fruits

You will never go hungry in Indonesia,

(unless you are out in the villages) as there is always a *warung* (food stall) around every corner. From early morning onwards they serve light snacks throughout the day.

In the small *toko* (stores), fruits are usually found, and they are one of the glorious pleasures of these islands. Sweet *pisang* (bananas), soft *nanas* (pineapples), juicy orange papaya and tangerine-like *jeruk* are commonly found. *Apels* are apples, usually expensive and not as fresh as the New Zealand or American varieties; it is better to go for the true Indonesian crops instead, such as sweet yellow star-shaped *belimbing,* the familiar *apokat* (avocado), the pink sweet-sour *jambu,* the snake-skinned *salak,* the tasty *mango* and the round, dark purple

Delicious soupy noodles sold at "restaurant" or wheels.

mangosteen.

Favourites are the hairy crimson "monkey balls" of sweet *rambutan* and the plentiful *kelapa* (coconut). There is also the infamous *durian* fruit, recognized by its spiky shell and distinct odour that most people despise. However, it is rumoured to light a fire of hunger and passion in tigers, elephants and humans – thus the seasonal saying of Kalimantan, "When the *durians* are down, *sarongs* (wrap around skirt-like garment) are up."

Light Snacks

Lighter snacks include *tahu* (soft square cake made of soya bean curd) that is somewhat reminiscent of a thin fried egg and is usually served with a couple of small peppers or a vegetable filling. *Tempe* (soya bean cake) is rich in protein and iron, it is often fried into *tempe goreng* (fried soya bean) with chillies and sugar.

Indonesians eat like their *roti* (bread) sliced, white and usually tinged with the taste of sugar. Smaller *roti* are usually found in street stalls or *toko*s (stores) where they are served for breakfast or snacks, and many have *coklat* (chocolate) or varied fruit fillings, or are covered in sugar or cinnamon similar to the western doughnut. *Madu* (honey), and jam are added to *roti bakar* (toast) which is topped with sweet chocolate sprinkles.

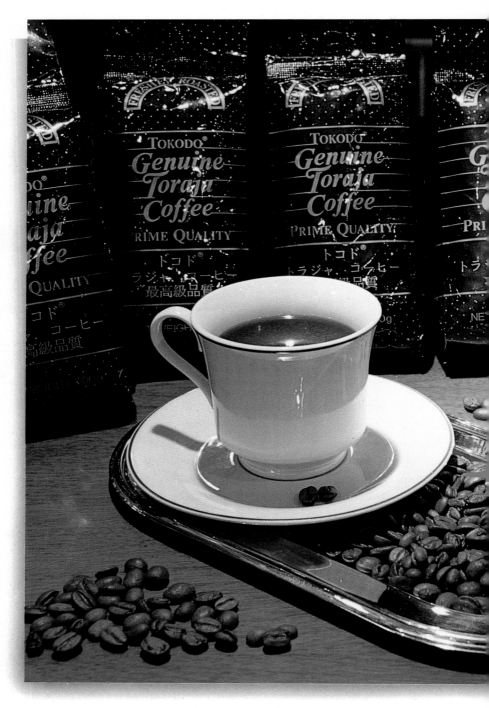

Coffee from the Celebes is exported widely.

Sweet Treats

If you have a sweet tooth, there will be no cravings here, for Indonesia has sugary treats that can put anyone into shock. Typical chewing gum and *gula gula* (bon bons, *or* candies), are available everywhere, as are chocolate bars, though they are not as rich or sweet as the familiar western versions.

Sweet *bubur* (rice porriage) cooked in coconut milk are filling snacks, as are the small *pisang goreng* (fried bananas) On hot afternoons, a bowl of *es* (crushed ice served with sugary syrups) makes a lovely cooling treat; try *es kacang* (ice with mung beans), *es buah buah*, (ice with slices of fresh fruit) or the colourful, syrup-striped *es campur* that mixes in a bit of everything. Though not as rich or sweet as European varieties, *es krim* (ice cream) is commonly found, in the form of frozen bars or scooped into dishes at special snack houses.

Minum, Mister?

To eat is *makan*, and to drink is *minum*, normally the last thing that is ordered with a meal. A glass of water is often served to each person at the table – feel it first; if it is hot, it has been boiled and is probably safe to drink. Still, the smarter option is to either ask for *air panas* (hot or boiled water), or order a boiled drink such as coffee or tea instead. Indonesian tea is perfect.

Nasi Goreng (Indonesian Fried Rice)

Everywhere across the archipelago, you'll find the dish *nasi goreng* (spicy fried rice) that is adored by all Indonesians at any time of the day. Both nutritious and filling, it is a tasty way to start the morning, a light afternoon snack or a delicious dinner meal that requires few utensils and just a little kitchen talent. This recipe is also conveniently flexible because, it traditionally only needs some rice, a bit of oil and a pile of leftovers! For the official recipe, however, here is what you will need:

Main Ingredients:
3 tablespoons vegetable oil
3 tablespoons chopped onion (any type will do)
4 minced cloves of garlic
2 tablespoons of *sambal* (red hot sauce – add more if you like it spicy, less if not)
1$\frac{1}{2}$ teaspoons salt,
1 cup diced meat (any mix works well – try beef, chicken or boiled eggs to see what you like best),
2 tablespoons sweet soy sauce,
3 cups white rice (cold rice works as well as steaming hot rice),
Added garnishes: Strips of fried egg (recipe follows) Crispy fried onions (recipe follows), Cucumber slices.

Method:
In a large *wok* (cast iron pan), heat the oil until sizzling, then add onion, garlic, *sambal* and salt and stir for about one minute.

Add the soy sauce and meat, then stir for about ten minutes, or until the meat is soaked with the seasonings.
Then, add the rice and stir until the entire meal is steaming hot – keep it moving or it may stick to the *wok*.
When heated, scoop the mixture into a large bowl or separate plates and sprinkle with crispy fried onions.
For decoration, lay a few omelette strips on top and arrange several slices of cucumber alongside the edge of the plate. Makes four servings.

To make Egg Strips
Simply beat together two eggs and a teaspoon of water, then melt a pat of butter in the bottom of a large frying pan and pour in the mixture to obtain a thin coating at the bottom of the skillet. When cooked through, roll up like a crêpe and cut into strips – then unroll and lay on top of the *nasi goreng* when ready.

To make Crispy Fried Onions:
Also known as *bawang goreng*, this crispy garnish is the perfect ingredient to a spicy meal. The most important technique is to begin with minced, dried onions – this can be done by slicing very thin strips of onion which are then cooked by being placed in a fine-mesh strainer which is immersed in hot vegetable oil until golden brown, (for half a minute or so). Dry on a paper towel to soak up the excess oil, then store in an air-tight container until ready to use.

Sweet, aromatic and pungent, tea will become a familiar scent as you travel, as it is probably the most common drink anytime and anywhere within the archipelogo. Some people find it too sweet; if so, ask for *te panas* (hot tea), rather than *te manis* (hot, sweet tea). Another instruction that works to lessen the sugar quantity is *sedikit gula*, ("just a little sugar"). *Te susu* comes with a thick bottom layer of sweet-ened, condensed milk – the Indonesian version of cream.

Coffee drinkers, get prepared for a shock – Indonesian *kopi* (coffee) is very different from western equivalents. Do not expect to find "de-caf" and be prepared to scoop silt-like grains from the top of the cup (and your teeth). Like *te* (tea), *kopi susu* has condensed milk stirred in producing a lighter brown liquid, and *kopi manis* is served with sugar.

A spit barbecue by the beach at Lovina, Bali.

Susu alone is like a glass of hot milk but sweeter versions are obtained by mixing condensed milk and hot water. Juices are usually fresh, but be careful of the use of unboiled ice to create a frothy effect. If you like your juice sugarless ask for *tidak gula* as sugar is usually added to every type of cold drink from banana, papaya and pineapple to *jeruk* (citrus fruit) and tomato. *Es kelapa* (ice coconut) is refreshing on hot afternoons especially served with shavings of coconut sweet coconut milk. Soy beans one of nature's healthiest products are used in another drink which is served throughout the islands: This drink is a watery mix similar to lemonade, but is light, sweet (as is almost everything in Indonesia) and absolutely refreshing!

Kelapa Muda

This is a cool, refreshing drink that is commonly drunk during long afternoons when the sunlight is nearly as unbearable as the heat. Not too sweet, this treat is light and tasty as an accompaniment to a midday snack or a before-bed thirst-quencher. It is also a popular diuretic for Indonesian women.

Ingredients:
1 coconut
1 lime
2 teaspoons sugar
ice shavings

Method:
Drain the juice of the coconut into a pitcher, and add an amount of water that is half that of the coconut milk.
Pour into two glasses of ice. Sweeten with sugar. Cut the lime into halves, each half being squeezed into separate glasses to give it a "tang". Delicious! Makes two servings.

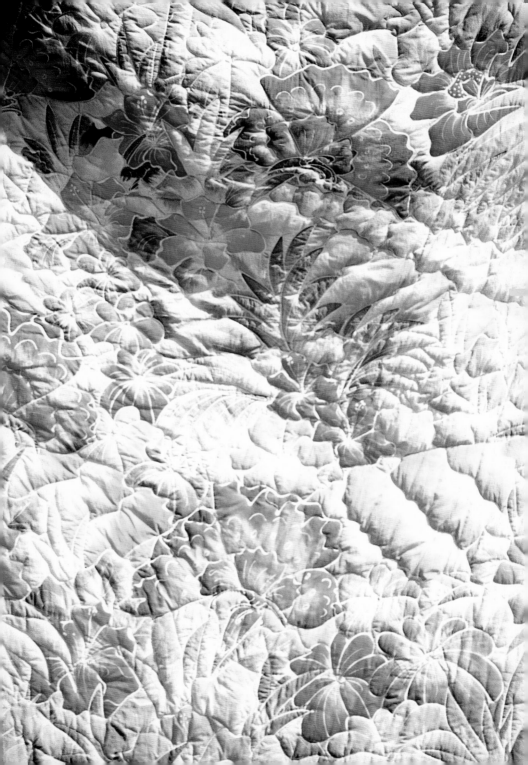

Shopping

Berapa harga, Missus?" "Mau apa?" "Murah, murah! Mau beli sekarang?" If you leave the main shopping malls and hotels you will soon become accustomed to these cries *"how much missy" "What do you want? "Cheap, cheap!"* These are the beckoning calls of the bright-eyed shopkeepers of Indonesia, men and women who run family-owned stalls, hawking everything from thongs to quail eggs and whistles.

The Pancasila spells out the five principals governing Indonesian life.

Shopping is half the fun of being in Indonesia; local goods are colourful and varied, and they reflect the cultural background of the area you are visiting. Best of all, things are unique, relatively inexpensive and often homemade. So, when you buy gifts and souvenirs there is a sense of pride, not only that you have received something special, but that your money probably helped someones family buy much-needed clothing, school books or a meal.

The Easy Way Out

Wherever you are in Indonesia markets are just

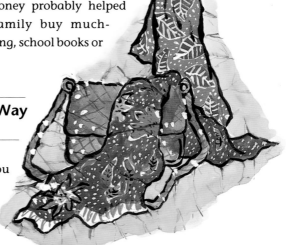

Ikats, songkets, batiks by the metres or sarong lengths make useful souvenirs.

around the corner. However, for travellers with limited time, there are also the glitzy, modern big-city stores that not only make one-stop souvenir and gift shopping a breeze, but also give you an overview of the different types of Indonesian handicrafts especially useful if you have only just arrived in the country.

Unless you are heading straight to the jungle, you will probably stay within or close to one of the major cities. And, if you are planning on bringing back things for your family and friends, it pays to take a day to relax and have fun "window shopping" various clothing, crafts and handiwork displayed in some of the larger stores, to get an idea of prices and where in the archipelago

these things can be bought. Then, when you return enroute to the airport, you can also pick up anything that you can not find elsewhere or might not have had time to purchase during your travels.

In Jakarta, the best-known all-in-one shopping store is **Sarinah** – located at Blok M in the suburb of Kebayoran and on Jalan Thamrin behind **McDonald's** and the **Hard Rock Cafe** in the centre of the city – which makes for a fun introduction to Indonesia and first exposure to the local culture. Once you get past the typical western clothing, perfume and music sections, you will find floors of interesting souvenirs from all over the archipelago; it can take hours to wander around!

Luckily, the goods are segregated according to island – for example, all the crafts from Sumatra are displayed in one area and sub-divided into cultural sections, so, the vast store becomes a bit like walking into a small island market. Here, too, because it is a department store, you can really examine the crafts without being entreatied by shop owners and vendors who think they might have a sale.

Bring some paper to make notes on if you like – colour, price, area, history and so on – this could be a useful reference later on when you shop in the rural areas and are left to your own bargaining skills. Those with more initiative might get the name of the artist and go and look for his work around the towns and villages that they visit.

In Jakarta, other good "overview" shopping areas include; **The Jakarta Handicraft Center** in Menteng, the **Indonesian Bazaar** at the Hilton Hotel and **Pasar Seni** at the Ancol Recreation Park. Other main cities such as Bandung, Cirebon, Solo, Surabaya and Yogyakarta have smaller versions of western-style department stores, but in these areas, especially Yogyakarta it is more enjoyable to simply walk and "window shop" before you decide to buy.

The Shopping Scene

You can find just about anything in Indonesia; the trick is having the patience to get around and really look for

Beautiful carvings may be shipped to one's home.

it within the area you are visiting. Unlike the precise, pristine organization of Singapore or other "western-style" large cities, Indonesian shopping has a reputation for chaos that is unfortunately well deserved. Instead of setting out with a mad desire for a particular item, begin with a general idea and an open mind – you may come back with something far more interesting than you originally intended!

Antiques are available almost everywhere and in every shape and form, but often at exorbitant prices. Unless you are fluent in *Bahasa Indonesia*, or you are absolutely certain about the authenticity and cost of an item, it is much safer to buy a good reproduction or pick up a similar antique at home.

Strawhats come in western styles, with Indonesian handiwork.

Batik

It is colourful, it is unusual, and it is everywhere, particularly in east Java and Bali. *Batik* fabrics, *batik sarongs* (waist wrap around skirt-like garment), *batik* tee-shirts, *batik* pants, *batik* handbags, *batik* bedsheets ... the list is unending. *Batik Tulis* means hand-painted, while *Batik Cap* is block – printed. Available in cotton, rayon, silk and other light fabrics, *batik* is usually easily washed in cold water and the colours should stay bright for years. However, look out for mass-manufactured designs before you buy, as there is nothing worse than thinking that you posses an original and then walking into someone who is wearing exactly the same design!

Books

Except for a few stores in Jakarta and the large city hotels, books are nearly impossible to find in Indonesia! The best small *"toko buku"* (bookstores) are full of Indonesian textbooks and Islamic religious texts, and the modern stores sell mostly magazines or bestseller-list novels. However, you can, pick up lovely photo books and travel publications about the archipelago's landscape and culture, which often make fine gifts or souvenirs since you can not find them at home (many are pubished in Jakarta or Singapore and have limited distribution outside Southeast Asia).

Brass

Dutch lamps and old chandeliers make unusual souvenirs, although they are sometimes difficult to find, look in antique shops and flea markets.

Clothes & Fashion

Because of the intense sunlight and heat, the Indonesian wardrobe is one of the most comfortable and attractive in the world. Not only will you always be able to find clothes that fit, no matter what your size, but you will soon find that there are a riot of colours and patterns available to suit anybody's taste or shape. Besides *batik* styles, hand-painted tee-shirts and linens are good souvenirs to take back with you, as you can tell the artist what you would like him or her to design.

Western clothes are another matter; if you are not the same size as the typical petite Indonesian, outside of the major cities you may have trouble finding even a simple pair of jeans. Alternatively, you could go for the "designer" clothes that are available at the various markets – some are the real thing, but there are some excellent lines of designer copies.

Tailoring is also an excellent option in Indonesia, for there are plenty of high-quality shops and a great selection

Irian Jaya weaving designs.

of materials available. It helps to have a sketch or picture of what you would like, and to shop around a little before you purchase materials to see who can sew it for the best quality and price – do not be afraid to ask for samples of the tailor's previous work, or for recommendations from the locals.

Computers & Electronics

We suggest that you forget electronics, unless you want to cart a television or refrigerator back with you, and you can probably buy it cheaper at home anyway. However small items like radios and cassette players can be good value. However, as far as computers go, a pur-

Bali is a great place to buy paintings.

chase can take weeks; you walk into the store, look through the brochures and decide what you want – and unless it is a Toshiba® it probably will not be available – then you wait for several hours (or days) for it to come from the mysterious "warehouse" – a frustrating and often unsuccessful experience.

Once you get the product there is little opportunity for questions, much less to try the machine before you buy it, although programmes (bootlegged, of course!) are included.

If you truly and absolutely determined to buy electronics, then, it is best to pay the extra airfare to Singapore and buy one there, where you will find a far better selection, genuine warranties, lessons and reliable service.

Furniture

Indonesia has a wealth of talented craftspeople who spend their lives fashioning beautiful four-poster beds, intricately carved dressers and comfortable chairs.

If you are certain you can get it home (many larger shops can help you arrange with the shipping) furniture can be one of the most unique and useful purchases you will find in Indonesia.

In the villages, you will probably also come across small-time furniture-makers who do personal work for family and friends. These carpenters often offer a more interesting version at a far lower price. Of course, in these situations you have to order ahead and arrange your own method of transporting the item back home.

Silver & Gold

One of the treasures since the time of pirates, gold can be found everywhere, and often at lower prices than in the west. Precious stones are also plentiful, but be prepared to pay for them, particularly in the tourist areas.

Silver bracelets, rings and other souvenirs are popular throughout the islands. Particularly beautiful are the elegant crafted silverwork ships and miniature houses found in various areas – look in **Sarinah** to see what is available. Indonesia is famous for the intricately designed filagree style of silverwork which can be bought in many forms of ornamentation.

Paintings

Almost every Indonesian is an aspiring artist, so you will find paintings everywhere. However, many are reproductions of something else, so for something original your best bet is to wander through the markets. Balinese paintings are lovely, and you will find plenty of galleries, though paintings by well-known artists will be rather pricey. The Balinese school of young artists is worth investing in.

Photography

Camera goods are available in the large cities and tourist centres. The film is usually Kodak® or Fuji®, and slide film is easy to find. However, processing often comes out under or over-exposed; ask others who have had film developed where it can be reliably done.

Textiles

Do not leave Indonesia without purchasing some kind of textile to remind you of the trip; such a variety of beautiful designs are available that it would be a shame to skip the one thing that really reflects the diversity of local culture. Again, wander through **Sarinah** for ideas and try to ascertain the type of textile you might like to purchase. *Batik*, *ikat* weaving, basketry, silks and other items are gorgeous gift ideas, and easy and light to carry with you too.

A Spree Throughout The Islands

Rows of shops line the gangs of Bali's beach areas, mixing denim jackets and surf boards with a brilliant variety of artwork and fashion. The best buys in Kuta and Legian are jewellery and clothing, (do not forget about the offers for hair braiding and massage). This area also boasts endless shops selling arts

A woodcarving materialises with meticulous chipping and chiselling.

and crafts. Ubud is a bit more quiet but offers the same variety around the river, on the road to Goa Gajah or along the Monkey Forest Road.

Best Bets

Bandung is the place for *wayang golek* (lifesize wooden puppets) and Sundanese musical instruments; Solo for antiques, *kerises* (wavy-bladed daggers) traditional richl coloured *luris* cloth and costumes; Yogyakarta for silverwork, textiles, *wayang kulit* (shadow puppets) and masks; Madura for teak furniture and Surabaya for just about everything, including street markets of Islamic clothing, oils, books, prayer beads and food.

Besides its beautiful gardens, Bogor offers **The Gong Foundary** and **Pak Sukarna**'s on Jalan Pancasan, where you can watch *gamelan* (percussion-type orcestra) instruments being made and even order instruments for personal purchase. Semarang also boasts two *jamu* (traditional medicine manufacturers). Each area of the archipelago also has its own style of *batik* – for example, Cirebon's Chinese-influenced designs. If you do not know much about the craft, there are plenty of small schools and shops that will be happy to demonstrate their expertise for you.

Gold and silver-threaded *songket* cloth is one of the beautiful souvenirs of Sumatra, usually found in the *sarongs* (waist wrap-around skirt) and scarves of the western areas such as the weaving

centres of Silungkang and Pandai Sikat. Fine silverwork is created at Kota Gede near Bukittinggi, while Bukittinggi itself is an excellent place to pick up Minangkabau craftworks like silver *salapah padusi* (boxes for storing betel nuts) and brass *salapah panjang* (boxes for keeping tobacco). Intricate cloths of needle weaving, embroidery and *songket* can also be bought here. Around Toba, Batak artefacts are common from musical instruments to magic books, wands, and wooden *topeng* (masks used in funeral dances). In Aceh, old weapons such as knives, swords a selection of Dutch porcelain, excellent silver and gold jewellery and rare Acehnese weaving can be found. Medan's markets offer a variety of carvings and crafts. In Sumatra ask around in the smaller villages and shops, for something special. Nusa Tenggara has a surprising number of markets that are all worth looking at to purchase various traditional goods.

At Ampenan in Lombok, you will find beautiful basketwork, woodcarving, weaving, even *songket* cloth and some antiques! Sumbawa, Besar and Sape have a lot of Islamic goods, including fabrics, and lovely *songket* shawls and ceremonial *sarongs;* young tourguide trainees will happily lead you to the home of the weavers. In Kampung Komodo, woodcarvers hone dragon likenesses according to your size and specifications, and pretty pearls for rings and necklaces are available from local fishermen. Although Flores' markets are bare, nevertheless they are good places

Pulutan pottery from Sulawesi.

to examine the different varieties of cloth and *sarongs. Ikat sarongs* and blankets are Timor specialties; in Kupang, you will also find *lontar* (leaf hats), *sirih* (bamboo boxes) and intricate silver jewellery. Sumba blankets are famous for their brilliant *ikat* colours and designs, and the textiles can be purchased throughout the island – browse along the Waingapu waterfront. In Sulawesi, Kendiri filigree jewellery is excellent value, as is Makassar brasswork, fine silk, Chinese pottery and interesting mounted butterflies that are found in the markets Ujung Pandang.

The tourist areas of Tanatoraja have some of the most interesting shops in the archipelago, crammed with everything from plant seed jewellery, "wind chime" calendars, silver and bamboo containers and odd hand-painted wooden chickens, to tacky picture frames, tasty Toraja coffee and replicas of traditional houses.

Manado

Manado and north Sulawesi have a variety of sea-oriented souvenirs and jewellery. Various Dayak crafts can be found at Kalimantan's markets in Banjarmasin and Samarinda, if you are travelling to the highlands it would be more meaningful to purchase something directly from a villager. In the Moluccas, Ambon's streets are packed with night markets offering pearl-shell

Bargaining Smart

One of the first things you will learn when shopping in the open markets of Indonesia is that bargaining is the key word. If the price is not listed, it will invariably be reduced if you haggle a bit; in fact, this is an established custom, and most shopkeepers will expect an enjoyable bargaining session. When you enter the street markets, you may be overwhelmed by the colour, action and noise. It will seem as if vendors are coming at you from all directions, trying to present you with everything, and always with a pleasant, hopeful smile. Its exciting to be in the midst of it all, for there are so many choices that the ambience and selections make western department store offerings seem boring and pristine. Just go slowly, and do not be afraid to look at things carefully.

If you are pursued by questions, simply smile back and say, "*Lihat, lihat sekarang*", – (pronounced this way: *lee-hat lee-hat se-kar-ang* – "I'm just looking now").

The next step, once you decide that you want something, will be to bargain for it, which can be an interesting and frustrating game. Vendors expect it, and they probably realize that you are neither familiar with the process nor have any idea how much it should cost. Often, the vendor will make up a price – sometimes a hilariously outrageous one – so ask the locals around you what the price is, or try several different vendors first to get a general idea.

Bargaining Basics

Bargaining can be fun, though sometimes exhausting, unless you are prepared to pay the immediate asking price – usually about a-third higher than the real price – it is practically impossible to make a purchase quickly. Thus, the rule when shopping is to make sure you

have plenty of time; after all, there is no point in trying to hurry the sale, so look around and be prepared to spend a lot of time talking to people.

Also, when shopping, *relax*. It is extremely easy to become excited in the heat of bargaining, but the Indonesian method is to take things slowly, and in a friendly manner. In the small stores, you may be offered a cup of tea while you look around, or you may be invited into the back room, or next door to someone's home to actually see the artist at work. Just a note: no matter what you buy, it is usually going to be of better quality and cost less in the small shops than in the regular city stores.

Another trick to bargaining: smile. Be friendly, patient, and gentle when looking around. Sometimes, a small token from your own country – a pin, flag, earrings – makes a good gift to soften up the seller if there is something you would really like to purchase. Talk with the vendors, ask how long they have been in the area, where they are from, if they have family, and other friendly questions to show interest in the culture and crafts. People are so used to the brash type of tourist that one who is genuinely interested in them makes a favourable impact and will probably get a better deal and make a lot of instant friends.

Some visitors become impatient at the amount of time it takes, or frustrated with a price that does not soon come down to their idea of a bargain. If you are not certain about the usual cost of something, simply wait to buy it, then look around at other shops and ask about prices; you can always return to the first store, or perhaps pick up the item somewhere else. The key to a good day of shopping is to enjoy it, so keep in mind where you are, and how the money that you spend can help the vendor and his family or village.

flower and animal designs, seashell artwork, jewellery and basketwork. As for Irian Jaya, apart from the tourist trade centres around the Baliem Valley the other main city markets tend to lack

good souvenirs. In Baliem, you can buy cowrie shell necklaces, woven *sekan* (rattan bracelets), woodcarvings, handbags and *horim* (penis guard) – a fun and shocking gift.

Wherever you travel in the archipelago, you will always find sporting activities a popular part of the culture.

Given the expanse of seas and coral reefs, lush jungle trails, steep mountains and wide fields, life in Indonesia has always been centred on exercise and physical action. Farming and fishing, gathering crops from the slopes of volcanoes and walking the distance between villages for centuries has resulted in a culture of strong people many of whom are all in great shape.

Bali, the popular playground of Indonesia.

453

Reefs & Rugged Coves

On every island, there are opportunities for watersports, from Bali's beaches to Java's sprawling west coast luxury hotels. Thousands of miles of coastline hide quiet bays and rugged coves, you can swim and sunbathe with a group of young children ... or next

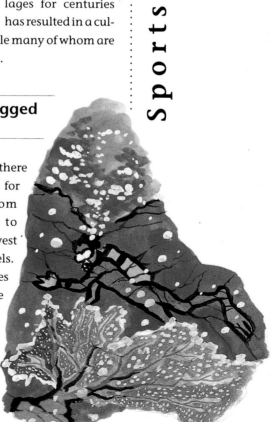

Surf-riding in Kuta, Bali.

to a private waterfall for a very romantic setting.

Cruise The Currents

More than 17,000 islands dot the aquamarine waves, where pods of killer whales, sea snakes and sharks cruise the currents over brilliant coral, delicate sea fans and enormous barrel sponges.

Nourished by Sunshine

Nourished by endless sunshine, there is plentiful plankton supply for smaller species of plants and fish, which in turn make a meal for the larger rays, mar-

lins, jackfish and barracuda found in the archipelago's waters.

Snorkelling & Scuba Diving

Snorkelling and scuba diving enthusiasts are drawn from all corners of the world to these reefs – particularly those of Moluccas' Spice Islands.

West of Bali

West of Bali, near Padangbai, divers are often surrounded by schools of friendly fish, and the Tulamben beach boasts the wreck of the **SS Liberty** to explore.

Underwater Sights

Stunning underwater sights are also found along the edges of Irian Jaya, between Biak and the main island, a pristine diving site that has recently been discovered.

Several live-aboard dive boats are available for charter at the Jayapura marina.

North of Flores

North of Flores, the coral gardens near Maumere hold such rich marine life that the area is the site for annual international photo competitions.

Visibility extends up to 70 metres and as recently as 1986 new species of aquatic life have been discovered.

Riau Archipelago

Another exciting area is above Sumatra, where the more than 3,000 islands of the Riau Archipelago are the site of many Japanese WWII shipwrecks.

Coral Gardens

Most are in shallow water, and there are gorgeous coral gardens as well. Boats can be hired from either Jakarta, Singapore, or smaller cities along the eastern Sumatran coastline.

Dugouts & Divers

Manado's Bunaken area is also a popular attraction, where dugout canoes take divers to shallow reefs around the islands. Equipment can be hired, but it's best to bring your own, and the nature reserve of Tangkoko-Batuangus makes a nice island break from the view underwater.

Around Pulau Seribu

Closer to the main metropolitan areas of Indonesia are the dive and snorkelling resorts around Pulau Seribu, or the Thousand Islands just north of Jakarta – the northern islands have been zoned as a national marine park to protect the biodiversity and beauty of the area.

Peucang & Panaitan Islands

Or, for a more unusual and peaceful underwater holiday, Peucang and Panaitan Islands off Java's west coast are part of Ujung Kulon National Park, and the reefs surrounding them are prime areas for exploration.

Boating & Sailing

Boating and sailing are part of coastal life, and both major cities and small towns will rent out or charter crafts for

A breezy ride in a perahu can be totally relaxing.

pleasure cruises or to explore the neighbouring islands. Fishing is popular, both in the deep seas and from local docks; at Java's west coast beach resorts, tournaments are often held between international competitors – contact the Tourist Office for details, or look in the Calendar of Events for contests throughout the islands.

Hang Ten, Dude!

Indonesia's proximity to Australia has given the archipelago a wave of popularity with surfers. Most arrive in Bali, boards only in hand, heading for the smooth southern waves of Nusa Dua and Sanur that roll in between October and March. April to September, crowded Kuta is the place to go ... and serious surfers challenge the long tubes of Ulu Watu off the south coast near the airport – experts only, as the waves are fast and strong, and the ocean floor lined with reefs of sharp coral.

There are however, surfing paradises past the Emerald Island: Java's southern coastline is good for beginners, where Batu Keras, near the Pangandaran resort, offers small but dependable "right-handers." Also favoured by surfers on the south coast is Pelabuhan Ratu, two hours south of Bogor, and the Blambangan peninsula off Java's eastern edge in the national park of Mehru Betiri.

In west Java, the beaches of Panaitan Island at Ujung Kulon national park are fun for camping in between sessions of riding the waves. Sumatra's Nias Island has been a long-favoured surfer's paradise as well.

Biking & Golf

Biking in Bali is a fun way to see the country; once out of Denpasar's tourist traffic, the northern roads lead up slim mountain sides and through sloping rice paddies, past temples and traditional villages and bicycles are for rent and sale throughout the main islands. It is possible to bike through Java, Sulawesi, Lombok and Sumbawa as well, particularly by mountain bike through the back roads. The mountains of Sumatra and Flores could make the going quite tough, while Kalimantan's trails are by river ... and Irian Jaya simply doesn't have any long roads at all, although biking the north coast or between villages is a bumpy but fun way to go.

Golf is quickly catching on, thanks to the influence of Westerners, although so far only in the major resort areas which cut into the pristine coastal forests of Java. If you're interested, try the Pulau Seribu Islands north of Jakarta, the west coast hotels around Anyer, and Bogor's posh northern recreational area.

For local sports, the most popular have to be badminton and football and volleyball - you'll see crowds of young kids batting birdies and whacking balls

Para-skiing in the islands for those who dare.

back and forth in the afternoons in nearly every small village. Indonesia won the Olympic gold medal in the couple's badminton competition for 1992 and has traditionally placed high in international competition for both badminton and ping pong. An seemingly odd sight, but one which is not so unusual, is a ping pong table or badminton net set up right in the middle of a dirt-road, thatched-roof home village.

Exploring Up & Down

Both the coastal and inland areas provide great opportunities for trekking and exploring, with rewards of rare wildlife sightings for those who are patient and

Bracing the chill on Gunung Bromo is exhilarating if one is keen on volcano climbing.

willing to stay in remote areas. The national parks are rarely crowded and have a high concentration of animals, so a week will usually provide and educational and rewarding journey into the Indonesian wilds.

Mountain Climbing

Mountain -climbing is always a favourite activity, particularly on the many volcanoes which form a line throughout the islands. Java's peaks of Bromo, Semaru, Merapi and, of course, the offshore Krakatau, are sometimes crowded attractions.

Bali's Agung and Batur, Lombok's Rinjani, Flores' Keli Mutu and Sumatra's Kerinci are summits well-known to avid climbers; tougher to reach are the slopes of Gunung Jayakesuma in Irian Jaya – at more than 5,000 metres, the highest peak in the country.

Whatever Your Preference ...

Whatever your preference, it can probably be found within the archipelago; however, note that for trekking and climbing, permits are often needed from the PHPA.

The Indonesian tourist offices are quite helpful with planning activities, but also ask the locals for ideas on the sports in which you're interested - you never know which adventures you might be invited on!

Nightlife

Above the traffic headlights, neon flashes through the night, colours keeping tempo with the sound of western style pop-music, played so loudly that it pulsates the sidewalk. Dressed in expensive dark suits and soft silk dresses, couples sit and sip cocktails, heads bent together as they laugh over some private amusement.

Traditional cultural performances fill evening programmes in Indonesia.

461

Down the street, the singles crowd fills the dance floor, whilst music floats around intimate conversations, while at quieter nightspots cigarette smoke provides an aromatic atmosphere for the soft saxophone melodies of live bands. In the cinemas, movies roll before elbow-to-elbow packed viewers, posh art openings light up museums, festi- vals fill the parks and thea-tres vibrate with a mix of odd modern and well-known tra-ditional shows. People are every-where, walk-ing, eating, observing, feeling very much a part of

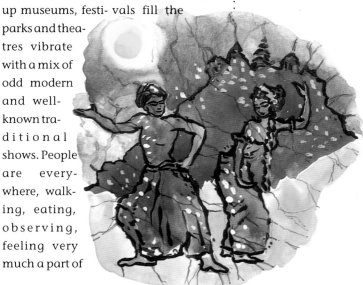

Jakarta's nightlife teems from restaurants to discos, bars and movie houses.

the big city's after dark beat.

Neverending Night

It could be Sydney or London, New York or Singapore, but rather surprisingly, the scene is Jakarta. "Southeast Asia's best-kept secret" is the term for nightlife in this city, where you can sample a bit of every culture. However western influence, is the most prevalent in Jakarta. Here, you can find enough familiar movies, concerts and shows at most of the major theatres to make you feel as if you are in Australia or North America. Most of the large hotels and bars have "happy hours" or similar discount-drink times that cater to non-Muslim cultures

and can actually be quite a good deal. Shortened versions of Indonesian traditional dances and music performances provide an introduction to understanding the local cultural scene. Upscale restaurants are first-time favourites, for the subtle dilution of spices easily suits Western culinary tastes – without incurring gastronomic revenge.

The evening might begin with a cocktail at one of the lively hotel bars, such as the **Tavern** at the Aryaduta Jakarta, **Pendopo Bar** at the Borobudur, **Kudus Bar** at the Hilton, or the Sari Pan Pacific's **Melati Lounge**. For an even earlier start to the night's festivities, try a "spot of tea" with confections often served in the lounges of these hotels – the **Fountain Lounge** at the Grand Hyatt

Jakarta even offers a monthly fashion show to highlight the afternoon. Please note when ordering hard liquor, that Indonesian bartenders usually pour more than the typical "shot" – they use a hefty "third-of-a-gill" measure that can knock you sideways if you are not careful!

Jakarta's Hot Spots

Popular Jakarta spots for cocktails and after-dinner drinks include **Amigos** on Jalan Kelurahan Bangka and Jalan Rasuna Said, **Pete's Tavern** on Jalan Gatot Subroto, **Bima**, **The Green Pub** at the Djakarta Theatre Building and **O'Reiley's** at the Grand Hyatt, all on Jalan MH Thamrin. Also on Jalan MH Thamrin in front of Sarinah and McDonalds is the "hip and happening" **Hard Rock Cafe**, with its enormous stained-glass motif of Elvis that dominates the back wall. Shopping areas like Blok M and Pasar Seni have a variety of smaller restaurants and bars that offer a nice pause. Jakarta has many restaurants which will meet any visitor's tastes; the only question is your preference of atmosphere and the whim of your stomach. If you know what you like, ask those who live and work in the area for ideas; most will be able to recommend several interesting choices that might be a bit off the well-eaten tourist path.

If you have no idea of what you might fancy –or what is available, pick up a copy of the **Guide to Jakarta** magazine available from the Tourism Office and most hotels, which provides a lengthy and detailed listing of restaurants and entertainment in the city. A lively Jakarta option are the supper clubs which offer entertainment with dinner; popular spots include the dazzling Las Vegas shows of **Halai** on Jalan Lodan in Ancol and the amusing acts at the **Blue Ocean** on Jalan Hayam Wuruk. Or, if you like a little music with your meal, wander through the main international hotels and chose your restaurant by the band playing inside – but first check out **The Jakarta Post's** list of major establishments.

For absolutely delicious Indonesian tidbits savoured in an atmosphere that reflects the excitement and chaos of the country, browse through the rows of street stalls peppered throughout the city. You will not be able to find better – and less expensive – seafood dishes than at the clean *warungs* (food stalls) off **Jalan Pecenongan**; for excellent *satay* and *soto*, head for the sizzling stalls of **Jalan Agus Halim** parallel to Jalan Jaksa in Jakarta Pusat.

After filling your stomach, you may want to feast on the country's cultural scene. **The Jakarta Post** and **Guide to Jakarta** list nightly and weekly guides, but most hotels can help you find out just what is going on. For an overview of cultural programs, **Taman Ismail Marzuki** on Jalan Cikini Raya is the performing arts centre where you can view dance, theatre and craft exhibi-

The strains of gamelan entertainment strikes more haunting in the evenings.

tions or listen to music and poetry readings. The **National Museum** often holds traditional *wayang kulit,* (shadow puppet) performances through Saturday nights. *Wayang orang* (symbolic dance plays) and *ketoprak* (a folk melodrama from Yogyakarta) dance performances can be seen at the **Bharata Theatre** on Jalan Pasar Senen. Dance and music are also the entertainment at **Gedung Kesenian** on Jalan Kesenian, while the **Pasar Seni Art Market** and the **Jaya Ancol Dreamland** complex feature lovely open-air restaurants and miles of crafts in addition to traditional cultural performances. For more cerebral entertainment, Jakarta's libraries, embassies, local organizations and universities often have a variety of intriguing lectures and exhibitions.

Discos and a surprising variety of other pulsating, late-night choices can be found at the various hotels – cover charges often include your first drink. **Earthquake**, on Jalan Silang Monas, could be the most infamous with its literally "rocking" dance floor, while **Ebony**, on Jalan Rasuna Said, takes you back to ancient Egyptian days.

At the casual and crowded **Tanamur** on Jalan Abang Timur you will find drinkers and dancers of every possible age, and style of dress – go for the experience, if not the enjoyment of people-watching! Tanamur is Jakarta's entertainment institution. **Dynasty**, on Jalan Pinangsia Raya in the Glodok Plaza, has a lively crowd, as does the

Cockerel comabt – a common evening sport for the locals.

Regent Space Place in the same area at the Glodok Jaya Building.

For variety show entertainment, try the international hotels; the Hotel Borobudur's **Music Room**, the Jakarta Hilton's **Oriental**, the Sari Pan Pacific's **Pitstop** and the Jakarta Tower Hotel's **Stardust**. Late-night bars and snack shops are gathered around the expatriate areas near Blok M, but you will find something open nearly anywhere as Jakarta is a 24-hour town.

A bit of advice: most pubs, bars and discos do have dress codes, and cover charges may change depending on the entertainment offered within. Single travellers – particularly women – should note that it pays to go with someone else, or in the midst of a group; other-wise you may wind up with a dozen or so "friends" you did not intend to make!

Cooler & Cultural

To make up for the heavy western beat of city nightlife, Indonesia's outer cities offer quite a bit more "true" cultural fare. Special traditional entertainment can be seen in different regional areas throughout the islands, and if you leave the typical "tourist" gatherings you will often run into smaller, impromptu practices and performances.

One of the best cities in which to find "real" Indonesian entertainment is in Yogyakarta, where every weekend is marked by performances of music, thea-

Like anywhere else in the world, the movies will take care of a few evening hours for not a princely sum.

tre and dance. During the dry season, monthly performances of the four-night **Ramayana** ballet take place at the Prambanan Temple, by the light of the full moon; beautiful, wistful, and magically performed to the soft music of the *gamelan* orchestra. On the second Saturday of each month, an authentic *wayang kulit* (shadow puppet) play is performed at night before an enthusiastic Indonesian crowd.

The audience here is informal, people wander about munching snacks, talking and even sleeping during the performance, which lasts till dawn. The *gamelan* orchestra's music can also be heard at the **Sultan's Palace**, where the staff put on a show for visitors once a week – you can also watch them practice for two hours on certain days. The South Palace Square often holds classical dance presentations, as does the **ASTI** (Academy of Dance) and **KONRI** (Conservatory of Classical Dance) schools – check with the Tourist Office to find out the times and dates of special performances. Yogyakarta is also an all-night city on the weekends, though in a much more relaxed, and less anonymous manner than Jakarta.

Cheap Thrills!

After a post-sunset meal at one of Jalan Malioboro's seemingly endless line of open-air *warungs* (foodstalls), in Yogyakarta you can wander through

For not just the dance movement and expressions but the costume and colour, the Legong is entertaining to watch.

the art galleries, watch *batik* students indulge in *batik* painting, stroll through parks filled with musicians and laughing children, take a windy *becak* (trishaw) ride through the wide streets or window-shop to your heart's content ... heading back along Jalan Malioboro for a late-night snack you will still find craggy musicians and wrinkled flower vendors even at the first light of dawn!

Alternative Night Scene

A suave, modern university town, Bandung has a wide choice of cultural things to see and a somewhat lively night life. If you do not care for the rowdy dance scene of **Thema** and **Studio East Disco** or the **Sunday ram fights**, try the rough-and-tumble Harley-Davidson leather atmosphere of the Saturday-night *debus* (mystical ceremony) at the **Sakadarna Homestay**. The *debus* is a white magic performance, where an odd wizard of sorts wiggles spikes through his cheeks, eats razors and glass and cracks coconuts with his head.

Sundanese dancing is a popular cultural attraction in Bandung that can be enjoyed at the **Kencana Wungu** nightclub and at the **Panghegar Hotel**. At **Padepokan Sani** on Jalan Lingkar Selatan there is a varied schedule of performances; also try the **Yayasan Pusat Kebudayaan**, (Cultural Center Foundation) on Jalan Naripan and the

A gamelan orchestra supporting dancers against a Balinese backdrop.

Performing Arts Academy on Jalan Buah Batu – ask the Tourist Information Centre for directions.

Balinese Fun

Bali's entertainment needs no introduction, as the infamous Kuta-Legian-Sanur beach areas are a magnet of western alcohol-soaked activity and gossip. But, it is all good fun, all-night long, as the bars and pubs rage with "happy hour" specials that include meals and entertainment: Cinemas blare out bad American movies and the rugged streets are crowded with young and old *batik*-dressed tourists.

"Happy hour" is fun in this area, as the vast variety of inebriative offerings can not be found anywhere else; everything from the deliciously sweet vodka-based *Soul Kiss* to the revolting petrol-tasting *Hair of the Dog*. For entertainment, walk the main street and pick the place that best suits your fancy – quiet moments can be found in small, back-alley bars while the lively crowds head for the "peanut area" with its leather-clad triad of loud, motorcycle-motif bars.

Denpasar

Denpasar's entertainment is mostly for the tourist crowd; get out to areas like Ubud for better music and artistic performances. In the outer areas of Bali, the best nightlife would be a peaceful walk along dark, star-lit roads, with the cool feel of the night breeze.

Sumatra

At night, Sumatra is quiet, even in the larger port cities like Medan and Padang. You will always find *warungs* (food stalls) open at midnight and people strolling around at all hours, but for culture, it is best to visit at festival times. In the westcoast cities, you might catch a Minang performance of the *tari payung* (umbrella dance), *tari lilin* (candle dance), or the *randai,* (an aggressive dance performed at harvest festivals and weddings).

During the late afternoons, horse racing and bull fighting events take place in the villages between Padang and Bukittinggi, and you can often stumble upon small, traditional festivals and music or dance performances.

Ujung Pandang

The final option is Ujung Pandang – where a large, central 24 hour port area of the city is alive throughout the night. As it lacks a bit in cultural performances; you could try the **THR Amusement Park** or the rather dry offerings at some of the international hotels. Your best option for fun is eating – at the open-air food markets everywhere; favourites are the **Central Market** on Jalan Andalas, the stalls near **Jalan G Bawa-**

karaeng or those along the pretty waterfront setting near the Makassar Golden Hotel.

The Real Experience

Unfortunately, in the more popular areas, traditions have often been watered down, condensed for tourists and business visitors who do not have the time to enjoy an authentic performance. Yet, there is a great diversity of "real" Indonesian nightlife and entertainment.

To find real Indonesian nightlife, you have to go further than the hotels – and not be afraid of exploring. Try the backstreets, talk to the locals, take a short trip to the rural areas; perhaps to the villages where older Indonesians still practice the music and crafts of their youth, or to the local schools where young students are trying to preserve these traditions for future generations.

Core of Tradition

To get a glimpse of Indonesia, canned culture will do, but you may find that it only whets your appetite and and encourages a search for the core of tradition.

And, it is these honest touches of culture which will exhibit the special sense of beauty and wonder contained within Indonesian life, reflected in the expressions of those whose heritage lies within the islands.

Kebyar

It began in Bali in 1914, borne as a creative interpretation of movement through dance to the crashing sounds of the newly popular *gamelan* orchestras. Soon *kebyar* (the "lightning" dance), was being performed throughout the island – a combination of wild music and imaginative choreography that burst through traditional movement to become one of the most exciting new forms of Balinese entertainment.

An Old Craze

What started at as a whim caught on quickly and grew into a craze, such that in 1918 the *kebyar* found its way into a ceremony held by the Balinese king of Tabanan. In the audience was a man so enchanted by the dance that he began creating his own forms and style of *kebyar,* to the music of the gamelan. The man's name was "Marya", and he became the most revered Balinese dance master of this century.

A true Balinese, Marya was born in Denpasar just before 1900, he was raised in Tabanan, under Anak Agung Ngurah Made Kaleran of the Puri Kaleran palace. As a young man he was both physically and musically talented, his skills being brought together during the surge of the *kebyar* dance forms. After he first saw the *kebyar* being performed at the Tabanan court, it took him five years before he introduced one of his most famous dances. Named the *kebyar duduk* ("sitting" *kebyar*), the movements involved only the upper body, arms and face, while the performer remained seated on the ground.

The Trompong Dance

A similar version is the "Trompong Dance," in which a solo performance involves the playing of the *trompong* while movements convey the various emotions and moods to the audience. It is known as one of Marya's most stunning works, with Marya – a legendary dancer himself – taking the role of the performer while at the same time beating beautiful sounds from the long, 14 kettle gong instrument.

The brilliance of *kebyar* is its ability to express mood and emotion that subtly shift with the sound and rhythmn of the music. Only the knees are allowed to change position; thus speed, grace and flexibility are part of its intricate styles. *Kebyar* the individual shines, he resembles a chameleon with shifting movements that are intricately woven into the accompanying music of the *gamelan* orchestra. The mood is often intense, yet relaxed, a sheer concentration on sound and rhythm, (not unlike meditation), that allows the dancer to seem as if he or she is driven by the notes of each individual instrument. The costume often involves a small fan held in the hand of the performer, although extremely talented dancers instead use their rapidly flickering fingers. The performer is bound in gold cloth from shoulder to torso, which is used as a silent display of flashing colour and light to the sudden crash of a gong or a shy mask which is placed over the lower facial area to enhance a whirlwind of eye movements.

Kebyar is not always performed solo, or by men. Women, too, can play a part in this dance form, often performing in a duet to the sound of the *gamelan* orchestra. In north Bali, there are house dances where two girls perform at the same time, with their movements highlighted with readings from the Javanese texts of the *kekawin*.

Usually, the *gamelan* sits stretches over the dance floor, surrounding the performer on all four sides. In this way, the interpretation of the music is greatly enhanced through the movements as seemingly unpredictable notes and levels of noise flow through the body of the dancer.

Hotel Performances

Some hotels in the Denpasar-Kuta-Sanur area offer *kebyar* performances – (try to see one if you can). The intricate blending of music and movement combines into an expressive performance that exhibits the incredible talent and diverse mixture of cultures that seems to encompass every aspect of Balinese tradition.

Accomodation

From the northern tip of Sumatra to Irian Jaya's most eastern edge, accommodation in Indonesia is, for the most part, incredibly safe, efficient and clean. An added bonus is that most places to stay are quite inexpensive compared with Western prices – often with better quality rooms and amenities – so whether you are a business, budget or holiday traveller, you will get a good night's sleep and excellent value for your budget. The well-known hotels of the big cities are of the best standard, providing the comfort of all the usual luxury Western standards and facilities at a cost equatable to typical Western prices.

Hotels nestled among the Indonesian foliage are more popular for those preferring less concrete environment.

Most of the big hotels are found in Jakarta, Denpasar, Medan, Ujung Pandang and a few other large, business-oriented travel centres that are used to accommodating international guests and important visitors. Smaller "hotels" are a bit different; modelled after the world-wide chains, they are often economical alternatives for business travellers who

Sanur Beach in Bali.

enjoy the Western style and amenities of the big hotels but are a bit more frugal with their budgets. However, these hotels sometimes compromise the extent of their facilities in exchange for savings of 10-30 per cent – check for availability of telephones, fax machines, business facilities, laundry services, car rental and so on *before* booking to ensure that you will be able to enjoy the amenities that you require.

A *wisma* is a smaller hotel with a friendlier feel, often differing from the hotels only in size and location. Hotels are used for larger meetings and conventions, and are conveniently located in the centre of the town, while a *wisma* accommodates a smaller number of guests and is often located outside of the city centre – an advantage if you prefer quieter quarters. A *wisma* is an accommodating introduction to the country; run by local Indonesian management, this type of lodging is more relaxed, the decor reflecting the culture of the area. This is an ideal get-away from yet another huge and anonymous Western business complex. However, *Losmen* (rooms to let) are the basis of inexpensive travel in Indonesia.

Just A Room...

Usually accommodation in a *losmen* consists of a simple room (with or without a desk), a chair and window, a small breakfast meal and tea. The toilet and

Losmen lodging can be very comfortable.

bathing area are usually shared. Basic, yes but for budget travellers, it is all you need. Most *losmen* have the advantage of being small, family run and friendly, and because of the flow of foreign clientele they will often have connected services such as travel and transportation agencies, information "libraries" and book exchanges, home-cooked restaurant meals, gardens and sitting areas. In similar style to the *losmen*, the type of lodging that *penginapans* (a cheap hotel with plain facilities) offer is small and friendly, but at the very, very bottom of the accommodation scale: "A bed and four walls" would be a good description, with a shared toilet of course – but at half the price of other rooms, *penginapan* are the perfect solution for true shoe

string travellers.

Resorts, Retreats & Remote Areas

Indonesia's hustling commercial centres are not just for business travellers and VIPs, students, explorers and holiday-makers are also lured by the offer of culture and entertainment. Therefore, a variety of accommodations for practically every combination of time, purpose and budget are available – made special by a bit of local charm. However, sometimes an escape from the real world is required; off-shore islands, mountain jungles or hidden river trails provide a setting of beauty and tranquillity for the

Deluxe suites and hillside pools rising from terraced ricefields in Ubud.

ideal break, and throughout the archipelago you will always find a friendly smile and a safe place to stay. South of Java, the coastal road south of Cilegon leads to a string of quiet beaches and hills that are a lovely respite from Jakarta's pulsating heat and noise. Just two or three hours from Jakarta by bus or car, this area is a pleasant weekend getaway or holiday hideout with a string of high-class resorts and comfortable, affordable *losmen* winding all the way south to the national park of Ujung Kulon. More of Java's escapes include the islands of Pulau Seribu, just north of Jakarta, where tour packages take care of all your accommodation needs – often resort hotels, but sometimes yachts or sailboats, and on several islands camping is al-

lowed. Six hours south of Bandung, the Pangandaran-Cilicap area is a lovely place to relax at the luxury beach-side bungalows or the less imposing *losmen* (rooms to let), which are still close enough for an easy walk to the sea.

For decades, Bali has been the not-so-secret haven for the holiday scene; not surprising, since the little island offers everything from quiet, hillside ponderings to sensuous beach-side massage. Just a quick wander through Kuta and Legian will be enough time to settle into the throng of *losmen* lining the thin village "gangs" or alleys; for more up-market accommodations, try the beach-front areas of Sanur and Nusa Dua, where package tours often fill bigger hotels.

Sumatran chalets by Lake Toba.

Inland Retreats

Inland retreats such as the Puncak Pass between Bogor and Bandung, the Dieng Plateau and the Bromo-Tengger mountain area all have modest accommodations that are clean and quiet, reflecting the peaceful ambience of the surrounding area.

To find true peace for the soul on Bali, Ubud is the answer, with charming *losmen* that capture the magic of the area all along Monkey Forest Road and the surrounding small villages. Lake Toba and Samosir Island are probably the best-known holiday areas, and there are plenty of relaxing, inexpensive, good-quality lodging options in Tuk Tuk and Ambarita near the lake. Off-shore islands like Nias, Mentawi and the Riau archipelago have less-fancy choices – although camping is one of them – and there are several options along the popular beaches and in nearby villages.

Adventure Travel

However, as a true "adventure" destination, the lodgings in Sumatra more often than not uphold the rugged reputation of this sparsely populated island – make sure you know enough *Bahasa Indonesia* to ask about price, meals and amenities before you travel here.

Tanatoraja's annual flood of European tourists has provided plenty of low

Jakarta's main thoroughfare, Thamrin, is dominated by the Grand Hyatt.

to mid-range hotels in Rantepao and Makale. When visiting central Kalimantan, however, the accommodation can be anything from basic *losmen* (rooms to let) to a place on the floor of the village leader's home – you have to take what you get where you go.

In the Baliem Valley of Irian Jaya, the village of Wamena has several basic *losmen* at upmarket prices for those interested in hiking and visiting tribes. Within Moluccas, most islands have standard hotels in the largest port cities such as Ambon and Ternate.

Outside of these areas, however, much like the small towns of Nusa Tenggara, losmen are the main fare; but you can usually count on clean and friendly lodging at very affordable prices.

A Few Important Terms

To save your system from shock when you stay in Indonesia, there are a few things for which you should prepare your mind and body. Unless you are planning on staying in only the most modern Western hotel chains, there are a few first "surprises" you will want to keep in mind before you travel. First, is the *toilet* – well, not really a Western "throne", but rather a "squat-and-aim" sort of structure that requires both balance and accuracy. Flush by scooping loads of water from the bucket/hand pail/sink provided. Note: in parts of Sulawesi, there may just be a hole in the floor. Do not forget, at any point of your trip, to bring your own tissue with you. At some point, you will also have to deal with the *mandi*. This is Indonesia's alternative to the Western method of taking a shower – and it is often a refreshing simplification. Just scoop water (often with the same scoop as that used to "flush" the toilet) from the bucket/hand pail/sink provided and pour it over your head and body. Lather, rinse, repeat. No hot water, by the way, so it is a wonderful way to perk up in the heat of the afternoon … and certainly an early morning eye-opener.

As for amenities, *electricity* is a flickering factor - literally - as you may or may not find it outside of the main cities, and if you do, you can count on it to fail at any time. Ditto for *telephones, faxes, telex machines* and the like, so leave business in the business centres and enjoy the free time in the more isolated parts of the islands.

Unless your room is buried in the central hills - or in the middle partition of a packed *losmen* - you are most likely to wake up early. That is, as early as in five or six o'clock. Children, chickens, mosque prayers and broom-sweeping aside, it is a lovely time of day to view the country … before the traffic and heat rush in to crowd the morning.

Special Considerations

Single travellers should not worry – Indonesia is not only safe, but very economical, though you will rarely find a dormitory or a single room. Most of the time, even as a single traveller you will have to fork out cash for a double-room, which actually will be rather pleasant if you are used to being squashed into small back rooms alone.

And, especially at *losmen* and *penginapan*, do not forget to bargain with the owner – often you will receive a substantial reduction in price. Indonesia is an excellent country in which to travel for women, even those who are moving around alone. Stories of fearsome, aggressive men have circulated the travel gossip trails, but with a little common sense, modest dress, and a firm "no" or "I'm already married" you will usually disarm the most persuasive of suitors that might knock on the door of your room. However, a good command of basic *Bahasa Indonesia* does help in these situations!

Research, Research & More Research

Unfortunately, Indonesia does not yet have many facilities for disabled travellers, though the larger hotel chains do provide for most needs. If you are planning to stay in less expensive places, you will need to do a little research first; stairs, street access, doorway measurements, animals and the availability of helpful facilities which can make all the difference in planning your trip.

Finally, families are a welcome addition to the Indonesian travel scene –

Five-star luxury and plush comforts at the Hyatt, Jakarta.

most hotels, *wisma* and *losmen* will be able to provide accommodation and extra service for those who stay.

Larger lodgings are better, as the greater number of rooms can give you a choice that best suits your needs, and will often have small added facilities such as kitchens, private toilets and *mandis*(type of shower), secluded play areas and so on to make your stay even more ideal.

A Few Questions...

A few questions to consider asking before you check in if you are staying anywhere except a well-known chain ...
• Does your stay include breakfast and other meals, or tea and coffee throughout the day?
• Are there facilities to accommodate your business needs if you are with a group?
• Can you count on the hotel's electrical power, telephones and other facilities?
• Is there a taxi service to the airport, or other transportation centres?
• Are there guest services for travel, laundry, meals, shopping, beauty, information, area tours and so on?
•How convenient is the lodging to the business or activities in which you plan to participate?

Hot Tips

And, a few tips: Ask to see more than

one room if you are looking at *losmen*, *wisma* or *penginapans*; often, the first will be the least desirable as the owner simply wants to rent it. For the same price, if you take time to look, you will often get much nicer accommodations.

Always try the electricity, fan and lights; just because a fan is in the room does not mean that it works – get a new one or change rooms if it does not – check out the toilet and *mandi*. A clean area reflects well on the rest of the place ... if it is abominable, you can always go somewhere else. Always ask for what you want. If you need blankets (not likely) or a fan, the owner can probably round them up somewhere; the same goes for mosquito coils, rope for clothesline, sewing tools, paper, etc.

Test the waters by looking around a little before you decide to stay at a place, especially if it is not crowded. A bit of hesitation often leads to a convenient reduction in price as a lure. Indonesia's stunning landscape, comforting climate and intriguing culture and diversity of wildlife make it an unforgettable destination to visit, regardless of your purpose, amount of time or budget.

However, what makes the country such a wonderful unforgettable destination is the generosity of its people. From *losmen* to top-end hotel, you will always receive a friendly smile and quality service that goes far beyond the usual expectations. Do not take it for granted, but instead say a sincere, "Terima Kasih!" (thank you) and return the service with a smile of your own.

TRAVEL TIPS

ARRIVAL

By Air

Indonesia's convenient location makes the country accessible from nearly every part of the world and by most international airlines. Daily flights to Jakarta and Denpasar are available from most major capitals in Southeast Asia, with easy connections to Medan, Ujung Pandang, Yogyakarta and other major city centres.

Within the archipelago, Garuda, Merpati and Sempati have an extensive flight network between the islands. Garuda offers a 25 per cent discount to students with an International Student Identity card (sometimes a formal letter from an advisor is requested, other agents set an age limit of 25 on validity – check around before purchasing). Merpati and Sempati also give varying price breaks when presented with this card, usually about 15 per cent.

A warning about purchasing airfares within Indonesia: sly agents will tack on a 10 per cent commission to the total – travel offices in the "budget" Jalan Jaksa area in Jakarta are famous for this move. When exploring ticket options, always first ask about extra "commission" charges, particularly when dealing with discounts, and do not forget about the unpredictable three per cent charge for using a credit card. Hot tip: Myanmar has a cheap Jakarta-Singapore flight on Sundays and Thursdays if you need a quick connection or a visa renewal. Purchase your ticket in Jakarta and it is about for US$70 one-way, US$140 roundtrip – but if you buy the same ticket in Singapore, it costs you close to US$100 one-way and double that for the return flight! **Hot tip**: When you are flying back to Jayapura from Wamena in the Baliem Valley, sit on the left for the best mountain views. If you are flying from Padang to Medan, Lake Toba, Samosir Island and Mount Leuser will also be on the left – an absolutely stunning sight to be enjoyed in the afternoon sunlight.

On Arrival

Except when they are being renovated, Indonesia's airports are organized, safe and clean. Currency change counters, banks, international telephones, postal services and other necessities are conveniently located in the arrival and departure areas. To and from the airport is not a problem, either, as many taxis and buses serve every major city.

In Jakarta, special air-conditioned buses run between Sukarno-Hatta airport and Blok M, Gambir and Grogol train stations for about Rp3,000; taxis from the city centre will cost Rp30,000-50,000 depending on the traffic and whether the driver decides to take the toll road in Bali. There are no buses in Denpasar, only *bemos* (small covered vehicle), which can be chartered for Rp10,000-20,000 to the city, Kuta and Sanur beaches or the terminal at Batubulan, where connections continue eastwards to Ubud and Padangbai – public *bemos* costing Rp3,000 ply the roads to these areas. Medan has no regular buses but the airport is close to the city centre and taxis cost Rp3,000. Taxis from the city to Ujung Pandang's airport cost approximately Rp15,000-20,000 and public *bemos* Rp500-1,000. In Irian Jaya, a taxi ride from Jayapura's airport, a mere 45 minutes from the city is an exorbitant Rp25,000, but a half-kilometre walk to the main road is where the pubic *bemos* will tranverse the same route for Rp500-1,000. In the Moluccas, the distance from the airport to Ambon is about as long, with fares running at about the same price for both taxis and public transportation.

Sea Travel

For a less-expensive and more adventurous alternative to inter-island travel, Pelni ships run sea routes between several dozen ports. However, it is a bit slow, and sometimes crowded, but definitely a different way to explore. If you have the time visit the Pelni office to find out about schedules. Trains and buses have neverending schedules throughout the islands, and most travel agencies will be able to help you with ticketing.

BANKING

Banking is a big industry in Indonesia, so nearly every international bank has at least one branch in Jakarta. Cash and traveller's cheques can be exchanged at most of these banks, as well as many of the national banks as well, although the rates may be lower and the amount of currency allowed in the exchange may be limited – money changers may offer a better rate. There are banks stretching from Banda Aceh to Wamena in central Irian Jaya. However, do not count on them to exchange traveller's cheques, particularly outside of the major cities. Most banks are open from 8.00 am to 3.00 pm Monday through Friday, and until about 2.00 pm on Saturdays.

BUSES

In Jakarta, various hot and crowded city buses run throughout the city, down the west coast to Labuan and over the Merak ferry terminal through Sumatra to Medan, or through Bogor and Bandung all the way to Cirebon, Yogyakarta, Surabaya and even Denpasar. Pick up the widely available **Krakatau Newsletter** from the tourist office or travel agency to check the schedules. Be warned: Though cheap, city buses are not for everyone and are notorious for pick-pockets. As most other modes of getting around – taxis, *oplets* (covered pick up truck with benches) and the like, cost relatively little more, a safer and far more comfortable method of inner-city travel is to use one of these options instead.

Bus systems also run in other major cities, as well as small mini-bus lines or *bemos* (small covered vehicle). No matter where you are, fares for these vehicles should be anywhere between Rp300 and 1,000 depending on the distance of the trip, unless you are in a high tourist locale like Bali's Kuta or Carita in west Java, where unsuspecting visitors are sometimes quoted exorbitant prices, watch out for this at airports, bus and train stations as well.

Final caution: Budget travellers looking for travel connections might be approached by a "helpful" taxi driver who will take them to a reliable ticket office for buses and trains. Indonesia is famous for the friendly helpfulness of its people ... *but* at arrival stations it is time to take care. The driver is probably charging far too much to take you to an out-of-the-way travel agency owned by family or friends. Once there, you will bargain over the ticket price and get a "special" discount on the price, – unbeknownst to you, at a markup price of around 50 per cent. At this point, you can either purchase your ticket or find your own transportation back to where you want to go. Insult is added to injury when at just about this time you realize all these "nice" people are in cahoots and the "helpful" driver is receiving a hefty commission for bringing you to that particular agency. Lesson learned: Do comparison shopping for prices first, and ask for the "terminal", where you can actually find the buses, as opposed to the bus "station", meaning the agent, who only sells tickets.

Another new trick – Surabaya travellers beware – is that when you buy your economy fare bus ticket from an agent, when they transport you to the actual site of the vehicle it will usually be "broken" down or "already full". After a bit of "arguing", you will be generously offered the chance to catch another, a deluxe-ultra-comfort bus leaving shortly – for another upgrade in price, of course. It is a shame it has to happen, but it does. Hold your ground, be patient, and smile.

For long-distance bus travel, the best advice (if you do not know a reliable local ticket agent) is to go straight to the terminal and book your ticket there. You can do this the day before you want to travel, or even just show up if you know when the bus is leaving; there will almost always be extra room for one more – though you will not be guaranteed any comfort or a choice of seats.

BUSINESS HOURS

Indonesians are early risers, so while the main city business centres and official commercial establishments keep traditional 9.00 am to 3.00 pm, the small stores and restaurants are usually open between 6.00 am to 7.00 am in the morning and stay open until 9.00 pm to 10.00 pm. In Muslim areas, Fridays are half-days, so everything closes down at around 11.00 am, and Saturdays are short days as well, although banks and business offices remain open. Official government office hours are from 8.00 am to 3.00 pm from Monday to Thursday and 11.00 am to 2.00 pm on Fridays and 2.00 pm on Saturdays. Keep an eye on the calendar for major holidays (there are many), so you can plan ahead if these offices will be closed.

CLIMATE

Settled close to the Equator, Indonesia's temperature varies between a cool mountain 21°-27°C to a comfortable coastal 28°-33°C. The strong sunlight adds a good deal of tropical humidity – usually 60-100 per cent, but it is brushed off by the breeze outside the stifling city areas. June to August is the best time to visit, when the sky is most clear; in October, the weather can be quite finicky, and in November the rainy season begins in most areas. In March, the rains lessen, but are unpredictable until mid-May – even so, during the wet season, the country is lush and refreshingly cool, and there is still a little sun everyday.

CLOTHING

Light and casual are the key words if you aim to remain in the cities, which are suppressingly sweltering with traffic and heat. Even so, everyone except forgiveably scruffy backpackers dresses both modestly and professionally. The men in clean, collared shirts and long pants, the women in pretty blouses and fashionable skirts and heels.

Outside of the cities, Indonesians still dress nicely, although more comfortable Western-styles of clothing are common. Sandals are a must, and sturdy boots or tennis shoes if you intend to do some hiking. In the mountains, and during the rainy season, things cool off quite nicely – bring a thin jacket or sweater for added warmth. Another hint is to bring a *sarong* (waist-wrap around skirt) or purchase one as a useful souvenir while you are in the country. It will be *the* most handy piece of clothing you have with you – it can fashion as a multi-purpose bed sheet, beach or bath towel, a picnic cloth, a window shade, a rain cover ... easily washed, rinsed and dried, it is so light you will not even feel it in your luggage.

A note to women: In Muslim areas like Banda Aceh, west Java and Sumbawa in particular, conservative dressing (skirts or shorts below the knees and sleeves covering your shoulders and upper arms) will improve your ease in travelling.

CREDIT CARDS

Outside of Jakarta and possibly Yogyakarta, Medan and Ujung Pandang, credit cards are not usually accepted, if even heard of at all. Luckily, most major airlines, hotels, restaurants and shopping malls like Jakarta's **Blok M** will usually accept well-known cards like **American Express**, **VISA** and **MasterCard**, which is especially handy

if you have to make an emergency purchase. However ask about additional fees beforehand, as often three to ten percent may be tacked on if you use a charge card.

CURRENCY

Not to be confused with the Indian or Nepalese *rupee,* the Indonesian *rupiah* (Rp) comes in notes of 100, 500, 1,000, 5,000, 10,000 and 20,000, and small coins of 10, 25, 50 and 100 rupiahs. Money can be changed at banks, large hotels, some supermarkets and department stores. Moneychangers are located in nearly every city and town throughout the islands, although rates can vary greatly. The most commonly accepted cash for exchange is the US dollar, but most places will trade in well-known traveller's cheques as well.

Hot Tip: Unless you are planning on purchasing something expensive in cash right away, or you feel like being a "millionaire" for a day, do not change more than the equivalent of US$300. The wad all the bills will make is not worth the trouble to carry around and things are relatively inexpensive here compared to the West or Southeast Asia. Also, ask for some *uans kecil* (small money) along with the 20,000 or 10,000 rupiah notes, as some taxi drivers or vendors will invariably be "out of change". Small value notes will be useful for things like snacks, public WC fees and small purchases in rural areas.

If you end up with too much cash at the end of your trip (and many people do), there is a Rp50,000 limit to the amount you can reconvert, which can be done at most airports before you leave.

CUSTOMS

The usual fare of "duty-free" items are allowed, including per-adult maximums of two litres of alcoholic beverages, a "reasonable amount" of perfume, and a choice of 200 cigarettes, 50 cigars or 100 grammes of tobacco.

What are *not* allowed are firearms and ammunition, Chinese medicines or materials printed in Chinese, and any type of narcotics, the use, sale, or purchase of which will result in long prison terms and heavy fines. All cars, photographic equipment, computers, typewriters and recorders must be declared to customs and advance approval is necessary for carrying transceivers.

All movie films and video cassettes must be censored by the Film Censor Board, while quarantine permits are required for animals, plants and fresh fruit. No more than Rp50,000 can be imported or exported from the country, although there is no restriction on the transport of foreign currency.

DEPARTURE

If your airline ticket does not already include it, the departure tax from Indonesian airports is between Rp1,500 and Rp5,000 for national flights, depending on the airport, while international jaunts raise the departure fee to Rp12,000. Always reconfirm your bookings 72 hours before your flight as airlines are always busy. Try to arrive at the airport an hour ahead of a domestic departure time and two hours before an international flight.

DISABLED TRAVELLERS

Sadly, wide doorways, low ramps and special facilities are little-known in this country except in the large hotel chains, restaurants and a few department stores. Be prepared for subtle stares and direct, curious questions. However, the availability of local transport is an advantage, as is the patience and open-mindedness of the people — do not hesitate to ask for assistance or extra service as it will be gladly provided.

ELECTRICITY

If you can get it, electricity runs at 220 volts and 50 cycles, but check with your hotel just to be sure as some areas still use the 110 voltage lines. For important business equipment and electronics, it is safest to bring a stabilizer, as well as an adapter if your plugs are not of the European two-pronged style. Whatever you do, do not depend on the electrical outlet to work even in the popular tourist areas of Bali and Java as the power dies out as often as once or twice a week! In Jakarta however, the supply is more stable.

HEALTH & HOSPITALS

Commonly misconstrued as a complete "jungle land", Indonesia does have modern medical facilities, pharmacies and hospitals. To the relief of most travellers, Western-trained doctors, common prescriptions and treatments are available in many towns outside of the major cities, and large hospitals are usually less than 24 hours away. As for health worries, the most common ailments for travellers to the country are sunburn, colds and the usual cuts and bruises. Bring an

antibiotic cream to help heal them quickly in the moist climate, and a strong suntan lotion and hat to prevent sunstroke. Dehydration and diarrhoea are two other medical catastrophes to be experienced in a country with both a hot climate and spicy food; salt tablets and an adequate intake of water will help the former ailment, while a gradual introduction to spices, plenty of tea and white rice will ease the latter. Just in case, bring some Immodium® or other anti-diarrhoea medicines.

A few precautions to take include some type of malaria prophylactic, as the disease is found in the islands, although it is mostly confined to Irian Jaya, Inner Kalimantan and the west Javan area of the Ujung Kulon National Park. Smart vaccinations to take include tetanus and hepatitis injections, as there are many rusty nails, *bemo* (small covered vehicle) doors and other unexpected hazards, and aside from the large hotel restaurants you can never be certain of the cleanliness of utensils with which you eat. You should always have some type of medical kit with you to at least tide you over until medical attention is available, or as a comfort to ease the small, annoying troubles.

Remember to include: aspirin, adhesive bandages, a needle and thread, cotton buds, scissors, iodine or water purification pills, glue, Immodium® anti-motion sickness medicine and a small bottle of alcohol to tide you over the little emergencies. Most items are commonly found at the *apotik* (pharmacy) and you will find round-the-clock physicians at major hotels and the *rumah sakit* (hospital). Your consulate or embassy may also be able to help you find a reliable hospital or doctor. Take comfort, however; if you have a real emergency, flights to Singapore with its excellent facilities are available for 24 hours a day.

HIRED TRANSPORT

Bicycles are a popular method of travel in Indonesia, especially in Bali and Java, for most of the land is flat and the roads are for the most part in decent shape. In the cities and many towns, bicycle shops sell modern-style frames more than rent them, but bargains can often be struck with a bit of discussion. Check the small hotels, too, as someone may have a bicycle that you can borrow. The best trips are down the dirt and gravel roads around small village areas — stay off the main roads as they are thin, crowded and filled with very unpredictable drivers.

Car Hire has become easier now that most

companies offer the service of a driver — by far the safest and sanest option available. In major cities, you can book through large hotels, travel agencies or directly through the company; check the telephone book or the Tourism Office for ideas as well. A selection of jeeps and luxury cars are the usual choices, but be ready for the shock of high rental prices. Note: Most car hire companies are located in Jakarta and the rental will usually be for day-trips unless you plan to drive yourself. To rent a car, a valid international driver's licence is required.

Motorcycle or Moped Hire is usually a Balinese adventure, although it is becoming more popular in Sumatra's mountainous areas and in parts of Java and Nusa Tenggara. In Bali, the typical bike is between 80 and 125 cc and is rented by individual owners by the day or the week. Prices are reached by bargaining and decrease with the length of time hired. You also need an International Driving Permit that is "endorsed for motorcycles"; if it is not you will need to go to Denpasar for written and driving tests. Get the bicycle's registration from the owner, as you will need to carry this with your licence at all times. Insurance is expensive and questionable – it is best to first get some at home if you think you are going to rent a vehicle.

Friendly Advice: Rent only if you have driven a motorcycle before or recently and only if you are comfortable riding it. Slippery gravel roads, crazy curves and wild traffic hamper these roads, and several tourists are killed every year. If you are uncertain of your abilities, travel with someone who is, or use the endless public transport available.

HOLIDAYS

January 1	–	New Year's Day;
February	–	*Isra Ji'raj Nabi Muhammad;*Prophet Mohammad's Ascension
March	–	*Nyepi;* Balinese New Year
April	–	*Idul Fitri;* End of Ramadan Fasting Month
April	–	Good Friday ;
April 21	–	Kartini Day;
May	–	*Waicak Day;* Anniversary of the Birth & Death of Buddha
May	–	*Kenaikan Isa Al–Masih;*

		Ascension of Christ
June	–	*Idul Adha;* Muslim Day of Sacrifice
July	–	*Tahun Baru Hijiriah;* Muslim New Year
August 17	–	Indonesian Independence Day;
September	–	*Maulid Nabi Muhammad;* Anniversary of the birth of the Prophet Mohammed
December 25	–	*Hari Raya Natal;* Christmas Day

LOCAL CUSTOMS

As a visitor, you will be forgiven by the very understanding Indonesians if you stumble over their customs, but even more so, you will be greatly respected for trying your best to observe them. This includes taking care that you should neither touch anyone, especially on the head, nor give or receive anything with the unclean left hand. Pointing at someone with the index finger is impolite (use your thumb or entire hand instead) and it is customary to remove your shoes before entering someone's home – this is much easier with sandals or thongs than hiking boots, but always ask first anyway. When dining as a guest, always wait until the food is placed in front of you and the host invites you to eat before you begin.

If someone prepares food or a drink for you, even if you did not ask for it, eat or drink it anyway as it is impolite to refuse. When having tea or coffee, always leave a little liquid in the cup from which you are drinking; an empty glass signals the host that you would like another. When others nearby are eating, you may be invited to share the meal – this is merely a polite formality that means "excuse us for eating when you are not" more than an invitation, so it is customary to refuse. Also, when you are having a cigarette or small sweets, it is polite to offer one to those around you.

NEWS

English-language newspapers that are widely available include **The Jakarta Post**, **Indonesian Observer**, **Indonesia Times** and Singapore's **Straits Times**. In airports, train stations and large city shopping areas, *toko buku* (bookstores), will often display Western news magazines such as **Newsweek** and **Time**. English-language newscasts are broadcast at various times on radio and television – check **The Jakarta Post** for the schedule in that city.

PHOTOGRAPHY

Brilliant scenery, vibrant colours and warm smiles are perfect photographic portraits that reflect the essence of Indonesia ... however, a few situations may crop up along the way. Fortunately, print and slide film are plentiful. Unfortunately, good developing techniques are not. Except for Jakarta, the time and quality of developing pictures within the country will probably not be worth the money – if you are anxious to view a roll of film, ask for recommendations on who does a good job before you have it overexposed or scratched by an inexpert printer. When you do find one, photo developing usually take about 30 minutes to an hour, while the time taken to develop slide film ranges from one to three days.

When shooting pictures, watch the light; early morning and late afternoon shots will result in stunning hues but midday photos will seem washed out because of the strong light. Photographers are free to shoot almost anything in Indonesia, but always ask before snapping your camera in people's faces or scrambling for a shot of the family grave site or temple. Also, areas of military importance are touchy subjects best left off film, these include certain bridges, airport facilities, ocean port sites, railway terminals and military bases – ask someone first before the film maybe unceremoniously yanked out of your camera.

POSTAL SERVICES

Although some people have never had any problems with the postal system, others warn that, whatever you do, do not rely on receiving mail on time, or at all. If something valuable or timely needs to be shipped, instead rely on one of the well-known courier services such as **DHL** in Jakarta and Surabaya, or **Eteha** and **Usaha Express**, which have offices in most major cities. When sending mail, add on a little extra postage for *kilat* (express) service, that supposedly saves a few days. However the good news is that the *Post Restante* system of receiving mail through the Post Office in central cities seems to be working smoothly. If you do not have a definite address or hotel, you can pick up your mail at the city's GPO (General Post Office), or main office if addressed to: YOUR NAME, Post Restante, GPO, Jakarta (or any other major city where you would like to receive mail), Indonesia.

TELECOMMUNICATIONS

The major international telephone company is **Telekom**, with the circular blue sign, and they are highly recommended as the only telephone office from which to call. Always organized and usually air-conditioned as well, **Telekom** is a welcome communication change that offers services like international faxing, telex, calling cards, and international direct dial calls – no more waiting hours in the humid weather for the operator to call back with the connection! Best of all, **Telekom** lines always seem to be working – and audible – an incredible concept if you are used to the frustrations of the Indonesian telephone system. There are **Telekom** offices in every major city and quite a few small towns, too. Head for one of these when the aggravation of confused communications hits you.

TIME

Bali, Nusa Tenggara, Sulawesi and East and South Kalimantan share the same Central Indonesia time zone, which is GMT + 8 hours – the same as Singapore. Western Indonesia time begins in Java, one hour behind (GMT + 7 hours) and includes Sumatra, Madura Island and West Kalimantan. Eastern Indonesia Standard Time, or GMT + 9 hours, is the zone for the Moluccas and Irian Jaya.

TIPPING

Tipping is not a custom in Indonesia. Usually major hotels and restaurants add a ten percent service charge, but if not, a five to ten percent tip for good service would be appropriate. Elsewhere, in regular restaurants, *warungs* (foodstalls), taxis and so on, there is no tipping. The exception is for airport porters, who might receive about Rp1,000 per bag. Hire car drivers and taxis that take special routes might earn an extra bonus.

TOURS

So many interesting areas have day-trips and tours that it is best to read up on the location you are visiting and then choose a few things you would like to do. Local travel agencies in the cities are well-versed in the major attractions, and many agents are from the area in which they work, so they may be able to suggest alternative, more unique places to explore and things to do. Your hotel may have a booking office for special sights. Otherwise, travel offices can be found in just about any town. The tourism offices are an excellent source of information about options available, and the staff usually speaks fluent English in order to communicate with international visitors. Check out local organizations if you are interested in particular sports, wildlife, culture and so on, as they may be a good source of ideas.

TRANSPORTATION
Around the Archipelago

Indonesia's transportation system is a refreshing change; unlike most countries, its organization is fast, efficient and constant. With 180 million people moving about the islands, the vehicles and vessels that travel the archipelago's roads, rails and seas are always on the go – at all hours, every day, – so you never have long to wait no matter where in the islands you would like to travel.

Local Air Travel: Garuda Indonesia is the country's national airline, with smaller branches in companies such as **Mandala, Merpati, Sempati** and **Bouraq.** Flights on these airlines will take you on a wide range of routes from northern Sumatra to southern Irian Jaya. International flights are available from most airlines, Garuda tends to be the most expensive, but the airline does give a hefty discount if you are a student with an International Student Identity card (available through the STA/Student Travel Association and the YHA/Youth Hostel Organization in Australia, Europe and North America) – 15 percent and 25 percent for national and international flights, respectively. Whatever age you are it is also worth noting that often, when booking, you will be told that the flight is "full". If so, get your ticket for the next available date and then show up for stand-by places at the airport. The chances are, with Garuda in particular, that there will still be plenty of seats available even on fully booked flights and you will have no trouble getting aboard.

Local Sea Travel: Because Indonesia is a country of islands, one of the most delightful and convenient ways of getting around them is by boat and ferry. At the docks of major port cities such as Jakarta, Medan, Ujung Pandang, Ambon and Jayapura, there are plenty of willing captains who do not mind taking travellers aboard. It is a great way to see the country – and inexpensive as well – as long as you are careful about the vessel and crew that you choose. The regular passenger ships in the country's **Pelni** fleet are safe vessels,

which make regular bi-weekly runs on more than a dozen routes between the islands. For those who want a "cruise line" experience, first-class cabins offer privacy, candle-light dinners and private washrooms in the price; budget travellers usually prefer the communal "deck" class which at a cheap price offers only a hard-wood floor and space between children and chickens, on which to sleep.

Indonesia's inter-island ferry system is another convenient way to travel across the archipelago, often with easy connections to the bus and rail lines. Schedules vary with distance and demand; there is a twenty-four hour timetable for the two-hour Sumatra-Java and half-hour Java-Bali crossings, while the four-hour Bali-Lombok and two-hour Lombok-Sumbawa ferries travel from dawn until dusk, and the eight-hour Sumbawa-Flores vessel – which also drops passengers off in the bay for jaunts to Komodo Island, – keeps a varying twice-weekly schedule.

Local Rail Travel: Rail travel is always scenic and fun, particularly along Java's stunning inland journey of peaks, plains and rice paddies between Jakarta, Yogyakarta and Surabaya. Elsewhere, train lines are limited, connecting only to the west coast and parts of Sumatra, though railroad transport provides a superior alternative to bus travel which is usually crowded and exhausting.

Local Bus Travel: Travel by bus is indeed the main means of moving about the islands. Most routes run from early morning (say, 5 am) to about midnight; popular lines travel 24 hours, especially the long hauls to and from the big cities such as the Jakarta to Mataram (Lombok) or Medan to Denpasar. In other areas, such as Flores, buses only run in the mornings, so it can take several days to make connections from one city to the next across the island. Just a note about bus travel; whatever anyone says, it is guaranteed to be an adventure. The new, huge air-conditioned, video-karaoke equipped vehicles that include snacks and meals are most likely to provide a smooth run for your money. However, to store up some anecdotes, endure if you want the spare tires, banana bunches and baskets of fish in the ancient, crammed-to-the-hilt non-airconditioned lines. For the most part, the major routes in Java and Bali run well ... however, outside of these areas, be prepared for flat tires, exploding engines, shrieking babies, grinding gears and sudden stops for dogs and cows sleeping in the middle of the road. The most notorious of all trips are those of the Sumatran bus lines (although those in Sulawesi take a close second place); bring food and water, ear plugs, a washcloth and soap and several plastic bags on these runs through the mountains – if not for your own refuse, they will come in handy for the dozen or so people whose stomachs invariably can not handle the jolting and rolling along classic cliff-hanging curves.

Self Hire: Renting your own vehicle is the last option – and one that is absolutely *not* recommended unless you have a suicidal tendency or can find an Indonesian driver to drive who is used to the traffic and roads. In Bali, moped rental can be safe ... if you are experienced, confident and careful; otherwise, forget it – ditto for the other islands. If you do not believe the warnings, wait until you see the conditions of the crowded roads, illogical street organization and absolutely crazy drivers weaving in and out between one another – and directly at each other – in near accidents close enough to make your skin tingle.

Other Methods: There is enough public transportation, with taxis, *bemos* (small covered vehicle), mini-buses and the like, so that getting around within and between cities is cheap and convenient. For travel within cities, here are a few helpful definitions: *Becaks* are the three-wheeled bicycle carts with two seats and a roof, usually pedalled by elderly Indonesians; *Bajajs* are the orange, pumpkin-shaped three-wheel vehicles found in Jakarta that scream and dart between huge buses at rush hour time and are generally responsible for all the pollution in the air; *Dokars*, also known as horse-carts or *benhurs* in east Sumbawa, are the merrily jingling wooden carts pulled by decorated horses; Enchanting! *Taxis* can be found in all major cities. If the driver refuses to use a meter, bargain hard.

TREKKING

To visit the national parks of Indonesia, a permit from the PHPA (Directorate-General of Forest Conservation) is usually required. Write to the tourism office or the PHPA Central Office in Bogor (Jalan Ir H Janda 100, Bogor), next to the Botanical Gardens for a list of parks, permit requirements and office locations. Irian Jaya has the added complication of the *surat jalan* (permit requirement) before visiting interior villages. Bring several black-and-white photos of yourself, make a couple of copies of the lengthy document you will be required to fill out by the police upon your arrival, and be prepared to spend a day (or longer) waiting for permission in Jayapura.

VISAS

With no visa required for a period of 60 days, all you need is a passport valid six months from your arrival date and proof, meaning a ticket, of your plans to leave the country if you are a national from the following countries: **Argentina, Australia, Austria, Belgium, Brazil, Brunei, Canada, Denmark, Finland, France, Germany, Greece, Iceland, Ireland, Italy, Japan, Lichtenstein, Luxemburg, Malaysia, Malta, Morocco, Mexico, Netherlands, New Zealand, Norway, Phillipines, Singapore, South Korea, Spain, Sweden, Switzerand, Taiwan, Thailand, United Kingdom (Great Britain), United States of America, Venezuela and Yugoslavia**.

If you are a national of a country not listed above, you may obtain a tourist visa from any Indonesian Embassy or Consulate. For visitors with a Hong Kong CI(Certificate of Identity), visas for group travel with a minimum of five people can be granted by the Consulate General of Indonesia in Hong Kong – if the visit is no more than 30 days. You must enter and exit the country from Jakarta, Denpasar or Medan, and all tour plans, including accommodation and travel, should be arranged by a tour operator.

All visitors entering and exiting Indonesia by air must do so through the approved gateways of Jakarta, Bali, Medan, Manado, Biak, Ambon, Surabaya and Batam Island. Arrivals and departures by sea must be done through the approved ports of Jakarta, Semarang, Bali, Pontianak, Balikpapan, Tanjung Pinang and Kupang.

Visas are required for all other ports of entry; see the Indonesian Embassy or Consulate in your country. Entry without a visa is valid for 60 days and is non-extendable without leaving the country. Conference delegates with prior official approval may also receive visa free entry.

WEIGHTS & MEASURES

Indonesia uses the celsius temperature system and the metric system of weights and measures; to convert to Fahrenheit, multiply by 1.8 and add 32. To convert centimetres to inches multiply by 0.39; for metres to feet multiply by 3.28; for kilometres to miles multiply by 0.62; for hectares to acres multiply by 2.47; for kilogrammes to pounds, multiply by 2.21; for grammes to ounces multiply by 0.035. When filling petrol, remember use litres rather than gallons.

DIRECTORY

AIRLINES
JAKARTA
Ailitalia
Jl H Agus Salim
Hotel Sabang Metropolitan
Tel: 379 5237/379 7409

Air Canada GSA
Jl H Agus Salim (Hotel Sabang)
Tel: 371 479/376 237

Air India
(Hotel Sari Pacific)
Jl M H Thamrin
Tel: 325 470/325 534

Air Niugini
Jl Lapangan Banteng
Hotel Borobudur
Tel: 379 1306/379 0108

British Airways
Jl M H Thamrin
(Hotel Mandarin)
Tel: 333 092/333 027

Canadian Airlines International
Jl M H Thamrin
Wisma Kasgoro
Tel: 336 573/336 521/324 742

Cathay Pacific
(Hotel Borobudur)
Jl Lapangan Banteng Selatan
Tel: 380 6664

China Airlines
Jl Gajah Mada (Duta Merlin)
Tel: 354 449/354 448

Garuda Indonesia
Jl Medan Merdeka Selatan
(Danareska Building)
Tel: 334 425/334 429/334 430/
334 434

Jl Jend Sudirman
(Wisma Dharmala-Sakti)
Tel: 588 707/588 708/588 797/
588 798

Japan Airlines
Mid Plaza Plaza Bldg
Jl Jend Sudirman
Tel: 582 758/5781708

KLM
Hotel Indonesia
Jl M H Thamrin
Tel: 320 708/320 053

Korean Air
Jl Jend Sudirman
Wisma Metropolitan
Tel: 578 0257/578 0236/
578 0258

Lufthansa
Jl Jend Sudirman
Panin Centre Building
Tel: 710 247/710 248

Malaysia Airlines System
Jl M H Thamrin
Tel: 320 909

Pakistan International
Jl M H Thamrin
(Oriental Building)

Tel: 345 278

Philippine Airlines
Hotel Borobudur
Jl Lapangan Banteng Selatan
Tel: 370 108

Quantas
Jl M H Thamrin (BDN Building)
Tel: 361 707/379 0108/327 707/
326 707/327 538

Royal Brunei Airlines
Jl M H Thamrin
Hotel Indonesia
Tel: 27 214/327 265

Sabena Airlines
Jl Lapangan Banteng
Hotel Borobudur
Tel: 370 108/327 039

Scandinavian Air System
Jl Jend Sudirman
S Wijoyo Building
Tel: 584 110

Singapore Airlines
Jl Jend Sudirman
Chase Plaza
Tel: 320909/584 011/584 021/
584 042

Swissair
Jl Lapangan Banteng
Hotel Borobudur
Tel: 373 608/379 8006/
379 6118

Trans World Airlines
Jl M H Thamrin
Wisma Nusantara Building
Tel: 331 500/337 874

United Airlines
Jl Lapangan Banteng
Hotel Borobudur

UTA
Jl M H Thamrin
Jaya Building
Tel: 323 507/323 609

BANKS

ABN
Jl Juanda 23-24
Tel: 362 309

American Express
Arthaloka Building
Jl Sudirman 2
Tel: 570 2398

Bank of America
Wisma Antara
Jl Merdeka Selatan 17
Tel: 348 031

Bank of Tokyo
Jl Sudirman kav 10-11
Tel: 578 0709

Chase Manhattan
Jl Sudirman kav 21
Tel: 578 2213

Citibank
Jl Sudirman kav 70A
Tel: 578 2007

Hong Kong & Shanghai
Wisma Metropolitan II
Jl Sudirman
Tel: 578 0075

CINEMAS

Most cities do not even have
cinemas, unless you enjoy the
rough-and-tumble Kungfu fare
that crackles over the screen in
shriekingly bad colour and
sound. For popular films, pick
up a copy of the *Jakarta Post* or

the major city papers. As cinemas tend to open and close at
a whim, these periodicals and
the Tourism Offices are probably your best bet for finding out
what is playing, when and
where.

DEPARTMENT STORES

Jakarta
Adiron Plaza
Jalan Melawai, Kemayoran Baru

Blok M
Kemayoran Baru suburb

Duta Merlin Shopping Centre
Jalan Gajahmada

Gajah Mada Plaza
Jalan Gajah Mada

Hayam Wuruk Plaza
Jalan Hayam Wuruk

Matahari Department Store
Ratu Plaza Shopping Centre
Blok M Shopping Area
Pasar Senen Shopping Area
Jatinegara Shopping Area

Pasar Senen
Jalan Pasar Senen

Pasar Tanah Abang
Tanah Abang suburb

Ramayana Department Store
Pasar Senen Shopping Area
Bok M Shopping Area
Jalan Melawai
Jalan Agus Salim No 22A

Ratu Plaza
Jalan Jendral Sudirman

Sarinah Department Stores
Jalan MH Thamrin II
Jalan Iskandarsyah II 2

DIPLOMATIC & CONSULAR MISSIONS ABROAD

Afghanistan
Indonesian Embassy
Wasir Akhbar Khas Mena, Dis-
trict No 10, Zone No 14
Road Mark 93, Jeem House
Kabut Afganistan
PO Box: 532 Kabul
Tel: 20632/20645 (6 lines)

Algerie, Guinea and Mali
Ambassade d'Indonesie
6 Rue Muhamed Chemial B P 62
El-Mauradia Algier
Tel: 60201/602 051

**Argentina, Chile, Uruguay and
Paraguay**
Indonesian Embassy
2901 Mariskal Ramon Castila
1425
Buenos Aires, Argentina
Tel: 801 6622/801 6655

Australia
Indonesian Embassy
8 Darwin Avenue Yarralumla
Canberra, Australia ACT 2600
Tel: (062) 733 222

Austria
Indonesian Embassy
Gustav Tschenmakgasse 5-7
1180 Wien Austria
Tel: (02220) 342 533/345 34/
342 535/316 663

Bangladesh
Indonesian Embassy
Gulshan Avenue 75
Gulshan Model Town,
Dhaka 12 Bangladesh
Tel: 601 1311/601 1312

Belgium, Luxembourg and EEC
Indonesian Embassy
294, Avenue de Turvueren 1150
Brussels Belgium
Tel: (02) 771 5060/771 1776/
771 2014

Brunei Darrusalam
Indonesian Embassy
EDR 4303 Lot 4498 KG Sungai
Hanching Baru Simpang 528

Jl Muara
Tel: 30180/30445

Canada
Indonesian Embassy
287 Maclaren Street
Tel: (613) 236 7403

Denmark
Indonesian Embassy
Rehj Alle I 2900 Hellerup
Copenhagen
Tel: (01) 624 422

Egypt, Sudan, Lebanon, Somalia, and Djibouti
Indonesian Embassy
13 Rue Aisha Elteinouria
Garden City, Cairo, Egypt
Tel: 352 7200

France
Indonesian Embassy
47-49 Rue Contambert
75116 Paris
Tel: 450 30760

German Federal Republic
Indonesian Embassy
Bernkasteler Strasse 2
5300 Boon 2
Tel: 0228-310091

India
Indonesian Embassy
50 A Hanakyapuri
New Delhi
Tel: 602 353

Italy and Malta
Indonesian Embassy
53 Via Campania
Rome
Tel: 475 9251

Japan
Indonesian Embassy
2-9 Higashi Gotanda 5 Chome
Shinagawa-Ku
Tokyo
Tel: 441-4201

Kenya
Indonesian Embassy

Utalli Hous 3rd Floor
Ururu Highway
Nairobi
Tel: 330 797

Republic of Korea
Indonesian Embassy
55 Yoido-Dong, Youg-Deong
Po-Ku
Seoul
Tel: 782 5116

Malaysia
Indonesian Embassy
Jl Tun Razak No. 233
Kuala Lumpur
Tel: 984 2101

New Zealand, Fiji, and West Samoa
Indonesian Embassy
70 Glen Road
Kelburn
Wellington, New Zealand
Tel: 75895

Netherlands
Indonesian Embassy
8 Tobias Asserlaan 5517
KCS Graven Hage
Tel: 070 469796

Pakistan
Indonesian Embassy
Diplomatic Enclave Rama 5/4
Tel: 820266

Philippines
Indonesian Embassy
Salcedo Street Lagaspi Village
185/187
Metro Manila
Tel: 85-50-61

Saudi Arabia, Yemen, and Oman
Indonesian Embassy
Diplomatic Quarter Riyadh
Tel: 488 2131

Singapore
Indonesian Embassy
7 Chatsworth Road
Tel: 737 7422

Spain
Indonesian Embassy
65 Calle de Agestia Madrid
28043
Tel: 413 0294

Sri Lanka and Maldives
Indonesian Embassy
1 Police Park
Colombo 5
Tel: 580 113

Thailand
Indonesian Embassy
600-602 Petchburi Road
Bangkok
Tel: 252 3135

United Kingom and Ireland
Indonesian Embassy
157 Edgware RD
London W2 2HR
Tel: 01-499-7661

United States of America
Indonesian Embassy
2020 Massachusetts Avenue
NW
Washington DC
Tel: (202) 775-5200

FOREIGN MISSIONS
Jakarta
Australia
Jl Thamrin 15
Tel: 323 109

Austria
Jl Diponegoro 44
Tel: 338 090/338 101

Belgium
Wisma BCA, 15th Floor
22/23 Jl Jend Sudirman
Tel: 578 0510

Canada
Wisma Metropolitan I5th Floor
Jl Sudirman Kav 29
Tel: 510 709

Denmark
Jl H R Rasuna Said Kav 10
Tel: 520 4350

Egypt
Jl Teuku Umar 68
Tel: 333 440/331 141

Finland
Bina Mulia Building 10th Floor
Jl H R Rasuna Said Kav 10
Tel: 516 980/517 408/517 376

France
Jl Thamrin 20
Tel: 332 807/333 2375/332 383/
332 367

Germany
Jl M H Thamrin 11
Tel: 323 908/324 292/324 357

India
S1 Jl HR Rasuna Said, Kuningan
Tel: 520 4150

Iran
Jl HOS Cokrominoto 110
Tel: 330 623/331 378

Italy
Jl Diponegoro 45
Tel: 337 422

Japan
Jl M H Thamrin 24
Tel: 324 308/324 948/325 396/
325 140

Malaysia
Jl Imam Bonjol 17
Tel: 332 170/332 864

Myanmar
Jl H A Salim 109
Tel: 327 204/320 440

Netherlands
Jl Rasuna Said Kav S-3
Tel: 511 515

New Zealand
Jl Diponegoro 41
Tel: 330 552/330 620/330 680

Norway
4th Floor Rasuna Said Kav 10
Tel: 517 140/511 990

Papua New Guinea
Panin Bank Centre 6th Floor
Jl Jend Sudirman
Tel: 711 218/711 225

Philippines
Jl Imam Bonjol 6-8
Tel: 348 917/310 0345

Saudi Arabia
3 Jl Imam Bonjol
Tel: 310 5499/310 5560

Singapore
Blok X/4, Kav 2,
Jl H R Rasuna Said
Tel: 520 1489

South Korea
Jl Jend Gatot Subroto
Tel: 512 309/516 234

Spain
Jl M H Thamrin 53
Wisma Kosgoro 6th Floor
Tel: 325 996/321 808

Sri Lanka
Jl Diponegoro 70
Tel: 321 018/321 896

Sweden
Bina Mulia Building
Jl HR Rasuna Said Kav 10
Tel: 520 1551/520 1553

Switzerland
Jl H R Rasuna Said Blok X/3/2,
Kuningan
Tel: 516 061/517 451

Thailand
Jl Imam Bonjol 74
Tel: 343 762/349 180

Turkey
Jl H R Rasuna Said Kav 1,
Kuningan
Tel: 516 250/516 258

United Kingdom
Jl Thamrin 75
Tel: 330 904

United States
Jl Merdeka Selatan 5
Tel: 360 360

HOTELS
Java
BANDUNG
Abadi Garden **
Jl Setiabudi No. 287
Bandung 40154
Tel: 210 987
Rooms: 40

Anggrek Golden **
Jl R E Martadinata 15
Bandung 40115
Tel: 52537/58199/431 536
Rooms: 46

Arjuna Plaza *
Jl Ciumbuleuit 128
Bandung 40141
Tel: 81328
Rooms: 30

Braga Hotel **
Jl Braga 8, Bandung
Tel: 51685
Rooms: 67

Bumi Asih **
Jl Cilamayaitu
Bandung 40135
Tel: 50419
Rooms: 27

**Cisitu's International
Sangkuriang Guest House** **
Jl Cisitu 45B, Bandung
Tel: 82420
Rooms: 45

Grand Hotel Preanger **
Jl Asia Afrika 81, Bandung
Tel: 430 682
Rooms: 103

Istana ***
Jl Lembang No. 22-24
Bandung 40111
Tel: 433 025
Rooms: 34

Kumala Panghegar ***
Jl Asia Afrika 140, Bandung
Tel: 52141
Rooms: 66

Panghegar Hotel ***
Jl Merdeka No 2
Bandung 40154
Tel: 432 286
Rooms: 201

Papandayan ****
Jl Gatot Subroto 83, Bandung
Tel: 430 788/430 799

Santika ***
Jl Sumatra 54, Bandung
Tel: 56491/56492

Savoy Homann Panghegar ***
Jl Asia Afrika 112, Bandung
Tel: 432 244
Rooms: 113

Sheraton Inn Bandung ****
Jl Ir H Juanda 390
Bandung 401144
Tel: 210 303
Rooms: 112

BOGOR
Bukit Indah Hotel
Jl Raya Ciloto No 116
Tel: 2904

Bukit Raya
Jl Raya Cipana No 219
Tel: 2605

Bogor Permai
Jl Jend Sudirman No. 23A
Tel: 2115

Bumi Parahyangan
Jl Raya Puncak No. 10
Tel: 27147

Evergreen Village
Jl Raya Tugu Puncak km 84
Tel: 4075

Lembah Byiur
Jl Raya Puncak km 79
Tel: 4891

Mars
Jl Raya Cipayung No 133
Tel: 4488

Orchid
Jl Ir H Juand No 8
Tel: 22091

Padang Sati
Jl Raya Cipans
Tel: 2722

Pendawa
Jl Raya Cipanas No 219
Tel: 2224

Puncak Pass
Jl Raya Puncak Sindanglaya
Tel: 250 314

Salak
Jl Ir H Juanda No 8
Tel: 22091

Sanggabuana
Jl Raya Cipanas No 4-6
Tel: 2227

Tunas Kembang
Jl Raya Puncak Sindanglaya
Tel: 2719

Ussu International Hotel
Jl Cisarua Puncak
Tel: 4499

Jakarta
**Borobudur Inter-
    Continental** *****
Jl Lapangan Banteng Selatan
Tel: 370 108
Rooms: 172

Cikini Sofyan ***
Jl Cikini Raya 79
Tel: 320 695
Rooms: 115

City Hotel ***
Jl Medan, Glodok No. 1
Tel: 629 70089
Rooms: 196

Dirgantara *
Jl Iskandarsyah Raya I,
Blok M Kebayoran Baru
Tel: 712 109
Rooms: 26

Djakarta **
Jl Hayam Wuruk 35
Tel: 377 709
Rooms: 111

Febiola **
Jl Gajah Mada 27 A
Tel: 639 4008
Rooms: 87

Gama Gundaling *
Jl Pal Putih 197 A, Kramat Raya
Tel: 354 251
Rooms: 47

Garden ***
Jl Kemang Raya, Kebayoran Baru
Tel: 798 0760
Rooms: 100

**Grand Hyatt, Plaza
    Indonesia** *****
Jl MH Thamrin
Tel: 310 7400
Rooms: 450

Grand Menteng ***
Jl Matraman Raya 21
Tel: 858 1524

Hasta **
Jl Asia Afrika Senayan
Tel: 582 034
Rooms: 105

Horison ****
Taman Impian Jaya Ancol
Tel: 680 008
Rooms: 321

Hotel Indonesia ****
Jl MH Thamrin
Tel: 320 608
Rooms: 655

Hyatt Aryaduta *****
Jl Prapatan 44-46
Tel: 376 008

Rooms: 340
Interhouse **
Jl Melawai Raya No 17-20
Tel: 716 408
Rooms: 140

**Jakarta Hilton
International** *****
Jl Gatot Subroto
Tel: 587 981
Rooms: 644

Jayakarta Tower ****
Jl Hayam Wuruk 126
Tel: 649 6760
Rooms: 377

Kartika Chandra ***
Jl. Gatot Subroto
Tel: 511 008
Rooms: 200

Kebayoran Inn **
Jl Senayan 87
Kebayoran Baru
Tel: 775 968
Rooms: 59

Kemang ***
Jl Kemang Raya
Kebayoran Baru
Tel: 799 3208
Rooms: 100

Mandarin Oriental *****
Jl MH Thamrin
Tel: 321 307
Rooms: 455

Marco Polo **
Jl Teuku Cik Ditiro No 19
Tel: 325 409
Rooms: 181

Melati *
Jl Hayam Wuruk I
Tel: 377 208
Rooms: 96

Menteng **
Jl Gondangdia Lama 28
Tel: 325 208
Rooms: 71

Menteng II **
Jl Cikini Raya 105
Tel: 324 071
Rooms: 70

Menteng III **
Jl Matraman Raya 21
Tel: 882 153
Rooms: 70

Metropole **
Jl Pintu Besar 60
Tel: 620 308
Rooms: 86

New City ***
Jl Medan Glodok
Tel: 629 7008
Rooms: 196

Nirwana *
Jl Otto Iskandardina 14
Tel: 819 1708
Rooms: 98

Nusantara *
Jl K H Mas Mansyur No. 36
Tel: 460 009
Rooms: 53

Orchid Palace ***
Jl Letjen S Parman Slipi
Tel: 596 911
Rooms: 82

Pardede International *
Jl Raden Saleh 9-11
Tel: 350 902
Rooms: 20

Paripurna *
Jl Hayam Wuruk 25-26
Tel: 376 311

Patra Jasa ***
Jl Jend A Yani No 2
Tel: 410 608
Rooms: 52

Peninsula *
Jl Mangga Besar Raya 60
Tel: 629 0308
Rooms: 60

Petamburan *
Jl K S Tubun 15-17
Tel: 548 1044
Rooms: 106

Prapanca *
Jl Prapanca Raya 30-31
Tel: 712 656
Rooms: 29

President ****
Jl MH Thamrin 59
Tel: 320 508
Rooms: 354

Pulau Ayer Resort ***
Seribu Island
Tel: 342 031
Rooms: 100

Putri Duyung Cottage ***
Taman Impina Jaya Ancol
Tel: 680 904
Rooms: 11 Cottages

Rena Sofyan *
Jl Duren Sawit Raya 108
Tel: 860 25509
Rooms: 20

Royal **
Jl Ir H Juanda 14
Tel: 380 4301
Rooms: 60

Sabang Metropolitan ***
Jl Haji Agus Salim 11
Tel: 354 031
Rooms: 151

Sabang Palace **
Jl Setia Budi Raya 24
Tel: 514 640
Rooms: 41

Sahid Jaya & Tower *****
Jl Jend Sudirman 86
Tel: 570 4444
Rooms: 132

Salemba Indah *
Jl Paseban 20A
Tel: 882 975
Rooms: 71

Sari Pan Pacific ****
Jl MH Thamrin 6
Tel: 323 707
Rooms: 474

Senen City Hotel *
Jl Bungur Besar 157
Tel: 420 9826
Rooms: 70

Sriwijaya *
Jl Veteran No. 1
Tel: 370 409
Rooms: 100

Surya **
Jl Batu Ceper 44-46
Tel: 378 108
Rooms: 72

Surya Baru **
Jl Batu Ceper 11A
Tel: 368 108
Rooms: 45

Tebet Sofyan *
Jl Prof Dr Soepomo,
SH No. 23
Tel: 829 3114
Rooms: 56

Transaera **
Jl Merdeka Timur 16
Tel: 357 059
Rooms: 34

Tugu Asri *
Jl Jatibaru 7-9
Tel: 336 706
Rooms: 27

Wisma Indra *
Jl KH Agus Salim 63
Tel: 334 556
Rooms: 26

Wisata International ***
Jl MH Thamrin
Tel: 320 308
Rooms: 165

Wisata Jaya *
Jl Hayam Wuruk 123
Tel: 649 8686

Rooms: 90

SEMARANG
Adem Ayem
Jl Sriwijaya 31-33
Tel: 314 506

Bali
Jl Imam Bonjol No. 146
Tel: 211 974

Candi Baru
Jl Rinjani No. 21
Tel: 315 272

Candi Baru
Jl Wahidin No. 112
Tel: 312 515

Dewa Asia
Jl Imam Bonjol 73
Tel: 22547

Dibya Puri
Jl Pemuda No. 11
Tel: 27821

Djelita
Jl M T Haryono 32
Tel: 23891

Gombel Indah
Jl Setyabudi No 12
Tel: 312 704

Graha Santika
Jl Pandanaran 116-120
Tel: 413 115

Green Guest House
Jl Kesambi 7
Tel: 312 642

Johar
Jl Empu Tantular No 1
Tel: 288 585

Merbabu
Jl Pemuda No 122
Tel: 27491

Metro Grand Park
Jl H Agus Salim No. 2-4
Tel: 314 441

Muria
Jl Dr Cipto 73
Tel: 22817

Patra Jasa
Jl Sisingamangaraja
Tel: 27371

Queen
Jl Gajah Mada No 44-52
Tel: 27603

Santika
Jl Jend A Yani No 189
Tel: 313 272

Siliwangi
Jl Mgr Sugiopranoto
Tel: 22636

Sky Garden
Jl Setiabudi No 5
Tel: 312 733

Surya
Jl Imam Bonjol
Tel: 24250

Telomoyo
Jl Gajah Mada No 138
Tel: 20926

SOLO/SURAKARTA
Cakra
Jl Brigjend Slamet Riyadi
No 171
Tel: 5847

Dana
Jl Brigjend Slamet Riyadi
No 232
Tel: 3890

Kusuma Sahid Prince
Jl Sugiyopranoto No 22
Tel: 6356

Mangkunegaran Palace
Jl Mangkunegaran
Tel: 5683

Sahid
Jl Gajah Mada No 104
Tel: 3889

SURABAYA

Elmi Hotel ***
Jl Panglima Sudirman 42-44
Tel: 471 571
Rooms: 140

Garden Hotel ***
Jl Pemuda 21
Tel: 470 000
Rooms: 100

Garden Palace Hotel ***
Jl Yos Sudarso 11
Tel: 479 251
Rooms: 203

Gunungsari Motel ***
Jl. Gunungsari
Tel: 65435
Rooms: 63

Hotel Bumi Hyatt ****
Jl Jend Basuki Rachmat 124
Tel: 511 234
Rooms: 268

Hotel Cendana *
Jl Kombes Pol M Duryat No 6
Tel: 42251
Rooms: 23

Hotel Lesmana *
Jl Bintoro 16
Tel: 67152
Rooms: 54

Hotel Majapahit ***
Jl Tunjungan 65
Tel: 43351
Rooms: 106

Hotel Mirama ***
Jl Raya Darmo 68-72
Tel: 69501
Rooms: 104

Hotel Pregolan *
Jl Pregolan 11-15
Tel: 41251
Rooms: 54

Hotel Ramayana **
Jl Jend Basuki Rachmat 67-69
Tel: 45395

Rooms: 100

Hotel Sarkies **
Jl Embong Malang 7-11
Tel: 44515
Rooms: 50

Hotel Semut *
Jl Samudra 9-15
Tel: 24578
Rooms: 48

Natour Hotel Simpang ***
Jl Pemuda No 1-3
Tel: 42151
Rooms: 100

New Grand Park Hotel ***
Jl Samudra 3-5
Tel: 331 515
Rooms: 100

Sahid Hotel
Jl Sumatra 1
Tel: 471 711
Rooms: 100

Tanjung Hotel *
Jl Panglima Sudirman 43-45
Tel: 44031
Rooms: 50

YOGYAKARTA

Ambarrukmo Palace Hotel ****
Jl Laksda Adisucipto 55281
Tel: 88488
Rooms: 257

Arjuna Plaza Hotel *
Jl P Mangkubumi 48
Tel: 86862
Rooms: 24

Hotel Garuda ****
Jl Malioboro 72
Tel: 2213
Rooms: 230

Hotel Mutiara ***
Jl Malioboro 18
Tel: 3272
Rooms: 137

Hotel Puri Artha ***
Jl Cendrawasih 9
Tel: 5934
Rooms: 73

Hotel Santika ***
Jl Jend Sudirman 19
Tel: 63036
Rooms: 148

Hotel Sri Wedari ***
Jl Adisucipto Km 5
Tel: 3599
Rooms: 70

New Batik Palace Hotel *
Jl P Mangkubumi 46
Tel: 2229
Rooms: 22

Sahid Garden Hotel ***
Jl Babarsari, Tambakbayan
Tel: 3697
Rooms: 134

Yogya International Hotel ***
Jl Laksda Adisucipto 38
Tel: 5318
Rooms: 79

Sumatra
BANDA ACEH

Aceh
Jl Muhammad Yamin No 1
Tel: 21354

Aceh Barat Hotel
Jl Khairil Anwar No 17
Tel: 23250

International
Jl Jend A Yani No 19
Tel: 21834

Kuala Tripa International
Jl Mesjid Raya
Tel: 21879

Lading
Jl Cut Meutia No 9
Tel: 21359

Medan
Jl Jend A Yani No 15

Tel: 21501

Rasa Sayang Ayu International Hotel
Jl Teuku Umar No 439
Tel: 21379

Sultan Hotel International
Jl Teuku Panglima Polim No 127
Tel: 22581

BATAM ISLAND
Batam Jaya Hotel **
Jl Raya Ali Haji
Tel: 58707
Rooms: 221

Batam View Hotel ****
Jl Hang Lekir, Nongsa
Tel: 22281
Rooms: 196

Bumi Nusantara Hotel *
Balai Indah, Lubuk Baja
Tel: 58481
Rooms: 62

Halmaya Hotel *
Jl Sriwijaya
Tel: 58138
Rooms: 35

Hilltop Hotel ***
Jl Ir Sutami No 8 Sekupang
Tel: 22840
Rooms: 70

Holiday Hotel *
Jl Imam Bonjol Blok B No 1
Lubuk Baja
Tel: 58616
Rooms: 65

Turi Beach Resort ****
Jl Teluk Mata Ikan, Nagoya
Tel: 21543
Rooms: 156

BUKITTINGGI
Dymen's International **
Jl Nawawi No 1-5
Tel: 21015
Rooms: 54

Hotel Limas *
Jl Kesehatan No 34
Tel: 22641
Rooms: 23

Hotel Benteng *
Jl Benteng No 1
Tel: 21115
Rooms: 30

Hotel Minang *
Jl Panorama No 20-A
Tel: 21120
Rooms: 8

JAMBI
Harisman Hotel
Jl Prof M Yamin
Tel: 24677

Hotel Telanaipura
Jl Kol H Abunjani
Tel: 23827

Losmen Abadi
Jl Gatot Subroto No 119
Tel: 24054

Losmen Garuda
Jl Dr Soetomo No 32
Tel: 22690

Losmen Matahari
Jl Sultan Agung No 67
Tel: 24610

KARO
Brastagi Cottage *
Jl Gundaling
Tel: 20908
Rooms: 34

Danau Toba International Hotel *
Jl Gundaling
Tel: 20946
Rooms: 34

GM Panggabean International *
Jl Merdeka No 9
Tel: 20832
Rooms: 22

Hotel Bere Karona *
Jl Pendidikan 148
Tel: 20888
Rooms: 25

Hotel Bukit Kubu
Jl Sempurna No 2
Tel: 20832

Hotel Rudang **
Jl Sempurna No 3
Rooms: 72

Hotel Sibayak International ***
Jl Merdeka
Tel: 323 200
Rooms: 163

LAMPUNG
Hotel Marco Polo **
Jl Dr Susilo No 4 Bandar
Lampung
Tel: 41511
Rooms: 104

Sahid Krakatau Hotel ***
Jl Yos Sudarso 294 Bandar
Lampung
Tel: 62766
Rooms: 64

Sheraton Inn Hotel ****
Jl Wolter Mongonsidi No 175
Bandar Lampung
Tel: 63696
Rooms: 113

MEDAN
Anantaboga Cottage *
Jl Letjen, Jamin Ginting Km 14
Rooms: 40

Danau Toba International ****
Jl Imam Bonjol 7
Tel: 327 000
Rooms: 259

Hotel Angkasa **
Jl Sutomo No 1
Tel: 321 244
Rooms: 57

Hotel Dharma Deli ***
Jl Balai Kota No 2

Tel: 327 999
Rooms: 176

Hotel Dirga Surya **
Jl Imam Bonjol No 6
Tel: 321 244
Rooms: 53

Hotel Elbruba *
Jl Perintis Kemerdekaan 19
Tel: 22477
Rooms: 48

Hotel Garuda **
Jl Sisingamangaraja 27
Tel: 22775
Rooms: 45

Hotel Garuda Plaza
Jl Sisingamangaraja 18
Tel: 326255
Rooms: 154

Hotel Pelangi *
Jl Letjen
Jamin Ginting Km 10.2
Tel: 28835
Rooms: 52

Hotel Petisah *
Jl Nibung II
Tel: 522 942
Rooms: 61

Hotel Sumatera *
Jl Sisingamangaraja 21
Tel: 24973
Rooms: 54

Hotel Tiara ****
Jl Cut Mutiah
Tel: 516 000
Rooms: 204

Hotel Waiyat *
Jl Asia No 44
Tel: 27575
Rooms: 79

Motel Danau Toba International
Jl Hayam Wuruk 2-6
Tel: 23979

Pardede International **
Jl Ir H Juanda 14
Tel: 323866
Rooms: 115
Polonia Hotel ***
Jl Jend Sudirman 14-18
Tel: 325 300
Rooms:178

PADANG
Hotel Bouganville *
Jl Baginda Azis Khan 2
Tel: 22149
Rooms: 20

Hotel Hang Tuah *
Jl Pemuda No 1
Tel: 26556
Rooms: 38

Hotel Muara **
Jl Gereja No 34
Tel: 25600
Rooms: 42

Hotel Padang
Jl Baginda Azis Khan 28
Tel: 22563
Rooms: 41

Hotel Pangeran **
Jl Dobi No 3-5
Tel: 26233
Rooms: 65

Hotel Putri Bungsu *
Jl Pasar Raya No 40
Tel: 22230
Rooms: 54

Mariani International Hotel **
Jl Bundo Kandung 35
Tel: 25410
Rooms: 30

Pangeran Beach Hotel **
Jl Juanda No 79
Tel: 26233
Rooms: 139

PEKANBARU
**Hotel Indrapura
  International** ***
Jl Dr Sutomo No 86

Tel: 25233
Rooms: 103

Hotel Mutiara Panghegar ***
Jl Yos Sudarso No 12-A
Tel: 23120
Rooms: 72

Hotel Sri Indrayani *
Jl Sam Ratulangi No 2
Tel: 24244
Rooms: 50

Hotel Tasia Ratu *
Jl Hasyim Ashari No 10
Tel: 21225
Rooms: 53

**PEMATANG SIATAR
SIMALUNGUN**
Astari Hotel & Bungalow **
Jl P Samosir No 9,
Parapat 21174
Tel: 41219
Rooms: 58

Danau Toba International **
Jl P. Samosir 17,
Parapat
Tel: 41583
Rooms: 32

**Danau Toba International
  Cottage** *
Jl Nelson Purba No 4,
Parapat 21174
Tel: 41172
Rooms:106

Hotel Budi Mulia *
Jl P Samosir No 9,
Parapat 21174
Tel: 41216
Rooms: 28

Hotel Patrajasa **
Jl Siuhan,
Parapat 21174
Tel: 41796
Rooms: 36

Natour Hotel Parapat ***
Jl Marihat 1,
Parapat 21174

Tel: 41012
Rooms: 85

Parapat View Hotel **
Jl Sidaka Pintu,
Parapat 21174
Tel: 41375
Rooms: 45

Siantar Hotel ***
Jl W R Spuratman No 3
Tel: 21091
Rooms: 31

Siansar Hotel Parapat *
Jl Sisingamangaraja No 8,
Parapat 21174
Tel: 41564
Rooms: 78

Tara Bunga Sibogo **
Jl Sibgo No 2, Parapat 21174
Tel: 41665
Rooms: 42

Wisma Danau Toba **
Jl P Samosir 3-6,
Parapat 21174
Tel: 41302
Rooms: 51

SAMOSIR ISLAND
Hotel Silintong **
Jl Durian No 5 Tuk-Tuk Siadog,
P Samosir,
Medan 20234
Tel: 41345
Rooms: 43

Toba Beach Hotel *
Tomok, Lake Toba, P Samosir
Jl Brigjen Katamso 62,
Medan
Tel: 41275
Rooms: 93

Bali
DENPASAR
Hotel Adyasa *
Jl Nakula 23
Tel: 22679
Rooms: 20

Hotel Artha
Jl Diponegoro 131-A
Tel: 27370

Hotel Damai *
Jl Diponegoro 117-A
Tel: 22476
Rooms: 30

Hotel Pamecutan Palace **
Jl Thamrin No 2
Tel: 23491
Rooms: 44

Natour Bali Hotel ***
Jl Veteran 2
Tel: 25681
Rooms: 71

KUTA
Bali Intan Cottages
Jl Melasti No 1
Tel: 51770
Rooms: 122

Hotel Bali Oberoi
Kayu Aya Legian
Tel: 25581

Kartika Plaza Beach Hotel *****
Jl Kartika
Tel: 22454
Rooms: 386

Kuta Beach Club Hotel **
Jl Bakungsari
Tel: 250 056
Rooms: 105

Kuta Cottages **
Jl Bakungsari
Tel: 24100
Rooms: 50

Kuta Palace Hotel ***
Jl Pura Bagus Taruna
Tel: 51461
Rooms: 281

Legian Beach Hotel ***
Jl Melasti
Tel: 23061
Rooms: 189

Natour Kuta Beach Hotel **
Jl Pantai Kuta
Tel: 25791
Rooms: 40

Pertamina Cottage *****
Jl Pantai Kuta
Tel: 51161
Rooms: 249

Ramayana Seaside Hotel *
Jl Bakungsari
Tel: 51864
Rooms: 60

NUSA DUA
Hotel Putri Bali *****
Lot N-3
Tel: 71020
Rooms: 393

Melia Bali Sol Hotel ****
Lot N-1
Tel: 71510
Rooms: 494

Nusa Dua Beach Hotel *****
Lot N-4
Tel: 71210
Rooms: 450

SANUR
Alit's Beach Bungalow **
Jl Raya Sanur
Tel: 8567
Rooms: 71

**Bali Beach Inter-
Continental** *****
Jl Hang Tuah
Tel: 8511
Rooms: 605

Bali Hyatt Hotel *****
Semawang Sanur
Tel: 8271
Rooms: 387

Bali Sanur Bungalows **
Jl Raya Sanur
Tel: 8421
Rooms: 175

Besakih Beach Hotel **
Jl Tanjungsari
Tel: 8423
Rooms: 50

Diwangkara Beach Hotel **
Jl Hang Tuah
Tel: 8577
Rooms: 36

Irama Bungalow *
Jl Tanjungsari
Tel: 8423
Rooms: 23

Gazebo Cottage **
Jl Tanjungsari
Tel: 8300
Rooms: 52

Paneeda View Hotel **
Jl Tanjungsari
Tel: 8425
Rooms: 46

Puri Dalem Hotel *
Jl Hang Tuah
Tel: 8421
Rooms: 36

**Sanur Beach and Seaside
  Bungalows** ****
PO Box 279
Tel: 8011
Rooms: 430

Segara Village Hotel ***
Jl Segara Ayu
Tel: 8407
Rooms: 130

Sindhu Beach Hotel ***
PO Box 181
Tel: 8351
Rooms: 59

Tanjungsari Hotel ***
Jl Tanjungsari
Tel: 8411
Rooms: 30

Sulawesi
MANADO
Ahlan City

Jl Sudirman No 103
Tel: 3454

Angin Mamiri
Jl Gajah Mada No 3
Tel: 2673

Garden Hotel
Jl WR Supratman No 1
Tel: 51688

Kawanua City
Jl Dr Sam Ratulangi No 1
Tel: 52222

Minahasa Hotel
Jl Dr Sam Ratulangi No 199
Tel: 2059

Nusa Tenggara
MATARAM
Hotel Granada
Jl Bung Karno, Mataram
Tel: 22275
Rooms: 50

Hotel Handika
Jl. Panca Usaha 3 Mataram
Tel: 23578
Rooms: 15

Hotel Kerta Yoga
Jl Pejanggik 64 Mataram
Tel: 21775
Rooms: 15

Hotel Melati
Jl Yos Sudarso 4 Mataram
Tel: 23780
Rooms: 20

Hotel Nusantara
Jl Suprapto 28 Mataram
Tel: 23492
Rooms: 35

Hotel Paradiso
Jl Angkasa 3 Mataram
Tel: 22074
Rooms: 36

Hotel Rinjani
Jl Panca Warca, Mataram
Tel: 21633

Rooms: 16

Hotel Suranadi *
Desa Selat,
Kecamatan Narmada,
Mataram
Tel: 23686
Rooms: 17

Hotel Tenang
Jl Panca Warga, Mataram
Tel: 23345
Rooms: 22

Hotel Triguna
Jl Koperasi, Palembak,
West Nusa Tenggara
Tel: 21705
Rooms: 22

UJUNG PANDANG
Hotel Ramayama **
Jl Gunung Bawakaraeng No 12
Tel: 22165

Losari Beach Inn **
Jl Pasar Ikan No 8
Tel: 4363

Makassar Golden Hotel *****
Jl Pasar Ikan 52
Tel: 22208

Marannu City Hotel ***
Jl Sultan Hasanuddin 3
Tel: 25087

Senggigi Beach Hotel
Batu Layar, Mataram
Tel: 23430
Rooms: 52

East Nusa Tenggara
Hotel Astiti *
Jl Jend Sudirman No 146-Kupang
Tel: 21810
Rooms: 35

Hotel Cendana *
Jl Raya El Tari No 15-Kupang
Tel: 21541
Rooms: 40

Hotel Flobamor II *
Jl Jend Sudirman No 21-Kupang
Tel: 21346
Rooms: 35

Hotel Sao Wisata **
Jl Don Thomas No 18
Waiara-Maumere
Tel: 342 555 666
Rooms: 45

Sasando International Hotel *
Jl Kartini No 1-Kupang
Tel: 22224
Rooms: 50

East Kalimantan
BALIKPAPAN
Andika
Jl Semoi, Balikpapan
Tel: 232 603

Bahtera Jaya Abadi
Jl Jend A Yani 2,
Balikpapan
Tel: 22563

Balikpapan ****
Jl P Antasari,
Balikpapan
Tel: 21804
Rooms: 186

Balikpapan
Jl Garuda 2,
Balikpapan
Tel: 21490

Blue Sky
Jl Letjen, Suprapto,
Balikpapan
Tel: 22267
Rooms: 72

Gajah Mada
Jl Gajah Mada 100,
Balikpapan 76113
Tel: 21046

Mama
Jl D I Panjaitan 95,
Balikpapan
Tel: 22104

Mirama *
Jl Mayjend Sutoyo II A/16,
Balikpapan
Tel: 22960
Rooms: 47

Piersa
Jl Sepingan By Pass Rt 52/1,
Balikpapan
Tel: 21064
Rooms: 38

Puri Kencana
Jl A Yani 10,
Balikpapan
Tel: 22981
Rooms: 34

Tirta Plaza
Jl Mayjend D I Panjaitan XX No
51 Balikpapan
Tel: 22324
Rooms: 29

Wisma Aida
Jl Mayjen D I Panjaitan 50,
Balikpapan
Tel: 21006
Rooms: 35

Wisma Patra
Jl Yos Sudarso, PO Box 198
Balikpapan
Rooms: 24

SAMARINDA
Andhika
Jl H Agus Salim 27, Samarinda
Tel: 22358
Rooms: 50

Diana Mas
Jl Veteran 11/8, Samarinda
Tel: 21882
Rooms: 30

Gelora
Jl Niaga Selatan 34,
Samarinda
Tel: 22024
Rooms: 29

Hayani
Jl Pirus 31, Samarinda

Tel: 22653
Rooms: 26

Hidayah
Jl K H Mas Temenggung 20,
Samarinda
Tel: 21712
Rooms: 32

Jakarta II
Jl Sartika,
Samarinda
Tel: 23895
Rooms: 50

Kota Tepian *
Jl Pahlawan No 4
Samarinda
Tel: 32510
Rooms: 30

Lamin Indah
Jl Bhayankaru,
Samarinda
Rooms: 18

Mesra International **
Jl Pahlawan No 1,
Samarinda
Tel: 21011
Rooms: 120

Nina
Jl Rajawali 176,
Samarinda
Tel: 22422
Rooms: 11

Rahayu
Jl KH Abdul Hassan 17,
Samarinda
Tel: 22422
Rooms: 11

Sewarga Indah *
Jl Jend Sudirman 43,
Samarinda
Tel: 22066
Rooms: 68

Sukarni
Jl Panglima Batur III,
Samarinda
Tel: 21134

Rooms: 20

Temindung
Jl Pelita II,
Samarinda
Tel: 21559
Rooms: 22

TARAKAN
Bahtera Jaya Abadi *
Jl Sulawesi No 1, Tarakan
Tel: 21821
Rooms: 55

Erli
Jl Kalimantan No 1, Tarakan
Tel: 21388
Rooms: 40

Mirama
Jl Jend Sudirman 63, Tarakan
Tel: 21637
Rooms: 22

Orchid
Jl Jend Sudirman 171, Tarakan
Tel: 21664
Rooms: 22

Oriental
Jl Sulawesi No 1, Tarakan
Tel: 21384
Rooms: 11

Sejahtera
Jl Karang Bali RT 1/74, Tarakan
Tel: 21472
Rooms: 53

Tarakan Plaza *
Jl Yos Sudarso, Tarakan
Tel: 21870
Rooms: 53

Wisata
Jl Jend Sudirman 46, Tarakan
Tel: 21245
Rooms: 17

Wisma Bunga Muda
Jl Yos Sudarso V/C/78, Tarakan
Tel: 21349

West Kalimantan
BANJARMASIN
Banjar Permai Inn *
Jl A Yani Km 33.5
Banjarbaru
Tel: 2280
Rooms: 52

Barito Palace ***
Jl Haryono MT16-20,
Banjarmasin
Tel: 67301
Rooms:

Maramin Hotel **
Jl Lambung Mangkurat 32,
Banjarmasin 70111
Tel: 688 944
Rooms: 68

Nabilla Palace Hotel ***
Jl Jend A Yani Km4.5,
Banjarmasin
Tel: 67007
Rooms: 71

New River City Hotel *
Jl R E Martadinata No 3,
Banjarmasin
Tel: 2983
Rooms: 43

Perdana *
Jl Brigien Katamso No 3,
Banjarmasin
Tel: 3276
Rooms: 33

Sampaga Hotel *
Jl Mayjen Soetoyo 3 No 128,
Banjarmasin 70117
Tel: 2753
Rooms: 25

The Kalimantan Hotel ***
Jl Bank Rakyat No 10,
Banjarmasin
Tel: 68309

BANTAENG
Hotel Ahriani*
Jl Lanto
Tel: 48
Rooms: 26

KENDARI
Kendari Beach Hotel *
Jl Sultan Hasanuddin No 44
Tel: 21988
Rooms: 26

PALOPO
Hotel Adipati *
Jl Pattimura No 2
Tel: 179
Rooms: 24

Hotel Palopo *
Jl Kelapa 11
Tel: 209
Rooms: 30

PALU
Bumi Anyiur Hotel *
Jl S Parman No 28
Tel: 21076
Rooms: 15

Hotel Alam Raya *
Jl Aljufri 27
Tel: 21643
Rooms: 24

New Dely Hotel *
Jl Tadulaho 17
Tel: 21037
Rooms: 25

Palu Beach Hotel *
Jl Raden Saleh No 22
Tel: 21126
Rooms: 55

Wisata Hotel *
Jl Letjen S Parman 39
Tel: 21175
Rooms: 27

PARE-PARE
Hotel Gandaria *
Jl Bau Messepe 171
Tel: 21093
Rooms: 17

Hotel Yusida
Jl Pinggir Laut
Tel: 21813
Rooms: 16

PONTIANAK
Kapuas Palace ***
Jl Imam Bonjol, Pontianak
Tel: 36122
Rooms: 76

Kartika Hotel
Jl Rahadi Usman, Pontianak
Tel: 34401
Rooms: 45

Mahkota Hotel
Jl Sidas 8, Pontianak
Tel: 36022
Rooms: 105

Orient Hotel
Jl Tanjungpura, Pontianak
Tel: 32650
Rooms: 61

Wisma Martani
Jl Tani 4, Pontianak
Tel: 32412
Rooms: 49

SENGKANG
Hotel Alsalam *
Jl Sentosa 27
Tel: 53
Rooms: 11

SINGKAWANG
Kalbar Hotel
Jl Kepolisian Mahmud,
Singkawang
Rooms: 76

Palapa Hotel
Jl Ismail Tahir
Singkawan

Moluccas
AMBON
Abdulali Hotel *
Jl St Babullah Ambon
Tel: 2057
Rooms: 38

Amboina Hotel *
Jl Kapitan Ulupaha No 5/A,
Ambon
Tel: 3354
Rooms: 28

Bahtera Hotel
Jl Christina Martha Tiahahu Sk
2-2/31 Ambon
Tel: 41088

Beta Hotel
Jl Wim Raewaru Ambon
Tel: 3463

Cendrawasih *
Jl Tulukabessy 39 Ambon
Tel: 2487
Rooms: 18

Eleonoor Hotel
Jl Anthone Rhebok 30
Tel: 2834

Irama Hotel
Jl Sultan Babullah Sk 30/22
Ambon
Tel: 3307

Jamila Hotel
Jl Soabali Ambon
Tel: 3054

Josiba Hotel
Jl Tulukabessy Ambon
Tel: 41280

Manise Hotel *
Jl W R Supratman No 1
Tel: 42905
Rooms: 60

Maulana Hotel *
Jl Pelabuhan Bandanaira
Tel: 21022
Rooms: 60

Mutiara Hotel **
Jl Pattimura Ambon
Tel: 3075
Rooms: 30

Ramayana Hotel
Jl Srimau 44/2/20
Tel: 3369

Rezfanny Hotel
Jl Wim Raewan 115
Tel: 2357

Rosemgen Hotel
Jl K Sasuit Tabun
Tel: 45

Sela Hotel
Jl Anthone Rhebok
Tel: 2422

Sentani Hotel
Jl Cendrawasih Sk 4/1-26
Tel: 2625

Silalou Hotel
Jl Sedap Malam 41
Tel: 3197

Tual Mirah
Jl Sapta Marga
Tel: 172

Wisma Aurei
Jl Wim Raewan 1/14
Tel: 3197

Wisata Hotel
Jl Mutiara Sk 3-15 Ambon 97125
Tel: 3298

Wisma Jaya
Jl Sultan Babullah Sk 45/30
Ambon
Tel: 41545

Irian Jaya
BIAK
Hotel Irian
Jl Prof Moh Yamin
Biak
Tel: 21139

Maju Hotel
Jl Imam Bonjol
Tel: 21218

Mapia Hotel
Jl Jend A Yani
Tel: 31383

Titawaka Hotel
Jl Selat Makassar No 3
Tel: 21835

JAYAPURA
Hotel Agung
Jl Argapura 47
Jayapura
Tel: 21777
Rooms: 9

Hotel Asia
Jl Pasar Central No 18
Tel: 41277

Hotel Dafonsoro
Jl Percetakan 22-24
Jayapura
Tel: 22285
Rooms: 25

Hotel Irian Plaza
Jl Setiapura 11
PO Box 40, Jayapura
Tel: 21575
Rooms: 40

Hotel Jayapura
Jl Olah Raga No 4, Jayapura
Tel: 21216
Rooms: 18

Hotel Matoa
Jl Jend A Yani 14
Jayapura
Tel: 22336

Hotel Sederhana
Jl Halmahera No 2
PO Box 45, Jayapura
Tel: 21291
Rooms: 20

Hotel Triton
Jl Jend A Yani No 52
PO Box 33, Jayapura
Tel: 21218
Rooms: 24

Hotel Wisma GKI
Jl Sam Ratulangi No 6
PO Box 222, Jayapura
Tel: 21574
Rooms: 14

Natour's Hotel Numbai
Jl Trikora Dok V Atas
PO Box 22, Jayapura

Tel: 21394
Rooms: 43

MERAUKE
Flora Hotel
Jl Raya Mandala No 221
Tel: 21879

Hotel Nirmala Merauke
Jl Raya Mandala No 62
Tel: 21038

SORONG
Batana Beach Hotel
Jl Barito No 2
PO Box 127, Sorong
Tel: 21347
Rooms: 24

Hotel Cenderawasih
Jl Sam Ratulangi 54
Sorong
Tel: 21740
Rooms: 22

Hotel Citra
Jl Pemuda 11
PO Box 8, Sorong
Tel: 21246
Rooms: 17

Hotel Memberamo
Jl Dr Sam Ratulangi
PO Box 318, Sorong
Tel: 21564
Rooms: 10

Hotel Pilihan
Jl Jend A Yani 85-87
Sorong
Tel: 21336
Rooms: 17

WAMENA
Hotel Baliem Cottages
Jl Thamrin, PO Box 32
Wamena
Rooms: 8

Jayawijaya Hotelama
PO Box 57, Wamena
Tel: 11
Rooms: 17

MUSEUMS
Northern Sumatra - Aceh
Art Museum
Jl Jati
Medan

Balige Museum
Jl Sanggrahan No 1
Balige

Bukit Barisan Museum
Jl Zaenal Arifin No 8
Medan
Tel: 21954

Gayo Museum
Jl Buntul-Buntul
Takengon, Central Aceh

Huta Bolon "Simanindo" Museum
Jl Kecamatan Simanindo
Pematang Siantar

Malikulsaleh Museum
Jl Mayjend T Hamsyah
Bendahara Lhokseumawe
North Aceh

Museum Joang 45
Jl Pemuda No 17
Medan
Tel: 324 110

Museum Negeri of North Sumatra
M H Yoni No 51
Medan
Tel: 25799

Museum Negri of Aceh
Jl Sultan Alaiddin
Machmudsah 12
Banda Aceh
Tel: 23241

Rumah Bolon "Pematang Purba" Museum
Jl Kampung Pematang Purba

Sepakat Segenap Museum
Jl Raya Babussalam
Kutacane
Southeast Aceh

Simalungun Museum
Jl Sudirman No 8
Pematang Siantar
Tel: 21954

Zoological Museum
Jl Kapten MH
Sitorus 10, Pematang Siantar
Tel: 21611

West Sumatra
Art Museum
Panorama No 22
Bukittingi
Tel: 22752Jl

Bundo Kandung Museum
Jl Cindur Mato
Bukittinggi
Tel: 21029

**Museum Negeri of West
  Sumatra**
Jl Diponegoro (Lapangan Tugu)
Padang
Tel: 22316

Tridaya Eka Dharma Museum
Jl Diponegoro, Padang
Tel: 22752

Zoological Museum
Jl Cindur Mato
Bukittinggi

RIAU
**Assejarah El Hasyimiah Palace
  Museum**
Jl Sukaramai Siak Sri Indapura
Bengkalis

Kendil Riau Museum
Jl Kijang Batu 11/76
Tanjung Pinang
Tel: 07712

South Sumatra
**Museum Negeri of South
  Sumatra**
Jl Sriwijaya
No 1 km 5.5, Palembang
Tel: 411 382

Museum U P T Balitung
Jl Melati, Tanjung Pandan,
Belitung
Tel: 278

Sultan Badaruddin Museum
Jl Pasar Hilir No 3
Palembang

JAMBI
Museum Negeri of Jambi
Jl Urip Sumoharjo No 1
Telanai Pura
Tel: 268 415

BENGKULU
Museum Negeri of Bengkulu
Jl Pembangunan Padang
Harapan
Bengkulu
Tel: 32099

Lampung
Museum Negeri of Lampung
Jl Teuku Umar
Meneng Building, Lampung
Tel: 55164

Jakarta
ASMAT Museum
Taman Mini Indonesia Indah,
Jakarta Timur

Adam Malik Museum
Jl Diponegoro No 29
Jakarta Pusat
Tel: 374 108

Anatomy FKUI Museum
Jl Salemba No 6
Jakarta Pusat
Tel: 330 363

Ancol Oceanarium Museum
Jl Lodan Timur Ancol
Jakarta Utara
Tel: 680 519

Art Museum
Jl Fatahillah No 6
Jakarta Kota
Tel: 271 062

Artha Suaka Museum
Jl Kebon Sirih 82-84
Jakarta Pusat
Tel: 374108

Criminal (MABAK) Museum
Jl Trunojoyo No 3,
Kebayoran Baru,
Jakarta Selatan
Tel: 7011

Fatahilla Museum
Jl Taman Fatahillah
Jakarta Kota
Tel: 679 101

Gedung Juang 45 Museum
Jl Menteng Raya No 31
Jakarta Pusat
Tel: 356 141

Indonesia Museum
Taman Mini Indonesia Indah
Jakarta Timur
Tel: 489 022

Kebangkitan National Museum
Jl Abdurrachman Saleh No 26
Jakarta Pusat
Tel: 336 143

Komodo Museum
Taman Mini Indonesia Indah
Jakarta Timur
Tel: 840 0525

Manggala Wanabhakti Museum
Jl Jend Gatot Suboto
Jakarta Selatan
Tel: 570 3246

Military Museum
Taman Mini Indonesia Indah
Jakarta Timur
Tel: 840 1081

National Museum
Jl Merdeka Barat No 12
Jakarta Pusat
Tel: 260 976

Planetarium
Jl Cikini Raya No 71
Jakarta Pusat
Tel: 346 610

Reksa Artha Museum
Jl Lebak Bulus 1
Cilandak Jakarta Selata
Tel: 739 5000

Sasmita Loka A Yani Museum
Jl Lembang, Jakarta Pusat
Tel: 547 431

Satria Mandala (ARMY)
  Museum
Jl Jend Gatot Subrot
Jakarta Pusat
Tel: 582 759

Science and Technology
  Museum
Taman Mini Indonesia Indah
Jakarta Timur

Taman Prasati Museum
Jl Tanah Abang 1 Jakarta Pusat
Tel: 377 907

Tugu National (MONAS)
  Museum
Jl Merdeka Utara, Jakarta Pusat
Tel: 340 451

Wayang Museum
Jl Pintu Besar Utara No 27 Ja-
karta Kota
Tel: 679 560

Young Pledge (Sumpah
  Pemuda) Museum
Jl Kramat Raya No 106
Jakarta Pusat
Tel: 310 3217

West Java
Bogor Botanic Garden
Jl Kebun Raya, Bogor

Geological Museum
Jl Diponegoro No 57,
Bandung
Tel: 73205

Herbarium Bogoriensis
  Museum
Jl Ir Hji Juanda No 22-24, Bogor
Tel: 22035

Mandala Wangsit Siliwangi
  Museum
Jl Mayor Lembong No 38
Bandung
Tel: 50393

Museum Asia Afrika
Jl Asia Afrika No 65, Bandung
Tel: 59505

Museum Negeri of West Java
Jl Otto Iskandar Dinata No 638
Bandung
Tel: 50976

Museum Perjuangan
Jl Merdeka No 28, Bogor

Pos and Giro Museum
Jl Cilaki No 3, Bandung
Tel: 56337

Pra Site Museum
Jl Mesjid Lama, Banten

Prabu Geusan Ulun Museum
Komplek Gedung Negara
Sumedang
Tel: 81714

Pusaka Kanoman Museum
Jl Dalam Kraton Cirebon,
Cirebon
Tel: 4001

Sejarah Mesjid Banten Museum
Jl Mesjid Banten Lama, Banten

Zoological Bogoriensis Museum
Jl Ir Haji Juanda No 3, Bogor
Tel: 24007

Central Java
AKPOL Museum
JlKomplek Akpol Candi
BaruSemarang
Tel: 411700

Batik Museum
Jl Pasar Ratu No 30
Pekalongan

Diponegoro Museum
Jl Diponegoro No 1

Magelang
Tel: 2308

Grobogan Museum
Jl Bhayangkara No 1
Purwodadi

Jamu Nyonya Menir Museum
Jl Raya Kaligawe km 4
Semarang
Tel: 285732

Kartini Museum
Jl Alon-alon, Jepara

Kartini Museum
Jl Jend Gatot Subroto No 8
Rembang
Tel: 25

Mandala Bakti Museum
Jl Merdeka 1
Semarang
Tel: 311 321

Museum Negeri of Central Java
Jl AbdurachmanSaleh
Semarang
Tel: 24389

Palagan Museum
Jl Mgr Sugiopranoto
Ambarawa

Pers Museum
Jl Gajah Mada 59
Surakarta/Solo

Pura Mangkunegara Museum
Jl Dalam Kraton Surakart,
Surakarta/Solo
Tel: 2016

Rekor Indonesia Museum/Jamu
  Jago
Jl Setiabudi No 179
Srondol, South Semarang
Tel: 312 762

Suaka Budaya Museum
Jl Dalam Kraton, Surakarta/Solo
Tel: 2889

Sudirman Museum
Jl Ade Irma Suryani C 7
Magelang

Sugar Museum
c/o. Pabrik Gula Gondang Baru
Klaten
Tel: 22328

Train Museum
Jl Komplek Stasiun Kereta Api
Ambarawa

YOGYAKARTA
"Affandi" Art Museum
Jl Solo No 167
Yogyakarta

Batik Museum
Jl Dr Sutomo No 9
Yogyakarta
Tel: 2338

Dewantara Kirti Griya Museum
Jl Taman Siswa No 31
Yogyakarta
Tel: 2093

Dharma Wiratama Museum
Jl Sudirman No 47
Yogyakarta
Tel: 86417

Dirgantara Mandala Museum
Jl Kolonel Sugiono, Yogyakarta
Tel: 3467 ext 205

Kraton Yogyakarta Museum
Jl Dalam Kraton Yogyakarta
Yogyakarta
Tel: 288

Pangeran Diponegoro Museum
Jl Tegalrojo
Yogyakarta
Tel: 3068

Pendidikan Islam Museum
Jl Kapten Tendean No 41
Yogyakarta
Tel: 4401

Perjuangan Museum
Jl Bintaran Wetan No 3

Yogyakarta
Tel: 2663

Sasmita Loka Museum
Jl Bintarn Wetan No 3
Yogyakarta
Tel: 2663

Sono Budoyo Museum
Jl Trikora No 6
Yogyakarta
Tel: 2775

UGM Biological Museum
Jl Sultan Agung 22
Yogyakarta
Tel: 4011

Yogya Kembali Museum
Jl Desa Kembaran Kab Sleman
Yogyakarta

East Java
Archaeological Museum Blitar
Jl Sodancho Supriyadi No 40
Blitar
Tel: 81365

Archaeological Museum Kediri
Jl Jend A Yani
Kediri

Archeological Mojokerto
Jl Jend Achmad Yani No 14
Mojokerto

Brawijaya Malang Museum
Jl Ijen No 25 A, Malang
Tel: 2394

Loka Jala Carana Museum
Jl Komplek AKABRI Laut
Morokembangan, Surabaya
Tel: 291 092

Museum Joang '45
Jl Mayjend Sungkono
Surabaya
Tel: 67206

Museum Negeri Mpu Tantular
Jl Taman Mayang Kara 6
Surabaya
Tel: 67037

Museum Sumenep
Jl Kantor Kabupaten II Sumenep

Statue Museum (Balai Arca)
Jl Arca
Nganjuk

Trowulan Archaeological Museum
Jl Raya Trowulan 13
Mojokerto
Tel: 61362

BALI
Art Museum
Jl Abian Kapas
Denpasar

Gedung Aca Museum
Jl Bedulu
Blahbatu, Gianyar

Kirtya Museum
Jl Veteran No 20
Singaraja
Tel: 938

Le Mayeur Museum
Jl Sanur, Sanur

Museum Negeri of Bali
Jl Letkol Wisnu No 8
Denpasar
Tel: 22680

Ratna Wartha Museum
Jl Ubud
Gianyar

Yadnya Museum
Jl Tangawi
Tangawi

West Nusa Tenggara
Museum Negeri of West Nusa Tenggara
Jl Panji Tilar Negara
Mataram
Tel: 22159

West Nusa Tenggara Museum
Jl Kekalik
Mataram

East Nusa Tenggara
Museum Negeri of East Nusa Tenggara
Jl Perintis Kemerdekaan
Kelapa Lima
Kupang

Udana Museum
Jl Jenderal Suharto
Kupang
West Kalimantan
Dara Yuanti Museum
Jl Dara Yuanti
Sintang

Mini Korem Museum
Jl Sintang, Sintang

Museum Negeri of West Kalimantan
Jl Jend A Yani
Pontianak
Tel: 4600

East Kalimantan
Mulawarman Museum
Jl Diponegoro, Tenggarong
Tel: 112

South Kalimantan
Museum Negeri of Lambung Mangkurat
Jl Jenderal A Yani Km 36
Banjar Baru Banjar
Tel: 2453

Central Kalimantan
Belanga Museum
Jl Tangkiling Km 2,
Palangkaraya

Museum of Central Kalimantan
Jl Cilik Riwut Km 2.5
Palangkaraya

South Sulawesi
Batara Guru Museum
Jl Andi Jemma No 1
Palopo

Goa Bala Lompoa Museum
Jl Sultan Hasanuddin 48
Sugguminasa

La Bangenge Museum
Jl Bau Masseppe 86
Pare-Pare

La Pawowoi Museum
Jl Petta Ponggawe
Watampone

Museum Negeri of La Galigo
Jl Banteng Ujung Padang
Ujung Padang
Tel: 21305

Nekara Museum
Jl Jend Sudirman No 2
Selayar

Central Sulawesi
Bangga and Lore Museum
Jl Kabupaten Poso
Poso

Museum Negeri of Central Sulawesi
Jl Sapiri No 23
Palu
Tel: 22290

Pugung Ulago Sembah Museum
Jl Tepi Laut Kaili Barat
Kab Donggala

North Sulawesi
Museum Negeri of North Sulawesi
Jl W R Supratman No 72
Manado
Tel: 2685

Wanau Paksinanta Museum
Jl Ki Hajar Dewantara 72
Manado
Tel: 2685

Southeast Sulawesi
Museum Negeri of Southeast Sulawesi
Jl Saranani, Wua-Wua

Moluccas
Istana Sultan Ternate Museum
Jl Kabupaten
North Maluku

Memorial Sultan Tidore Museum
Jl Salero
Tidore

Museum Negeri of Siwa Lima
Jl Taman Makmur, Ambon
Tel: 42891

Sonyine Malige Museum
Jl Soa Sio Tidore
Central Halmahera

Irian Jaya
Loka Budaya Museum
Jl Uncen, Sentani Abepura
Jayapura

Museum Kebudayaan dan Kemajuan Asmat
Jl Keuskupan Agats, Irian Jaya

Museum Negeri of Irian Jaya
Jl Raya Sentani Km 17.8
Jayapura

Timor-Timor
Museum Negeri of Timor-Timur
Jl Lecue Kotak Pos 48, Dili
Tel: 2756

Waemena Museum
Jl Waemena, Irian Jaya

PHOTO CREDITS

Antiques of the Orient : 10/11, 14, 25, 50/51

Glenn A Baker Archives/Glenn A Baker : xvii (top), 104, 140/141, 158, 250, 266, 267, 269, 270 (top), 270 (bottom), 271 (bottom), 272, 273, 274/275, 283, 284, 287 (top), 290/291, 310, 319, 322 (bottom),323, 370, 397, 398, 398/399, 400/401, 404/405, 406/407, 409, 444, 457, 477

Glenn A Baker Archives/Bob King : xv (bottom), 103, 104, 116/117, 118, 146 (bottom), 193 (bottom),238, 246, 268, 271 (top), 285, 286, 292, 293, 294, 301 (bottom), 361, 403, 409, 435, 458/459

Randa Bishop : xv (top), 100, 108, 164 (top), 230, 312, 358, 367, 380, 381, 382/383, 384/385, 386, 387, 390, 400/401, 450, 452, 462

Wendy Chan : 115, 161, 200, 482

M Clarborough : xi (top), xi (bottom), xiii (top), 68, 70/71, 78 (bottom), 79 (top), 81 (top), 86, 87 (bottom), 88, 90/91, 253 (bottom), 254 (top), 254 (bottom), 256, 257, 368

V Deschamps : v, xii, xiii (bottom), 74, 77 (top), 78 (top), 87(top), 218 (bottom), 241, 282, 287 (bottom)

Alain Evrard : 123, 142, 153, 306, 306/307, 322 (top)

Jill Gocher : 106, 108

Holzbachova/Benet : Back cover (top right), Back cover (bottom), viii, ix, xiv, xvi, xvii (bottom), 1, 17, 20 (top), 20 (bottom), 21, 22, 24, 26/27, 28 (top), 28 (bottom), 29, 30, 32, 33, 38, 42/43, 44/45, 49, 55, 56, 77 (bottom), 92, 94, 95, 96/97, 98, 102, 107, 109, 112, 113, 114, 117, 119, 121, 124 (top), 124 (bottom), 125, 135 (top), 135 (bottom), 136 (top), 136 (bottom), 137 (bottom), 138, 140, 147, 148, 150, 154, 159, 160, 174 (top), 174 (bottom), 176, 178, 179 (top), 179 (bottom), 180 (top), 180 (bottom), 181, 186, 188, 191, 192, 193 (top), 194 (top), 195 (top), 195 (bottom), 196, 203, 207, 258, 261, 265, 280, 300, 301 (top), 304, 305, 311, 314 (top), 317 (top), 318 (top), 318 (bottom left), 364, 364/365, 371, 372, 376, 378 (top), 378 (bottom), 379, 394, 395, 428, 430, 431, 432, 433, 434, 436/437, 439, 454, 460, 464, 465, 466, 467, 472, 475, 478

Images of the East/Kaushik Ramanathan : 149

Images of the East/Deniek G Sukarya : Back cover (top left), 128, 130, 134, 202, 214/215, 320/321

Aileen Lau : 79 (bottom), 99 (bottom), 476

Gilles Massot : Back cover (bottom), End paper (back), 3, 63, 64/65, 120, 126/127, 162, 165, 166, 201, 226/227, 234, 235, 303, 308/309, 314 (bottom)

Alan Peterson : xvi, 8, 23, 41, 99 (top), 137 (top), 144, 156, 167, 210, 212, 279, 302, 315 (top), 315 (bottom), 316, 318 (bottom right), 328, 334, 340, 440, 442, 443, 446

R Ian Lloyd Productions/R Ian Lloyd : 172, 244/245, 357

R Ian Lloyd Productions/Bob Witkowski : 353

Andy Smith : 67, 105, 410, 414, 415, 417, 418, 422, 425, 426, 427

Holly S Smith :2, 6/7, 12, 75, 89, 168/169, 263, 317 (bottom), 336/337, 341, 342, 343, 344/345, 346/347, 348, 350/351, 363, 393, 396, 416, 419, 420 (top), 420 (bottom), 445

Stockphotos/Wanda Warming : 204/205

Morten Strange : 72, 82 (top), 82 (bottom), 83 (top), 83 (bottom), 84 (top), 84 (bottom), 182, 183, 184, 216 (bottom), 217 (top), 217 (bottom), 218 (top), 253 (top), 276, 281, 288, 289, 295, 369, 421, 424

The Image Bank/P & G Bowater : 40, 48, 52, 53, 58/59, 216 (top), 259, 260 (top), 260 (bottom), 262/263, 480, 486/487

The Image Bank/Wendy Chan : 60, 264, 482

The Image Bank/Paulo Curto : Front cover, 335

The Image Bank/Peter Hendrie : 146 (top), 296, 448

The Image Bank/Don King : 301 (bottom)

The Image Bank/Butch Martin : 488/489

The Image Bank/Robbi Newman : 456, 468/469

The Image Bank/Andrea Pistolesi : 110, 163, 164 (bottom), 194 (bottom), 199, 236/237, 255, 352, 362, 374, 474

The Image Bank/Anne Rippy : 485

The Image Bank/Guido Alberto Rossi : End paper (front), 36/37, 46, 152/153, 206, 208/209, 219, 249

The Image Bank/Nevada Wier : 132/133, 313

INDEX

NOTES

NOTES